Possessives in English

Possessives in English

An Exploration in Cognitive Grammar

John R. Taylor

OXFORD
UNIVERSITY PRESS

OXFORD

UNIVERSITY PRESS

Great Clarendon Street, Oxford OX2 6DP
Oxford University Press is a department of the University of Oxford.
It furthers the University's objective of excellence in research, scholarship,
and education by publishing worldwide in
Oxford New York

Athens Auckland Bangkok Bogotá Buenos Aires Calcutta
Cape Town Chennai Dar es Salaam Delhi Florence Hong Kong Istanbul
Karachi Kuala Lumpur Madrid Melbourne Mexico City Mumbai
Nairobi Paris São Paulo Shanghai Singapore Taipei Tokyo Toronto Warsaw
and associated companies in Berlin Ibadan

Oxford is a registered trade mark of Oxford University Press
in the UK and certain other countries

Published in the United States
by Oxford University Press Inc., New York

British Library Cataloguing in Publication Data
Data available

Library of Congress Cataloging in Publication Data
   Possessives in English : an exploration in cognitive grammar
John R. Taylor.
   Includes bibliographical references and index.
   1. English language—Possessives.   2. Cognitive grammar.
I. Title.
PE1221.T39   1996   425—dc20   96–16385
ISBN 0–19–823586–0 (hbk)
ISBN 0–19–829982–6 (pbk)

10 9 8 7 6 5 4 3 2 1

Typeset by Graphicraft Limited, Hong Kong
Printed in Great Britain on acid-free paper by
Biddles Ltd., Guildford and King's Lynn

To my most precious possession of all

Acknowledgements

Research for this book was partially supported by a grant from the Centre for Science Development of the Human Sciences Research Council, Pretoria; the book's completion was made possible by the congenial working conditions of the University of Otago. Special thanks go to René Dirven, Dirk Geeraerts, Ron Langacker, and Ken-ichi Seto for their comments on earlier versions of the manuscript; to audiences at universities in Leuven, Osaka, Pietermaritzburg, and Thessaloniki, at which parts of it were aired; and, not least, to Frances Morphy of Oxford University Press for her assistance in guiding the book through to publication.

Contents

List of Figures

1 Preliminaries

THIS book is about a single morpheme in English and the constructions in which it occurs. The morpheme in question is the one that attaches to the ends of noun phrases to give the forms *John's*, *the city's*, *the children's*, and the like.

I shall refer to it as the possessive morpheme, and denote it by the mnemonic abbreviation POSS. I have opted for this designation over its chief competitor—the genitive—mainly because genitive could suggest that the morpheme is an exponent of genitive case, and that the items to which it attaches inflect for genitive case. As I shall argue later, whatever POSS is, it is definitely not a marker of genitive case, as this notion is generally understood especially with respect to the Indo-European languages. On the other hand, possessive is not an ideal term, either, since it could imply too intimate a link between the morpheme and the semantic relation of possession, in the everyday sense of the word. We shall see that the notion of possession does indeed play an important role in the semantics of POSS and of the constructions in which it occurs. However, at the outset of the investigation, it would be better not to pre-judge the issue, and to regard the term possessive merely as a convenient label for a morpheme whose semantic value will emerge in due course.

Phonologically, POSS is realized by /əz/, /s/, /z/, or zero; orthographically, it is represented by *'s*, or by the apostrophe alone. Factors governing the distribution of these phonological and orthographic variants are well known,[1] and for the time being at least, need not concern us.

We need to say a word or two about the forms *my*, *your*, *his*, *her*, *our*, and *their*. Older grammarians, such as Jespersen, Poutsma, and Curme, as well as, more recently, Quirk *et al.* (1985), made a terminological distinction between 'genitive nouns' (*John's*, etc.) and 'possessive pronouns'. Diachronically, there may be some justification for such a distinction; synchronically, there is little basis for it. *His* is distributed very much like *John's*; if the latter can be analysed as [John + POSS], *his* is surely its pronominal equivalent, i.e. [he + POSS]. I shall therefore regard *my* etc. as opaque fusions of a pronoun + POSS.[2] There is also the question of the forms *mine*, *yours*, *hers*, *ours*, and *theirs*. I shall

---

[1] See e.g. Quirk *et al.* (1985: 319–21). Orthographic conventions governing the use of the 'possessive apostrophe' became fully standardized only towards the end of the last century. For more on this, see below, section 11.3.

[2] For a similar view, see Seppänen (1980). Note that *whose* (*who* + POSS) and *its* (*it* + POSS) idiosyncratically omit the apostrophe. Phonologically, though, the forms are perfectly regular.

address this issue in Chapter 12, arguing that these are phonologically strong forms of *my*, *your*, *her*, *our*, and *their*.

One of the main uses of the possessive morpheme is in *prenominal possessives*, of the kind exemplified in (1).

(1)   *a.* John's wife.
       b. the neighbour's car.
       c. the country's population.
       d. yesterday's news.
       e. the train's arrival.
       f. Rome's destruction.

These expressions have the status of noun phrases, with the schematic structure [[X POSS] Y], where X and Y are nominal expressions. I shall sometimes refer to the [X POSS] constituent as the possessor phrase, to X as the possessor nominal, and to Y as the possessee. Again, these terms should not be taken to imply any a priori commitment to the semantic roles of the constituents; the entity denoted by a possessor nominal does not necessarily 'possess' (in the everyday, legalistic sense of the term) the entity denoted by the possessee.

Prenominal possessives (or possessives for short) will be our main focus of interest in this book. The possessive morpheme, however, is used in a number of other environments, which will claim our attention in due course. One environment is *gerundive nominalizations*, as exemplified in (2).

(2)   *a.* Amy's removing (of) the picture.
       b. if you don't mind my saying so.
       c. in spite of its being spring.

We will need to recognize several kinds of gerundive nominalization. The properties of these constructions, and some differences (and commonalities) between them and regular prenominal possessives, will be addressed in Chapter 10.

A second environment is *possessive compounds*. Examples include *woman's magazine*, *driver's licence*, *boys' school*. Whereas prenominal possessives constitute noun phrases, possessive compounds resemble regular nominal compounds (*dog food*, *elevator operator*, and the like) in being nouns. The contrast is illustrated in (3). Observe that in the prenominal expressions, *the woman* and *my driver* are constituents, whilst in the compound expressions *woman's magazine*, *driver's licence* are constituents. As the rough paraphrases show, the alternative constituencies correlate with different readings.

(3)   *a.* [the woman]'s magazine.
          "the magazine belonging to the woman"
          the [woman's magazine].
          "the magazine aimed at a female readership"
       b. [my driver]'s licence.
          "the licence belonging to my driver"

my [driver's licence].
"the licence permitting me to drive"

The semantic and structural characteristics of possessive compounds, and their status *vis-à-vis* prenominal possessives, will be the topic of Chapter 11.

There are a few other environments in which the possessive morpheme occurs. In *postnominal possessives*, the morpheme attaches to a nominal in a postnominal *of*-phrase.

(4) *a.* a friend of John's.
     b. that brother of his.

In *predicative possessives*, the morpheme attaches to a nominal in predicative position.

(5) *a.* This car is John's.
     b. These photographs look like his.

In *pronominal possessives*, [NP POSS] functions as a pronominal form *vis-à-vis* a full prenominal possessive.

(6) John's car is new. What about Mike's?

These constructions will be discussed in Chapter 12.

My account of the possessive morpheme, and of the constructions in which it occurs, will be embedded in the theory of Cognitive Grammar, as this has been elaborated by Ronald Langacker and others. I will argue that this theoretical approach is able to offer a more comprehensive and more insightful account of the data than some other theories, especially those associated with Chomskyan generative grammar. A second theme of the book, therefore, will be a critical examination of the theoretical bases of these approaches, and their evaluation especially in light of their treatment of possessives.

I.I THE CHALLENGE OF POSSESSIVES

Why should anyone be interested in possessives? The expressions in (1) look innocuous enough. Why devote a whole book to expressions like these?

In spite of their seemingly transparent nature, possessives do present a number of rather special challenges, and raise a number of intriguing problems, which touch on the very basis of linguistic theory. Here I shall mention some of the more immediate.

I.I.I *Possessive nominalizations*

For the professional linguist, the most immediate reason for being interested in possessives is that there already exists a substantial literature on possessives, more precisely on a restricted subset of possessives. This is the subset of *possessive nominalizations.* Possessive nominalizations are expressions whose possessee is a derived (usually deverbal) noun, and whose possessor stands in some kind of argument relation (analogous to that of the subject or direct object of a transitive verb) to the possessee.

A major theme has been the analogies, and disanalogies, between finite clauses and their nominalized counterparts. Consider the following examples.

(7) *a.* The enemy destroyed the city.
         the enemy's destruction of the city.
     b. *The enemy destroyed.
         *the enemy's destruction. [with *enemy* as Agent]
     c. The city was destroyed by the enemy.
         the city's destruction by the enemy.
     d. The city was destroyed.
         the city's destruction. [with *city* as Patient]

The parallels between the clauses and their nominal equivalents are striking. In each case, the possessor corresponds to the subject of the finite clause (irrespective of whether the finite clause is active or passive); a postnominal *of*-phrase corresponds to the direct object of the active clause (7*a*); whilst a *by*-phrase encodes the Agent, both in the passive clause and the corresponding nominalization (7*c*). We also see that the clausal and the nominal expressions in (7*b*) are equally unacceptable, and presumably for the same reason, i.e. both are semantically incomplete, in that we need to know in each case who, or what, was destroyed. Even so, the parallels are not perfect. For example, the finite verb appears in both active and passive forms (*destroy* vs. *be destroyed*); there is, however, no passive form of the derived noun *destruction*.

Not all deverbal nouns pattern like *destruction*. Consider the following paradigm.

(8) *a.* The voters admired the politician.
         the voters' admiration {of/for} the politician.
     b. *The voters admired.
         the voters' admiration. [with *voters* as Experiencer]
     c. The politician was admired by the voters.
         *the politician's admiration by the voters.
     d. The politician was admired.
         *the politician's admiration. [with *politician* as Stimulus]

Although *admire*, like *destroy*, readily passivizes, there are no 'passive' nominalizations corresponding to the passive clauses. The possessor, in other words, corresponds only to the active subject, i.e. it denotes only the Experiencer of the admiration, never the Stimulus that triggers the admiration. Furthermore, whereas the notional direct object of *destruction* may be introduced only by the preposition *of* (7*a*), the 'direct object' of *admiration* may be introduced by a different preposition, i.e. *for* (8*a*). Another disanalogy may be mentioned. Whereas **the* *voters admired* is ungrammatical (because syntactically and semantically incomplete: we need to know *who* or *what* the voters admired), the corresponding nominalization *the voters' admiration* is perfectly acceptable, even though the object of the voters' attitude is not stated.

At least since Chomsky's seminal paper 'Remarks on nominalization' (Chomsky 1970), a leitmotif, especially of the generative-transformational literature, has been the proper treatment of the relation between clauses and noun phrases; a further concern has been the search for general principles which will account for the differences between the *admiration*-paradigm in (8) and the *destruction*-paradigm in (7). We shall review a number of generative approaches in Chapter 6. Here, just one aspect may be mentioned. This is that generative accounts have tended to treat deverbal nominalizations, of the kind *the city's destruction*, as a category apart from run-of-the-mill possessives like *my car, John's wife*. Whatever principles may be relevant to the structure and interpretation of the one kind of expression, some quite different principles are presumed to be applicable to the other kind.

The account that I shall develop in this book will emphasize the unity of the possessive construction. The special properties of possessive nominalizations, as these have been extensively documented in the literature, as well as constraints on their acceptability and interpretation, will be seen to fall out from a more general characterization of the possessive morpheme, in interaction with the properties of the lexical items that participate in the construction. In later chapters, I show that the special properties of other possessive constructions, such as the postnominal, pronominal, and predicative possessives, can also be derived from the unitary value of the possessive morpheme.

1.1.2 *Semantic issues*

To assume the unity of the possessive construction is to raise a number of questions which are essentially semantic in nature. The basic issue concerns the proper treatment of meaning variation, i.e. the fact that a linguistic form can designate different states of affairs according to its use in context. That this should be a central concern in lexical semantics is readily accepted. Less obvious is the fact that the very same issue arises when we deal with the grammatical resources, including the bound morphemes, of a language. Consider the question: What does the possessive morpheme actually *mean*?

Although I earlier expressed reservations about the suitability of the term possessive, intuitively, the prenominal possessive construction does seem to be rather intimately connected with the notion of possession, in the everyday sense of the term. To ask *Whose car were you driving?* is to enquire after the legal owner of the car, and to respond *It was John's car* is to name the owner. But in other situations, *John's car* could invoke many other kinds of relation besides that of possession. For example, the expression could denote the car that John has rented from a car-hire company, in which case the car is not strictly speaking one of John's 'possessions'. Or it could be the car that the car-hire company intends to allocate to John. Alternatively, supposing John to be a car-designer, *John's car* could be a car that John has designed. And so on. In fact, one might even be inclined to say that *John's car* could invoke any one of an indefinite number of pragmatically plausible relations that could hold between a car and a person. This said, there are situations in which the notion of possession does seem to predominate over other interpretations. Consider the following scenario. You lend me your car, which I later smash. I could approach a third party for assistance, and truthfully (i.e. without intent to deceive) report the event with the statement *I've had an accident with my car*. Here, *my car* has the sense "the car I was driving". But I could scarcely report the accident to you, the legal owner, in this way. In speaking to you about the accident, I would have to say that I smashed *your car*, not *my car*!

With respect to at least some of the possible interpretations of *John's car*, one could, perhaps, say that they involve some 'loose', or 'extended' notion of possession, having to do, say, with a person's short- or long-term rights of access to the car. But this move seems less appropriate for *John's wife*, not to mention *John's ex-wife*. A man does not 'own' his wife, even less does a man's ex-wife count as one of his possessions, even on a *very* loose understanding of 'possession'! And when we turn to possessive nominalizations, of the kind *the train's arrival* and *the city's destruction*, the notion of possession seems even more remote.

The traditional approach to this issue has been to set up taxonomies of the kinds of semantic relation encoded by the possessive construction. We may take Poutsma as an early and representative example. Poutsma (1914–16: 41) identifies the following types of genitives (as he called them):

(a) genitive of possession: *my brother's books, the earth's crust*;
(b) genitive of origin: *the pheasant's nest, nature's work*;
(c) the subjective genitive:[3] *Elizabeth's reign, the horse's breathing*;
(d) the objective genitive:[4] *Gordon's murder, their kingdom's loss*;
(e) the genitive of measure: *an hour's interval, a shilling's worth*;
(f) the genitive of apposition:[5] *Tweed's fair river, treason's charge*.

It should be noted that Poutsma construes possession rather broadly, to encompass 'a great many other relations of a kindred nature' (p. 41), such as kinship and other interpersonal relations (*John's wife, John's friends*), as well as whole–part relations (*the earth's crust*). He further surmises that the prevalence of the

---

[3] So called, because the possessor bears a semantic relation to the possessee analogous to that of a subject nominal to a verb.
[4] So called, because the semantic relation between possessee and possessor is analogous to that between a transitive verb and its direct object.
[5] So called, because possessor and possessee refer to the same entity, i.e. they are in apposition.

possession relation (broadly construed) explains the frequent use of the term possessive as an alternative name for the genitive.

It would be tedious to review the alternatives to Poutsma's taxonomy (itself based on descriptions of the Classical languages) that are to be found in the work of other commentators on the English language.[6] Suffice it to say that the taxonomic approach has a number of weaknesses. We note, first, the absence of any clear criteria for the identification and differentiation of the various types. Poutsma classifies kinship and whole–part relations as 'possessive' relations, on account of their 'kindred nature'. Yet it is anything but obvious why *John's wife*, *the earth's crust*, and *John's books* should form one semantic category, while *Elizabeth's reign* and *the horse's breathing* should form another. (And how would expressions with locative or temporal possessors, such as *Birmingham's population*, *today's weather*, fit into the traditional classification?) On the other hand, given that each of the semantic relations receives exactly the same linguistic expression (by means of the possessive morpheme), one might well wonder whether anything tangible actually hinges on whether *the man's mistakes*, to take one of Poutsma's examples (p. 41), counts as a subjective genitive, a genitive of origin, or a genitive of possession.

However, the major criticism of the taxonomic approach must be that it fails to offer any explanation of how one and the same morpheme comes to express such highly diverse semantic relations as possession, subject-of, object-of, etc. Poutsma, like others before and since, simply presents us with a list of the meanings that the possessive construction *can* have, passing over the question of why just these meanings should be involved. We are left with the impression that the possessive construction is not so much multiply polysemous (in that it expresses a range of different semantic relations), but that it is multiply homonymous (in that the different semantic relations are not related to each other).

Dissatisfaction with this aspect of traditional accounts motivates Nikiforidou's (1991) study. She recognizes, much as traditional grammarians before her, a number of distinct senses of the possessive (or genitive, in her terminology). Taking her cue from Lakoff (1987) and Lakoff and Johnson (1980), she argues that the different meanings are related in a 'radial category', by a variety of metaphorical links. She proposes possession as the basic, or 'literal' meaning. Whole–part expressions (*my hand*), kinship expressions (*John's wife*), experiencer–experienced relations (*the woman's anger*), objective possessives (*the President's murder*), and so on, are sanctioned by a metaphorical construal of the respective domains in terms of possession.

Nikiforidou's programme to analyse the possessive as a case of structured polysemy is laudible, and we shall return to it again at the conclusion of our investigation, in Chapter 13. However, her implementation of the programme is

---

[6] For taxonomies in the same tradition as Poutsma's, see e.g. Curme (1931: 78–88) and, more recently, Quirk *et al.* (1985: 321–2). A rather elaborate taxonomy based on different principles, namely Fillmorean case relations, is proposed by Altenberg (1982: ch. 5).

far from convincing. Part of the problem is that she nowhere attempts to characterize what she takes to be the literal meaning of the possessive, i.e. 'possession'. This aside, a major weakness of her analysis concerns the kind of evidence which is supposed to demonstrate the widespread existence, in English and other languages, of conceptual metaphors such as PARTS ARE POSSESSIONS, RELATIVES ARE POSSESSIONS, EXPERIENCERS ARE POSSESSORS (OF THE EXPERIENCES), THINGS THAT HAPPEN (TO US) ARE (OUR) POSSESSIONS. Her evidence is that other morphemes testify to exactly the same metaphorical extensions as those attributed to the possessive. Thus, in English, *have* (*got*) can be used, not only to denote literal possession (*I have a car*), but also a whole–part relation (*She's got arms and legs, let her do it herself*), a kinship relation (*I have a brother*), an experiencer–experienced relation (*She has no feelings*), and a patient relation (*I had an accident*). Even so, we do not have **The President had a murder*, in the sense "the President was murdered", which could count as evidence for the claim that the patient relation in *the President's murder* is construed metaphorically in terms of possession.

By attempting in this way to document the ubiquity of the conceptual metaphors, Nikiforidou is merely presupposing the truth of what she is intent on proving. She gratuitously assumes that *have*, just like POSS, has a basic, 'literal' meaning of possession (the very same meaning, it would seem), all other uses of *have* being metaphorical extensions therefrom. *I have a brother* is thus taken as evidence for the existence of the metaphor RELATIVES ARE POSSESSIONS, and, hence, of the metaphorical nature of *my brother*. But it is no more evident that *I have a brother* is metaphorical, than that *my brother* is metaphorical. All that Nikiforidou has demonstrated is that the range of semantic relations expressible by POSS partially coincides with the range of semantic relations expressible by *have*. The links between the supposedly different meanings are not really addressed at all.

There are some further problems of principle with the polysemy approach, as pursued by Nikiforidou. Polysemy engenders ambiguity. If the possessive construction were genuinely polysemous, we should expect possessive expressions to be multiply ambiguous, at least potentially.[7] Yet this does not appear, in general, to be the case. We would not, for example, want to say that *the car's headlights* is ambiguous between a whole–part reading, a kinship reading, and a participant–event reading! The way in which many possessives are interpreted hinges, rather transparently, on the identity of the possessor and possessee. *The car's headlights* evokes a whole–part relation simply because we know that headlights are part of a car. Likewise, *John's wife* invokes a kinship relation because *wife* is a kinship term; and *the train's arrival* invokes the relation between an event and a participant because *arrival* is derived from an event

---

[7] In fact, given the indeterminate number of interpretations that may be assigned to an expression like *John's car*, we should have to say that some possessives are not only ambiguous, but ambiguous in an indeterminate number of ways.

verb. The notion of a whole–part relation, a kinship relation, or a participant–event relation, may not therefore be inherent to the semantics of the possessive construction.

A radical alternative to taxonomic approaches has been to deny that the possessive construction is associated with any inherent semantic content at all. The construction merely conveys that there exists *some* semantic relation between possessor and possessee, the nature of this relation being extrinsic to the construction itself. Kempson, after considering the range (and open-endedness) of interpretations that may be assigned to *John's book*, *John's train*, *John's sheets*, writes:

> In the face of this variety, it seems clear that we can say little about the meaning of possessive constructions other than that there must be some relation of association between the 'possessor' and the 'possessed'. The meaning is otherwise quite indeterminate. (Kempson 1977: 125)

A similar line is taken by Kay and Zimmer (1990: 240), as well as by adherents to Relevance Theory. For Sinclair and Winckler (1991: 28), the only meaning of the possessive morpheme is 'somehow associated with'. Sperber and Wilson (1986: 188) find it 'hard to believe that the genitive [i.e. possessive: JRT] is ambiguous, with as many senses as there are types of relationship it may be used to denote'. Instead, they regard the construction as 'semantically incomplete'. Specific readings of a possessive expression emerge through the fleshing out of this underdetermined meaning, in accordance with contextual information. 'Contextual information is needed to resolve what should be seen as the semantic incompleteness, rather than the ambiguity, of the genitive' (p. 188).

This approach, too, has its problems. In the first place, it ignores the fact, already noted, that a rather specific semantic relation—viz. possession—does emerge as the preferred, or at least as the default interpretation of some possessives, such as *John's car*. We must also take issue with the statement (Williams 1982: 283) that the relation encoded by the possessive morpheme can be 'any relation at all'. It is true that the range of semantic relations that may be associated with the construction is indeed very wide, but it is not unrestrictedly so. It is certainly *not* the case that any two nominals can be adjoined in a possessive construction, just in case they can be linked by *some* relation of association. There is a 'relation of association' between fish and chips (at least in British culture). Yet the relation is incompatible with a possessive; we cannot speak of **the fish's chips*, or of **the chips' fish*. Significant, too, is the fact that the nominals in a possessive expression may not normally be reversed. We have *the car's headlights*, but hardly **the headlights' car*. And whilst a participant in an event can sometimes function as the possessor of the event (*the train's arrival*), the event can under no circumstances be the possessor of the participant (**the arrival's train*). There are, in fact, strong constraints on the nominals that can function as possessors to a deverbal noun. We have *the city's destruction*, but not **the fact's knowledge*.

Constraints on the acceptability and interpretation of possessives show the inadequacy of viewing the construction simply in terms of some general, essentially contentless semantic relation. Some other considerations lead to much the same conclusion.

Many prenominal possessives coexist alongside alternative wordings, usually involving a postnominal *of*-phrase. Alongside *the king's daughter, the company's director, the car's headlights*, we have *the daughter of the king, the director of the company, the headlights of the car*. We might be inclined to say that the one expression is a mere stylistic variant of the other, one factor influencing a speaker's choice being, for example, the 'weight' of the possessor nominal. We would probably prefer *the wife of a colleague of mine* over *a colleague of mine's wife*. Yet the alternative wording is not always available. In general, the usage range of postnominal *of* is much broader than that of the prenominal possessive. Alongside *the foot of the hill, the woman of the year, the knowledge of the facts*, we do not have **the hill's foot, *the year's woman, *the facts' knowledge*. On the other hand, there seems to be something radically wrong with *the car of John* as a paraphrase of *John's car*, over and above the 'weight' of the *of*-complement. After all, there is nothing wrong at all with *a photograph of John*, or even with *a photograph of him*.

Concerning postnominal *of*-expressions, we might be tempted to say, in the style of Kempson and others, that this construction, too, is semantically indeterminate, its interpretation having to do with the semantics of the participating nominals, and other contextual factors. Yet the different usage ranges of postnominal *of* and the prenominal possessive should alert us to the possibility of important differences in the values of the two constructions. This suspicion is confirmed when we consider that sometimes the prenominal and postnominal wordings are more than just stylistic variants, they can mean quite different things (i.e. they can have different truth conditions). *News of yesterday* need not be *yesterday's news*. *News of yesterday* is news about events that happened yesterday, whereas *yesterday's news* could be news that was reported, or which was received, yesterday. Likewise, *students of Chomsky* are not necessarily *Chomsky's students*. Nominalizations provide us with many more examples. *The politician's admiration* is admiration that the politician felt, whereas *the admiration of the politician* could be admiration felt towards the politician. Similarly, *the enemy's fear* means that the enemy was afraid, whereas *the fear of the enemy* could mean that the enemy was feared.

In brief, even though we might not be satisfied with a mere listing of the different meanings of the possessive construction, we cannot content ourselves either with statements of the construction's semantic 'indeterminacy'. What is needed is an analysis which will capture the unity of the construction, and which will characterize it in such a way as to allow us to derive the various constraints that we have noted. A further condition is that the analysis will have to differentiate the possessive from other constructions with which it is, so to speak, in competition. A first sketch of such an analysis will be presented in section 1.2.

1.1.3 *The language specificity of the English prenominal possessive*

A comparison of English with some other languages also points to the need for a rather precise characterization of the English construction. The presence of some kind of possessive construction would appear to be a universal feature of the world's languages. As the typological surveys in Seiler (1983) and Croft (1990: 27–38) show, possessive constructions differ widely in their internal syntax. What these scholars tend not to emphasize, however, is that possessive constructions also differ widely in their range of uses. It is certainly the case that the distribution of the prenominal possessive in English rarely corresponds exactly with the distribution of any single construction in other languages. Consider a couple of examples, from French, Zulu, and German.

French, like other Romance languages, has a series of possessive adjectives. Although these are superficially comparable with English *my*, *your*, etc., their usage range does not correspond exactly with that of their English counterparts. *Its* (= the problem's) *understanding* is only marginally acceptable in English, and then only in special supporting contexts. An analogous reading of *sa compréhension* "his/her/its understanding" is much easier to obtain (see below, section 8.3.1). Full NP possessors must be expressed in French in a postnominal *de*-phrase: *le père de Jean* "John's father", *la voiture du voisin* "the neighbour's car". But the range of postnominal *de* is very much broader than that of the English prenominal possessive. Corresponding to *l'idée de Dieu* we do not have **God's idea*, *l'amour de la patrie* cannot be rendered as **the fatherland's love*, *l'amour de Dieu* can mean, not only the love that emanates from God (like English *God's love*), but also the love of which God is the object.

The possessive in Zulu has an even wider range of uses. Zulu possessives (Doke 1930: 115–23) correspond, not only to English prenominal possessives (9a–b) and post-modifying *of*-expressions (9c), but to nominal compounds (9d–e) and adjective–noun combinations (9f), and even to non-finite clausal modifiers (9g–h).[8]

(9) *a.* indlu ye-ndoda.
     house POSS-man
     "the man's house"

    b. uku-fika   kwe-sitimela.
     NMLZ-arrive POSS-train
     "the train's arrival"

---

[8] Abbreviations: NMLZ: nominalizing prefix; APPL: applied verbal extension; LOC: locative suffix. The possessive morpheme is *a*, which coalesces with the noun prefix of the possessor. Hence the somewhat opaque morphology of the examples in (9).

    c. ubukhulu bo-tamatisi.
        size   POSS-tomato
        "the size of the tomato"
    d. indlu yo-tshani.
        hut   POSS-grass,
        "grass hut"
    e. umfundisi we-sifazane.
        teacher   POSS-woman
        "woman teacher"
    f. isifundo se-sine.
        lesson   POSS-four
        "fourth lesson"
    g. indlu yo-ku-dl-ela.
        room POSS-NMLZ-eat-APPL
        "room for eating in", "dining-room"
    h. indoda yo-ku-sebenza   ensim-ini.
        man   POSS-NMLZ-work garden-LOC
        "a man to work in the garden"

It is clear from these examples that any general characterization of the Zulu possessive is going to differ considerably from that of the English prenominal possessive (and from English postnominal *of*, as well).[9]

A different picture is presented by German. In addition to a series of possessive adjectives, there are in standard German three distinct constructions which may translate an English prenominal possessive; a fourth is quite widespread in the informal spoken language.[10] The constructions are as follows:

(*a*) The possessor appears in the genitive case, as a postnominal adjunct to the possessee.

(10)   das Auto des   Vaters.
        the car   the-GEN father-GEN,
        "father's car"

The usage range of the adnominal genitive is broader than that of the English possessive (*die Liebe des Vaterlandes* vs. **the fatherland's love*). Furthermore, genitive-case nominals have uses which have no parallels at all in English, e.g. as complements of certain verbs (*sich einer Sache erinnern* "to remember something", *einer Sache bedürfen* "to need something"), as complements of certain adjectives (*einer Sache ledig* "deprived of something") and prepositions (*wegen des Regens* "because of the rain"), also as sentence adverbials (*eines Tages* "one day", *Montags* "on Mondays").

---

[9] Indicative of its wider semantic value is the fact that the cognate of the Zulu possessive morpheme in other Bantu languages (e.g. Chichewa, see Bresnan 1994) is sometimes called the 'associative morpheme'.

[10] Haider (1988) discusses, within a government and binding (GB) framework, a number of restrictions on some of these constructions.

(*b*) A genitive-case possessor appears before the possessee, and functions as a definite determiner to it, very much like [NP POSS] in English. This construction has a distinctly archaic flavour, and in the modern idiom is largely restricted to a few fixed expressions.[11]

(11)   *a.* des   Vaters   Segen.
        the-GEN father-GEN blessing
        "the Father's blessing"
     b. auf des   Messers   Schneide.
        on the-GEN knife-GEN blade
        "on a knife-edge"

The prenominal construction is, however, rather more productive if the possessor nominal lacks an article (the set of article-less nominals corresponds, in the main, to proper names). A further similarity to English is the fact that the possessor generally takes an -*s* inflection. Although -*s* is the normal marker of genitive case on masculine and neuter singular nouns, the inflection also occurs on feminine nouns (which suggests that German -*s* may not be a genitive-case inflection after all).

(12)   *a.* Amerikas Entdeckung.
        "America's discovery"
     b. Vaters Auto.
        "Father's car"
     c. Marias Freund.
        "Maria's friend"

Being restricted to possessor nominals which lack an article, the usage range of German -*s* is obviously much narrower than that of the possessive morpheme in English.

(*c*) A postnominal phrase is introduced by *von* "of, from".

(13)   *a.* Das Auto vom Nachbarn.
        "the car of the neighbour"
     b. Die Entdeckung von Amerika.
        "the discovery of America"
     c. Briefe von Milena.
        "Letters of/from Milena"

As with (*a*), this construction has a much wider usage range than the English prenominal possessive.

---

[11] The construction was very frequent in certain poetic styles. Here are some examples from the first few poems that Schubert set to music in his *Winterreise*: 'und auf den weißen Matten | such ich *des Wildes Tritt*' "and on the white fields I search for the deer's track"; 'Der Wind spielt mit der Wetterfahne | auf *meines schönen Liebchens Haus*' "The wind plays with the weather-vane on my sweetheart's house"; 'Er hätte es eher bemerken sollen, | *des Hauses aufgestecktes Schild*' "He should have noticed before the sign attached to the house"; 'Da ist *meiner Liebsten Haus*' "There is my beloved's house".

(*d*) Especially in informal registers, the possessor appears in the dative case, followed by the possessee in association with a resumptive possessive adjective.

(14)   dem   Mann seine Frau.
       the-DAT man   his   wife
       "the man's wife"

This construction is used only with human possessors: **dem Flugzeug sein Abflug* "the plane's departure" (cf. *der Abflug des Flugzeuges*). First and second person possessors are also excluded (Seiler 1983: 71). Corresponding to *ihm sein Haus* "his house", we do not have **dir dein Haus* "your house" or **mir mein Haus* "my house".

The upshot of this brief survey must be that the usage range of the English prenominal possessive is *highly language-specific* (or, if one prefers, highly parochial). Several observations are pertinent.

Given the possessive construction in English, with its distinctive usage range, and a possessive construction in some other language, with *its* distinctive usage range, on what basis can we make meaningful comparisons between the two constructions? How can we even justify using the same term, i.e. 'possessive', to designate constructions whose usages may only partially overlap? The issue is crucial in typological studies (see, for example, Keenen's 1976 discussion of the notion of 'subject of'). Wierzbicka (1996) has pointed out that the criteria are largely semantic. The Polish imperative has uses which do not match those of the English imperative, and vice versa. We recognize both devices as imperatives, and are able to make comparisons between them, on the assumption that there is a 'core' imperative meaning, of cross-linguistic validity, and that a device that a language uses to express this core meaning is *eo ipso* an imperative. By the same token, we can identify a possessive morpheme in Zulu largely because this morpheme is used to express, among many other things, a core possessive meaning ("the man's house"). Thus we come back, albeit by a different route, to the need to recognize the centrality (in a sense that we shall need to clarify) of the possession relation in the semantics of the possessive construction.

At the same time, even a cursory glance at some other languages underlines the need to offer precise characterizations of the semantic values of supposedly equivalent devices in different languages. Kempson's formula—that the English possessive requires only that there exists 'some relation of association' between possessor and possessee—would be quite useless as a basis for a comparative study of English and Zulu possessives (or, for that matter, for distinguishing the English prenominal possessive from the postnominal *of*-construction).

Although cross-language comparisons will not be our concern in this book, I would suggest, none the less, that a detailed account of the English construction, along the lines to be pursued here, is a precondition for meaningful contrastive and typological studies. Only when possessive constructions in other languages

have been characterized in similar detail do we have a basis for drawing insightful comparisons between possessives in English and other languages.

1.2 THE MEANING OF THE PRENOMINAL POSSESSIVE: A FIRST SKETCH

Having pointed to the desirability of a unified account of the English possessive,
I should like, at this point, to sketch the outlines of the approach that I shall develop in subsequent chapters.

The accounts of the possessive construction that were mentioned in 1.1.2
focused exclusively on the semantic relation between possessor and possessee.
Some linguists, like Kempson and Williams, were content to state that the construction could encode any relation at all. Others, like Poutsma, offered a taxonomy of possessive relations. As our brief discussion showed, both approaches
are unsatisfactory, perhaps inherently so. The one fails to account for the constraints to which the construction is subject, whilst the other ignores the possibility that there might be a unifying principle which sanctions the range of
attested semantic relations.

Nikiforidou (1991: 164) rightly observes that there is no 'objective' link (that
is, no link 'that would be verifiable in the real world') between the various
meanings of the possessive. She takes this as evidence that the different meanings are related by metaphor. I would like to propose a different tack, and
consider the *function* of a prenominal possessive. The first point to note is that
prenominal possessives (almost invariably) have specific reference; generally,
prenominal possessives also have definite reference. (Referential aspects of the
construction, and the need to hedge statements about the definiteness and
specificity of possessives, will be addressed in Chapter 7.) A nominal has specific reference if the speaker uses the nominal to refer to an entity that she, the
speaker, has uniquely identified, and singled out for attention. *A car*, in *There's
a car I want to buy*, has specific reference. With this expression the speaker
intends to refer, not to any car, but to one particular car, which she has uniquely
identified, in contradistinction to all other entities that might be appropriately
designated by the word *car*. Definite reference obtains when a speaker assumes,
further, that the hearer, also, is able to uniquely identify the specific referent that
the speaker has in mind. If I say *I bought the car*, I assume that my hearer will
be able to uniquely identify which car I am talking about. Of course, my assumption may turn out to be ill-founded, in which case the hearer can legitimately ask
for clarification. He may turn to me and ask, 'Which car are you talking about?',
or 'Which car is that?', or some such.

On what basis, then, may a speaker assume that the hearer is able to uniquely
identify the intended referent? There are various possibilities. Sometimes, it may
be possible for the speaker to make an ostensive gesture towards the intended
referent (*that man over there*). In other cases, the intended referent may be

known to both speaker and hearer by a unique name (*the Thames, Oxford, Queen Anne*), in which case the name alone is sufficient to ensure definite reference. Alternatively, the referent may be unique within the context of situation, including the context created by preceding discourse. In such cases, it will be sufficient to use a simple noun in association with the definite article (*light the fire, answer the question*). Often, however, the speaker will need to supply additional information which will guarantee (or which the speaker presumes will guarantee, or at least facilitate) the referent's unique identification. A typical strategy is for the speaker to incorporate into the referring NP, in the form of modifying or adjunct phrases, material whose function is to restrict the referential possibilities of the construction's headnoun (*the girl with green eyes, the spy who came in from the cold*). In the limiting case, the incorporated material restricts the referential possibility of the nominal down to a single, unique entity (*the day I was born, the present Queen of England*).

Before proceeding, we need to say a few words about the nature of the 'entities' that a speaker refers to. The above examples could suggest that the entities that a speaker refers to are entities existing in the 'real world'. It is clear, however, that a person can equally well refer to entities that have no objective existence 'in the real world'. *The book I want to write* has definite reference, but it identifies an entity that exists only in the mental world of the speaker's intentions. But even expressions that might appear to be referring to entities existing in the real world, are not, strictly speaking, 'about' the real world, or at least, not 'directly' about the real world. A person has conscious access only to what Jackendoff (1983: 29) calls the 'projected world', i.e. 'the world as unconsciously organized by the mind'. Consequently, 'we can talk about things only insofar as they have achieved mental representation through these processes of organization'.

Reference, therefore, involves the establishment of 'mental contact' (Langacker 1991: 97) with an entity in a mental world. Specific reference entails the singling out of an entity for individual conscious awareness. Definite reference obtains when the speaker presupposes that the hearer, also, is able to establish mental contact with a parallel concept in *his* mental world.

The prenominal possessive construction provides the speaker of English with a rather special device for ensuring definite reference, in that the construction gives the hearer a clue as to how he, too, can establish mental contact with the referent intended by the speaker. The special character of the construction lies not so much in the fact that it conveys *that* the speaker is referring to a uniquely identified entity (such is the import of the definite determiners in *the car, that man*), but in the fact that it gives instructions to the hearer as to *how* the referent can be identified. To this extent, the possessive construction does not convey definiteness directly, through the presence of an inherently definite morpheme, such as *the* or *this*, but indirectly, by directing the hearer's attention to an entity that the speaker has uniquely identified.

The account that I shall propose develops Langacker's reference point analysis of the construction. Langacker introduces the notion of reference point as follows.

The world is conceived as being populated by countless objects of diverse character. These objects vary greatly in their salience to a given observer; like stars in a nighttime sky, some are immediately apparent to the viewer, whereas others become apparent only if special effort is devoted to seeking them out. Salient objects serve as *reference points* for this purpose: if the viewer knows that a non-salient object lies near a salient one, he can find it by directing his attention to the latter and searching in its vicinity. (Langacker 1991: 170; author's emphasis)

Like the stars in the night-time sky, not all entities are equally salient in a person's mental world, i.e. equally available for conscious awareness. Some, we may suppose, are inherently salient, because of their centrality to our mental life, because of their status as cognitive landmarks, or because of the frequency with which they are evoked by ourselves and by others. Other entities are variably salient, as determined by context. Others, yet again, are inherently non-salient, whilst others may need to be created as the occasion demands.

The point of the analogy with the night-time sky, therefore, is that when we single out a less salient entity for individual conscious attention, we frequently do so *via* the prior conceptualization of another, more salient entity. The special character of the possessive construction lies in the fact that it invites the hearer to first evoke the possessor entity, and conveys that the referent of the possessee nominal is to be located in the neighbourhood of the possessor. The import of the possessor phrase is thus to *make explicit the mental path that the hearer must follow in order to identify the target.* Slightly elaborating on Langacker's analysis, we may say that in opting to use a possessive expression, the speaker is *instructing the hearer on how best to identify the referent that he, the speaker, intends.* The speaker, that is, invites the hearer to first conceptualize ('establish mental contact with') the one entity (the possessor), with the guarantee that this will facilitate identification of the target entity (the possessee).

The strategy may, of course, fail, in which case the hearer can legitimately ask for clarification. But the kinds of difficulties that a hearer may experience only confirm the general validity of the reference point model. Consider some of the queries that a hearer may raise with respect to *John's car*. In using this expression, a speaker presupposes that the hearer can identify, from amongst the innumerable entities that can be appropriately designated by the word *car*, just that car that is located in the neighbourhood of a uniquely identified individual, John. The possessor nominal *John* may, however, turn out to be inadequate as a means of establishing the reference point. So the hearer asks, 'Who's John?', or 'Which John do you mean?'. Even if the hearer is able to correctly identify the reference point, he may still be unable to uniquely identify the target entity in its neighbourhood. So he asks, 'Which of John's cars do you mean?' Or he may be unable to locate any suitable referent within the neighbourhood of the reference point. An appropriate remark in this situation might be 'I didn't know John had a car'.

I shall argue that the reference point analysis, suitably elaborated, provides a characterization of the possessive construction that is both sufficiently general, in that it covers the range of attested uses, and at the same time sufficiently specific, in that it enables us to derive constraints on its acceptability and interpretation; the account also serves as a basis for differentiating the prenominal possessive from its close competitor in English (i.e. postnominal *of*), perhaps also from possessive constructions in many other languages.

Consider, for example, a seemingly trivial aspect of the English construction —the fact that the possessor is named *before* the possessee. Constituent order *iconically diagrams* the mental route that the conceptualizer needs to follow in order to identify the possessee. This aspect alone distinguishes the prenominal possessive from possessive constructions in many other languages, as well as from postnominal *of*-expressions in English.[12] Langacker (1992) suggests that the semantic value of *of* is to designate an *inherent relation* between entities; one of its characteristic uses, therefore, is to introduce a complement phrase, which enriches the semantic structure of a relational noun.

Compare a prenominal possessive, such as *the company's director*, with a non-possessive wording, e.g. *the director of the company*. Both expressions are definite, i.e. both designate a specific individual, which the speaker presumes the hearer will be able to uniquely identify, and both characterize the 'director' in terms of his relation (the very same relation, one might want to say) to 'the company'. To this extent, the expressions are functionally (and semantically) equivalent. At first blush, therefore, one might be inclined to say that the import of the possessor phrase is exactly equivalent to that of the postnominal phrase. But while *of* explicitly elaborates the relational character of *director* (a 'director' is necessarily the director *of* something), the prenominal possessive does not encode any specific relation at all between possessor and possessee. Secondly, while both expressions are definite, they achieve definite reference by radically different means. The prenominal possessive instructs the hearer to first identify the (presumably) highly salient entity *the company*, and conveys that the referent of *director* is to be identified with respect to the company. In contrast, *the director of the company* achieves definite reference in virtue of initial *the*.

Numerous aspects of the possessive construction will fall out from the reference point analysis. We may suppose that certain kinds of nominals will in general be better able to discharge a reference point function than others. In Chapter 8 we explore the hypothesis that possessor nominals will need to be high in topicworthiness, topicworthiness being defined in terms of the cognitive accessibility of a concept. I shall argue that this aspect of possessor nominals

---

[12] Claims concerning the iconicity of a linguistic expression (which postulate a homology between an expression's form and the conceptualization that it symbolizes) are easily misinterpreted. If the English prenominal possessive is iconic, in the way suggested, it might be asked whether possessives in French or Zulu are therefore not iconic. The point is that the English construction needs to be analysed in its own terms; other languages are irrelevant to the enterprise.

underlies a good many of the grammaticality judgements that have been discussed from alternative viewpoints in the literature. Similar arguments may be brought to bear on the distribution of possessee nouns, in that entities that are low in inherent salience, or which display a high degree of conceptual dependence, will typically need to be identified *via* a reference point entity.

As a further line of enquiry, I shall explore, in Chapter 9, the thesis that with respect to some targets, certain kinds of entities will be better suited to discharging the reference point function than others. I shall pursue this enquiry in terms of the relative 'cue validity' of potential reference points. The notion of cue validity will enable us to solve one of the puzzles already referred to, i.e. the impossibility of objective readings of *the fact's knowledge, the politician's admiration*, in contrast to the ready availability of subjective readings of *the student's knowledge, the voters' admiration*. Specifically, we will want to say that the Experiencer of a cognitive state is a better cue for the identification of the target than is the Stimulus that causes the cognitive state.

Finally, there is the question of the semantic relation between possessor and possessee. To the extent that the reference point account does not explicitly invoke any specific semantic relation, it is compatible with the views of Kempson and others, who declined to associate the possessive construction with any specific semantic content. Nevertheless, as we have seen, the relation of possession, or ownership, does have special prominence in the semantics of the construction, for a certain range of expressions, at least.

A closer look at the nature of possession suggests why this should be so. A distinctive characteristic of the possession relation is that it is an *exclusive* relation. Barring cases of disputed or communal ownership, there exists, for each possessed entity, only one possessor. A possessed entity can therefore be uniquely identified, given the identity of the person who possesses it. Possession thus offers itself as a paradigm for what we would claim to be the essential character of the possessive construction, i.e. unique identification of the referent of the possessee noun.

There is a further aspect of the possession relation. Typically, a person has direct and easy access to his possessions. Just as the possession relation affords a person physical access to his possessions, so the possessive construction affords the conceptualizer mental access to the possessee concept. The distinctive character of the English prenominal possessive lies in the fact that it has grammaticalized this component of a relation of paradigmatic possession.

1.3 STRUCTURE OF THE BOOK

This book is not only about the possessive morpheme, it is also motivated by metatheoretical concerns. I make no apologies, therefore, for the fact that the discussion of possessives only really gets started about a third of the way into the book.

In Chapter 2, I position the cognitive grammar approach within the current theoretical linguistic landscape, and in Chapters 3 and 4 I introduce some technical aspects of the cognitive grammar approach I shall adopt. (Readers already familiar with Langacker's cognitive grammar may prefer to skip these chapters, at least on a first reading.) Chapter 5 focuses on the constituent structure of prenominal possessives, and especially on the nature of the possessive morpheme itself. Departing from Langacker's analysis, which takes the possessive morpheme to be relational in character, and thus analogous to the prepositions, I argue that the possessive morpheme is akin to a determiner, and that it designates a schematic instance of the possessee. Chapter 6 critically reviews the accounts of possessives that have been proposed in the generative-transformational tradition, with a focus on the various constraints on the acceptability and interpretation of possessives that these accounts have highlighted. Chapter 7 addresses the referential properties of possessives, against the background of some configurational approaches to this issue, whilst Chapter 8 focuses on some properties of possessor nominals, in particular, their topicality. Chapter 9 deals with semantic constraints on possessives, and on possessive nominalizations in particular, showing how these fall out from the reference point analysis. Chapters 10, 11, and 12 deal with other possessive constructions—*ing*-nominalizations, possessive compounds, and the remaining uses of the possessive morpheme. Chapter 13 returns to the issue of possession, and its relation to the reference point analysis.

2 Theoretical Orientation

THE theoretical approach underlying my treatment of the possessive is cognitive grammar, as this has been developed by Ronald Langacker and others. In this book, besides presenting a cognitive grammar analysis of the possessive, I also undertake a confrontation of the cognitive grammar approach with some alternatives, in particular, those that have been pursued within the generative, and more recently, the government and binding (GB) paradigm, and its newest progeny, principles and parameters. The aim will be to show that cognitive grammar can offer a more economical, and more insightful account of the English possessive than these theoretical alternatives.

In this chapter I discuss some aspects of the theoretical background to the study, focusing in particular on general points of contrast between cognitive grammar and generative approaches, as I see them. The chapter concludes (section 2.10) with a discussion of learnability, an issue where the contrasts between the approaches are particularly conspicuous.

2.1 COGNITIVISM

A feature of the current linguistic scene is a general commitment to cognitive realism, i.e. to the thesis that language is a mental, or cognitive phenomenon. There are, to be sure, approaches which fall outside this generalization, such as Montague grammar, or generalized phrase structure grammar. Thus, GPSG (Gazdar *et al.* 1985) aims at a maximally explicit statement of the formal properties of sentences, with little regard for whether the postulated rules for the generation and parsing of sentences might correspond to anything inside a person's head.[1]

Many of today's linguists, however, certainly *would* want to make such a claim. There is, namely, a rather general consensus that the goal of linguistic analysis is not just a description of a person's linguistic behaviour, but an account of the mental structures and processes that cause that behaviour. This goal is shared by linguists of such diverse theoretical orientations as Chomsky and Langacker, Jackendoff and Lakoff, Bierwisch and Hudson. A grammar of a

---

[1] Actually, the same was true of Chomsky's early work; see below, section 2.7. As Gazdar (1987: 123) observes, grammars in the style of GPSG attempt to follow the line set by Chomsky in his early work, but since abandoned by him.

language is meant to be, quite literally, a description, or, perhaps better, a hypothesis, of what a speaker of a language actually knows. On this, Chomskyan generative grammar and Langackerian cognitive grammar are in full agreement. To this extent, these (and other) approaches can legitimately claim to be 'cognitive grammars'. The term cognitive grammar is therefore potentially confusing. Unless otherwise specified, I shall use the term to refer to Langacker's specific approach, rather than in the broad sense of any grammatical approach committed to cognitive realism.

The cognitive commitment, as just outlined, is highly programmatic and does not, of itself, dictate a specific research strategy, nor does it bring with it any specific requirements on the content or form of a linguistic description. And indeed, Chomskyan generative grammar and Langackerian cognitive grammar do represent radically divergent implementations of the cognitive commitment.

Broadly speaking, the approach of Langacker and other cognitive linguists (in a narrow sense) has been to constrain linguistic description by psychological considerations. Lakoff (1987), for example, in his analysis of a wide range of linguistic phenomena, appeals to prototype categorization, a phenomenon independently established by cognitive psychologists (Rosch 1978); likewise, Deane (1992) draws heavily on theories of information processing in his attempts to explain various kinds of syntactic constraints. Langacker's position is actually rather ambiguous. While Langacker (1987a: 12) does state that '[a]n account of linguistic structure should articulate with what is known about cognitive processing in general', there are scant references to the psychological literature in his work. Rather, he motivates his approach largely by appeal to what one might call common-sense psychology—aspects of mental experience that are said to be 'mostly self-evident' (p. 99), and presumably readily accessible to introspection. It is on this basis that Langacker rejects many features of the contemporary linguistic landscape, such as mathematical-logical formalism as a model of linguistic semantics, and the idea that intervening between the meaning of an utterance and its overt linguistic form there might exist layers of structure that are independent both of meaning and of the overt form.

An alternative approach—implemented by Chomsky and his sympathizers— has been to use linguistic analyses as input to the construction of hypotheses about cognition. These hypotheses in turn constrain the further development of the theory. Consider the issues of autonomy and modularity, to be mentioned below. Autonomy (the notion that a person's linguistic competence is independent of other cognitive abilities) and modularity (the idea that linguistic competence itself is the product of an interaction of a number of distinct modules), did not have (and for that matter, to this day still do not have) the status of independently discovered facts about cognition; nor, it seems safe to say, can the issues be settled by appeal to common-sense intuitions. Autonomy and modularity are hypotheses put forward, by linguists, to explain linguistic data, as these have been analysed within the constraints of the linguistic theory.

In spite of a shared commitment to cognitive realism, then, cognitive linguists (in the broad sense) have made, and continue to make, incompatible assumptions about the mental representation and processing of language. Inevitably, the question arises whether cognitive realism might not be a final arbiter in evaluating the competing theories. If two parties claim that their (incompatible) linguistic models are to be taken as hypotheses about the mental representation of language, there are, surely, certain facts of the matter, which we may call upon in order to empirically (dis)confirm one or the other of the theories?

Unfortunately, linguistic debates cannot be settled so straightforwardly. The knowledge that resides in a person's brain can only be inferred on the basis of a person's performance, it cannot be directly observed.[2] When arguing the mental representation of linguistic knowledge, a linguist's primary, indeed, sole source of evidence is nothing other than the linguistic data itself. While linguists can (and do) make reference (some more frequently than others) to empirical findings from the cognitive sciences, the 'facts of the matter' to which linguists, in their capacity as linguists, appeal in arguing their conflicting theories are linguistic facts. Linguistic theories, even cognitive linguistic theories, tend therefore to be evaluated, first and foremost, on purely linguistic criteria. The most important of these must be descriptive adequacy. Any hypothesis about the mental representation of linguistic knowledge which fails to account for linguistic data, in all their variety and complexity (what people actually *say*), is automatically invalidated. Other criteria include economy, constrainedness, explicitness, and motivation. A theory is economical to the extent that it makes minimal assumptions about the domain which the theory aims to cover. An economical theory is also likely to be constrained; the possible accounts of a set of data will be limited, in the ideal case, to only one. A theory is explicit to the extent that the entities that the theory postulates are precisely characterized. (It will not be enough to give a name to a theoretical construct; it will be necessary to say what that entity actually *is*.) A theory will be motivated to the extent that it will be possible to say *why* the theory, or some component of it, should be as it is, independently of the facts that the theory is intended to explain.

In my account of the possessive morpheme in English, I can do no more than appeal to these criteria. I can offer no 'proof' that my account of possessives is more 'correct' than competing accounts, in the sense that my account describes what actually resides in the mind of a speaker of English. All I can do is try to demonstrate that its coverage of the data is more parsimonious, more comprehensive, and more motivated than that of competing approaches.

---

[2] The point has also been made by Rosch, who declines to extrapolate her findings on prototype effects to theories of mental representation. Facts about prototype categorization constitute, at most, a constraint on cognitive models; cognitive models should not make predictions which are inconsistent with the known facts of behaviour. See Rosch (1978: esp. 40–1); also Rosch (1987: 158–60).

2.2 THE LANGUAGE FACULTY

Fodor (1983) made a broad distinction between 'vertical' and 'horizontal' mental faculties. A horizontal faculty is one which underlies many different kinds of skills and knowledge, in widely different domains of activity. A vertical capacity is restricted to a single cognitive domain.

A general question that has divided cognitive linguists (in the broad sense) has been whether a person's linguistic knowledge derives from a special-purpose, i.e. specifically linguistic, vertical faculty, or whether it derives from a specialization of general-purpose faculties. The first position—that language is autonomous—informs Chomskyan generative linguistics. The alternative view has been promoted by Langacker (1987a: 13), Hudson (1984: 37–41; 1990a: 53–6), Foley and Van Valin (1984), and many others.

It should be stressed that controversies over autonomy do not put in question the fact that language is a peculiarly *human* phenomenon. It is beyond dispute that ability to acquire and use language must be innate, or genetically determined, in the sense that human beings are able to acquire and use language in virtue of some special mental capacities, which other creatures presumably do not possess.[3] The issue, rather, is whether these special mental capacities are specific to language knowledge and language processing, or whether they are of a more general nature.

Of these two positions, the second is undoubtedly the more parsimonious. From a general methodological perspective, therefore, it is the thesis of the non-autonomy of language that ought to constitute the linguist's null hypothesis. Only when attempts to derive linguistic phenomena from more general cognitive abilities have manifestly failed might there be reason to postulate a specialized linguistic component of mind. The burden of proof lies with supporters of autonomy (Hudson 1984: 37).

All too often, however, claims for the autonomy of language are put forward, with little serious attention being given to the possible alternatives. On a first inspection, many phenomena in a language may not seem to be motivated, in any obvious or transparent manner, by general cognitive principles. In the absence of a coherent and well worked-out alternative, the temptation may be very great to offer purely formal accounts of them. It is then but a short step to declaring that these phenomena, and the formal accounts of them, are evidence for the correctness of the autonomy position. (Chomsky is a past master at this rhetorical device.)

Moreover, as Foley and Van Valin (1984: 13) point out, a premature appeal to autonomy can actually inhibit exploration of alternatives. If we postulate a syntactic constraint, and claim that this constraint reflects some property of the

---

[3] But see Givón (1989) on the continuities between human linguistic behaviour and the non-linguistic behaviour of non-humans.

language faculty, we in effect put an end to further investigation of it. We may, of course, study the effects of the constraint, in interaction, possibly, with other constraints. We may debate the proper characterization of the constraint. But the question of why the constraint should be as it is, is ruled out a priori.

In recent years, though, careful study has suggested that a number of allegedly autonomous aspects of language may well be motivated by more general cognitive factors. I shall mention just one example. So-called 'island constraints'— the fact that NPs may not be 'extracted' out of certain kinds of environment—have long been cited as paradigm examples of autonomous linguistic principles (Newmeyer 1991 is a recent instance). Acceptable extraction is exemplified in (1); *who* is said to have been extracted from its position to the right of the verb, where it functions as the verb's direct object, and moved to the beginning of the sentence.

(1)   Who did you see——?

In (2*a*), however, extraction is not possible, even though the 'echo question' (2*b*), in which *who* appears in its 'original' position, is fine.

(2)   *a.* *Who did you know the man that saw——?
      b. You knew the man that saw *who*?

The formal generalization that was made is that an NP cannot be extracted over more than one clause or NP boundary. (Thus, in (2*a*), *who* has been moved over the relative clause boundary before *that*, as well as the NP boundary before *the man*.) This is the principle of subjacency, proposed by Chomsky (1973) in an attempt to unify various syntactic constraints noted by Ross (1967).

Yet it has long been known that there are numerous exceptions to subjacency. This fact in itself ought to arouse one's suspicions about the status of subjacency as a property of the language faculty. Chomsky (1980: 236) likened the development of the language faculty in the child to the growth of an embryo, in accordance with a genetic plan; a child no more learns the principles of the language faculty than he learns to grow a pair of arms, instead of a pair of wings. The analogy invites the inference that formal constraints which constitute the language faculty ought not to tolerate any exceptions at all. That a speaker can violate a formal linguistic constraint and still find the resulting sentence grammatical, should be just as remarkable an event as a human embryo growing a pair of wings.

The exceptions to subjacency are reviewed by Deane (1991, 1992), who proposes an alternative account of extraction in terms of a rather general cognitive mechanism. Successful extraction, Deane claims, requires that attention be focused both on the extracted item, and on the constituent from which extraction has taken place, in order that a connection between the two can be established. (Note, by the way, that Deane's account does not entail an underlying structure in which the 'extracted' item appears in its 'original' position.) A person's powers of attention are limited—we can focus attention only on a restricted number of things at the same time. Extraction is possible just in case various factors conspire to render both the extracted item and the extraction site cognitively salient, and simultaneously available for attention. Specifically, Deane claims that the extracted item needs to achieve cognitive salience through being the information focus (it is *selected* as an object of attention), whilst the extraction site achieves cognitive salience through its topicality (it attracts attention *automatically*, in virtue of preceding context, its activation by frame-based knowledge, or simply though familiarity, or entrenchment). A further condition is that the material intervening between the extracted item and the extraction site should be 'inconspicuous', and not deflect processing attention to itself.

Compare, now, the following sentences (Deane 1992: 42).

(3)   *a.* Which guild did he make the suggestion that we join?
      b. ?Which guild did he retract the suggestion that we join?
      c. *Which guild did he photocopy the suggestion that we join?

The sentences share an identical syntactic structure, and all three violate subjacency. Yet (3*a*) is (reasonably) acceptable, (3*b*) rather less so, and (3*c*) is definitely out. The decrease in acceptability correlates with the increasing informativity of the intervening expressions *make the suggestion, retract the suggestion,* and *photocopy the suggestion. Make a suggestion* is an established idiom, roughly equivalent, semantically, to the simple verb *suggest.* After all, suggestions are things that one typically *makes. Make* is therefore relatively inconspicuous. One may also, of course, *retract* a suggestion. But one can only retract a suggestion if the suggestion has already been made. *Retract the suggestion* therefore carries presuppositions that *make the suggestion* lacks. *Photocopy* is an even more unexpected thing to do to a suggestion; in addition, the word presupposes, not only that the suggestion has been made, but also that it has been written down. The amount of information, including presupposed information, packed into the middle of (3*c*) will make it even less likely that a person's limited attention resources can be focused simultaneously on the extracted item and the extraction site.

This example (and Deane gives many others) suggests that the possibility of extraction is not really a formal syntactic property of a sentence at all, but reflects the way in which a sentence is processed. And the processing strategies that Deane refers to are plausibly regarded as horizontal faculties, in Fodor's sense; as such, they are not specific to the domain of language.

2.3 MODULARITY

How should we set about studying the complexity of a natural language? Fodor's distinction between vertical and horizontal faculties suggests that one approach could be to construe the complexity as due to the interaction of different mental faculties. The contribution of each faculty may then be investigated in isolation from the others, leaving to a later date the study of the interaction between them.

Thus, Chomsky (1980: 28) concedes that actual languages, as they are spoken around us, might well 'incorporate elements derived by faculties other than the language faculty'. One such faculty is the conceptual system, having to do with matters of knowledge and belief, as well as with the perception, categorization, and symbolization of experience. Another faculty is pragmatic, or social knowledge, which determines the appropriate use of language in specific settings. Linguistics in the Chomskyan mould has, as its primary object of study, linguistic knowledge proper, i.e. linguistic knowledge 'purified' of conceptual and social knowledge.

Chomsky himself has not been particularly concerned with the structure and content of non-linguistic faculties, nor with their interaction with the language faculty. Others, however, have explicitly incorporated these topics into their research programmes. A notable example is Manfred Bierwisch (Bierwisch 1981, 1983; also Bierwisch and Schreuder 1992). Bierwisch assumes a strict separation between linguistic and conceptual knowledge. Accordingly, for each expression, he postulates a level of linguistic meaning, compositionally derived from the linguistic meanings of its parts, and a level of conceptual meaning, at which linguistic meaning gets interpreted relative to conceptual knowledge. The following sentence has two readings.

(4)   John left the University a short time ago.

On one reading, John departed from the University premises, on the other, he severed a relation of association with the University (he graduated, or resigned his position). These two readings, Bierwisch insists, reflect alternative conceptual interpretations of a unitary linguistic meaning. Bierwisch (1983: 65) even hints at a third level, at which conceptual meaning gets interpreted relative to an interactional context. The fact that in (5) *the University* could refer to a building or an institution is a matter of conceptual interpretation, not of linguistic meaning proper.

(5)   This is the University.

However, the fact that (5) could be meant as a request for payment (if spoken, say, by a taxi-driver upon arriving at the passenger's destination) is a matter of the interactional interpretation of a conceptual meaning.[4]

Perhaps closer in spirit to Fodor's original proposal is Relevance Theory (Sperber and Wilson 1986). Sperber and Wilson propose that the vertical linguistic faculty delivers the linguistically determined meaning of an utterance. The linguistic meaning will typically be incomplete in many respects, and may actually be at variance with the speaker's intended meaning. The 'enrichment' of linguistic meaning, and the computation of intended meaning, are the tasks

---

[4] For a critical appraisal of some aspects of Bierwisch's approach, see Taylor (1994c).

of the horizontal faculty, i.e. the central thought processes. Whereas the vertical capacity has no access to information outside itself (in Fodor's terminology, the vertical capacity is 'informationally encapsulated'), the horizontal faculty can refer to information from the vertical faculties, and to the vast store of encyclopedic knowledge residing in memory. Whereas the language faculty operates rapidly and automatically, beyond conscious introspection, according to genetically determined mechanisms unique to the module in question, central thought processes operate inferentially; their output is subject to revision; and their progress may be slow and subject to introspection. Crucially, it is claimed (Wilson and Sperber 1986: 67) that grammar and pragmatics have nothing substantive in common—apart from the trivial fact that both involve mental activity, and both involve language (the grammar, necessarily, and pragmatics, circumstantially).

In contrast to modular approaches, Langackerian cognitive grammar rejects a strict compartmentalization of linguistic and non-linguistic knowledge. Language is assumed to be essentially symbolic in nature. Meaning is equated with conceptualization, and language serves to encode a speaker's conceptualizations. There can therefore be no grounds for postulating a purely linguistic meaning of a linguistic expression, ontologically distinct from the meaning that the expression might have in virtue of a person's conceptualization of a state of affairs. Such a view might not seem too outlandish in as far as the meanings of lexical items are concerned. (What, *pace* Bierwisch, would the linguistic-semantic meanings of words like *leave* and *university* be, if not the concepts designated by these words in actual utterances?) One might still wonder, though, whether there might be more substantial grounds for supposing that syntax—the mechanism by which smaller linguistic units combine together to form larger, more complex units—is organized according to uniquely linguistic principles, independent of general conceptual principles. Even here, however, cognitive grammar strongly rejects the autonomy thesis. This follows from the assumption that syntax itself is symbolic, and therefore inherently meaningful. Syntax, no less than the lexicon, has to be approached from the perspective of the conceptualizations that linguistic expressions encode.

2.4 THE MODULARITY OF THE LANGUAGE FACULTY

Not only does Chomskyan linguistics postulate a language faculty that is encapsulated from other mental faculties, a central claim is that the language faculty itself has a modular structure. That is to say, the language faculty is taken to be constituted by a number of independent principles, each of which imposes its own conditions on the grammaticality of a linguistic expression. None of the principles can be reduced to any of the others, nor can the different principles be derived from a more general cognitive principle.

A full account of these principles may be found in any of the standard introductions (e.g. Radford 1988, Haegeman 1991). Here I shall briefly characterize those principles to which we shall need to refer in the following chapters of this book.

(a) The X-bar principle

The X-bar principle determines the range of admissible phrase structures in a language. Presupposed is a small, finite set of lexical categories (these may be identified, in the main, with the traditional 'parts of speech': noun, verb, preposition, etc.), and, corresponding to these, an equal number of phrasal categories (noun phrase, verb phrase, etc.). The basic idea is that a member of a lexical category X combines optionally with a complement, to give a constituent of type X′. X′ combines optionally with one or more modifiers, or adjuncts. The phrasal category XP (or X″) consists of an X′ constituent in combination with an (optional) specifier. Schematically, a phrasal category has the following structure. Constituent X is said to 'head', or to be the head, of the phrasal category XP; XP is the 'maximal projection' of X.

(6)

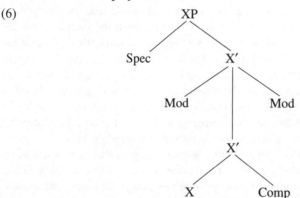

The position of the complement, modifiers, and specifier with respect to the head is language-specific; (6) gives the sequence that is characteristic of English. Applying these notions to the category NP, we get, for the noun phrase *the student of physics with long hair*, the following structure.

(7)

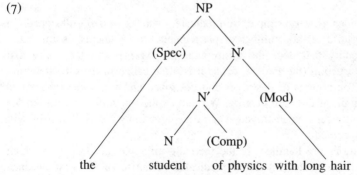

Salient aspects of the X-bar principle are the following.

(i)   All phrasal categories have the status of an XP, and are headed by an item of category X. This is the 'endocentric constraint' (Radford 1988: 259).

(ii) All phrasal categories, irrespective of the category of the head, share essentially the same internal structure.

(iii) The modifier(s) and complement in any given phrase are themselves phrasal categories. In (7), the complement (*of physics*) and the adjunct (*with long hair*) each constitutes a phrasal category, viz. a prepositional phrase (PP), headed by a preposition (*of*, *with*) followed by a complement. The complement is in each case a noun phrase (NP), viz. *physics* and *long hair*.

The above remarks outline a 'conservative' version of X-bar theory. Problematic, in the conservative theory, is the status of the specifier. If (iii) is to have maximum generality (and the search for cross-category generalizations is indeed a motivating force in X-bar theory), we should have to say that the specifier of any phrasal category is itself a phrasal category. However, the specifier in (7), i.e. the determiner *the*, is a word, not an XP. Considerations such as these led in the late 1980s to some radical revisions of the conservative theory (see especially Abney 1987 and Stowell 1989). These involve recognizing 'functional' morphemes, such as determiners, tense inflections, and complementizers, as phrasal heads. As a consequence, the traditional noun phrase gets reanalysed as a determiner phrase (DP). On one version, the determiner phrase is headed by the determiner, which takes an NP complement. In like manner, the traditional verb phrase becomes an inflection phrase (IP), and a sentence becomes a complementizer phrase (CP). Subsequently, further categories of functional heads have been proposed, including, for nominal phrases, markers of case and number, as well as (for some languages) possessive affixes; these developments are discussed in Spencer (1992).

(b) Thematic theory

Whereas X-bar theory establishes the possible phrase structures in a language, thematic theory determines the kinds of complement that a head may (or must) take.

The basic idea is very simple. A predicate, such as *destroy*, designates a relation between a certain number of participants, or arguments, in this case, between an entity that does the destroying (the Agent), and the entity that undergoes destruction (the Patient, or, as it is often called in the GB literature, the Theme). The notions of destroyer and destroyed are in a sense inherent to the very meaning of the verb *destroy*. Without explicit mention of who did the destroying, and what was destroyed, a sentence containing the verb *destroy* will tend to be ill-formed.

These intuitions are handled by the thematic principle, according to which each relational predicate (relational predicates comprise in the first instance verbs and prepositions, as well as some adjectives and nouns) is associated with a thematic grid. The thematic grid states (i) the number of arguments associated with the predicate, (ii) the semantic relation between each argument and the predicate, expressed in terms of the theta-role (θ-role) of the argument with respect to the head, and (iii) the syntactic position that the argument occupies. In the case of *destroy*, the thematic grid specifies that the verb takes Theme as NP complement, and Agent as its subject; in other words, the verb assigns the θ-role of Theme to its NP complement, and the θ-role of Agent to the subject. Following a distinction introduced by Williams (1981), it has become usual to refer to the complement(s) of a predicate as internal arguments, since these are assigned θ-roles within the domain of the phrasal category headed by the predicate. The subject of a verb, in contrast, is an external argument, since this is assigned a θ-role outside the VP. A specific constraint imposed by thematic theory is that each argument in a syntactic configuration must be assigned one, and only one θ-role, and that each θ-role is assigned to one, and only one argument.

Although the thematic principle seems straightforward enough (it amounts, basically, to the claim that each nominal constituent in a phrase has to bear some semantic relation to the head of the phrase, and that semantic notions that are inherent to the meaning of the head need to be explicitly elaborated), there are many controversial aspects (Dowty 1986, Ladusaw and Dowty 1988). For example, there is the question of how many θ-roles there actually are. One view would be that the relation between an argument and its predicate is unique to that predicate, and is to be defined in terms of the semantic structure specific to the predicate. Alternatively, we might postulate a small number of more general θ-roles (Agent, Theme, Experiencer, and a few others), such that each argument can be uniquely categorized with respect to one of these relation-types. An extreme view would be that the semantic content of a thematic relation is actually irrelevant to the syntax; it is merely necessary that each argument be assigned *a* thematic role, in accordance with the thematic grid of the predicate, and that every θ-role (irrespective of its semantic content) be assigned to some argument. This possibility raises a further question, namely, whether the thematic principle is a principle of syntactic or of semantic well-formedness. Imagine a situation in which an argument is inherent to the meaning of a predicate, but the argument does not have to be expressed syntactically. Such a possibility suggests that at the end of the day, the thematic principle, although motivated by semantic considerations, is a principle of syntactic well-formedness. The matter becomes particularly acute with respect to nominalizations. *Destruction*, no less than *destroy*, implies a destroyer and a destroyed. We might therefore say that the noun 'inherits' the thematic grid of the verb. But whereas any use of the verb *destroy* will require that the internal argument (and usually also the external argument) be explicitly stated, the noun *destruction* may be used without any mention whatever of the Agent or Theme.

(c) Case theory

Case is a familiar category of traditional grammar, having to do with noun inflection as a function of the syntactic and semantic role of an NP within a larger configuration. The GB notion of case is at once broader than the traditional notion, and narrower. It is broader in that case is not limited to matters of morphological marking. Case is therefore just as relevant to English (where it is not generally marked by the morphology), as it is to Russian and Latin (where it is so marked). It is narrower in that case would appear to be an essentially structural property, having little, if any, semantic import.

Case is assigned under certain structural conditions. The crucial notion is that of government. The definition of government comes in several versions; its essential features are as follows.

(i) Only the categories N, V, A, P, and INFL (i.e. inflection, that component of a finite sentence that expresses tense, as well as person and number agreement of a verb with its subject), and their projections (i.e. N', NP, etc.) can be governors.

(ii) Only phrasal categories (XP) are governed.

(iii) Governors and governed c-command each other.

(iv) The c-command relation holds between an element α and all elements dominated by the least phrasal category (XP) which contains α, but which are not dominated by α.

GB theory, as expounded in Chomsky (1981), recognizes four cases: nominative, accusative (or objective), oblique, and genitive. A noun phrase is assigned one of these cases under certain structural conditions, as follows (Chomsky 1981: 170).

(i) An NP is assigned nominative case if it is governed by INFL.

(ii) An NP is assigned accusative case if it is governed by a verb.

(iii) An NP is assigned oblique case if it is governed by a preposition.

(iv) An NP is assigned genitive case if it appears in the environment $[_{NP}\underline{\quad} X']$.

The overt marker of genitive case in English is the morpheme POSS. By (iv), POSS is inserted into $[_{NP}[John] [_{N'}book]]$, $[_{NP}[The city] [_{N'}destruction]]$, $[_{NP}[John] [_{V'}reading the book]]$, to give, respectively, *John's book*, *the city's destruction*, *John's reading the book*.

Although the four cases are given traditional names in GB theory, it is actually a moot point whether any significance attaches to the different categories. The terms nominative, accusative, etc. would appear to be little more than mnemonic aids for the different circumstances in which case is assigned. The important point is simply that each NP in a phrase must be assigned *some* case. By the 'case filter', a caseless nominal renders the sentence in which it occurs ungrammatical.

Generally, case assignment and θ-role assignment go hand in hand. In the VP *destroy the city, the city* is assigned accusative case, since the NP is governed by the verb, as well as the θ-role of Theme, in virtue of its status as the complement of the verb. The need to separate case assignment from θ-role assignment is motivated by examples like the following.

(8)   I secretly believed him to be right.

Here, *him* is assigned accusative case under government from *believe*. There is, or so the argument goes, no thematic relation between *believe* and *him*; what is believed is not the person, but the proposition 'he is right'.[5] *Him* receives its thematic role from the verb phrase *to be right*. At the same time, *him* fails to receive nominative case from *to be right*, since this non-finite verb phrase lacks the INFL constituent.

Case will be relevant to our investigation of the possessive to the extent that the possessive morpheme, both in traditional grammars and in GB theory, is said to be a marker of genitive case. We will therefore need to undertake a careful examination of the nature of case, and will need to revise the notion of case as a purely structural relation between an NP and its governor.

Already at this point, however, we might observe that even within the GB framework of Chomsky (1981), genitive case turns out to be rather anomalous *vis-à-vis* the other three cases. It is, namely, the only case which is assigned, not under government, but in an arbitrarily stated syntactic environment. Whereas (i)–(iii) might well be applicable, in principle, to most, if not all languages, (iv) is idiosyncratic to English (and perhaps also to one or two other Germanic languages). Furthermore, in English, genitive case would be the only one of the four cases that receives phonological expression.

(d) Movement and traces

Early versions of generative grammar (up to about 1970) were dominated by transformations. These performed structural changes on a syntactic representation, and thereby made it possible to relate some syntactic configurations to others.

An important motivation for transformations was the desire to capture regular correspondences between expressions of different syntactic structures. Classic examples are the relation between active and passive sentences (*They destroyed the city/The city was destroyed*), between sentences with raised and unraised constituents (*It seems an error was made/An error seems to have been made*), and between sentences and nominalizations (*They destroyed the city/their destruction of the city*).

Nevertheless, from the earliest days of transformational grammar, doubts were

---

[5] Bolinger (1977: ch. 6), however, has pointed out that the construction in (8) would be slightly odd, just in case the accusative object of *believe* is not, in fact, believed. Hence *I believe him to be telling the truth* is better than ?*I believe him to be telling a lie*.

raised about the psychological reality of transformations (Johnson-Laird 1970). There seemed to be little evidence that speakers did actually create passive sentences from their active counterparts, or, conversely, that they understood passive sentences by un-doing the passive transformation. Such considerations lay behind one of the earliest break-away movements from mainstream generative grammar, lexical functional grammar (Bresnan 1978). In LFG, the relation between, say, an active and a passive sentence was captured, not by means of a transformation on a syntactic structure, but by means of a lexical rule, which derived a passive verb, e.g. (*be*) *destroyed*, from its active counterpart, *destroy*. Even though the relation between an active verb and its passive counterpart might be quite predictable, in many cases, the passive still needed to be entered into the lexicon.

Since the 1970s, transformations have played a decreasing role in mainstream generative grammar, too. The motivation for this trend has been, not so much a striving for psychological realism, but a desire to place constraints on the free-for-all transformations that had been permitted in earlier work in this tradition. Whereas previously, the surface form of a sentence might be far removed from the underlying structure from which it was derived, more recent versions have been characterized by an increased shallowness of derivation. Essentially, in GB theory, deep structures (D-structures) represent thematic relations in their purest, most direct form, with the arguments of a predicate appearing as close as possible (in the ideal case, adjacent) to the predicate which assigns thematic roles to them. The only permissible transformation is the movement of an argument away from its canonical thematic position, as when the complement of a verb is moved into subject position (as in a passive sentence), or when the external argument of a verb is moved to become the subject of a higher verb (as in raising constructions). Furthermore, whenever an item is displaced, it is said to leave a trace, symbolized by *t*, in its original position. The surface structure (S-structure) of a sentence thereby comes with evidence of its derivational history.

Although in principle GB theory permits anything to be moved anywhere (this is the import of the rule Move-α; Chomsky 1981: 7), the theory places various constraints on movement. Given the above characterization of D-structure, only NPs that are in an argument position, i.e. that are able to be θ-marked, can move. Other constraints follow from the thematic principle and from the case principle. An NP can be θ-marked only once. Hence, it can move only into a position that is not θ-marked. Likewise, an NP in S-structure must receive case. Hence, an NP can only move into a position where it can be case-marked.

Even though the scope of transformations has been severely reduced over the decades, there is still reason to be sceptical about the idea that there might exist layers of syntactic organization distinct from the surface form of a sentence. Whilst demands for psychological realism are relevant here, the main issue, again, is the need to constrain a grammatical theory. A constrained theory is one which permits a small number of analyses (in the ideal case, only one) of the language data. An unconstrained theory permits many possible analyses, and provides few means for evaluating the one analysis over the others. Now, GB theory, in spite of much talk of constraints, is in many crucial respects remarkably *un*constrained. In the first place, the theory makes available to the linguist a range of constructs—such as deep structures, movement rules, invisible (and inaudible!) elements like traces—which cannot be directly observed in the primary linguistic data. The characteristics of these entities, indeed, their very existence, cannot therefore be checked out by inspection of the linguistic data. The analyst is therefore at liberty to propose deep structures and movement transformations for which there exists *no direct evidence whatsoever*. Since deep structures cannot be validated against language data, the only mode of argumentation that is available is in terms of the internal consistency of the theory, as constituted at a given period.

That a theoretical construct might not be directly observable in the primary data is not, of itself, a reason to excise the construct from one's theoretical arsenal. Some linguists like to appeal to other disciplines, such as physics or astronomy, pointing out that no one has directly observed a quark, either, or the inside of the sun. At issue here is the same metatheoretical principle that we invoked earlier, in connection with the supposed autonomy vs. non-autonomy of linguistic knowledge. The most parsimonious account of syntactic structure would be in terms of entities that are immanent in the linguistic data, and whose properties can be readily observed by any competent speaker of the language. A linguist's null hypotheses, therefore, ought to be that there are no levels of syntactic organization that diverge from the surface form of a sentence (e.g. with respect to the order of elements), that there are no transformations which map one level of representation into another, and that there are no invisible (inaudible) constituents in a surface structure. Only after the null hypothesis has been fully tried and tested, and shown to be manifestly inadequate, might there be a reason to postulate deep structures, movement transformations, and invisible constituents.

Many linguists have taken up the challenge of the null hypothesis. Strict monostratalism (the thesis that there exists only one level of linguistic structure) has been espoused by, amongst others, Starosta (1988), Hudson (1984, 1990*a*), and Gazdar *et al.* (1985). Langacker (1987*a*: 46), too, assumes that 'grammatical structure is almost entirely overt'. It is perhaps not coincidental that with respect to the range of theoretical constructs which it postulates, Langacker's cognitive grammar must count amongst the most parsimonious, and hence most highly constrained theories available today.

This is not to say that cognitive grammar makes no reference to such notions as head of phrase, complement, thematic relations, or case relations. Probably, these notions are inherent to the very nature of grammatical organization, and will need to be incorporated into any grammatical model. A distinctive contribution of cognitive grammar, however, is that these fundamental grammatical notions receive a natural explanation in terms of the restricted ontology of the theory. Furthermore, Langacker has initiated discussion of the conceptual foundation of these, and other fundamental grammatical concepts.

The contrast with GB theory is striking. In view of the central role in GB theory of such notions as case assignment, thematic relations, NP-movement, traces, complements, specifiers, and the like, it is remarkable that there has been so little discussion of the conceptual foundations of these notions. The main object of attention has been the conditions under which, say, case, or thematic roles, are assigned, with scant concern for the question of what case, or thematic roles, actually *are*. Likewise, the literature teems with proposals for constraining the circumstances under which one constituent of a sentence may move to another location in the sentence. But little, if anything, has been done to clarify the ontological status of the postulated underlying, or deep structures, which get transformed into surface structures by the operation of these movement rules. For this observer of the generative linguistic scene, at least, a major obstacle to my endorsement of the generative programme is, precisely, the lack of conceptual clarification of the theoretical constructs that it proposes.

2.5 FUNCTIONALISM

Non-autonomous linguistics attempts to derive linguistic phenomena from more general cognitive principles. Functionalism is one such approach.

The study of language functions is not, in itself, inconsistent with the autonomy thesis. There is no contradiction in supposing that the form of a sentence is determined by purely linguistic factors, and then investigating the functions that that sentence may have. This, certainly, is Newmeyer's (1991) position.

A stronger functionalist claim would be that the properties of a language have been shaped by the functions that the language is called upon to serve, and that, therefore, each element in a language 'can be explained, ultimately, by reference to how language is used' (Halliday 1985a: p. xiii). Functionalism in this sense has been pursued by Givón, Chafe, Foley and Van Valin, and many others.

Chomsky (1980: 229–31) has rejected outright the possibility of functional explanation. He has argued strongly for the view that syntax is organized by its own, system-specific rules and principles, and that the function, or functions, of language are but parasitic on, and quite incidental to, its true nature. In particular, he has dismissed (p. 230) any suggestion that the 'essential purpose' of language could be 'communication', pointing out that the notion of communication is vague and ill-defined, and that no 'substantive proposals' can follow from it.

Chomsky's strictures on the vagueness of the term communication have some legitimacy. The viability of a functional explanation will certainly depend on the precision with which the functions of language can be articulated.

Let us consider, briefly, how some of the functions of language could be spelled out. Any stretch of language has to be 'about' something—people, things, concepts, ideas, and suchlike. A speaker needs to refer to these entities; he has to introduce them into the discourse; he has to keep track of them as the discourse proceeds; and he has to make reasonably certain that his (potential or actual) interlocutor is able to correctly identify just which entities he (the speaker) has in mind. In brief, a person is under the obligation to ensure that his interlocutor knows what he is talking about. One might even want to say: A person has to make sure that he himself knows what he is talking about! In order to achieve this aim, a speaker must needs draw on the resources made available by his language. A functional account would study the palette of available resources, investigate their properties, and consider the factors that might motivate the choice of one, rather than another of these resources in a given situation, matching each device with its function, in order to see in what ways the device is adapted, in virtue of its structural properties, to its function.

Or, consider another tack. The ideas, concepts, etc. that a discourse is about, do not just spring from nowhere. Any discourse (even an internal monologue, or internal musing) takes place against a background of existing, or presupposed knowledge. The background knowledge may be very general in nature (e.g. that things have parts, that people have names, that objects have locations), it may be knowledge pertaining to the meanings of individual words (if a person X is called a 'student', then there will be some domain of knowledge that X is studying), or it may be knowledge pertaining to a specific interactional context, or that has been built up in the course of preceding discourse. We might expect, therefore, that a language will have various devices for anchoring a current discourse in the conceptual background of speaker and hearer. Again, a functional approach would strive to identify these resources, and attempt to correlate their formal properties with the functions that they serve.

The account of the prenominal possessive that was sketched in section 1.2 has a strong functional component, in that the construction is seen as a device that facilitates the identification of an entity from the vantage of a previously named entity presumed to be cognitively salient to both speaker and hearer. There is, therefore, a close homology between the structure of the construction and its function. We shall see in due course how a number of formal properties of the construction fall out quite naturally from this functional account.

2.6 MENTAL PROCESSING

The term mental processing may be construed very broadly. Indeed, given the assumption that language is a mental phenomenon, all aspects of language knowledge and language use will be reducible, ultimately, to matters of mental processing. It will subsume the attention effects invoked by Deane (1992), matters of reference and referent tracking, as studied by Givón (1979) and Chafe (1987), as well as such matters as parsing strategies (Hawkins 1990), and constraints imposed by limitations on working memory.

In particular, meaning will be seen in terms of mental processing. Indeed, Langacker equates the meaning of a linguistic expression with a conceptualization, or 'mental experience'. The term conceptualization, for Langacker,

> is meant to include not just fixed concepts, but also novel conceptions and experiences, even as they occur. It includes not just abstract, 'intellectual' conceptions, but also such phenomena as sensory, emotive, and kinesthetic sensations. It further embraces a person's awareness of the physical, social, and linguistic context of speech events. There is nothing inherently mysterious about conceptualization: it is simply cognitive processing (neurological activity). Entertaining a particular conceptualization, or having a certain mental experience, resides in the occurrence of some complex 'cognitive event' (reducing ultimately to the coordinated firing of neurons). (Langacker 1988b: 6)

Here, I want to mention two aspects of mental processing that will prove useful in our subsequent discussion. These are the notions of 'mental route' and 'conceptual dependence'.

Langacker (1991: 97) has discussed reference in terms of the metaphor of establishing mental contact, defined as the singling out of a concept for conscious awareness in a person's current psychological state. Now, some entities may be more easily, or more directly, singled out than others. Extending Langacker's metaphor, we may speak of the 'mental route' by which contact is established.

The experiential basis of the metaphor is quite transparent. Suppose I wish to establish telephonic contact with someone. One way would be to do so directly, by looking up the person's telephone number and dialling it. Suppose, though, that I know the person, not as a private individual, but as the manager of a company. In this case, I might ring the company, and ask to be connected with the manager. I establish telephonic contact with the person *via* prior contact with the company. Or suppose I wish to locate a place on a map. If the place is a major landmark, I may be able to zoom in on it directly. Alternatively, I may have to locate the place with respect to a major landmark. The one entity thus serves as a reference point for the location of another, less salient entity.

Analogously, it may be possible to establish mental contact directly with a concept. In other cases, contact is established through prior contact with a related concept. Suppose I wish to say something about 'the headlights of my car', that they need adjusting, for example. The very expression that I have had to use to introduce the example illustrates the point. To conceptualize (establish mental contact with) the headlights, it is necessary to make reference to a car. And in order to conceptualize the specific car that is intended, namely, *my* car, I make reference to myself (by means of the possessive *my*). There is a further point. Not only are headlights conceptualized *via* the notion of the car of which they are a part, headlights have status as 'headlights' only to the extent that they constitute a part (potential or actual) of a car, or some similar kind of vehicle. If we divorce the notion of 'headlights' from any notion of 'car', we would probably not call them headlights at all, but something else; searchlights, perhaps.

The example has also illustrated the important notions of *conceptual autonomy* and *conceptual dependence* (Langacker 1991: 286–91). An entity is conceptually autonomous to the extent that it is possible to conceptualize the entity in and of itself, without making necessary reference to anything outside the entity. An entity is conceptually dependent to the extent that conceptualization of that entity presupposes, or requires, reference to other entities; these latter entities, we shall say, are *intrinsic* to the conceptually dependent entity. Conceptual dependence and conceptual autonomy are, of course, matters of degree. Probably, no concept is fully autonomous, in the manner suggested. And just as the ease with which a place can be located on a map may well be a function of a person's familiarity with the map, and with the terrain which it represents, so degree of conceptual autonomy might vary according to a person's previous use of the concept. Even so, there is a fairly clear sense in which the concept of 'headlights' is less autonomous than the concept of 'car'. For, as pointed out, if we were to excise all notion of a car from our conceptualization of headlights, there would be little basis for their conceptualization as headlights in the first place.

The notions of mental route and conceptual dependence have far-reaching linguistic consequences. I will cite just two examples. The first is from Deane (1992: 41). A part is conceptually dependent *vis-à-vis* the whole. Conceptualization of a part needs to make inherent reference to the whole. In contrast, the notion of a whole is typically autonomous *vis-à-vis* the parts of which the whole is composed. We can, generally, conceptualize a whole as a gestalt, without having to enumerate, or even be aware of, its various parts. Consider now the following pair of examples.

(9)   *a.* I saw headlights coming straight at me, but I was able to get out of its [= the car's] way.
      b. *As a car came at me, I noticed they [= its headlights] were bright.

In (9*a*) mention of *headlights* has already invoked the notion of a car. Consequently, *it* can be taken to refer to this highly salient aspect of the conceptualization. In contrast, mention of conceptually autonomous *car* does not evoke the notion of headlights. In the absence of contextual information, which might render the notion of headlights cognitively salient, *they* cannot be taken to refer to the headlights.

A second reflex concerns the possessive construction. On the reference point analysis, the possessor names a salient, i.e. cognitively accessible entity, which serves as a reference point for the subsequent identification of an otherwise difficult-to-access entity, i.e. the possessee. Now compare the following.

(10) *a.* the car's headlights.
      b. ??the headlights' car.

(10*a*) is perfectly normal, whilst (10*b*) is decidedly odd.[6] The difference is plausibly attributed to the conceptual autonomy vs. conceptual dependence of *car* and *headlights*.

In order to conceptualize (or establish mental contact with) the conceptually dependent *headlights*, it is normal first to conceptualize an entity that is intrinsic to that conceptualization, i.e. *car*. Thus (10*a*) iconically maps the mental route that the conceptualizer takes. But (10*b*) is unacceptable because conceptually incoherent. The reference point (by definition) needs to be more salient, i.e. more easily accessible, than the target entity. (If the target entity were already accessible, there would be no need to employ a possessive construction to identify it!) A conceptually dependent entity is less accessible than a conceptually autonomous entity, in that it cannot be conceptualized in and of itself, but must involve necessary reference to another entity. Furthermore, the accessibility of the conceptually dependent *headlights* would presuppose the accessibility of *car*, the notion of car being inherent to a conceptualization of headlights. The status of *the headlights* in (10*b*) as a reference point for the subsequent identification of the car would therefore conflict with the very *raison d'être* of the possessive construction.

This is not to say that a conceptually dependent entity, like headlights, may never function as a reference point. The target, however, would have to be an entity which is itself conceptually dependent, and for whose conceptualization the notion of headlights (or some schematically characterized entity, of which 'headlights' is an instance) is intrinsic. The following examples exactly parallel those in (10).

(11)   *a.* the headlights' price.
       b. *the price's headlights.
(12)   *a.* the headlights' size.
       b. *the size's headlights.

The notion of price presupposes an entity which bears that price. The possessor nominal names such an entity. Likewise, the notion of size presupposes an entity with physical dimensions. Again, the possessor nominal names some such entity.

2.7 THE SCOPE OF SEMANTICS

A frequent strategy for non-autonomous linguistics has been to propose semantic explanations for an ever increasing range of syntactic phenomena. As a

---

[6] This is not to say that it might not be possible to engineer a situation in which something like (10*b*) might be marginally acceptable. Imagine a scrapyard, where cars are being demolished. Someone investigating the provenance of a set of headlights which he is holding in his hands could point to several wrecks and ask *Which is their car?* Such a possibility depends on the headlights being the centre of a person's interest (and therefore cognitively accessible, in the circumstances), and on cars being conceptualized only with respect to the headlights. The situation would entail a reversal of the usual autonomy–dependence asymmetry.

'deeper and deeper semantic wedge' (Jackendoff 1990: 285) is driven into the syntax, an autonomous level of syntactic organization could become increasingly difficult to justify.

Some caution, however, is called for. Just as the study of language functions is not, in itself, inconsistent with the autonomy position, so the study of the semantic correlates of syntactic phenomena need not conflict with a commitment to the autonomy of syntax.

Few linguists, I imagine, would want to quibble with Langacker's (1987*a*: 12) assertion that 'meaning is what language is all about'. A language is, uncontroversially, a device for linking meaning (a quintessentially mental entity) with some perceptible event, prototypically, an acoustic signal. At issue is whether we need to postulate a level, or levels, of organization intervening between sound and meaning, levels which are structured according to principles which are independent of phonological (or orthographic, pictographic, or gestural) expression on the one hand, and semantic content on the other.

Thus, Chomsky's early monograph, *Syntactic Structures* (1957), was 'an attempt to construct a formalized general theory of linguistic structure' (p. 5). 'Linguistic structure' here comprised only the sequential patterning of 'formatives', i.e. words and morphemes, without regard to their meaning; and a 'grammar' was taken to be the set of rules which generated, or defined, all and only the well-formed strings of formatives. The meaning of the formatives, and of the well-formed strings, was said to be quite irrelevant to the enterprise; as irrelevant, Chomsky tells us with a rhetorical flourish, as 'knowledge of the hair color of speakers' (p. 93).

Even at this time, however, Chomsky did not deny that there might be 'correlations', even 'important correlations' (p. 108), between syntax and semantics, between the strings of formal objects that the grammar defines, and the meanings that speakers might wish to symbolize in using them, nor that these correlations might be the 'subject matter for a more general theory of language'. Chomsky's main point appears to have been that in order to establish such correlations, syntax and semantics *have* to be studied independently of each other. The exclusion of semantic considerations from the study of syntax was therefore a matter of methodological principle, it did not arise from any commitment to the psychological reality of autonomous syntax.[7]

The study of the correlations between syntax and semantics has become rather prominent in recent years. Symptomatic is the attention devoted to lexical argument structure, and to the relation of lexical argument structure with lexical

[7] Observe that commitment to a 'completely formal and non-semantic' (Chomsky 1957: 93) theory of language pre-dated attempts to cognitivize, and to biologize, the language faculty. There is therefore some substance to the claim that the twin theses of autonomy and modularity arose as elaborations of the formalist commitment; the idea of a language faculty encapsulated from conceptual knowledge did not arise in response to known facts about the structure of the mind, or the status of language knowledge in the mind.

semantic structure on the one hand, and with subcategorization frames on the other.

These terms perhaps need some explanation. Lexical semantic structure (or lexical conceptual structure, sometimes abbreviated to LCS) would appear to be but a fancy name for word meaning, in all its complexity and subtlety. Subcategorization frames define the syntactic environment(s) in which the word may occur, and specify the kinds of complements that the item may (or must) take. Take the example of the verb *cut*. Guerssel *et al.* (1985: 51) propose the following as a statement of the meaning (or, perhaps better, some aspects of the meaning) of the verb.

(13)   *cut* LCS: x produce CUT on y, by sharp edge coming into contact with
       y

The subcategorization frame associates the transitive verb with an obligatory NP complement.

(14)   *cut*: _____ NP

The NP complement names the Patient, corresponding to the variable y in (13), of the activity denoted by the verb *cut*, whilst the subject expresses the Agent, corresponding to the variable x in (13). The lexical argument structure (often abbreviated to A-structure) states the number of arguments associated with the predicate, and their semantic relation (Agent, Patient, etc.) to the predicate.

(15)   *cut* A-structure: Agent, Patient

Subcategorization frames, by definition, are a matter of syntax. Lexical semantic structure, again by defintion, is a matter of semantics. Argument structure is a kind of bridge between the two domains, in that it specifies syntactically relevant aspects of the semantics.

The crucial question is whether, and to what extent, subcategorization frames may be derived from (or, more strongly, may be predicted from) lexical argument structure; likewise, whether lexical argument structure is derivable from (or predictable from) lexical semantic structure. For if it should turn out that subcategorization frames are derivable from argument structure, and argument structure is derivable from semantic structure, it follows that the syntactic properties of a word are derivable from the word's semantics. The strongest claim, therefore, would be that to know the meaning of a word is to know the syntactic properties of the word.

Many linguists have been reluctant to take this step. Thus, for Grimshaw (1990: 4), the syntactic properties of predicates may not be 'reduced to their semantics'. The syntactic properties may well be predictable, but not from argument structure alone, but from argument structure *in interaction with* independent formal principles of the language. Secondly, she states that the argument structure of a predicate 'has its own internal structure' (p. 3). Although argument structure may be 'a reflection' of a word's meaning, and may even be derivable from 'key characteristics' of a word's meaning' (p. 3), argument structure and lexical conceptual structure need to be separately specified. The matter will be of some interest to us, in that it bears directly on the analysis of certain possessive nominalizations. We might want to say that conceptually, the verb *examine* and the noun *examination* equally presuppose an Agent (one who examines) and a Patient (an entity that is examined). In (16), according to Grimshaw (pp. 51–2), both the verb and the noun do indeed have an argument structure, requiring the expression of Agent and Patient.

(16)   *a.* The instructor intentionally examined the papers.
       b. The instructor's intentional examination of the papers took a long time.

In (17), however, *examination* is claimed not to have an argument structure.

(17)   The instructor's examination took a long time.

While the possessor NP in (17) may well be interpreted as Agent, *the instructor* does not fill this role in virtue of the argument structure of *examination*. One piece of evidence for the difference between (16*b*) and (17) is the fact that an agent-oriented adverbial may not be inserted into (17).

(18)   *The instructor's intentional examination took a long time.

In a similar vein, Jackendoff (1990: 252) points out that not all constituents in lexical conceptual structure necessarily have the status of arguments. And even if the syntactically relevant participants were to be specially marked as such (e.g. by an essentially *ad hoc* device of 'A-marking'), Jackendoff still says that he 'would hesitate to endorse without more careful research the claim that *all* syntactic argument structure is determined by conceptual structure plus A-marking' (p. 257). Jackendoff's position, in fact, is rather close to that of Chomsky in *Syntactic Structures*. Jackendoff proposes an autonomous level of conceptual (i.e. semantic) structure, and an autonomous level of syntactic structure. Each level is organized around its own constituent elements, and principles for their combination. But now, going beyond Chomsky's original suggestions, a *third* component becomes necessary—'*logically* necessary', according to Jackendoff (p. 286). This is a component which interfaces between the syntax and the semantics. This is the domain of 'correspondence rules', or 'linking rules', which 'must crucially involve the vocabularies of both autonomous components', but which are themselves autonomous of syntax and semantics, with 'their own properties and typology'.[8]

Others, however, have been prepared to pursue a reductionist programme with more enthusiasm. Ironically, the lead may have come from Chomsky himself (Chomsky 1986: 86–92). While admitting that 'many problems remain' (p. 92), Chomsky does seem rather optimistic that a word's syntactic properties may

---

[8] Observe how modularity feeds itself. To postulate one module creates the need for a further module, to interface between it and an already postulated module.

be fully predictable from its semantics, albeit in interaction with principles of Universal Grammar. A clearly reductionist approach may be noted in various studies conducted within the lexical semantic tradition established by Jackendoff (1983, 1990) and Pinker (1989). Consider the methodology of Levin and Rappaport Hovav (1991). They set out to identify classes of verbs that occur in similar syntactic environments, and seek to isolate just those 'components of meaning' that the different classes have in common, and hypothesize that these meaning components are 'syntactically relevant' (p. 126), in as far as it is they that determine the syntactic configuration in which the verbs occur. A similar line has been taken by linguists working outside of the generative paradigm. Thus, in his detailed study of the kinds of complement (*that*-clause, *to*-infinitive, and so on) that English verbs can take, Dixon (1991) assumes 'a principled interaction between the meaning of a word and its grammatical properties'. He continues:

Once a learner knows the meaning and grammatical behaviour of most of the words in a language, then from the meaning of a new word he can infer its likely grammatical possibilities; or, from observing the grammatical use of a new word, he may be able to infer a good deal about what it means. (Dixon 1991: 6)

At this point, one may wonder whether there are any matters of substance differentiating a reductionist programme of the kind envisaged by Chomsky and pursued by Levin and Rappaport Hovav, and the position of linguists outside the generative stream, such as Dixon and Langacker. While a certain convergence cannot be denied, there still remain, I think, a number of important differences between the two approaches.

The first concerns the nature of syntactic organization. To reject the autonomy of syntax position does not, of course, bring with it a denial of the rather obvious fact that sentences have syntactic structure. But neither does the existence of syntactic structure of itself legitimize a level of organization that is autonomous of semantics. Langacker's claim is not so much that syntactic configurations (statable in purely syntactic terms) are predictable from word meanings (the essence of the reductionist programme), but that syntax is itself inherently meaningful. To this extent there is no principled distinction between the meaning of a word or morpheme, and the meaning of a grammatical pattern.

I contend that grammar itself, i.e. patterns for grouping morphemes into progressively larger configurations, is inherently symbolic and hence meaningful. Thus it makes no more sense to posit separate grammatical and semantic components than it does to divide a dictionary into two components, one listing lexical forms and the other listing lexical meanings. Grammar is simply the structuring and symbolization of semantic content. (Langacker 1987a: 12)

It is therefore not just a question of predicting a word's syntactic behaviour from its semantics, but rather of deriving the meaning of a complex expression from the meaning of its component morphemes, and from the meaning of the syntactic configurations in which they occur. Much the same point has been made by Wierzbicka. The possibility of using a word in a certain construction, she says, 'is determined both by the meaning of the [word] AND by the meaning of the construction' (Wierzbicka 1988: 8).

A second difference between the reductionist programme and the non-autonomy position (especially as the latter has been implemented by Wierzbicka and Langacker) concerns the content and scope of semantic characterizations. Semantic characterizations as proposed by Jackendoff, Grimshaw, Levin, and Rappaport Hovav, are *partial* characterizations of word meanings. The aim has been to identify just those aspects of a word's meaning which are claimed to be syntactically relevant. On the other hand, Wierzbicka (e.g. 1988) has pursued a programme of full semantic characterization. Only in this way, she claims, is it possible to explicate the subtle differences between superficially similar words, and between superficially similar constructions, both within a single language, and in different languages.

Let us look at an example in more detail. Jackendoff (1990: 34) claims that the verbs *run* and *jog* are 'syntactically parallel', and can thus be assigned an identical conceptual structure, along the following lines (p. 45).

(19) $[_{Event}GO \, ([_{Thing} \quad], [_{Path} \quad])]$

Since (19) treats both verbs simply as motion verbs, it can obviously only count as a *very* partial characterization of the meanings of *run* and *jog*. Jackendoff, however, claims that whatever we may know about running and jogging over and above what is present in this formula, is 'invisible to syntax' (p. 34; see also p. 88). In other words, (19) is meant to capture the syntactically relevant aspects of the meaning of the two verbs.

But the alleged syntactic parallelism between the two verbs only holds at a *very* coarse level of description, the level, that is, at which we merely say that both verbs take a path-denoting complement. On closer inspection (and even ignoring the fact that all manner of non-human entities, like dogs, car engines, water taps, noses, and stomachs, can 'run', but not 'jog'), very many differences emerge. You can *run to catch the bus*, but it would be odd to say of a person that he *jogged to catch the bus*. A child can *run into the road* (*after his ball*), but you can hardly say of a person that he *jogged into the road after something*. While running, you can *run into a lamppost* (because of a temporary distraction), but you cannot *jog into a lamppost* while jogging. You can *run a race*, *run in a race*, or *run against someone in a race*, but you cannot *jog a race*, *jog in a race*, or *jog against someone in a race*. You can *outrun* someone, but not *outjog* them. You can *run on the spot*, but not *jog on the spot*.

These differences (and they are clearly *syntactic* differences, having to do with the kind of complements with which the verbs are compatible) surely require, for their explanation, a rather detailed understanding of what jogging is, in contrast to mere running. One crucial aspect, it seems to me, is that jogging is pursued as a form of non-competitive physical exercise, like doing aerobics, and is thereby associated with a certain category of person (such as health-conscious yuppies). The syntactic restrictions on *jog*, in contrast to *run*, fall out from this characterization. For example, if you jog, then necessarily you have to jog along some route, past certain landmarks. But you do not jog *in order to get to* the places that lie on the route. That is why you cannot 'jog to catch the bus'. There is even, I would maintain, a subtle difference of interpretation between the 'syntactically parallel' sentences in (20).

(20)   *a*. I ran to the post-office.
       b. I jogged to the post-office.

If I run to the post-office, it is probably because I need to get there quickly, before the post-office closes; that is why I run, rather than walk, or drive through the traffic. But if I jog to the post-office it is not because I need to get to the post-office at all. It just happens that the post-office lies at the end of my jogging route.

2.8 CONVENTIONALITY

If syntax is autonomous, the possibility exists that a sentence may be conceptually well-formed, but syntactically deviant, because of the violation of a purely formal constraint. On the other hand, if syntax is inherently meaningful, the distinction between 'semantically deviant' and 'syntactically deviant' falls away. 'Ungrammatical' becomes synonymous with 'conceptually incoherent'.

Even a person who is sympathetic to the non-autonomy position is likely to protest that at least some aspects of a language are evidence of purely formal principles of organization, of no semantic or functional import whatsoever. If a speaker of French construes *silence* as a feminine noun, if he says, for example, *la silence*, he has produced an ungrammatical utterance, whose deviance, surely, cannot be put down to its conceptual incoherence? The speaker has simply violated a purely arbitrary, formal principle of the French language.

The arbitrariness of gender assignment is a clear challenge to a claim that formal aspects of a language are semantically motivated. But I do not think that it proves the correctness of the autonomy position. Consider more carefully the notion of arbitrariness. Saussure (1964: 100) spoke of the arbitrariness of the linguistic sign. The phonetic form /tri:/ is associated with the concept "tree". The relation is arbitrary in the sense that there is no reason why just this signifier should be associated with just this signified; in principle, any other phonetic form would do just as well. (In fact, there is no reason why the concept "tree" should be lexicalized at all.) From the perspective of an uninvolved observer of the English language, all this may well be true. But from the perspective of an

English speaker, there is a perfectly good reason why *he* should associate the concept "tree" with the phonetic form /tri:/. The reason is that everyone else who speaks English does the same! From the perspective of a speaker of the language, the relation between signifier and signified might be more appropriately termed 'conventional', rather than 'arbitrary'.

Conventionality—the notion is crucial to cognitive grammar—is used here in very much its everyday sense. A convention is simply a generally accepted way of doing something. Humans, in their daily lives, are constrained by all kinds of conventions, which they contravene at their peril. There are conventional ways of dressing, and conventional ways of eating. There are also conventional ways of saying things—as well as conventional things to say. It would not be too far-fetched to say that a language is just a large repository of conventions, which are sanctioned by the linguistic community, and which are available to a speaker for his individual use.

Conventionality pervades all aspects of a language's resources, most obviously, its lexical resources. Even expressions which are compositionally motivated, i.e. are analysable into their component parts, and whose meaning reflects their internal composition, may still be conventional, to some degree. Take the example *pencil sharpener* (Langacker 1988*b*: 24). Its meaning is derivable from the meanings of the component morphemes (*pencil*, *sharp*, *-en*, *-er*), and general patterns for their combination. Yet the expression is still conventional, in two respects. First, it denotes a particular kind of mechanical device; it does not denote, or at least does not conventionally denote, a person who sharpens a pencil,[9] nor *any* instrument that may be used to sharpen a pencil (such as a bread knife). Secondly, the expression is conventional to the extent that the mechanical device could have been called something else (*pencil-pointer*, or some such).

Bierwisch and Schreuder (1992) observe that there is no one-to-one correspondence between the concepts that a person may entertain and the meanings of linguistic expressions; this is one of their arguments for the existence of a specifically linguistic level of meaning, distinct from conceptualization. The point loses its validity if we accept that linguistic meanings are not just 'conceptual structures' but 'conventionalized conceptual structures' (Langacker 1982: 23). It follows that a person has to mould his conceptualizations to match the symbolic resources made available to him by his language. English forces its speakers to make a conceptual distinction between *snails* and *slugs* (the former carry their shells with them, the latter do not); German does not (snails and slugs are both *Schnecken*). British English requires its speakers to make a conceptual distinction between a singular and plural construal of certain collective nouns; they have the choice between *the government has . . .* and *the government have . . .* Speakers of American English do not, in general, have this option

---

[9] But think of Gogol's *Diary of a Madman*. Would it be so outrageous to refer to the chief protagonist of the story as a 'deluded pencil-sharpener'?

(Langacker 1988*b*: 37–8). Neither do speakers of many other languages. (German, for example, does not make available the choice between *die Regierung hat* . . . and *die Regierung haben* . . .)

This last example touches on the conventional character also of the syntactic resources of a language. It is certainly worth emphasizing here the conventional character of possessive constructions in English. I have already pointed to the close homology between the form and the meaning of the prenominal possessive. The construction therefore possesses a high degree of 'naturalness'. Still, a speaker of English has had to learn that *this* is the way to identify the target entity in English, given the prior identity of a reference point. (The question, sometimes raised in this connection, of whether possessive constructions in other languages are therefore somehow 'less natural' is not really an issue at all. It is a bit like making a value-judgement between chopsticks and a knife and fork.) And whilst I shall argue (in section 12.4) that [NP POSS] in the postnominal possessive (*a friend of Bill's*) has exactly the same semantic value as it has in the prenominal possessive (*Bill's friend*), the former construction still constitutes a conventional resource of the language, in that a speaker of English has to learn of the availability of just this construction, and of its suitability for certain expressive needs.

It might be objected that conventionality is just a way to reintroduce a level of formal grammatical organization, by the back door, as it were. I do not think that this objection is valid. Conventionality itself has a firm cognitive foundation. Givón (1989: ch. 7) has drawn attention to two 'modes' of cognitive processing: automated processing, and attended processing. Attended processing is slow, and is applied to tasks that are novel and unpredictable. Automated processing is rapid, and is applied to routine, predictable tasks.

Many aspects of language use are highly automated. This is most obvious with respect to articulation. In speaking our native tongue, we do not need to consciously attend to the movements of the articulators; these are coordinated automatically, in virtue of the practice of a lifetime. Givón argues that automaticity also pertains to matters of conceptualization, and to the linguistic encoding of conceptualizations. On the one hand, the lexical stock of a language makes available a set of pre-established concepts, whilst syntactic constructions supply a set of pre-established routines for the combining of concepts. The automaticity of production and comprehension largely rests on the conventionality of a language's resources, in both its lexicon and its grammar.

2.9 LEXICALISM AND CONSTRUCTIONISM

Recent years have seen a striking convergence, by linguists of various theoretical persuasions, towards lexicalism, i.e. the thesis that properties of syntactic configurations derive from properties of lexical items which feature in the

configurations. In generative grammar, the trend towards lexicalism was initiated by Chomsky's 'Remarks on nominalization' (1970). In this paper, Chomsky
argued that properties of a phrase could be derived from general principles of
syntactic well-formedness, in interaction with the properties of the word that
heads the phrase. The advance of the lexicalist thesis was accompanied by a
decrease in the scope of syntactic transformations. Thus, Chomsky proposed that
the relatedness of different kinds of phrase—such as the verbal phrase *destroy
the city* and the nominal phrase *destruction of the city*—should be captured, not
by means of a transformation, but by statements about the words that head the
phrases, i.e. *destroy* and *destruction*. The subsequent elaboration of these ideas
gave rise, on the one hand, to the development of general principles of syntactic
well-formedness (the X-bar principle, the theta principle, principles of case-
assignment, etc.) that together constitute government and binding theory, and,
on the other hand, to an increased interest in properties of lexical items, in
particular their lexical argument structure (Jackendoff 1990).

Lexicalism characterizes not only mainstream generative grammar, but certain offshoots as well, such as lexical functional grammar, and generalized phrase
structure grammar. Other approaches, such as Montague grammar and categorial
grammar, as well as dependency grammars, also tend to construe syntagmatic
combination as the reflex of properties of words. Indeed, the crucial importance
of this aspect is nicely captured in the very name of one kind of dependency
grammar: Hudson's 'word grammar'.

Seemingly inconsistent with lexicalism has been a trend towards constructionism. According to the constructionist thesis, syntactic constructions may have
properties over and above, or even at variance with those that could be predicted
from the properties of their constituents and the manner of their combination;
consequently, constructions, i.e. established patterns for the syntagmatic combination of words and phrases, need to be separately represented in the grammar
of a language. Many approaches accord no theoretical significance at all to
syntactic constructions. Constructions are merely 'taxonomic epiphenomena'
(Chomsky 1991: 417)—structures created as the output of various kinds of
rules and principles.[10] This is just as true of current GB theories as it was of
transformational grammars of the 1960s. Yet there is compelling evidence
that a full account of a language will need to incorporate construction-specific
information.

Lakoff (1987: 533) discusses the case of the negative polar question in English. On a strictly compositional view of syntax (and semantics), an affirmative
question (*Did Harry leave?*) and a negative question (*Didn't Harry leave?*)
ought to boil down to the same thing; to ask whether or not it is the case that
p should be no different from asking whether or not it is the case that *not p*. Yet,

---

[10] Lakoff (1987: 467) made the same point: 'In most contemporary formal theories, grammatical
constructions . . . are considered epiphenomena—consequences of more general rules of a very different character'.

as is well known, negative questions have properties beyond what might be expected from the addition of negation to a polar interrogative. In fact, negative questions are not really requests about polarity at all ('Is it, or is it not the case that *not p*?'), they function rather as hedged (affirmative) assertions. This semantic-pragmatic property has syntactic consequences, in that negative questions can sometimes occur in environments normally reserved for statements. A negative question can occur verbatim in certain subordinate clauses, whereas a 'genuine' (i.e. non-negative) question normally may not. *I'm surprised that you ask about Harry, because didn't Harry leave?* is fine, whereas **I'm surprised that you ask about Harry, because did Harry leave?* is out.

Examples such as these suggest that knowledge of a language comprises, not only knowledge of words and their properties, and knowledge of general principles for the combination of words, but also knowledge of specific constructions and their properties (syntactic, semantic, pragmatic, and even phonological). This position informs Construction Grammar (Fillmore 1988, and especially Fillmore *et al.* 1988; also Taylor 1995*b*: 198–220). Constructions, as theoretical linguistic entities, are also of fundamental importance in work by Wierzbicka and Langacker. Wierzbicka (1988: 12) states that 'the grammatical constructions of any natural language encode certain meanings', and argues that the meaning (and grammaticality) of an expression is determined jointly by the meanings of its component words and by the meanings of various grammatical devices, including the meanings of grammatical construction(s) which the expression instantiates. And as the presentation in the following chapters will show, Langacker handles matters of syntax principally by means of construction schemas, which sanction the syntagmatic combination of words into units of increasing internal complexity, and whose meaning can be characterized with varying degrees of abstraction.

For Fillmore, one dimension of a construction is its degree of idiomaticity. Some constructions have highly idiosyncratic properties; their meaning cannot be derived from the meanings of their parts, and even their permissible instantiations may need to be separately listed (and separately learned by the language user). Other constructions are so productive, and their properties so predictable, that their characterization might even be functionally equivalent to a phrase structure rule. (Take the case of the 'transitive clause' construction.) Langacker highlights a different kind of continuum, between lexicon and grammar, the difference residing, essentially, in the degree of schematicity with which an item needs to be characterized. (As a consequence, constructionism need not be seen as inconsistent with lexicalism.) Lexical items tend to be associated with rather specific semantic (and phonological) content, whereas construction schemas generally need to be defined in such a way as to capture the commonality of their permissible instantiations. These matters will be touched on in the next two chapters. Here, I would merely emphasize that when I speak, in this book, of possessive *constructions*, I do so quite deliberately, and so distance myself from the view that the syntactic configurations in which the possessive morpheme appears are merely epiphenomenal by-products of general syntactic principles.

2.10 LEARNABILITY

I would like to bring together some of the points made so far in this chapter by considering the issue of learnability.

According to the cognitive commitment, a linguistic description is a hypothesis of what it is that a person who knows a language actually knows. But the cognitive commitment, as just stated, prompts a further question. How did a person who knows a language acquire that knowledge? This, for Chomsky (1977: 81), is 'the fundamental empirical problem of linguistics'. It is both empirical, and fundamental, to the extent that the kind of knowledge that we may attribute to the mature speaker of a language is severely constrained by accounts of how that knowledge could plausibly be acquired.

It is well known how the dialectic of the acquisition of language knowledge, and the proper characterization of that knowledge, has informed the generative enterprise. Prima facie, we should want to say that a linguistic description which incorporates elements that are in principle unlearnable, given the circumstances in which languages are acquired, is fundamentally flawed. Generative linguists have been the first to concede that GB theory incorporates formal principles which are so abstract, and so remote from primary linguistic input, that they could not plausibly be learned, by induction or generalization, from an inspection of a limited range of data, and certainly not by a pre-school child. Indeed, many have tended to make a virtue out of this fact, claiming that the very unlearnability of syntactic principles is prima-facie evidence that these principles do not have to be learned, for the reason that human beings are genetically predisposed to acquire just these formal principles. The need to postulate the genetic encoding of Universal Grammar is in turn taken as evidence for the correctness of the autonomy position, and of linguistic analyses conducted within its parameters.

Countless examples of this mode of argumentation could be cited. I will mention just one. Giorgi and Longobardi (1991: 135) point to the grammaticality contrast in (21).

(21)   *a.* I disapprove of the destruction of the ship to collect the insurance.
       b. *I disapprove of {its/the ship's} destruction to collect the insurance.

They state (p. 135) that the 'sentence types' exemplified by these expressions are rather rare, 'almost non-occurring', in fact. They doubt therefore that intuitions concerning the grammaticality contrast in (21) could ever be acquired 'by direct exposure' (p. 134) to input sentences; indeed, they believe it 'unlikely that the relevant evidence may ever be available in the primary data to any language learner' (pp. 135–6). The grammaticality contrast would therefore be 'completely unlearnable' (p. 135), were it not for the fact that speakers of English have access to certain genetically transmitted principles of Universal Grammar. The grammaticality contrast in (21) thus acquires the status of crucial empirical evidence in favour of the elaboration of GB theory that Giorgi and Longobardi are intent on promoting.

We shall have occasion to return to examples like those in (21) later in this book, where I will suggest that Giorgi and Longobardi's pessimism concerning the complete unlearnability of the contrast, given only a limited range of primary data, is overstated (section 8.3.2). I will claim, on the contrary, that the contrast is indeed 'learnable', and that the principles involved are readily derivable from some general and rather transparent properties of prenominal possessives on the one hand, and of subjectless purpose clauses on the other. The data in (21) need not therefore be taken as conclusive evidence for the autonomous position defended by Giorgi and Longobardi.

Leaving aside particular examples like this, what are we to say in general of the argument from unlearnability? I have to admit that the argument does have a certain attraction, a fascination even, and to the extent that we concern ourselves only with *very* general principles of syntactic organization, the argument could well go through. As observed earlier, for it to be possible at all for a person to acquire a language, certain genetically inherited capacities have to be presupposed. Disputable is whether these genetically inherited capacities are of a general cognitive nature, or whether they are specific to a language faculty. I suspect, however, that the moment we address more specific linguistic phenomena, such as the behaviour of a single lexical item in a given syntactic environment, the argument from unlearnability will quickly begin to look suspect. Indeed, rather than supporting the autonomy hypothesis, the learnability issue could well be its Achilles' heel.

I will discuss one example in some detail, and then note a comparable state of affairs with respect to prenominal possessives. The example pertains to the so-called dative shift alternation in English.

Consider, first, the following kind of situation. There are, in a given language, two grammatical constructions, C_1 and C_2, and two lexical items, L_1 and L_2. Semantically, the two constructions appear to differ but little. The one could be said to constitute a mere stylistic variant of the other, and in earlier versions of generative grammar the one construction might have been derived from the other, by means of a (meaning-preserving) transformation. In like manner, the two lexical items, at least on a cursory examination, appear to be mere stylistic variants, with little of semantic substance differentiating them. We observe, however, that L_1 and L_2 behave very differently with respect to C_1 and C_2. We find, for example, that L_1 may appear freely in both C_1 and C_2, whereas L_2 may occur only in C_1, the insertion of L_2 in C_2 resulting in ungrammaticality. Schematically, the situation may be represented as follows.

(22)

	C_1	C_2
L_1	+	+
L_2	+	

The following paradigms illustrate the situation sketched in (22).

(23) *a.* They gave a prize to the best pupil.
      b. They gave the best pupil a prize.
      c. They donated £1,000 to the charity.
      d. *They donated the charity £1,000.
(24) *a.* He told the story to his friends.
      b. He told his friends the story.
      c. The Prime Minister announced his resignation to the press.
      d. *The Prime Minister announced the press his resignation.

The constructions exemplified here are the dative construction [NP V NP_1 to NP_2] and the double object construction [NP V NP_2 NP_1]. The lexical items *give* and *tell* may appear freely in either construction. However, the semantically rather similar lexical items *donate* and *announce* may only occur in the dative construction; their insertion in the double object construction results in ungrammaticality.

Examples such as these present the linguist with a problem of great subtlety. Describing the facts of usage is, of course, no big issue. One simply states that *give* and *tell* may be used in both the dative construction and the double object construction, whereas *donate* and *announce* may only be used in the dative construction. More formally, *give* and *tell* might be assigned the subcategorization frames in (25), whereas *donate* and *announce* have only the subcategorization frame in (26).

(25) give, tell [_____ NP_1 to NP_2], [_____ NP_2 NP_1]
(26) donate, announce [_____ NP_2 to NP_1]

Beyond purely descriptive matters, however, lurks the question of learnability. How does the speaker of English come to know that *donate* and *announce* may not be used in the double object construction? If *give* and *tell* may be freely used in both constructions, why does the speaker of English not generalize this knowledge to the semantically rather similar verbs *donate* and *announce*?

Clearly, native speakers of English—unlike, possibly, (some) foreign learners—have not learned these facts in the course of formal instruction in English grammar, such that, had they not received instruction in the relevant facts, they would readily accept the starred sentences in (23) and (24).

One could suppose that people reject the use of *donate* and *announce* in the double object construction because they have never before heard the words used in that construction. But this will clearly not do. A vast number of the expressions that a person encounters, and judges to be grammatical, have never been heard before.[11] It is, furthermore, common cause that speakers do extend their usage ranges, if somewhat cautiously,[12] from known usage patterns. The verbs *to fax* and *to e-mail* are very recent innovations in the English language. Yet we do not need to have first heard expressions of the kind *Fax me your reply, E-mail me the data*, or to have been instructed in the fact that these sentences are grammatical, to know intuitively that *to fax* and *to e-mail* may be used in the double object construction. How does an English speaker know that these verbs pattern like *give* and *tell*, whereas *donate* and *announce* do not?

Appeal to innateness does not get us very far, either, although Neil Smith does in fact take this tack. Smith (1989: 144), discussing the examples *tell* and *report*, writes that our knowledge about the ungrammatical member of the paradigm in (23) 'must be due at least in part to properties of the mind that are independent of experience, i.e. must be innate or genetically determined'. But what, precisely, are these genetically determined properties of the mind supposed to be, that might cause an English speaker to reject (23d)? I see only two possibilities. The one possibility, which Smith appears to favour, is that human beings possess the genetically determined knowledge that 'only some "analogies" are possible' (p. 144). Smith, in other words, appears to be claiming that people have the innate knowledge that whatever generalizations they may make over linguistic data, these generalizations are apt to have exceptions. But this account is trivial, in that a person is still left with the task of identifying just *which* linguistic items fail to participate in any given generalization—which is, of course, the very essence of the problem under discussion. The other possibility is that what is genetically determined is an inventory of exceptions to each and every generalization—a truly bizarre claim. We would have to say that all human beings born over the past 50,000 years (or however long the 'language

---

[11] To claim that a person judges the grammaticality of an expression solely on the basis of previous encounters would indeed have some very undesirable ramifications. The reader of this book, having now encountered examples (23d) and (24d), ought to be inclined to judge these sentences in a somewhat favourable light. And this inclination ought to increase on each rereading of the sentences! What is more, the mere fact that someone, somewhere, once produced an at the time ungrammatical expression, through some lapse of attention for example, could legitimize the grammaticality of that expression for anyone who happened to hear it. The hearers in turn could employ the expression, legitimizing its grammaticality for their hearers, and so on, until eventually its grammaticality could extend to the whole linguistic community. Grammaticality would be a matter of original baptism.

[12] For speakers' conservatism in this regard, see Gropen *et al.* (1989).

faculty' is supposed to have been part of the human genotype) have innate knowledge of the subcategorization frames of the verbs of modern English.

We appear, then, to be faced with a paradox. Speakers of English know that certain words may not be used in certain constructions. The knowledge that some uses of a word are ungrammatical cannot be based on the fact that the ungrammatical expressions have never been heard before. At the same time, the knowledge is so highly language-specific, pertaining to particular lexical items and particular constructions, that it cannot reasonably be regarded as genetically encoded.

The dative and the double object constructions have been the subject of intense interest in recent years. The discussions in Wierzbicka (1988), Pinker (1989), Langacker (1991: 359–60), and Goldberg (1992) suggest a way out of the paradox. Drawing on these accounts, the kind of solution I would propose amounts to the claim that the ungrammatical sentences in (23) and (24) are rejected, not because the sentences violate some syntactic rule, or lexical subcategorization frame, or other kind of formal constraint, but simply because the sentences are semantically incoherent. With respect to (22), the cell in the bottom right is empty because the meaning of L_2 is incompatible with the semantics of C_2.

There are several stages to the substantiation of this claim. It is necessary, first, to presuppose that syntactic constructions have meaning. Then it must be shown that the competing constructions, C_1 and C_2, while similar in meaning, are not identical in meaning. Further, the meanings of the constructions must be readily inferable from the surface form of the constructions, by appeal to general linguistic-cognitive principles; the meanings, in other words, must be learnable. (These general linguistic-cognitive principles might themselves, of course, be innate. As observed before, language acquisition would be not be possible at all unless *some* cognitive capacities are genetically determined.) Then, it will be necessary to establish that the lexical items, L_1 and L_2, while again similar in meaning, nevertheless differ in some crucial respects, also that these differences are readily inferable from how the words are used independently of the constructions under discussion. Finally, it must be shown that the meaning of L_2, while compatible with the meaning of C_1, conflicts in some crucial respect(s) with the meaning of C_2.

I take it as given that syntactic constructions do have meaning, even though their semantic content may be rather more abstract, or 'schematic', than the meanings of lexical items. With respect to the dative and the double object constructions, some relevant aspects may be derived by Lakoff and Johnson's 'spatialization of form' hypothesis.

We speak in linear order; in a sentence, we say some words earlier and others later. Since speaking is correlated with time and time is metaphorically conceptualized in terms of space, it is natural for us to conceptualize language metaphorically in terms of space. . . .

Because we conceptualize linguistic form in spatial terms, it is possible for certain spatial metaphors to apply directly to the *form* of a sentence, as we conceive of it spatially. This can provide automatic direct links between form and content, based on general metaphors in our conceptual system. Such links make the relationship between form and content anything but arbitrary, and some of the meaning of a sentence can be due to the precise form the sentence takes. (Lakoff and Johnson 1980: 126)

The dative and the double object construction contrast, most conspicuously, with respect to the linear order of the constituents. In the double object construction, the so-called 'indirect object', which encodes the thematic role of Benefactor, is adjacent to the verb, while in the dative construction, the indirect object appears in a peripheral prepositional phrase. According to the metaphor CLOSENESS IS STRENGTH OF EFFECT (Lakoff and Johnson 1980: 128), the double object construction thus conveys that the Benefactor is more directly, or more immediately, involved in, or affected by the action or activity denoted by the verb than is the case with the dative construction. These considerations are supported by the well-known contrast in (27).

(27)   *a.* Tom taught his wife Spanish.
       b. Tom taught Spanish to his wife.

While these two sentences could be truth-conditionally equivalent (whence the impression that the one is a mere stylistic variant of the other), (*a*) might be more appropriate if Tom's wife now speaks Spanish, i.e. if Tom's teaching activity 'affected' his wife in a significant way. In contrast, (*b*) might be more appropriate if Tom's wife gained nothing from Tom's teaching.

The notion that the first NP in the double object construction is affected by the action denoted by the verb, in virtue of the fact that the NP stands adjacent to the verb, legitimizes the inference that a verb can slot into the double object construction to the extent that the verb denotes an action or activity which is directed at the beneficiary or recipient. To put it another way: A verb slots into the double object construction to the extent that the notion of the Benefactor is inherent to the very meaning of the verb.

Consider now Wierzbicka's (1988: 373) explications of the semantics of the verbs *tell* and *announce*.

TELL: (I say this because) I want to cause you to know
ANNOUNCE: (I say this because) I want this important fact to be known

Announce focuses on the message, rather than on the person(s) to whom the message is addressed. Several facts substantiate this claim. To begin with, *announce* requires that the message be important. I may 'tell' my wife that we've run out of sugar, but scarcely 'announce' this fact to her. That the message is inherent to the semantics of *announce* is suggested by the fact that the message constitutes an obligatory complement of the verb; furthermore, the message may not be demoted to a prepositional phrase. **The Minister announced* is syntactically (and conceptually) incomplete, whilst *The Minister announced about his res-ignation* is syntactically (and conceptually) contrived. On the other hand, *tell* readily tolerates the omission of the message: *Who told you? Nobody told me.* Alternatively, the message may easily be demoted to a peripheral prepositional phrase: *She told me about her new appointment.* Furthermore, an 'announce-ment' is typically made, not to a specific individual, or individuals, but to an audience, whose individual members are, of themselves, not the focus of inter-est. Thus, one announces something in the press, on television, to a congregated assembly, but not usually (or if so, only ironically) to a named individual. Symptomatic of the low salience of the addressee(s) in the verb's semantics is the fact that the addressee need not even be mentioned: *The Minister announced his resignation.* The conclusion must be that *tell* and *announce* are by no means synonymous, or mere stylistic variants. Whilst the two verbs have much in common—both have to do with verbal communication—*announce* differs se-mantically from *tell* precisely in those respects that are relevant to a verb's appropriateness in the double object construction. Given an independent charac-terization of the double object construction, the low salience of the addressee in the semantic structure of *announce* is plausibly the reason why the addressee is barred from functioning as the first object of the construction.

This example was meant to illustrate how a semantic characterization of a construction, in combination with a semantic analysis of lexical items that are candidates for insertion into the construction, can offer a way out of the learnability paradox. For further examples pertaining to the dative and double object con-structions, the interested reader is referred to the work of Wierzbicka, Pinker, and others, cited earlier.

But what, the reader may be asking, has all this to do with possessives? The point is that possessives, too, present us with a learnability paradox. Consider: *the city's destruction* readily receives an objective interpretation, according to which the city is the entity destroyed, not the entity that destroys. How does the speaker of English come to know that *the enemy's fear*, *Herbie's love*, and *Mary's knowledge* may not likewise receive an objective interpretation? Given that speakers do extend their expressive repertoires by analogy, why does the known possibility of an objective reading of *the city's destruction* not sanction an objective reading of *the enemy's fear*; or, conversely, that the known possib-ility of a subjective reading of *the enemy's fear* does not sanction the possibility of a subjective reading of *the city's destruction*? Or again: given that *the city's destruction* is an acceptable paraphrase of *the destruction of the city*, how come speakers of English do not accept *the cliff's avoidance* as a paraphrase of *the avoidance of the cliff*? My answers to these questions (in Chapters 8 and 9) will require an investigation of the semantics of the participating nominals, in asso-ciation with a characterization of the semantics of the possessive construction.

3 Some Basic Notions of Cognitive Grammar

IN this chapter I introduce some basic concepts of cognitive grammar. For a fuller presentation of the theory, the reader is referred to Langacker (1987a, 1990a, 1991). A succinct overview may be found in the four chapters that Langacker contributed to Rudzka-Ostyn (1988), i.e. Langacker (1988a,b,c,d).

Cognitive grammar is characterized by extreme austerity with regard to the entities that it posits. In keeping with the thesis that language is essentially symbolic in nature, only three kinds of entity are recognized. These are (a) phonological structures, (b) semantic structures, and (c) symbolic units, each associating a phonological structure with a semantic structure.

Notable, in this ontology, is the absence of any strictly syntactic elements. A very strong claim of cognitive grammar is that syntactic organization is fully describable without recourse either to syntactic primitives, or to exclusively syntactic principles of organization. This is not to say that traditional syntactic categories such as noun, noun phrase, prepositional phrase, and so on, play no part in cognitive grammar. These categories, however, are not taken to be uniquely syntactic elements, axiomatically defined, but as symbolic units, each associating a phonological representation with a semantic representation. As we shall see in Chapter 4, notions of constituency, such as head, complement, and modifier, can also receive a natural interpretation in terms of the symbolic thesis.

3.1 SYMBOLIC UNITS

Central to cognitive grammar is the notion of the *symbolic unit*. Langacker (1987a: 11) has characterized a language as simply an open-ended set of symbolic units. As he observes (p. 11), the symbolic unit of cognitive grammar is, in essence, nothing other than the familiar 'linguistic sign', which, for Saussure, had linked a 'mental concept' to an 'acoustic image'.

Traditionally, the Saussurian sign has been identified with the lexical items of a language (Saussure 1964: 98–9). Saussure himself illustrated the notion on the example of the word *arbre* "tree". But Saussure clearly intended the notion of linguistic sign to apply to a wider range of phenomena than just the lexical items of a language; for, as he stated, 'ce qui est dit des mots s'applique à n'importe quel terme de la langue, par exemple aux entités grammaticales' (p. 161).[1] And in his own practice, as recorded in the posthumous *Cours de linguistique générale*, morphophonemic categories like singular and plural, and categories of tense and aspect, were treated as signs.

Cognitive grammar extends the notion of linguistic sign, both 'horizontally' and 'vertically': horizontally, to comprise units larger than lexical items and morphemes, and vertically, to comprise units that are schematic for more fully characterized units.

Accordingly, not only are the words and morphemes of a language regarded as symbolic units, fixed idiomatic expressions, such as *Good morning, How do you do?*, *Dear Sir, Yours sincerely*, also have symbolic unit status. These expressions have a fixed form, conventionally associated with a rather specific meaning.[2] In addition, phrasal expressions, even those that are fully compositional, i.e. expressions that are fully analysable with respect to both their form and their meaning, may acquire the status of symbolic units, to the extent, namely, that these expressions, through repeated use, have become 'entrenched', or 'automated', and are employed by a speaker as integrated wholes, without attention to their internal structure. Such expressions do not need to be constructed afresh from their component parts, on each occasion of their use. For many speakers, I would imagine, expressions such as *my wife* (or *my husband*), *roast turkey, in the kitchen, to some extent, go for a walk, Have you fed the dog?, Did anybody phone?, Is there anything on television?*, and countless more, have the status of symbolic units, which are stored as integrated wholes, and which are retrieved as such from memory.[3]

Cognitive grammar also attributes symbolic unit status to units that are more abstract, or 'schematic', than individual morphemes, words, and expressions. Langacker defines a *schema* as

an abstract characterization that is fully compatible with all the members of the category it defines . . . it is an integrated structure that embodies the commonality of its members, which are conceptions of greater specificity and detail that elaborate the schema in contrasting ways. (Langacker 1987a: 371)

[1] 'What is said of words applies to any other term of the language, for example, the grammatical entities.'

[2] Note that 'meaning' is being used here (and elsewhere) in a rather broad sense, to include not only referential meaning, but also pragmatic aspects, including conditions for the appropriate use of an expression. See section 3.5.

[3] A similar point has been made by Pawley and Syder (1983), who maintain that 'fluent and idiomatic control of a language rests to a considerable extent on knowledge of a body of "sentence stems" which are "institutionalized" or "lexicalized". A lexicalized sentence stem is a unit of clause length or longer whose grammatical form and lexical content is wholly or largely fixed; its fixed elements form a standard label for a culturally recognized concept, a term in the language. Although lexicalized in this sense, most such units are not true idioms but rather are regular form–meaning pairings' (Pawley and Syder 1983: 191–2). Pawley and Syder speculate that the number of such units memorized by speakers of a language may run into 'hundreds of thousands'. Psycholinguistic evidence that speakers do indeed store, and access, complex units of this kind comes from Potter and Faulconer (1979).

Not only does the lexical item [TREE] constitute a symbolic unit, we will want to say that [COUNT NOUN] also has symbolic unit status, [TREE] being an instance of the more abstract, schematic unit [COUNT NOUN]. [COUNT NOUN] is likewise an instance of the still more abstract and schematic unit [NOUN].

Crucially, the set of symbolic units comprises what Langacker calls *construction schemas*. These constitute abstractions over what is common to combinations of simpler units, which in turn provide a pattern for the creation and interpretation of new expressions. The construction schema [ADJ N] abstracts the commonality of expressions such as *big tree, old man, young child*; conversely, each of these expressions is an instance of the construction schema [ADJ N]. Prenominal possessives were characterized in Chapter 1 by way of a construction schema [NP POSS N]. The schema sanctions the combination of a unit characterized as [NP] with the morpheme POSS and another unit characterized as [N]. A more detailed analysis might recognize [NP POSS] as a kind of determiner to the possessee noun, i.e. [NP POSS N] could be seen as an instance of the more schematic unit [DET N]. At an even more schematic level, we might want to say that [NP POSS N] and [DET N] themselves instantiate the symbolic unit [NP].

The device of the construction schema, together with the possibility of embedding one construction schema inside another (as when [NP POSS] features as a component of [NP POSS N]), makes possible generalizations that might appear, at first sight, to be exactly equivalent to those that are captured by means of traditional phrase structure rules, as in (1).

(1)   NP → DET N
       DET → NP POSS

It is certainly true that both phrase structure grammar and cognitive grammar postulate a hierarchy of syntactic organization, whereby a particular expression may be represented, on one level, say, as [NP POSS] [N], on a 'higher' level as [DET] [N], and on a still higher level as [NP]. Yet it is important to emphasize that the cognitive grammar account is by no means a paraphrase of the phrase structure rules.

In a phrase structure grammar, the elements N, NP, DET, and so on, are syntactic primitives—formal objects which are devoid of semantic (and phonological) content. Phrase structure rules generate strings of such objects, comprising a set of initial strings, and a set of terminal strings. A sentence's 'phrase marker'—often represented by means of the familiar tree diagram, or by labelled bracketing—summarizes the derivation of a terminal string from its initial string. Importantly, the strings can only receive semantic (and phonological) content through interpretation by the semantic and phonological components of the grammar.

In cognitive grammar, on the other hand, syntactic elements such as N, NP have the status of symbolic units, which emerge through the process of schema abstraction from their instances. Hierarchical structure is therefore not a matter of a sentence's derivation, but of the categorizing relations between units of different degrees of schematicity. Neither does a cognitive grammar 'generate' the set of well-formed sentences. It merely provides the language user with the resources for creating and interpreting utterances, according to patterns already abstracted through previous linguistic experience. Since schemas are abstracted from their instances (ultimately, from semantically and phonologically fully specified instances), syntactic elements are both inherently meaningful (albeit at a very schematic level), and phonologically contentful (even though in many cases the phonological content will be so schematic as to be essentially vacuous). A further point of contrast is that grammaticality, in a phrase structure grammar, is a clear-cut matter; a string is either well-formed, in accordance with the phrase structure rules, or it is not. Hierarchical structures in cognitive grammar are a matter of categorizing relationships between units at different degrees of schematicity. Categorizing relationships can permit degrees of goodness; consequently, the well-formedness of an expression will typically be a matter of more or less.

It is also worth bearing in mind that the notions of schema, and instantiation of a schema, are not unique to matters of syntactic structure, but apply much more widely within language, and in domains outside language. For both phonological and semantic structures we can recognize a hierarchy of units of increasing schematicity. In phonology, a phoneme is schematic for the allophones which may instantiate it, whilst [CONSONANT] and [VOWEL] are schematic for the consonant and vowel segments, respectively. Likewise, [SYLLABLE] is schematic for its various instantiations, such as [CV], [CVC]. With respect to semantic structures, the concept 'dog' is schematic for 'poodle', 'terrier', 'alsatian', and so on; while to identify a creature as a dog is to recognize the creature as an instance of a schematic conceptual unit 'dog'. Very often, discussion as to whether a word is polysemous or not hinges on the level of schematicity at which the meaning of the word is characterized (Taylor 1995*b*: ch. 14). We may wish to distinguish two different *in*-relations: *money in the box* (containment in a hollow internal region) and *crack in the vase* (containment within the material substance). At this level of analysis, *in* could be regarded as polysemous. At the same time, the two *in*-relations might be seen as instantiations of a more schematically characterized containment relation; at this level of analysis, the relation symbolized by *in* is indeterminate *vis-à-vis* the more specific senses.

3.2 THE SYMBOLIC THESIS

Having pointed to the Saussurian quality of the symbolic unit, we should also mention that the notion of construction schema, too, was prefigured by Saussure. As is well known, there is relatively little discussion of syntactic matters in the

Cours. In this respect, Saussure was typical of his time. Most linguists of the nineteenth and early twentieth century (and of earlier centuries, too, for that matter) also had very little to say about syntax, in the modern sense. The cursory remarks in the following passage on the way words combine to form larger syntagma are therefore all the more arresting.

[I]l faut attribuer à la langue, non à la parole, tous les types de syntagmes construits sur des formes régulières. En effet, comme il n'y a rien d'abstrait dans la langue, ces types n'existent que si elle en a enregistré des spécimens suffisamment nombreux. Quand un mot comme *indécorable* surgit dans la parole . . . , il suppose un type déterminé, et celui-ci à son tour n'est possible que par le souvenir d'un nombre suffisant de mots semblables appartenant à la langue (*impardonnable, intolérable, infatigable,* etc.). Il en est exactement de même des phrases et des groupes de mots établis sur des patrons réguliers; des combinaisons comme *la terre tourne, que vous dit-il?* etc., répondent à des types généraux, qui ont à leur tour leur support dans la langue sous forme de souvenirs concrets.[4] (Saussure 1964: 173)

Surprising, perhaps, for the modern reader, is Saussure's statement that *langue,* i.e. the socially sanctioned language system, as opposed to *parole,* i.e. an individual's linguistic acts, contains 'nothing abstract', it is merely a vast repository of 'concrete memories', presumably, memories of actual linguistic utterances. We can imagine, therefore, that Saussure would not have been sympathetic to the idea of a person's linguistic competence being constituted by knowledge of phrase structure rules, and other abstract principles postulated by many modern theories! Rather, Saussure saw syntax as a matter of combining words in accordance with 'regular patterns', or 'general types'. These emerge in a speaker's mind through acquaintance with countless expressions, or 'specimens', deposited in memory, which instantiate the patterns. Essentially, therefore, syntax is a matter of analogy. New expressions (the province of *parole*) are sanctioned by their compatibility with the 'general patterns' instantiated by already familiar expressions.

It is not clear from his brief remarks whether Saussure would have wanted to attribute semantic content to the syntactic patterns instantiated by expressions such as *La terre tourne* and *Que vous dit-il?*, or even whether he would have wanted to claim that such patterns have any permanent status within *langue.* Even so, there is a clear affinity between Saussure's 'regular patterns' and the construction schemas of cognitive grammar, in that both emerge on the basis of

[4] 'We must attribute to *langue* all kinds of syntagmatic types that are constructed on regular forms. Indeed, since there is nothing abstract in *langue,* these types exist only if a sufficient number of specimens of these types have been registered in *langue.* When a word like *indécorable* emerges in the act of speaking . . . , this presupposes a fixed type, which in turn is possible only in virtue of the memory of a sufficient number of similar words belonging to *langue* (*impardonnable, intolérable, infatigable,* etc.). It is exactly the same with sentences and phrases formed according to regular patterns; combinations such as *la terre tourne* "the earth turns", *que vous dit-il?* "what does he say to you?", etc. conform to general types, which in turn are supported in *langue* by concrete memories.' (My translation)

a person's familiarity with their instantiations (or 'specimens'). Since, in cognitive grammar, construction schemas are assimilated to the broader category of symbolic units, each of which, by definition, associates a phonological representation with a semantic representation, construction schemas will necessarily be associated both with a semantic content, and with a phonological content.

The thesis that language is inherently symbolic in nature is far from being universally accepted. Perhaps the most loquacious critic of what he calls the 'fixed-code fallacy' has been Roy Harris (e.g. Harris 1981). Harris points out that the uses (and range of pronunciations) of a word are in principle open-ended. Some of the things a speaker may say and mean are perhaps routine and conventionalized, others testify to the speaker's innovation and creativity, and are highly context-dependent. According to Harris, there can, therefore, be no fixed, predetermined meanings for each and every word of a language, nor can there be fixed rules, which govern the way a speaker can combine words and the way in which these combinations are to be understood. Harris also argues that the symbolic thesis, if true, would require that speaker and hearer have access to *exactly the same* form–meaning relationships. On the assumption that 'each individual's private mental world is always in certain respects different from that of any other individual, there is no cast-iron guarantee that the same words are similarly understood by those who use them' (Harris 1988: 98). If I meet a person who 'speaks English', but whose biography has at no previous point intersected with mine, and whose collective experiences (of the language, and much else) are therefore quite different from mine (a fairly everyday happening), what right have I to assume that the semantic representations that this person associates with the words he is using will be commensurate, let alone identical, with mine?

Harris goes further in his critique of the Saussurian thesis, querying the very notion that there might exist such things as 'meanings' that are attached, as in a code book, to 'forms'. Harris's rejection of 'meanings' has affinities with the position popularized by certain philosophers. Austin (1979: 56) surmised that the very expression 'the meaning of a word' could be a 'dangerous nonsense-phrase'; sentences may have meanings, yes, but words 'have meanings' only in a secondary, derivative sense. 'To say a word or a phrase "has a meaning" is to say that there are sentences in which it occurs which "have meanings"' (p. 56). Austin's remarks echo Wittgenstein's aphorism that a word has meaning 'only as part of a sentence'.[5] Indeed, the *Philosophical Investigations* can be read as a multi-pronged attack on the very notion of word meanings.

Cognitive grammar, I think, is able to maintain the symbolic thesis, without at the same time exposing itself to the kinds of criticism raised by Harris and

---

[5] In §49 of the *Philosophical Investigations*, Wittgenstein attributes this aphorism to Frege. Its centrality to Wittgenstein's own thought is inferable from the fact that Baker and Hacker (1980) adopt it as the title of their ch. 8.

others. Part of the enterprise will consist in a proper characterization of semantic and phonological representations.[6] We will also need to take account of the variability of the semantic and phonological value of a linguistic unit, as it is used on different occasions. And there is a further point that we should keep in mind. It is self-evident that speakers can and do construct new and meaningful expressions by assembling their component parts, and that hearers are able, on the whole, to comprehend these novel utterances (more or less) as intended. The facts of compositionality and creativity constitute perhaps the strongest empirical evidence in favour of the thesis that the parts themselves are not only inherently meaningful (cf. Fodor and Pylyshyn 1988), but also that their meanings are reasonably stable. If it were not so, there would be no constraints at all on what can be combined with what, nor on how a novel combination (such as the one you are reading at the moment) could be interpreted.

Generative linguists have a quite different quarrel with the symbolic thesis. At issue is not so much whether the component parts of an expression have meanings (this is not denied, at least with respect to *some* constituent elements), as whether there exists an intermediate level (or levels) of organization intervening between meaning and sound, and autonomous of both. It is no coincidence that Newmeyer, a defender of the autonomy of syntax, should be so keen to establish the implausibility of a direct pairing of sound and meaning.

[S]ound and meaning are too different from each other [for a one-to-one pairing between them] to have ever been a *practical* possibility. Meanings, whatever their ultimate nature, are first and foremost *mental* realities, with no obvious physical instantiation. Sounds, physical realities *par excellence*, are produced by a coordinated set of articulations in the vocal tract, under control of a very different area of the brain from that responsible for meaning. (Newmeyer 1991: 7; author's emphasis)

An acoustic signal, Newmeyer continues, unfolds in time; typically, its constituent elements (formant frequencies, pitch levels) vary continuously, rather than in discrete jumps. Meanings, in contrast, are not linear, and their conceptual constituents (agent, patient, process, etc.) are discrete, they do not merge into each other at the edges like the events of the acoustic signal. In brief, conceptual units do not correspond directly with any units of phonetic substance. Even the introduction of a phonological representation, organized around such units as segments, syllables, and feet, will alleviate the mismatch 'only slightly'. It is, Newmeyer argues, the very incompatibility of sound and meaning, the fact that they constitute 'inherently disparate components of language' (p. 8), that created the need for an intermediate level, a 'switchboard' (p. 7), that could facilitate the

---

[6] Wittgenstein (1978: 181) asked, 'How do the meanings of the individual words make up the sense of the sentence "I still haven't seen him yet"?', presumably taking the line that simply asking the question showed the impossibility of a coherent answer. But whether the question does admit of a coherent answer will obviously depend on our theory of semantics, and on how we wish to characterize the 'meanings of the individual words'.

coordination of the two. The emergence of the intermediate level of autonomous syntax (actually, a cluster of intermediate levels, in many current theories), was the 'major evolutionary step' (p. 7) which made possible the development of human language.

Newmeyer's rejection of the symbolic thesis rests on the premiss that there can be no one-to-one pairing of elements from radically different domains. Now, it is certainly true that sound and meaning do constitute radically different domains, in terms of their inherent content and its organization.[7] But it is not clear how the two levels might be rendered more compatible by the postulation of an intermediate level of autonomous syntax, which, by definition, is also constituted by domain-specific elements, structured according to domain-specific principles. On Newmeyer's premiss, there can be no one-to-one relation between the elements of autonomous syntax and sound, either, or between elements of autonomous syntax and meaning, since autonomous syntax will differ radically, in content and organization, from both. And no matter how many intermediate levels we postulate, the symbolization problem, as Newmeyer construes it, will remain.

To be fair, Newmeyer rejects a one-to-one pairing of sound and meaning, not on the grounds of logical necessity, but as a 'practical possibility'. In the passage cited above, Newmeyer is adopting an evolutionary perspective. In this context, 'practical' would appear to mean 'conferring evolutionary advantage upon the species'. But it is also tempting to take 'practical' in another sense. A pairing of sound and meaning is a practical possibility to the extent that it is a valid option for contemporary linguistic theory. The most effective rebuttal of Newmeyer's position would be to demonstrate the practicality of the symbolic thesis, to show, in other words, that the facts of language *can* be adequately described without appeal to intermediate levels of organization.

But is the symbolic thesis a practical possibility? Can it, in other words, really be shown to work?

The practical difficulties may seem quite daunting. To repeat: A symbolic unit, by definition, associates a phonological representation and a semantic representation. In the case of a good many lexical items, such as *tree*, the matter seems relatively straightforward, in principle at least. It may turn out to be quite difficult, in practice, to state the meaning even of such an everyday word as *tree*, and there may be disagreements over the correct phonological representation. Even so, there is not likely to be much disagreement that *tree* does in fact mean something, and that it does have a pronunciation.

---

[7] Even so, we would do well not to overstate the differences. In the first place, phonological representations are also cognitive entities, no less than conceptual structures (Langacker 1987a: 78). Furthermore, vocalizations, even non-linguistic vocalizations, can sometimes be integrated into the syntactic-conceptual structure of a sentence, as in *She went* [SCREAM]. Nor does the complement have to be a vocalization: *She went* [OBSCENE GESTURE]. Here, the scream or gesture functions as a complement of the verb *go*. For discussion of examples like these, see Langacker (1987a: 61) and Hudson (1990a: 68–9).

But with respect to some other words and morphemes, the symbolic thesis may seem less defensible. Consider the preposition *of*, or the possessive morpheme. In comparison with semantically more contentful prepositions (such as *on*, *in*, or *under*), *of* does seem to lack a clearly definable meaning. What, for example, is the semantic contribution of *of* to the following expressions?[8]

(2)   *a.* the centre of the lawn.
       b. a man of integrity.
       c. three of my friends.
       d. the destruction of the city.
       e. the author of the book.
       f. her knowledge of history.
       g. the state of California.
       h. a friend of Jill's.

Chomsky (1981: 50), for one, has spoken of *of* as 'devoid of semantic content'; it is a 'vacuous preposition' (Chomsky 1988: 111), which gets inserted into certain environments in order that purely syntactic constraints (in particular, case assignment) can be satisfied.

Likewise with the possessive morpheme. While there are hints (e.g. Chomsky 1986: 195) that in some expressions (such as *John's book*), the morpheme may denote a possession relation, the prevailing view in the generative literature appears to be that the possessive morpheme, too, is a purely grammatical marker, of no semantic import, which gets inserted into certain configurations in order that grammatical constraints (again regarding case assignment) can be met.

And when we turn to more schematic units—to grammatical categories like [NOUN], or to construction schemas like [DET N]—the thesis that these units associate a sound with a meaning seems even harder to defend.

Consider, first, the phonological representations. For many of the more abstract symbolic units, phonological representations will be essentially vacuous. We can probably do no more (for English, at least[9]) than state that [NOUN] associates a semantic representation with *some* phonological content. Even so, such a statement will not be totally vacuous. For a start, the symbolic thesis rules out the possibility that there might exist 'invisible', or 'inaudible' nouns—nouns, that is, which are claimed to occur in the (surface) structure of a sentence but which lack any phonological manifestation. Such disembodied elements do in fact play a quite major role in current generative theories, in the guise of NP traces, and the invisible pronouns, pro and PRO.[10] Secondly, phonological

---

[8] For Langacker's account of the preposition, see Langacker (1992).

[9] For other languages, a slightly more contentful phonological representation may be possible, concerning, for example, the minimum number of syllables, or the location of stress.

[10] pro is the understood subject of e.g. Italian *canta* "he/she sings", while PRO is the understood subject in subjectless non-finite clauses: *They sank the ship* [PRO] *to collect the insurance.* Cognitive grammar recognizes the existence of an 'understood' subject in the semantic structure of *canta* and of the non-finite clause in English. But whereas, in cognitive grammar, these are (unelaborated)

representations that are associated with a construction schema, such as [ADJ N], or [NP POSS N], will contain the crucial information that the adjective, in English, conventionally precedes the noun, and that the possessor NP precedes the possessee.

With respect to their meaning, the standard view is that grammatical categories are *sui generis*, with no semantic basis. Consider again the case of nouns. Newmeyer (1991: 20–1) points out that *tree* names an 'entity', *explosion* names a 'process', and *nuisance* names an 'attribute' of a thing or process. Given the wide range of semantic values that can be associated with nouns, Newmeyer doubts whether the noun category 'can be defined semantically'. Jackendoff, who is in general sympathetic to the view that syntax should reflect semantics,[11] also accepts without question that some syntactic notions, such as noun and grammatical subject 'cannot be identified with any coherent semantic category' (Jackendoff 1983: 14). It is, of course, generally accepted that many nouns, in English and other languages, do denote concrete things or substances, conversely, that concrete things and substances are typically denoted by nouns. But in order to identify the nouns of English (or of any other language), we would be well advised to ignore the semantics! We identify a word as a noun on purely distributional grounds, i.e. on the basis of the kinds of syntactic environment in which it can occur. (This is not to say, however, that distributional criteria will always be unambiguous; purely formal criteria may well suggest degrees of nounhood.[12]) The mainstream view, then, is that there is no semantic content common to all nouns, and that there can therefore be no general meaning of the word class, such that all nouns in a language instantiate this general meaning.

One possibility for a defender of the symbolic thesis might be to say that the semantic representation associated with [NOUN] is, like the phonological representation, essentially vacuous; the unit merely associates *some* semantic content with *some* phonological content. But even this proposal, unsatisfactory as it is, will again not be entirely vacuous, in that it will rule out the existence of nouns which are completely devoid of meaning. And, once again, Chomskyan theory does indeed postulate semantically empty nouns, such as 'expletive' *there* and *it*, as in *There seems to be a mistake, It is thought that he left, It is raining.* There are, however, good reasons to suspect that a more contentful characterization of [NOUN] is both possible, and desirable.

Consider the fact that a speaker, wishing to conceptualize and linguistically encode a given situation, typically has a number of options at her disposal. Let

elements of semantic structure, which can have a bearing on how a sentence is interpreted, in GB theory the invisible elements have exactly the same kinds of properties (regarding case theory, thematic theory, etc.) as phonetically overt NPs, and are therefore considered to be full components of surface structure.

[11] Cf. Jackendoff's (1983: 13) 'grammatical constraint', according to which 'one should prefer a semantic theory that explains otherwise arbitrary generalizations about the syntax and the lexicon'.

[12] On the 'squishiness' of grammatical categories, see Ross (1972). There is also some discussion in Taylor (1995b: 183–90).

us look more closely at one of Newmeyer's examples. Newmeyer (1991: 20) states that *explosion* 'encode[s] grammatically what semantically' is a process. Presumably, the point of this remark is that semantically, the noun *explosion* does not differ from the verb *explode*, which likewise encodes grammatically what semantically is a process. Certainly, in wishing to report a certain kind of event, a speaker may use either the noun (3*a*), or the verb (3*b*).

(3)   *a.* There was an explosion.
     b. Something exploded.

These two expressions are obviously very similar in meaning (and, as suggested, they could well be truth-conditionally equivalent). Yet I do not think that it would be correct to say that they are identical in meaning, i.e. that they encode exactly the same conceptualization of the situation. The supposition that there might in fact be quite substantial differences between the nominal wording and the verbal wording receives some confirmation when we consider how a speaker might linguistically encode a more complex situation. Consider (4) and (5).

(4)   *a.* We heard three loud explosions.
     b. We heard three things explode loudly.
     c. We heard something explode loudly three times.
(5)   *a.* The bomb failed to explode.
     b. The bomb failed to cause an explosion.
     c. There was a bomb, but there was no explosion.

The (*b*) and (*c*) expressions not only sound rather odd—this in itself is a fact in need of explanation—the (*b*) and (*c*) expressions clearly differ in meaning from each other, and neither is a satisfactory paraphrase of the (*a*) expressions. In fact, it is by no means obvious how the nominal wording in (4*a*) could be para-phrased at all by means of the verb, nor how the verbal wording in (5*a*) could be paraphrased by means of the noun.

    These few examples (which could be readily multiplied) suggest that *explosion* and *explode* are not simply alternative grammatical forms for encoding the same meaning, i.e. the conception of a process, but that the two words encode different conceptualizations. A reasonable inference might be that the semantic difference is crucially dependent on the difference in grammatical category, and might even be derivable from it. Pursuing this line, we might say that the distinctive meaning of *explosion* resides in the fact that *explosion* imposes a 'nominal' construal on the situation, whilst the verb *explode* imposes a 'verbal', or 'processual' construal. The nominal construal suppresses the internal struc-ture of the event, and removes the event from its temporal setting. We can talk of 'an explosion' without reference to what, exactly, exploded, and without reference to when the explosion occurred; furthermore, the event can be quan-tified (*three explosions, how many explosions?*), and we can attribute qualities to it (*a loud explosion, a terrifying explosion*). The verbal construal brings into focus the participant(s) in the event, as well as the temporal setting, the temporal progress, and ontological status of the event. We are obliged to say *what* exploded; the verb is marked for polarity (*explode* vs. *not explode*), and (if the verb is finite) it must be marked for tense. It should now be clear why (4*b*) and (4*c*) would be slightly odd things to say, in comparison with (4*a*). If a speaker wishes to convey only the acoustic effect of the event, and the number of events, she will opt for the noun. The verb would force her to include information on the participant. This information may not only be redundant, it may even distract from her communicative intentions (not to mention that a person who reports on 'an explosion' may be ignorant of the identity of the participant.) In contrast, the use of the noun in (5*b*) and (5*c*) is less than satisfactory, mainly, it would seem, because the nominal construal forces the speaker to separate the event from its participants and from its temporal setting.

These few examples will also indicate that any semantic value that we wish to attribute to a schematic grammatical category, such as [NOUN], is itself going to be highly schematic; 'name of a physical entity' will clearly not do. We can expect the semantic value of construction schemas, such as [NP POSS N], and of morphemes such as POSS and *of*, also to be highly schematic, and certainly not reducible to a notion such as possession (in the everyday sense of the word).

It is one thing to state, as a matter of theoretical principle, that grammatical categories and construction schemas, as well as each and every morpheme in a language, are symbolic, and hence inherently meaningful. It is another thing to propose substantive characterizations of these meanings. Langacker has devoted considerable effort to just this task, and we shall be considering some of his proposals in due course.[13] This book develops his approach, arguing that many seemingly unrelated properties of possessive expressions are derivable from the semantics of the construction (in combination with the semantics of the nominals which participate in it). The approach, to the extent that it is successful, will demonstrate, *pace* Newmeyer, that a symbolic pairing of sound and meaning is indeed a 'practical possibility'.

3.3 THE SYMBOLIC THESIS: SOME FURTHER ISSUES

According to the symbolic thesis, all linguistic units associate a phonological representation and a semantic representation.

The wording I have used, both here and earlier, could be taken to imply that the phonological and semantic poles of a symbolic unit are entities whose values are fixed and unchanging, that on each occasion of a unit's use, it is always the *same* phonological representation that is associated with the *same* semantic representation. Especially linguists of a Saussurian orientation have been eager

---

[13] Wierzbicka (1988) has also made proposals for the semantic characterization, not only of the noun-class, but of various subcategories of the class.

to defend the 'one form–one meaning' hypothesis. One of the most vigorous defenders was Jakobson. In his introductory remarks to his essay on the Russian cases, Jakobson (1936) argued that if one should admit to the possibility that a linguistic sign may have a range of distinct semantic values ('Sonderbedeutungen'), then its very essence as a sign will be destroyed, in that the sign will disintegrate into a multiplicity of sound–meaning relations. He even rejects the notion of a 'Grundbedeutung', or 'basic meaning', to which other meanings can be related. Rather, Jakobson goes for a 'Gesamtbedeutung', or unitary meaning, which covers the full range of particular meanings ('Sonderbedeutungen'). The search for unitary representations has also motivated members of the so-called Columbia school. Kirsner (1993: 85) characterizes the Columbia school as a 'sign-oriented approach', whose Saussurian orientation leads to the 'working hypothesis that the basic units of language will . . . be signs: invariant signals of invariant meaning'.[14] In spite of his very different theoretical orientation, Bierwisch (1983: 76), too, proposes the 'methodological principle' that word meanings should be represented, as far as possible, by unitary semantic entries.

On the other hand, many sceptical voices have been raised against the one form–one meaning thesis. Wierzbicka (1980: p. xix) points out that Jakobson's formulas for the Russian cases are so lacking in inherent content, that they are quite useless as a means of predicting the range of uses of the cases. The speaker of Russian has to know the range of *specific* semantic values associated with each case. (For the Russian instrumental, Wierzbicka 1980 identifies fourteen distinct Sonderbedeutungen.) Kirsner (1993: 86), too, acknowledges that general meanings may be inadequate predictors of usage. Consequently, he has to allow that knowledge of general meanings may need to be enriched by knowledge of 'conventionalized strategies for the communicative exploitation of meanings'. But if general meanings have to be supplemented with a statement of their more specific instantiations, the question arises of the relation between general meanings and specific meanings; one might even ask whether general meanings are needed at all. Observe that, given a commitment to cognitive realism, these questions will involve, not only the status of general and specific meanings as theoretical entities, but also their status as cognitive entities, i.e. as mental representations to which speakers have access in their production and understanding of language.

The cognitive grammar approach to these issues cannot be reduced to a simple slogan, of the kind 'one form–one meaning'. On the contrary, it is recognized that for a given symbolic unit language users may have access to a range of representations—both phonological and semantic—which may vary with respect to their schematicity.

---

[14] For examples of the Columbia school approach, see the references in Kirsner (1993). See also Ruhl (1989) for a tenacious attempt to attribute unitary meanings even to such apparently multi-valued items as the English verb (*to*) *bear*.

Consider the Saussurean example of *tree*. It would probably be an over-simplification to say, following Saussure, that a person's knowledge of this lexical item associates a (unitary) semantic representation with a (unitary) acoustic image. For example, on my normal pronunciation of *tree*, I heavily affricate the initial consonant cluster. Presumably, this pronunciation is highly salient in my phonological representation of the word. At the same time, I am able to recognize as valid instances of the word a range of pronunciations which diverge very considerably from my own. Alongside the more specific representation, which captures my own pronunciation, therefore, it seems plausible to postulate a more abstract representation, which is schematic for the full range of pronunciations that I may encounter. Likewise with the semantic pole. Quite salient in my understanding of the word is the image of a large, leafy, deciduous plant, supported on a bare, central trunk (the image is not too dissimilar, in fact, to the little drawing that illustrates Saussure's *Cours*). But in addition to this rather specific image, it is plausible to postulate a more schematic representation, which is able to encompass, not only large oak-trees in leaf, but also young saplings, pine trees, and perhaps even palm trees (not to mention phrase structure trees and family trees!).

There is therefore no inconsistency in principle between proposing, on the one hand, highly schematic and maximally general representations, and, at the same time, a range of more specific values, which instantiate the schemas. Langacker (1988c: 132–3), in fact, surmises that often the lower-level representations may actually be more directly involved in production and comprehension than the maximally schematic representations. Furthermore, for many symbolic units, it has to be recognized that it may simply not be possible at all to bring the range of specific uses under a more general representation.

Thus, for the noun *ring*, Langacker (1988d: 51–2) identifies a number of specific meanings, including "circular piece of jewelry worn around finger", "circular piece of jewelry worn through nose", and "arena (for sporting event)". The first two can certainly be assimilated to the schematic notion of "circular entity". On the other hand, an ear-ring need not be circular, and a boxing-ring is typically rectangular. The possibility of an overarching general meaning for *ring* is therefore remote, and Langacker makes no attempt to offer one. *Ring*, in other words, is simply regarded as polysemous. Indeed, Langacker (p. 50) takes it for granted that polysemy will be 'the norm for lexical units', especially for lexical units that are in frequent use (p. 49). Yet when it comes to characterizing the semantic content of grammatical units, such as the word classes and the construction schemas, Langacker has tended to opt for abstract schematic meanings, claiming, in the case of nouns, that '*all* members of the noun class' (Langacker 1987b: 54; author's emphasis) instantiate the very same general meaning; likewise with all members of the verb class.

Langacker has stated (personal communication) that there is no theoretical principle at stake in his differential treatment of lexical items (for which sometimes quite extensive polysemy is tolerated) and grammatical units (for which unitary, and highly abstract meanings tend to preferred). Each case is evaluated on its merits, and there is no difference in principle between the kind of analysis suited for lexical items, and the kind of analysis indicated for grammatical items. Nevertheless, the differential treatment that emerges from Langacker's work may not be without theoretical significance. We can gain some insight into this matter from Langacker's (1993: 2–5) discussion of certain mental abilities which he takes to be innate. These abilities facilitate the emergence of some very general concepts, or 'conceptual archetypes', of a high level of abstraction. Thus, the supposedly innate ability of conceptual reification underlies the concept of a discrete physical object, whilst the conception of force dynamics underlies the construal of an agent–patient interaction in a canonical transitive event. These are precisely the kinds of highly schematic notions that make up the semantic pole of word classes and construction schemas. The reference point analysis of the possessive also appeals to a very general (and, Langacker surmises, innate) mental ability, namely the ability to identify one entity from the reference point of another. Again, the highly schematic content that we wish to attribute to the possessive construction is plausibly based in this cognitive ability. In contrast, the rich conceptual content of individual lexical items is unlikely to be innately determined—although such a possibilty has indeed been argued by Fodor (1980), and is hinted at by Chomsky (1988: 31–4). For one thing, word meanings tend to be highly language-specific, and in many cases are clearly culture-dependent. Their content, then, will typically be rich in experientially based information.

But the dual approach to lexical items and to grammatical categories may also have a theory-internal rationale, which derives from the symbolic thesis itself. Recall Jakobson's concern about preserving the integrity of the linguistic sign. Whilst Jakobson rejected a polysemy account of the Russian cases, he seems not to have been unduly worried by the absence of a unitary phonological exponent of any of the cases. For the integrity of the sign to be guaranteed, it was apparently sufficient for him that a constant value could be attributed to *one* pole of the sign; variability at both semantic and phonological poles, however, could not be tolerated. Now, the integrity of the noun *ring* as a symbolic unit is guaranteed by the relative stability of the phonological pole; we can reliably identify any instance of the word on the basis of its phonological expression. The item is therefore free to associate at its semantic pole with a wide range of distinct meanings. In contrast, the stability of [NOUN] as a symbolic unit cannot be assured at the phonological pole; the phonological instantiation of [NOUN] could be anything at all. Yet the stability of the unit is required by the symbolic thesis. If word classes, in virtue of a multiplicity of form–meaning relations, were to disintegrate as symbolic units, we would be forced to fall back on purely distributional criteria for their identification and definition; we would, in other words, be implicitly giving recognition to a level of autonomous syntax. It therefore becomes a theoretical imperative that syntactic categories be associated with a stable semantic content.

With respect to its phonological stability, the possessive morpheme in English falls somewhere between a lexical item proper, such as *ring*, and a grammatical unit, such as [NOUN]. There is clearly a substantive phonetic commonality between some realizations of the possessive morpheme, between, for example, /z/ in *dog's*, /s/ in *cat's*, /əz/ in *horse's*. On the other hand, these phonological forms are homophonous with expressions of plurality. We can, of course, identify /s/ as an instance of the possessive rather than [PLURAL] on distributional grounds, in most cases, at least.[15] But, again, to appeal to an item's distribution is implicitly to acknowledge the autonomy of a syntactic level of organization. The same issue arises in connection with items such as *my*, *mine*, etc. We have suggested that these should be analysed as [I + POSS]. There is certainly no phonological motivation for this analysis. In order to maintain the symbolic thesis, we must identity *my* as [I + POSS] on the basis of a stable semantic value of its supposed constituents.

Although in this book I pursue a unitary account of the possessive morpheme, it must be emphasized once again that the search for maximally general meanings is not in itself incompatible with the postulation of a range of specific meanings. On the contrary, it seems reasonable to suppose that a person's knowledge of a language contains a good deal of redundancy, with highly schematic knowledge coexisting with a good deal of rather specific knowledge of how the general schemas may be instantiated.[16]

3.4 SEMANTIC REPRESENTATIONS

Any claim that a language (including what would normally be called its syntax) can be exhaustively described in terms of a set of symbolic units, each associating a phonological representation with a semantic representation, clearly places a heavy descriptive burden on the characterizations of phonological and semantic representations. In this section I address the question of the content of the semantic representations.

As already noted several times, meanings, in cognitive grammar, are identified with conceptualizations. This is not to say that any conceptualization that a person may care to entertain *ipso facto* has the status of a linguistic meaning. Many aspects of conceptual life—those pertaining to musical cognition, for example—clearly have no direct linguistic expression. The point would hardly be worth making, were it not that some linguists (e.g. Bierwisch and Schreuder 1992: 31) have cited this state of affairs as evidence for the need to make a

---

[15] But not always. See below, section 11.3.
[16] For discussion of these issues, see Taylor (1995*b*: ch. 14).

principled distinction between a level of (non-conceptual) linguistic meaning and a level of (non-linguistic) conceptualization.

Another argument, advanced by Bierwisch and Schreuder (1992: 28, 56), is that to equate linguistic meanings and conceptualizations would entail a correspondence, or strict isomorphy, between the meanings of linguistic expressions and the conceptualizations that a person may entertain. Such a strict isomorphy clearly does not exist. Suppose, on the one hand, that we want to claim that all human beings share essentially the same cognitive capacities, and are able to entertain the same range of conceptualizations. Yet the expressions of different languages manifestly do not encode the same meanings. On the other hand, suppose we insist on the uniqueness of each person's mental life. Yet, given the fact of linguistic communication, speakers of a language presumably do share semantic representations which, if not identical across all speakers, are at least commensurate, for most practical purposes. On either score, it seems, we will need to postulate a set of linguistic meanings, which are distinct from, and non-isomorphic with, more general conceptual abilities.

Cognitive grammar meets these objections by claiming that semantic representations constitute 'conventionalized conceptual structure' (Langacker 1982: 23). A language makes certain symbolic resources available to its speakers. For the purpose of linguistic expression, a speaker needs to shape her conceptualizations in accordance with the resources made available by her language. At the same time, a speaker's expressive needs may lead to one-off innovations, and these innovations, if used sufficiently frequently, can themselves achieve conventionalized status within the language. Cognitive grammar thus foresees a dynamic, dialectic relation between conceptualization on the one hand, and the symbolic resources of a language on the other.

Having cleared away these potential sources of misunderstanding, let us now turn to the content of semantic representations. A good way to introduce the cognitive grammar approach is through the notion of presupposition, in the everyday, non-technical sense of the word. The presuppositions of an expression are simply those aspects of a person's knowledge which are necessary for a proper understanding of the expression, as used by a speaker on a specific occasion.

Suppose someone asks you *How old is Fred's uncle?* In order for this utterance to be understood, there has to be an individual, Fred, known to both speaker and hearer by this name; Fred must have at least one uncle; should Fred have more than one uncle, both speaker and hearer must be able to identify which of the uncles is being talked about. Should any of these presuppositions not be met, the hearer can legitimately ask for clarification: *Who's Fred? Which of Fred's uncles do you mean? I didn't know Fred had an uncle*, and so on.

How old is Fred's uncle? presupposes much else as well, of course: that people have names; that we refer to people by their names; that we find it useful, or interesting, to characterize people in terms of their age; that in certain circumstances it is legitimate, and socially acceptable, to enquire after a person's age; that a person's age is measured in years; that years are defined by the cycle of the seasons, as codified in the calendar. Or consider the presuppositions of the single word *uncle*. This word can only be understood against the knowledge of a kinship network and kinship relations. Kinship relations, in turn, presuppose knowledge of such things as gender, procreation, marriage relations, procreation and parenting of children within a marriage relation. These notions, in turn, presuppose yet others. Even such a seemingly banal query as *How old is Fred's uncle?* thus presupposes a vast conceptual network, which reaches into many aspects of a person's beliefs, knowledge, and assumptions.

Presuppositions (in the informal sense in which I am using the term) do not merely provide a conceptual context against which expressions are interpreted. Presuppositions constitute the very substance of semantic structure. Remove from the word *uncle* all knowledge of a kinship network, and the word simply ceases to mean anything at all. To put it another way: A person who did not know anything about kinship and kinship networks, and all that they presuppose, would have no basis for understanding the meaning of the word. If this point is accepted, any attempt to separate out the purely linguistic meaning of linguistic units from the conceptual knowledge against which these meanings are interpreted will become fruitless. Of course, there might be some heuristic value in distinguishing between presuppositions that are context-dependent, and that are in principle negotiable between speaker and hearer, and presuppositions that are shared by all fully socialized members of a speech community, and which are rarely, if ever, up for revision. The distinction, however, is a matter of degree, it is not one of principle. We might also find it useful to distinguish between presuppositions that concern highly specialized fields of knowledge, and which thus might need to be spelled out for the hearer, and those that are the common property of all members of a speech community. But even highly specialized knowledge will be based, ultimately, in more general knowledge configurations; and, given the appropriate conditions, erstwhile specialized knowledge may become, in time, general knowledge. A third distinction might be useful, for some purposes. This is between lexical presuppositions, having to do with the meanings of lexical items; pragmatic presuppositions, pertaining to the acceptability of an utterance in a given situation; and cultural presuppositions, pertaining to certain cultural practices. To some extent, the distinction would reflect a distinction between the semantic structures of different kinds of linguistic unit. Lexical presuppositions concern, obviously, the meanings of lexical items (*uncle*, *old*, etc.). Some pragmatic presuppositions (e.g. that a person, in speaking of *Fred's uncle*, intends to refer to an individual that is uniquely identifiable by both speaker and hearer) are associated with the meanings of grammatical constructions (in this case, the prenominal possessive construction). Likewise, the fact that a person who asks *How old is Fred's uncle?* expects the hearer to be able and willing to provide the information requested, could be taken as part of the meaning of a schematically characterized [INFORMATION QUESTION]. Cultural presuppositions cut across these distinctions. The appropriate utterance of an information question presupposes certain cultural norms for verbal interaction; the appropriate use of a proper name presupposes the cultural practice of naming; and the very fact that we have kinship terms in English presupposes the cultural salience of the kinship network, and of just those kinship relations that are lexicalized in the language. In the last analysis, therefore, all presuppositions will be grounded in conceptual knowledge.[17]

Langacker (1987a: ch. 4) uses the term *domain*, or *cognitive domain*, to designate any knowledge configuration, of whatever degree of complexity or sophistication, which provides the context, as it were, for the proper understanding of an expression. Typically, more than one cognitive domain will be involved. Consider another example, taken more or less at random. The word *book* presupposes the domain of physical objects (books are objects with a range of characteristic shapes and sizes), which in turn presupposes notions of three-dimensional space; *book* also presupposes the domain of writing, and, more generally, the domain of linguistic communication. It presupposes, further, the domain of knowledge dissemination; the domain of the publishing industry, which in turn presupposes the technologies of printing and type-setting; also the domain of commercial transactions and the retail trade (books are things that are bought and sold). The *domain matrix* is the in principle open-ended set of domains necessary for a proper understanding of an expression. However, specific domains, selected from the domain matrix, may be invoked in the interpretation of a given sentence. For example, (6) would typically be interpreted differently, according to whether John is known to be an avid reader, a prolific writer, a translator, or a type-setter.

(6)   John has just begun a new book.

Alternatively, suppose John to be a book-worm (literally). This would activate the conception of books as edible entities![18]

It may be instructive to compare Langacker's notion of domain matrix with Searle's notion of 'the Background'. Searle[19] construes the background as the network of knowledge, beliefs, and skills which makes it possible for a person to interact with the world, and to talk meaningfully about it. Consider the expressions *open the door* and *open a wound* (Searle 1983: 145–7). These two

---

[17] The reader may have noticed that I have avoided distinguishing between 'sentences', and the 'utterances' of sentences. Although this distinction is usually taken as axiomatic in discussions of semantics and pragmatics, it has no privileged status in cognitive grammar. The relation between a sentence and its utterance is the familiar relation of a schema and its instantiation; an utterance of *How old is Fred's uncle?* is simply an instance of the sentence 'How old is Fred's uncle?', whilst the latter is an instance of the more schematic unit [INFORMATION QUESTION]. The sentence is just one level in a hierarchy of schematic characterizations (albeit a highly salient one, no doubt).

[18] There is some affinity between Langacker's domain matrix and the 'qualia structure' of semantic entries postulated by Pustejovsky (1991a).

[19] See especially Searle (1979, 1980, 1983). For an update, see Searle (1992).

expressions denote activities of a very different kind. (Imagine trying to open the door by making incisions in it with a surgical scalpel!) Our knowledge of just what is involved in 'opening a door' and 'opening a wound' derives, according to Searle, from our familiarity with the relevant 'practices', which in turn constitute aspects of the background. An expression like *open the sun* (Searle 1983: 147) is so odd because there is no generally accepted practice in terms of which we can interpret the expression.

In spite of some obvious affinities, there are important differences between Searle's account and ours. Although background knowledge is constantly involved in the interpretation of expressions, Searle rejects the idea that background knowledge constitutes part of the linguistic meaning of an expression. He insists, for example, that *open*, in *open the door*, *open the wound*, and even *open the sun*, contributes *exactly the same* semantic information to the meanings of the complex expressions. Searle's approach, in fact, prefigured that of Bierwisch, who likewise proposes a distinction between the linguistic meaning of an expression, compositionally derived from the linguistic meanings of its parts, and the manner in which an expression is interpreted, relative to conceptual knowledge. On an encyclopedist view of meaning, however, background knowledge is an intrinsic aspect of meaning, to the extent that expressions (and parts of expressions) can only have meanings in the context of background knowledge. Remove all traces of background knowledge from the semantic representation of *open*, and the verb simply ceases to mean anything at all.

A second difference follows. For Searle, the background is so all-pervasive that it is generally taken for granted. Only in bizarre situations does the background force itself upon our attention. Suppose a cat and a mat were floating around in gravity-free space (the example is from Searle 1979: 121). On what basis might we say that the cat is *on* the mat, rather than *under* it, *next to* it, or *against* it? The example shows that the presence of a gravitational force is a precondition for the use of certain spatial predicates. For most practical purposes, the background does not need to be explicitly described, nor need it enter into statements of the meaning of linguistic expressions. Indeed, Searle is at pains to stress that it would, in principle, be impossible to explicate all aspects of the background, since whatever aspects of the background we might succeed in explicating would themselves need to be explicated against yet other aspects of the background. On a cognitive grammar view, in contrast, the pursuit of semantics requires that background knowledge be made explicit—perhaps not all aspects of background knowledge (for this could well be an impossible task, if, as Langacker 1987a: 64 suggests, a full explication of linguistic meanings could be coextensive with a full description of human cognition), then at least those aspects of background knowledge that are most immediately relevant to the characterization of an expression's semantic value.

For on any particular occasion of its use, some aspects of background knowledge are likely to be of more immediate relevance than others. In the case of *uncle*, the relevant background knowledge will be, not the notion of a total kinship network, but only that portion of the network that specifically relates the uncle to his nephew(s) and/or niece(s). Those aspects of a cognitive domain specifically invoked by a linguistic expression constitute the *scope*, or *base of predication* of the expression. Within the scope of predication, one component is *profiled*, or *designated*, by the linguistic form in question. Thus *uncle* (in its standard uses) designates nothing more than a male human being; the relation of this person to his nephew(s)/niece(s), as well as, of course, the nephew(s)/niece(s) themselves, are *unprofiled* elements within the noun's scope of predication.

Whereas the designation, or profile, of an expression is a fairly constant aspect of the expression's semantic structure (whence the impression, perhaps, that linguistic items, especially many lexical items, do tend to be associated with constant semantic values), the scope of predication and the wider domain matrix evoked by an expression are highly variable, and open. Thus, *uncle* may evoke, not only the cognitive domain of kinship relations, but also stereotypical knowledge associated with uncles, for example, that a child's uncle is typically an adult male who is on friendly terms with the child's parents, and who takes a benevolent interest in the child's welfare. This stereotypical knowledge constitutes the cognitive domain for the designation, as *uncle*, of any adult male who conforms to the stereotype, irrespective of his kinship relation to a particular child; the important thing is merely that the person is a friend of the family, and displays a typically 'avuncular' behaviour towards the child. Another stereotype might be that of the 'uncle' as an older person with useful connections, in business or politics, who is able to further the career of a younger colleague. *He has an uncle in the party*, as an explanation of why a person's career has advanced so rapidly, might be understood against this stereotypical knowledge. Yet another stereotype could be the idea of an uncle as a person to whom one turns in times of trouble; whence the expression *cry uncle*, in the sense 'shout for help'.

In principle, any bit of knowledge, no matter how idiosyncratic or circumstantial, can be associated with the semantic structure of a linguistic expression. Langacker (1987a: 160) observes that Jimmy Carter's presidency had a substantial, if transient, effect on the semantic value of *peanut*. In the same vein, one could say that Ronald Reagan's presidency has left its mark on the semantic value of *former movie actor*, while—to take an example from the British political scene—*grocer's daughter* cannot but be coloured by memories of Margaret Thatcher's career. These examples are perhaps not so bizarre as they might appear. Historical semantics provides countless instances of how circumstantial facts associated with the use of an expression have triggered changes, not only in scope of predication, but also in designation. The classic example is *bead*, in its semantic evolution from "prayer" to "spherical object on a string" (discussed in Langacker 1987a: 383–4). The cognitive domain which made the change possible was the practice of keeping track of the number of repetitions of a prayer by counting off the beads on a rosary. Such facts of semantic change possibly provide the most compelling empirical evidence for the correctness of the encyclopedist conception of meaning promoted by cognitive grammar.

The open-endedness of the domain matrix—the fact that *any* bit of background knowledge *could* be relevant for a proper understanding of a linguistic expression—does not entail that *all* bits of background knowledge are equally likely to figure, on every occasion of its use, in the expression's scope of predication. Certain aspects of domain-based knowledge are clearly more intrinsic to an expression's semantic value than others, and are likely to figure quite prominently in most instances of its use. Other aspects are less central, to the point of being, for just about any use of the expression, irrelevant. Centrality, however, is a matter of degree, and, as facts of historical change show, the peripheral and circumstantial can, in special circumstances, acquire centrality.

Consider some of the word definitions that Wierzbicka has recently proposed. In earlier work, Wierzbicka declined to offer substantive characterizations of the meanings of many words, in particular, words denoting natural kinds. Her definition of *horse* (in Wierzbicka 1972: 54) was 'an animal called "horse"'. More recently (Wierzbicka 1996), she has seen the need to propose much fuller definitions. Her definition of *mouse*, for example, includes such aspects as the characteristic shape, size, and colour of mice, the fact that mice are thought of as inconspicuous and timorous, also that cats chase them, and that mice are reputed to be attracted to cheese. (That some people, stereotypically women, have a phobic terror of mice, however, is not included in the definition.)

Wierzbicka motivates the content of her definitions by appeal to the linguistic evidence. Her definition of *mouse* reflects the way in which the word *mouse* is used in various idioms, set expressions, and so on. She goes on to make two further claims. The first is that her proposed definition of *mouse* captures the linguistic meaning of the word, which needs to be clearly distinguished from encyclopedic knowledge about mice. There are, she says, many things that a person could know about mice, for example, facts pertaining to their geographical distribution, to the length of the gestation period of the female mouse, to the size of a mouse litter, which are extraneous to the concept designated by the word *mouse*, and that it is to the encyclopedia that a person would turn in order to find out such facts. In spite, therefore, of the apparently encyclopedic nature of her defintion, she still insists on a clean distinction between the 'encyclopedia' and the 'dictionary'. Her second claim is that whereas encyclopedic knowledge about mice may be open-ended, the meaning of the word *mouse* is not. A person's encyclopedic knowledge depends on all sorts of non-linguistic factors, such as a person's professional or other interests. In contrast, the dictionary definition is 'determinate' and 'clearly delimited', and is presumably shared by all members of a speech community, in virtue, namely, of their knowledge of the word *mouse*.

A first observation on Wierzbicka's definition is that, by simply amalgamating aspects from many different uses of the word, it fails to reflect the particularity of individual uses. If I speak of a person as a 'grey mouse', I do not intend to convey that the person so designated is partial to Cheddar cheese. Likewise, the characteristic colour of mice is irrelevant to my characterization of a cat as a 'good mouser', or to my talk of a 'computer mouse'. At best, then, Wierzbicka's definition provides a pool of information which may be selectively drawn upon in order to understand a specific use of the word *mouse*.

Wierzbicka also makes the claim that this pool of information can be rigorously circumscribed. Here, I think, Wierzbicka falls prey to the determinacy myth (as Roy Harris might put it), in two of its manifestations; first, to the myth of a speech community as a clearly demarcated, homogeneous construct, and secondly, to the myth of a person's linguistic knowledge as fixed and immutable. It may be true that the overwhelming majority of English speakers know nothing at all about, and are not at all interested in finding out about, the gestation period of a female mouse, or the typical size of a mouse litter. Most people are just not interested in mouse sexuality. Such notions, therefore, are hardly likely to figure in the scope of predication of *mouse*, on any occasion of its use. It is rather different, of course, with human sexuality. The 'gestation period' of the human female probably does figure quite prominently in the semantic structure of *The secretary is pregnant again*, and knowledge of the typical size of the 'human litter' certainly does guide us in interpreting *His wife gave birth*. The point is, given a context in which speakers, for whatever reason, become interested in the breeding habits of mice, the relevant encyclopedic knowledge *could* impact on the semantic structure of *mouse*; these notions, that is, could come to constitute facets of the base of predication presupposed by some uses of the word, for these speakers, at least. (These speculations are not quite so far-fetched as they might appear. See, for example, the transcript entitled 'Mice', in Crystal and Davy 1975.)

To round off the discussion, let us return to Roy Harris's objections to the determinacy of the Saussurian linguistic sign, and to the fixed-code fallacy that it entailed. Hopefully, it will now be clear how cognitive grammar is able to maintain the symbolic thesis, without exposing itself to the kinds of objections that Harris had raised. It is definitely not assumed that the phonological and semantic poles of the linguistic sign are the unitary, invariant representations of many Saussurian approaches, but comprise an open-ended set of units of varying degrees of schematicity. Concerning the semantic units themselves, these are open in two related respects. First, the domain matrix is open, in that any piece of associated knowledge could constitute a presupposition for an appropriate use of an expression. Secondly, just which aspects of domain-based knowledge are relevant to the understanding of an expression is variable, and context-dependent. This is not to say that all bits of background knowledge are equally likely to be relevant. Some aspects will be highly intrinsic to the semantic value of a linguistic unit, and are likely to be invoked on all, or almost all, occasions of its use; others will be relatively extrinsic, but may still play a role in non-routine situations.

4   Syntax in Cognitive Grammar

IN this chapter I address some aspects of the treatment of syntax and syntactic categories in cognitive grammar, especially as these bear on the possessive construction.

I begin by devoting a few pages to a distinction, fundamental to cognitive grammar, between two kinds of linguistic unit: those that designate things, and those that designate relations.[1] All linguistic units belong to one of these two categories. Nouns and nominal expressions designate things, whilst expressions of other syntactic categories (clausal, prepositional, adjectival, adverbial, etc.) designate relations. The distinction is fundamental, not only to a characterization of syntactic categories, but also to the mechanism by which symbolic units combine to form units of increasing internal complexity.[2]

4.1   THINGS AND RELATIONS

In line with the symbolic thesis, the distinction between nominal and relational expressions will need to be motivated in conceptual terms. Ultimately, the validity of the distinction will rest on the possibility of offering substantive conceptual definitions of thing and relation.

In section 3.2 we already touched on some of the difficulties associated with a conceptual characterization of grammatical categories like noun. One approach, that we can briefly mention here, has been to identify prototypical instances of the grammatical categories, and to assimilate other instances to the categories on the basis of some kind of similarity. Thus, Givón (1984: 51) characterizes the prototypical noun referent as concrete, physical, compact, and, above all, time-stable. Prototypical verb referents, in contrast, are 'experiential clusters denoting

---

[1] Note that 'thing' and 'relation' are technical terms in cognitive grammar. 'Entity' is a cover term for both.

[2] Miller (1985) also proposes semantic structures comprising only two kinds of element, viz. 'entities' and 'relators' (Miller's 'entities' would appear to correspond to Langacker's 'things'). Miller's approach differs fundamentally from that pursued here. Miller assumes that syntax is autonomous of semantics. Syntax and semantics therefore need to be characterized in terms of their own, system-specific principles, and he denies that there could be a strict one-to-one correspondence between units of the one level and units of the other. In fact, Miller proposes that all major syntactic categories (nouns, verbs, adjectives, adverbs, and prepositions) denote 'entities', of one kind or another, whilst 'relators' are exclusively elements of semantic structure.

rapid changes' (p. 52; author's emphasis). Adjectives, on this approach, occupy a position midway between time-stable 'things' and temporally changing 'events'.

It is easy, of course, to cite crushing counterexamples to these characterizations. *Thunder*, as a noun, denotes a brief, dynamic situation; in what sense, therefore, might one say that the noun *thunder* designates a thing? On the other hand, the verbs *be* and *remain*, the adjectives *old* and *dead*, and even prepositions such as *in* and *around*, could denote time-stable situations. Recall also my earlier discussion (section 3.2) of *(to) explode* vs. *explosion*. This example, in fact, points to a major shortcoming of the prototype approach, namely, its inability to deal insightfully with the phenomenon of nominalization. *The bomb exploded* and *the bomb's explosion* could refer to exactly the same situation. The temporal properties of the situation can therefore have no bearing on the choice between a verbal and a nominal wording. It is perhaps significant that Givón (1984: 498–501) discusses nominalization in terms of 'structural adjustments', saying little about the semantic-conceptual import of the phenomenon.[3]

A further problematic aspect of Givón's approach, for our purposes at least, is the postulation of a continuum (established on the basis of time stability) from nouns, through adjectives, to verbs. The approach thus fails to capture the, for us, crucial distinction between nominal expressions on the one hand, and non-nominal expressions on the other, that is, between those expressions that designate things, and all other expressions, including verbs and adjectives, which designate relations.

Langacker's approach has been to search for maximally general characterizations of thing and relation. Citing examples like *explosion* and *explode*, *circle* and *round*, *group* and *together*, he (1987*b*: 68) points out that the thing–relation contrast does not necessarily reside in a difference in conceptual content, but rather has to do with the manner in which the content is structured. His claim is that

[a] nominal predication presupposes the interconnections among a set of conceived entities, and profiles the region thus established. By contrast, a relational predication presupposes a set of entities, and it *profiles* the *interconnections* among these entities. (Langacker 1987*b*: 68; author's emphasis)

Thus, *together* (a relational predicate[4]) profiles relations (of spatial proximity, or whatever) between individuals; *group* (a nominal predicate) presupposes that entities are related (for example, by spatial proximity), and profiles the region comprising the related entities.

---

[3] Thus, Givón (1984: 740) observes that when a process is topicalized, it is 'almost always nominalized', i.e. it becomes 'morphologically and syntactically noun-like'. He gives a purely structural motivation for nominalization: the topicalized process is made noun-like because it comes to occupy a position in a clause typical for nouns, i.e. it functions as the subject, object, or indirect object of a verb.

[4] Following Langacker's usage, 'predicate' denotes the semantic pole of a morpheme, whilst 'predication' denotes the semantic pole of any linguistic expression (including morphemes).

In brief, then, the 'defining property of a nominal predication is that it designates a region in some domain' (Langacker 1987a: 198), whereby 'region' is defined as 'a set of interconnected entities', and entities become interconnected 'by their co-conception' (p. 199). Langacker suggests that this characterization 'exhausts the content of the [THING] schema' (p. 198). Moreover, he (1987b: 54) makes the very strong claim that '*all* members of the noun class . . . instantiate [the] abstract noun schema' (author's emphasis). Although Langacker has not stated so explicitly, the converse, it would seem, also holds, namely that no non-nominal expression profiles a thing.

We have already commented on the inclusiveness of the noun schema, and possible reasons for it (section 3.3). Another aspect is worth mentioning. Most distinctions in cognitive grammar, such as the distinction between grammar and lexicon, between syntax and morphology, between word and affix, are seen as gradual, rather than absolute (Tuggy 1992: 239). The above remarks show, however, that for Langacker the distinction between thing and relation is clear-cut. An expression either profiles a thing, or it profiles a relation; it is either nominal in character, or it is relational. The possibility of borderline, or fuzzy cases, it would seem, is not entertained.

Langacker's approach to the word classes has been queried by Hudson (1990b), who points out that the characterizations of thing and relation could be ultimately circular. Especially problematic for Hudson is the notion of 'region', defined as a 'set of interconnected entities' (Langacker 1987a: 198), and the claim that all nominals profile such a region. Hudson (1990b: 277) remarks that he 'would hate to have to use this as a criterion in deciding whether a particular word was a verb or a noun'. Whether, in any particular case, we have to do with a 'region' comprising interconnections, or with 'interconnections' within a region, would probably be decided by reference to the grammatical properties of an expression, i.e. to whether the expression functions grammatically as a nominal or as something else.

Thus, on syntactic criteria, *today*, in *today's weather*, is a noun; again, on syntactic criteria, *today*, in *I saw John today*, is an adverbial. In the former case, we should have to say that the word designates a period of time construed as a thing, while in the second example it designates a relation between an event (*I saw John*) and a period of time. Hudson's point is that the only evidence for the different construals of the time period is, precisely, the different syntactic statuses of the word, which we determine primarily, or even solely, by reference to its distribution. Appeal to different construals of the time period, once in terms of a region, and once in terms of interconnections, plays no part at all in the syntactic analysis of the word.

Langacker (1987b: 55) attempted to pre-empt this line of criticism by distinguishing between procedures for the discovery of category members, and the 'ultimate characterization' of the category, adding that the grammatical behaviour of a word is symptomatic of its semantic value, it is not the sole or final basis for its categorization as noun or verb, or whatever. A further point is that highly schematic characterizations, like that proposed for the noun class, typic-ally lack predictive power; they will, in any case, need to be supplemented by more contentful sub-schemas. (To this extent, therefore, Langacker's highly schematic characterizations are not inconsistent with the more contentful char-acterizations offered by Givón.) Even so, the suspicion of circularity remains, and it could threaten the thesis that *all* nouns share a common semantic content, namely, the property of profiling a region in some domain.

I believe it will still be possible to maintain the conceptual basis of the thing–relation distinction, without incurring the censure of circularity. To begin with, note that an analogous state of affairs occurs in phonology. If the distinction between nominal and relational predicates is crucial to syntax and semantics, an equally crucial distinction in phonology is that between vowels and consonants. Although some phonetic segments may have ambivalent status *vis-à-vis* the vowel–consonant distinction (just as certain concepts may be ambivalent be-tween construal as a thing and construal as a relation), it is neverthess quite clear, in any particular instance, whether the segment is to be taken as a vowel or as a consonant. In many varieties of English, the final segment of *say* and the initial segment of *yes* are, from an acoustic or articulatory point of view, to all intents and purposes identical. Yet we should have little hesitation in saying that the [j] of *say* is vocalic, whilst the [j] of *yes* is consonantal.

The phonological analogy turns out to be rather instructive (cf. Seiler 1993: 120). Let us pursue it further, and consider some of the parallels.

(*a*) The distinction between vowels and consonants is firmly based in phonetic substance. Likewise, the distinction between things and relations is firmly based in conceptual substance.

The substantive basis of the phonological distinction has to do with sonority, which in turn is a function of degree of constriction of the vocal tract. Vocalic segments are produced with a relatively free flow of air through the vocal tract, whilst the production of consonantal segments involves constriction of the air flow at some point (or points). The segment [ɑ] involves minimal constriction; it counts unambiguously as a vowel. Voiceless stops involve maximal constric-tion; they count unambiguously as consonants.

What might be the substantive basis of the distinction between things and relations? A plausible answer is that it concerns conceptual autonomy vs. con-ceptual dependence, that is, the extent to which it is possible to conceptualize an entity without making necessary and intrinsic reference to another entity. A relation necessarily presupposes some conception, however vague or schematic, of the entities that are related. The very notion of 'in', for example, needs to make reference to a container and to a contained. Remove all notion of a con-tainer and a contained, and the notion of 'in' simply dissipates. Schematic conceptualizations of a container and contained are therefore inherent to the profile of the preposition. A thing, in contrast, is relatively self-sufficient. Whilst the notion of 'book' may evoke relations with entities from various cognitive domains, these entities are not inherent to the notion of book, in the sense that they do not need to be profiled in order for the notion of 'book' to be coherent. Pursuing the analogy between semantics and phonology further, we might even reinterpret the vowel–consonant dichotomy in terms of phonological autonomy vs. phonological dependence. Highly sonorous sounds can easily be produced in isolation, without the support of any adjacent sound, and their articulation can be sustained for a significant period of time; sonorous segments could be described as phonologically autonomous. Many consonantal segments, especially those which require a high degree of constriction, cannot be articulated in isolation, but require the support of a neighbouring vocalic segment. Sounds of low sonority could be described as phonologically dependent.

(*b*) Vowels and consonants, things and relations, are both 'correlative categories' (Seiler 1993: 120), that is to say, both distinctions are inherently oppositional.

Vowels are characterized in contrast to consonants, and vice versa. The very notion of a 'sonority peak' (identified with a vocalic segment) presupposes that there are 'sonority troughs' (identified with consonantal segments), and vice versa. Likewise, the notions of thing and relation are mutually dependent. A relation presupposes that there are things that can be related; whilst a thing is a potential participant in a relation. We can no more conceive of a language whose phonology comprised only vowels, than of a language whose phonology comprised only consonants. Likewise, we could no more entertain a conceptual structure comprising only relations (there being no things that were related), any more than there could be a conceptualization comprising only things (there being no relations amongst these things).

(*c*) The substantive basis for both distinctions is inherently gradable, and thus a matter of degree.

There is a gradient between a maximally constricted stop consonant [p] and a minimally constricted open vowel [ɑ]. The voiced fricative [v] is somewhat less constricted than [p], and the mid-high vowel [e] is rather more constricted than [ɑ]. Nevertheless, [v] is sufficiently constricted, and [e] sufficiently unconstricted, for these segments to be unambiguously categorized as consonant and vowel, respectively. But some sounds fall midway on the continuum, such as the glides [j, w] and the nasals [m, n, ŋ]. And indeed, we sometimes find these sounds functioning, now as vocalic segments, now as consonantal segments.

There is a similar gradience with respect to conceptual dependence vs. conceptual autonomy. The notion of 'uncle' contains a relational component lacking in the notion of 'man'. Although we might say that *uncle* is a relational noun, the word is nevertheless uncontroversially a noun, in that it designates the man, not the relation. But there are certainly borderline cases, analogous to the glides and nasals, where a conceptualization can sometimes count as a thing, sometimes as a relation.

Hudson drew attention to the ambivalent status of *today*. Consider also some notions of place. The notion of 'under', we would want to say, is conceptually dependent and therefore unambiguously relational (cf. our earlier remarks on 'in'). But what about *under the bed*? On the one hand, we might say that *under the bed* is also conceptually dependent, in that it invokes a relation between a place and a schematically characterized entity located with respect to that place. In the nominal expression *the book under the bed*, *under the bed* does indeed count as a relational expression, more specifically, as a prepositional phrase.

(1)   [$_{NP}$the book [$_{PP}$under the bed]]

But consider (2).

(2)   Take the book from under the bed.

The standard X-bar syntax approach (e.g. Jackendoff 1973) has been to say that *from* takes as its complement the prepositional phrase *under the bed*.

(3)   Take the book [$_{PP}$[$_{P}$from [$_{PP}$under the bed]]]

Conceptually, however, this doesn't make much sense. The book is to be taken from *a place*, construed as a conceptually autonomous region characterized with respect to the bed. Conceptually, the sentence is exactly parallel to *Take the book from the bookshelf*. We might therefore want to say that *under the bed* has a nominal profile. Although the following syntactic structure would be forbidden by standard phrase structure theories, it corresponds, I think, rather closely to the conceptual structure of the sentence.

(4)   Take the book [$_{PP}$[$_{P}$from [$_{NP}$under the bed]]]

There are other contexts in which *under the bed* appears to have a nominal profile, in that it denotes a place construed as a conceptually autonomous region.

(5)   *a.* [Under the bed] is where I put it.
      b. [pointing to a place 'under the bed']
         That is where I put it.
      c. [Under the bed] is dusty.

Conversely, expressions which look like noun phrases can designate what conceptually is a relation (Taylor 1991*b*).

(6)   *a.* The burglar came in [the back door].
      b. The cat jumped out [the window].

The back door and *the window* do not designate conceptually autonomous things, but places construed with respect to the path followed by the burglar and the cat. The above sentences might be considered elliptical for the more explicit sentences in (7).

(7)   *a.* The burglar came in [through the back door].
      b. The cat jumped out [through the window].

Interestingly, it is not possible to replace *the back door* and *the window* in (6) by the pronominal forms *this* or *it*. The only acceptable pronominal forms are *here* and *there*, which Jackendoff (1973) takes to be prepositional phrases (equivalent to *at/to this place, at/to that place*), not nominals.

(8)   a. The burglar came in {*this/here}.
       b. *The cat jumped out {*it/there}.

The ambiguous character of locatives is apparent also in many Bantu languages. In Tshiluba (spoken in Shaba province of Zaïre), the *in*-relation is expressed by prefixing *mu*- to a noun.[5]

(9)   a. nzi-bo "room"; mu-nzi-bo "in the room"
       b. mo-bo "rooms"; mu-mo-bo "in the rooms"
       c. ino-nzi-bo "this room"; mu-ino-nzi-bo "in this room"

The locatives, so formed, may function as relational predicates, as in (10); here they designate the relation between a place and a state or activity, exactly like the prepositional phrases in the English glosses.

(10)   a. Ba-na   ba-di mu-nzi-bo.
            NPREF-children SC-be LOC-NPREF-room[6]
            "The children are in the room"
        b. Ba-na   ba-kaya mu-mo-bo.
            NPREF-children SC-play LOC-NPREF-room
            "The children play in the rooms"

But in following examples, the locatives function as nominals, specifically, as subjects of the verb, as shown by agreement between the locative prefix *mu*- and the subject concord *mu*- on the verb.

(11)   a. Mu-nzi-bo   mu-di ba-na.
            LOC-NPREF-children SC-be NPREF-children
            "In the room (there) are children"
        b. Mu-mo-bo   mu-di ba-na.
            LOC-NPREF-room SC-be NPREF-children
            "In the rooms (there) are children"
(12)   a. Mu-nzi-bo   mu-di kyanga.
            LOC-NPREF-room SC-be hot
            "In the room (it) is hot"
        b. Mu-ino-nzi-bo   mu-di kyanga.
            LOC-this-NPREF-room SC-be hot
            "In this room (it) is hot"

One analysis of these data would be in terms of profile shift (see below, section 9.3); this, for example, is Langacker's (1993: 16) approach to (5c). He takes the nominal construal of the basically relational *under the bed* to be an instance of the very general conceptual-grammatical process of nominalization.

---

[5] Comparable data from Chichewa are discussed in Bresnan (1994).
[6] In these examples, NPREF = noun prefix, LOC = locative morpheme, and SC = subject concord.

On the other hand, the absence of any overt morphological marking of the relational–nominal contrast (either in English or Bantu) would make this instance of nominalization a case of zero derivation, which could be problematic for the symbolic thesis.[7] The analysis also gives rise to the kind of uneasiness that Hudson expresses, in that there can be no independent evidence for nominal vs. relational construal, other than the syntactic environment in which the expression occurs.

(*d*) In spite of the inherent gradability of the two domains (sonority and conceptual dependence), the distinction between vowels and consonants, like that between things and relations, does turn out to be fairly clear-cut, in the vast majority of cases. We need to ask ourselves why this should be so.

The reason, I suggest, is that membership in one or other of the 'correlative categories' is determined not only on the basis of the substantive content of the element in question, but also with respect to the function of the element within some higher, more inclusive unit. In phonology, this higher unit is the syllable. It is only in the context of the syllable that degrees of sonority acquire functional significance. Even though one and the same acoustic/articulatory event might be phonetically ambiguous, its status in a syllabic configuration as consonant or vowel is usually quite clear.

The higher order unit for the thing–relation contrast is the more inclusive conceptualization encoded by a containing syntactic expression. The relational vs. nominal character of *under the bed* in (1)–(5), and *munzibo* in (10*a*) and (11*a*), cannot be determined solely on the basis of the conceptualization itself (just as the consonantal vs. vocalic status of [j] cannot be determined solely by inspection of articulatory-acoustic properties of the segment), but only by considering the contribution of the expression to the larger syntactic-conceptual unit.

This brings us to the crux of the matter. Why are the distinctions (between vowels and consonants, things and relations) of such central importance anyway to phonology and syntax?

(*e*) Both distinctions are needed in order to account for the syntagmatic combination of simpler units in higher-order units.

Without the vowel–consonant distinction, we would be at a loss to account meaningfully for patterns of segment concatenation, in that permissible sequences of segments are governed by constraints statable at the level of the syllable;[8] to put it another way: syllables are structured with respect to the vowel–consonant opposition.

---

[7] It is problematic, in as far as it postulates a distinction in semantic value which receives no phonological expression. This is not to say that zero derivation must be ruled out in principle. *Dream* can function both as a noun and as a verb. But here we clearly have to do with two distinct lexical items, which need to be listed as such. There is no general principle, in English, which zero-derives a noun from a relational predicate.

[8] As well as at levels higher than the syllable, such as the foot and phonological phrase. On phonological hierarchies of this nature, see Nespor and Vogel (1986).

Likewise, the thing–relation distinction is of such fundamental importance in syntax because it provides the basis for describing the syntagmatic combination of units into expressions of progressively increasing complexity. This is because complex expressions are structured on the basis of the thing–relation distinction.

4.2 KINDS OF RELATION

So far, I have spoken of relational predicates only in contrast to nominal predicates. Relational predicates comprise such diverse items as prepositions, verbs, adverbs, and adjectives. In order to explicate these categories, we need to make some subdivisions within the broad category of relational predicates.

First, we must introduce two more terms. Whenever a relation is designated, the entities participating in the relation are not of equal status. One of the participating entities is the prime focus of attention; this is the *trajector* (tr) of the relation. The trajector is characterized relative to the less salient entity(ies), i.e. the *landmark* (lm). The following expressions could well be true of exactly the same objective situation.

(13)   *a*. The picture above the sofa.
       b. The sofa below the picture.

The two expressions construe the situation differently. The difference lies in a reversal of the trajector–landmark roles. The first characterizes the location of the picture (tr) with respect to the sofa (lm), whereas (13*b*) locates the sofa (tr) with respect to the picture (lm).

A first distinction amongst relational predicates is between those that designate an *atemporal relation* and those that designate a temporal relation, or *process*. Compare:

(14)   *a*. The picture above the sofa.
       b. Mike watched the film.

Both expressions designate a relation between things. But whereas the preposition designates a relation without reference to its instantiation in time, the verb designates the relation through time. The temporal course of the relation is therefore part of the verb's profile.

A second distinction has to do with whether the trajector and/or landmark of a relation are things or are themselves relations. In (15*a*), *before* designates a relation between things, whereas in (15*b*) the trajector is itself a relation (the process designated by *Mike watched the film*). In (15*c*), *before* designates a relation whose trajector and landmark are both temporal relations.

(15)   *a*. The day before yesterday.
       b. Mike watched the film before supper.
       c. Mike watched the film before he did his homework.

Traditionally, *before* would be assigned to different lexical categories in these examples. In (15*a*, *b*) it is a preposition, whereas in (15*c*) it is a conjunction. Jackendoff (1973) argues for the categorial unity of the traditional class of prepositions and certain conjunctions (as well as certain adverbials and some so-called particles), by allowing that a preposition (broadly construed) can take either an NP complement, or a clausal complement. His views had been prefigured by Jespersen (1924: 87–90). In cognitive grammar terms, the distinction is simply a matter of the thing vs. relational character of the landmark.

A third distinction concerns the possibility that the landmark may be 'incorporated' into the relational predicate. Prime examples include the adjectives and adverbs. In (16*a*), *intelligent* designates a relation between its trajector (*pupil*) and a region in excess of some norm in the domain of mental ability; the notional landmark is not expressed independently of the adjective, since it is already contained within the semantic structure of the adjective.

(16)   *a*. An intelligent pupil.
       b. The pupil answered the question intelligently.

A principal difference between adjectives and adverbs lies in the nature of the trajector; the trajector of an adjective is a thing, whilst the trajector of an adverb is a relation. The trajector of *intelligently* in (16*b*) is the temporal relation designated by *the pupil answered the question*. Certain items commonly regarded as adverbials, such as *there* in *Go there, Stay there*, are plausibly analysed as prepositions with an incorporated landmark, i.e. *there* is equivalent to 'to that place', 'at that place'. Arguably, the distinction between transitive and intransitive verbs also has to do with the incorporation of the landmark. As a transitive verb, *say* requires that its landmark be overtly expressed. *Talk*, in contrast, is normally intransitive; its landmark ('a verbal utterance') is already part of its semantic structure.

Distinct from incorporation is the possibility that either the trajector or the landmark may be sublexical. The trajector or landmark entity is schematically represented in the semantic structure of the predicate; its identity, however, is not explicitly specified, but is subject to contextual interpretation. Compare.

(17)   *a*. The boss is in the office.
       b. The boss is in.

Traditionally, the *in* of (17*b*) would be categorized as a particle, or (perhaps) as an adverbial. However, it differs from the *in* of (17*a*) only in that its landmark fails to receive overt lexical expression. Depending on context, the landmark would probably be interpreted to be 'the office', 'the factory', 'the house', or the like. The elements pro and PRO in GB theory are plausibly analysed as sublexical trajectors. The Italian finite verb-form *canta* "he/she sings", or a non-finite infinitival or participial verb-form in English, contain within their semantic profiles a schematically characterized trajector. The notional trajector receives

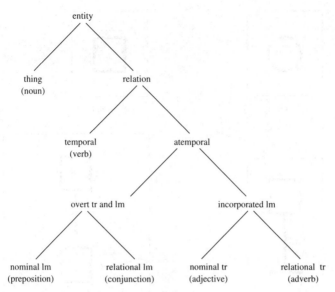

FIG. 4.1. A taxonomy of grammatical categories

conceptual substance, not through an overt nominal expression, but by context-dependent interpretation.

The above remarks suggest how word classes can be conceptually motivated, given only the assumptions of cognitive grammar (see Figure 4.1). The basic distinction is between items with a nominal profile, and those with a relational profile. The latter divide into two broad classes, those which scan the relation through time (verbs), and those with an atemporal profile. The latter again divide into two broad categories, those whose landmark may be expressed overtly (prepositions and conjuctions), and those whose landmark is incorporated (adjectives and adverbs). Prepositions differ from conjunctions according to the nominal vs. relational character of their landmark, whereas adjectives differ from adverbs according to the nominal vs. relational character of their trajector. It will be observed that, apart from some problems with the traditional class of adverbials, the classification matches up rather closely with traditional taxonomies.

Cross-cutting the distinctions we have introduced is the degree of schematicity of the designated entity. The profiles of so-called content words—(*to*) *watch*, *pupil*, *intelligent*, and the the like—are generally rather rich in conceptual content. Other symbolic units designate highly schematic entities; their semantic structures therefore lack inherent conceptual substance. Prime examples are the so-called functional morphemes, such as case markers, markers of number and tense, and the determiners. The plural morpheme in English, for example, profiles multiple instances of a thing; the number of instances, or the kind of thing,

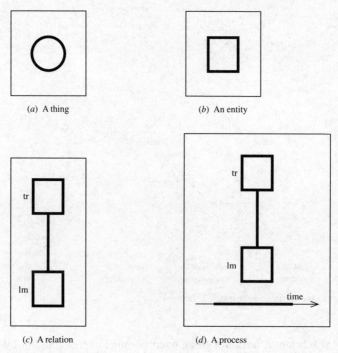

(a) A thing   (b) An entity

(c) A relation   (d) A process

FIG. 4.2. Representation of (a) a thing, (b) an entity, (c) a relation, and (d) a process

are not specified in the morpheme's semantic structure. In order to receive conceptual substance, the schematic profile will need to 'unify' (see below, section 4.3) with a semantically more contentful predicate, namely, a noun stem. Likewise, the verb (*to*) *be* profiles only the persistence through time of a relation. The relation only receives conceptual substance through the syntagmatic combination of *be* with a more contentful relational predicate, as in the expressions *be old, be here, be watching*.

Langacker has devised a range of pictorial conventions for representing the concepts that we have introduced. Some of these are shown in Figure 4.2. A thing is represented by a circle, an entity (which may be either a thing or a relation) by a square, and a relation by a line joining two entities. Boxes surrounding the figures represent the scope of predication of the respective items. Heavy lines mark the profiled elements of the diagrammed semantic structures. Diagrammed in Figure 4.2 are schematic representations of (a) a thing, (b) an entity (i.e. thing or relation), (c) an atemporal relation, and (d) a temporal relation, or process, i.e. a relation scanned through time.

This descriptive apparatus enables us to represent the structure of some semantically more complex predicates. Take the word *uncle*. We could represent

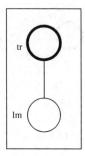

FIG. 4.3. A relational noun

the meaning of the word, quite simply, as in Figure 4.2(*a*), thereby capturing the fact that *uncle* designates a thing. But this misses an important aspect of the word's meaning, namely that *uncle* (in many of its uses) invokes a specific kind of kinship relation. *Uncle* does not profile this relation, nor does it profile the relation's landmark, i.e. the nephew(s) and/or niece(s). Using the device of heavy lining to represent profiled entities, these properties of *uncle* may be diagrammed as in Figure 4.3.

4.3 VALENCE

We now turn to the issue which is central to any theory of syntax: The combination of linguistic units to form increasingly complex structures.

Most linguistic theories handle syntagmatic combination by means of formal rules which operate on grammatical categories such as N, NP, V, and so on. Since cognitive grammar rejects a purely syntactic level of linguistic organization, these formal devices are not available. In accordance with the symbolic thesis, syntagmatic combination is seen as a matter of the conceptual integration of the semantic structures of the component items. Conceptual integration proceeds in parallel with integration of phonological structures. This latter aspect will be largely ignored here.

Langacker addresses the issue of conceptual integration in terms of the establishment of *valence relations*.

A valence relation between two predications is possible just in case these predications overlap, in the sense that some substructure within one corresponds to a substructure within the other and is construed as identical to it. (Langacker 1988*a*: 102)

Let us consider a simple example. Diagrammed in Figure 4.4 is the integration of the component parts of the expression *book on the table*. At the bottom left of Figure 4.4 is a schematic representation of the semantic structure of the preposition *on*. *On* profiles a particular kind of spatial relation (whose details we

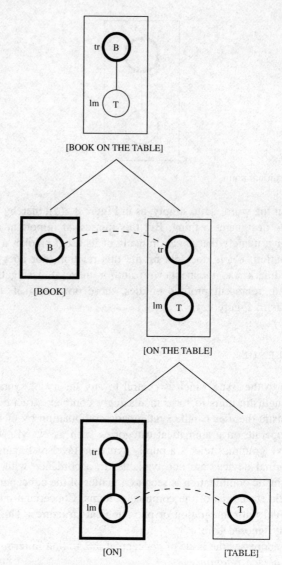

FIG. 4.4. Integration of a complex expression
Source: After Langacker 1991: 92.

may ignore) between a trajector and a landmark. The tr and lm are represented simply as open circles, as befits the fact that *on*, of itself, gives no conceptual substance to the tr and lm entities.[9] The tr and lm constitute *elaboration sites*: 'holes' in semantic structure which need to be given conceptual content by the expressions with which *on* combines. Diagrammed in the lower half of Figure 4.4 is the combination of *on* with *the table*, to give the composite expression *on the table*. (We ignore for the time being the contribution of the definite article *the*.) The combination is possible to the extent that *the table* is construed as identical with the lm of *on*, and can therefore be unified with it. Note that *on the table*, like *on*, designates a relation (namely, a relation between the still schematic tr and the fully specified lm, *the table*). The expression, in other words, inherits the profile of *on*; *on* is said to be the *profile determinant* of the expression. (In the diagram, the profile determinant, at any level of constituency, is represented by the heavy box surrounding the expression.) Subsequently, *on the table* combines with *book* in the manner shown at the top of Figure 4.4. *Book* elaborates the schematic tr of *on the table*, and the composite expression is itself a noun, i.e. *book* constitutes the profile determinant.

Several things need to be noted about this account.

(*a*) The account provides the framework for a natural explication of a number of traditional grammatical notions. Thus profile determinant corresponds rather closely to the traditional notion of phrasal head. *On the table* is headed by its profile determinant *on*, since the expression inherits the relational profile of *on*; *book on the table* is headed by its profile determinant *book*, since the expression inherits the nominal profile of *book*.

The account also enables us to characterize the traditional distinction between complement and modifier. A *complement elaborates a schematic entity in the semantic structure of the profile determinant*; in other words, a complement adds conceptual substance to a notion which is already implicit within the semantic structure of its head (and which is therefore intrinsic to the head). A *modifier has a schematic entity in its semantic structure which is elaborated by the profile determinant*; generally, therefore, a modifier adds specifications over and above those that are implicit in the semantic structure of the head (and which are therefore non-intrinsic to the head). In accordance with these characterizations, we can say that *the table* is a complement of *on*, whilst *on the table* is a modifier of *book*. Although, in this instance, the cognitive grammar account coincides exactly with mainstream accounts, this will not always be the case. For example, on the cognitive grammar definition of complement, the subject of a finite verb turns out to be a complement, no less than the direct object.

Also contrary to received wisdom is the fact that the cognitive grammar account does not treat the categories of complement and modifier as mutually

---

[9] This is an over-simplification, in that *on* requires, as its lm, an entity that is, or that can be construed as, a one- or two-dimensional line or surface. To this extent, *on* already incorporates within its semantic structure some schematic aspects of its lm.

exclusive. Consider the expression *father of twins*. The expression is headed by *father*, but what is the status of *of twins*? On the one hand, *of twins* elaborates a notion already implicit in the semantic structure of *father* (a father is necessarily a father of somebody); the prepositional phrase is therefore a complement. At the same time, *father* elaborates the schematic trajector of the relational expression *of twins*; to this extent, the prepositional phrase is a modifier. *Of twins* exhibits properties both of a complement and of a modifer.

(*b*) The notions of thematic grid and thematic role shed much of their formalistic mystique. The thematic grid, alias argument structure, of a lexical item is simply the array of elaboration sites in the item's semantic structure, sites that are given conceptual substance as the item enters into valence relations in complex expressions. The thematic role of a complement follows from aspects of the head's meaning. Given that *on* (in many of its uses) designates a spatial relation, the thematic role of its complement is the specification of a location.

(*c*) It will be evident that a very large number of expressions are assembled in a manner comparable to that diagrammed in Figure 4.4: *book on the bed*, *man in the moon*, *dust under the bed*. By extracting what is common to these expressions we obtain a *construction schema*, i.e. a kind of template for the creation (and interpretation) of these, and countless other expressions. It is the construction schemas, and the valence relations on which they are based, that in cognitive grammar perform the work which is delegated to the syntactic component, in most grammatical theories.

(*d*) A further observation concerns the sequence in which elements combine into a composite structure. The sequence determines the *constituency* of an expression. The constituency of *book on the table*, as diagrammed in Figure 4.4, is [book [on [the table]]], which corresponds, of course, with the traditional phrase structure account. This particular constituency is motivated by the fact that a complement is more intrinsic to its head than is a modifier. The relation of complement to head therefore needs to be satisfied before the relation of modifier to its head. This said, constituency does not constitute an autonomous level of syntactic structure, neither is it a major issue of contention in cognitive grammar. For example, there are no compelling reasons why *Mike watched the film* should have the constituency [Mike [watched the film]]—this corresponds to the traditional subject–predicate, or NP–VP division—rather than [[Mike watched] the film]. Which way the components are assembled, in this example, has few, if any consequences for the meaning of the composite expression, and indeed, many expressions can have alternative, and equally valid constituencies.

The example we have discussed illustrates the relations of modification and complementation. A third syntagmatic relation needs to be recognized. This is the relation of *apposition*. (Although I shall not pursue the matter here, I suspect that *all* syntagmatic combinations can be exhaustively analysed in terms of these three relations.) Two items are in apposition if they both designate the same entity, and their profiles are unified to produce a richer conception of the designated entity (Langacker 1991: 432). Typical examples of apposition are the expressions *our neighbour the butcher* and *we the people*.

Apposition tends to be ignored by mainstream grammatical theory. (The textbooks of Radford 1988 and Haegeman 1991 do not even mention it in their index.) Yet apposition is probably of no lesser importance in syntax than modification and complementation. Furthermore, just as one and the same expression can exhibit properties both of a modifier and of a complement, so too an appositional relation can share properties especially of complementation. Consider *the fact that pigs can't fly*. The *that*-clause can plausibly be analysed as a nominal expression in apposition to *the fact*. At the same time, a 'fact' is necessarily (intrinsically) a fact *that* something is the case. The *that*-clause thus elaborates a notion that is already schematic in the semantic structure of *fact*, and to this extent functions as the complement of *fact*.

4.4 DETERMINERS

I have spoken so far of nominal expressions, and ignored the role of determiners. However, a distinction obviously needs to be made between a 'bare' noun (an N or N', in traditional X-bar terms), and a noun phrase.[10] Both nouns and noun phrases designate things, on Langacker's schematic definition of thing. The difference is that whereas a noun (an N or N') designates a kind, or type of thing, a noun phrase designates an instance of the kind (or instances, in case the noun phrase is plural). Two aspects are involved: some notion of number or quantity, and some process of *grounding*. Grounding involves a relation between the designated instance and the ground, i.e. the circumstances of the speech situation, and the participants that are involved in it. Some nominals (those with definite reference) convey that the instance can be uniquely identified by both speaker and hearer, whilst nominals with non-specific reference pick out an instance (or instances) that cannot be uniquely identified.

We might note in passing that grounding applies not only to noun phrases, but also to finite clauses. Grounding, in a finite clause, establishes the relation of the designated process to the speech event. Grounding is effected by tense, which specifies the time, relative to a reference point (normally, the time of utterance), at which the conceived process is instantiated; alternatively, by various epistemic modalities, which convey the speaker's assessment of the likelihood of the process being instantiated. The grounding element of the finite clause corresponds by and large to the INFL constituent of GB theory.

I have spoken of grounding as a *relation* between instance and ground. Let us consider how this relation is to be represented in the semantic structure of a

---

[10] Langacker reserves the term 'noun' for the traditional N or N', and uses 'nominal' to refer to the traditional noun phrase.

noun phrase. One possibility would be to say that, in a grounded expression such as *the car*, the determiner profiles a relation between its trajector (a schematically characterized instance) and its landmark (the ground). *The* combines with *car* through the establishment of a valence relation between the nominal profile of *car* and the schematically characterized instance within the relational profile of *the*. The resultant expression then inherits the nominal profile of *car*. On this account, *the car* turns out to be headed by *car*, and *the* is a modifier of the head. This analysis corresponds, by and large, with the traditional account, in which a noun phrase is indeed headed by the noun, and articles are assimilated to the more general category of adjectival modifiers.[11]

There are, however, a number of reasons why this account should be questioned. If *the* is a modifier to *car*, we should have to say that the semantic contribution of *the* to the composite expression *the car* is comparable to the contribution of the modifier *in the garage* to the complex expression *car in the garage*, or to the contribution of the modifier *expensive* to the complex expression *expensive car*. This is surely incorrect. Modifiers enrich the conceptual content of their head, by adding specifications over and above those that are implicit in the semantic structure of the head. Modifiers, therefore, are generally optional. Omission of a modifier may result in an impoverishment of semantic structure, it will not normally result in conceptual incoherence (or grammatical ill-formedness). *I bought the car* is no less coherent than *I bought the expensive car*, or *I bought the car in the garage*. *The*, however, does not add optional conceptual substance to *car*, neither can *the* be omitted. *I bought car* is simply conceptually incoherent (and grammatically ill-formed), the expression cannot be regarded as semantically less elaborated than *I bought the car*.

Something which might speak in favour of the relational profile of *the* is the fact that the definite article cannot stand alone; the article must always be attached to a noun. This would be an expected consequence of the conceptual dependence of an element with a relational profile. On the other hand, if we say that *the* has a relational profile, we should presumably want to say the same of other determiners, such as *this, that, these, those*, and unstressed *some*, all of which, as prenominal determiners, are in paradigmatic contrast with *the*. These words can, however, stand alone, unattached to a noun: *I bought this, Those have been sold*. Here, *this* and *those* function as fully grounded nominals (although the entities that they designate are characterized only schematically). The fact that these words *can* stand alone as nominals suggests an alternative analysis of the determiners, namely, that determiners have a nominal profile.

On this account, the relational character of grounding would be captured by means of an unprofiled relation in the semantic structure of the determiner. The semantic structure of a determiner would be analogous to the semantic structure of an inherently relational noun like *uncle*. A determiner, that is, designates a

---

[11] The *Shorter OED* defines *article* (as a grammatical notion) as 'a name for the adjectives *a, an, the*'.

thing, the thing, however, is construed as a participant in an unprofiled relation. What distinguishes determiners from nouns like *uncle* is, above all, the conceptual content of the profile. The profile of a determiner lacks any inherent conceptual content; in the case of *the* its profile is merely 'instance(s) of a thing'. *The* therefore lacks even a specification for number. (The profile of *this*, however, is somewhat richer, in that *this* does contain a specification for number, in addition to designating an entity in proximity to the speech act participants; its slightly more contentful profile possibly accounts for the fact that *this* can stand alone as a nominal, whereas *the* may not.) In order for the profile of a determiner to acquire conceptual content, it needs to be put into correspondence with a conceptually richer nominal profile. In *the car*, the profile of *car* unifies with the nominal profile of *the*. The resultant expression construes the profiled thing with respect to the grounding relation.

On the account so far, the relation between a determiner and a noun is a relation of apposition. There is, however, a wrinkle to be ironed out. Recall Langacker's characterization of valence, cited earlier. A valence relation between semantic structures requires that some substructure in the one can be construed *as identical to* some substructure within the other. The nominal profile of a determiner cannot be construed as identical to the nominal profile of the associated noun, for the reason that the determiner profiles an instance, the noun profiles a kind, or type. (Precisely the same problem, of course, arises in connection with our first account of nominals, in which the determiner functioned as a modifier to the noun.) We therefore need to propose a more elaborate semantic structure for the grounding predication. The semantic structure of the determiner needs to include within its scope of predication not only the notion of the type (this is what gets unified with the associated noun), but also the notion of *domain of instantiation* of the type. The domain of instantiation of *car* will, typically, be three-dimensional space (cars, namely, are artefacts in three-dimensional space). Langacker suggests that we can think of a type specification as 'floating about unattached through the domain of instantiation, with the potential to be manifested anywhere within it. This potential is realized, and an instance conception obtained, when the specification is anchored at a particular spot' (Langacker 1991: 57).

We are now in a position to diagram the semantic structure of a grounded nominal, such as *the car* (Figure 4.5). The determiner, diagrammed on the left, profiles an instance (I) of a type (T). The profiled instance is selected from indefinitely many potential instances, and is singled out by the speech act participants (SP) from the perspective of the ground. (The broken line linking SP and I indicates the mental path taken by the speech act participants). A valence relation between the determiner and the noun becomes possible through the unification of the schematically characterized type in the structure of the determiner with the nominal profile of the noun.

This account leads to a radically revised view of the structure of a noun phrase. If, on the first account, a noun phrase was headed by the noun, and the

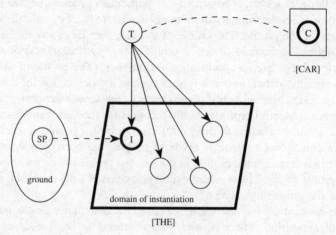

FIG. 4.5. A grounded nominal (after Langacker 1991:92)

determiner was a modifier to the noun, we now propose that the noun phrase is headed by the determiner, and the noun turns out to be a complement to the determiner.[12] To recapitulate the argumentation: The determiner heads the noun phrase in that the noun phrase inherits the instance-of-a-thing profile of the determiner; the noun is a complement in that it gives greater conceptual substance to a schematically characterized type specification present in the semantic structure of the head.

This account is broadly consistent with some independent developments in other syntactic theories. Hudson, pursuing a particular version of dependency grammar, has long argued for the thesis of 'determiners as heads' (see especially Hudson 1984: 90–2.) Recent developments in X-bar syntax have also analysed the traditional noun phrase, which used to be headed by the noun, as a determiner phrase, or DP, headed by the determiner (Abney 1987; Stowell 1989). Within the determiner phrase, the N, or N′ constituent of the erstwhile noun phrase functions as an NP complement to D. (18), therefore, has been replaced by (19).

(18)

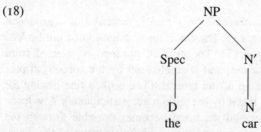

[12] For a defence of the determiner as head thesis within cognitive linguistics, see Hewson (1991); and, for arguments in favour of the traditional analysis, Van Langendonck (1994). Within the GB framework, doubts about the determiner as head thesis are raised by Ernst (1992) and Spencer (1992).

(19)

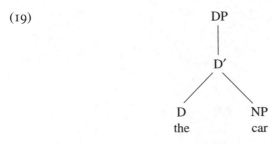

A similar kind of analysis is available for a wide range of 'functional' elements in a language, such as derivational and inflectional affixes (including
markers of tense, aspect, case, and number) and auxiliary verbs. The semantic
content of these elements is highly schematic. Since they lack inherent conceptual substance, these elements generally cannot occur independently of a conceptually more contentful host. In combination with a host, the profile of the
functional element acquires conceptual substance through unification with some
component of the semantic structure of the host. By the arguments presented
above, the functional element turns out to be the head of the composite expression, with the host as its complement.

Take, for example, the plural morpheme in English. Concerning its semantic
value, we can say little more than that the plural morpheme profiles an indeterminate number (greater than one) of instances of a type specification. Lacking
any inherent conceptual substance itself, the plural morpheme cannot occur
independently of a host—it is, in other words, a typical bound morpheme. In
order to acquire inherent conceptual substance, the plural morpheme needs to
enter into a valence relation with a type specification. The type specification,
profiled by the noun stem, is thereby unified with the schematic type specification in the semantic structure of the plural morpheme. A plural noun, such as
dogs, is headed by the plural morpheme, in that the plural morpheme is the
profile determinant of the complex expression. Since the noun stem gives greater
conceptual substance to an unprofiled element in the semantic structure of the
head, the noun stem is the complement of the plural morpheme.

Note, by the way, that plural marking (in English) is internal to grounding.
Grounding, as effected by the definite determiner, applies to a noun that is
already specified for number. We can express this fact in terms of constituency.
The constituency of *the dogs* is [the [[dog][s]]], or, schematically, [GROUND-
ING [[NOUN] [PLURAL]]].

Recent developments in X-bar syntax have come up with a rather similar
analysis of number marking in the noun phrase. Whereas the older generative
tradition, as exemplified by Chomsky (1965: 170–6), treated number as a syntactic feature on a noun, recent versions of the theory postulate a 'number
phrase' (NmP), headed by the functional category Nm, i.e. 'number' (cf. Spencer 1992: 315). The constituent structure of *the dogs* would be approximately as
in (20).

(20)

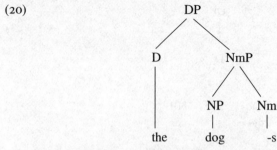

In cognitive grammar terms, this diagram captures the fact that the definite determiner is schematic for the class of definite nominals, and that the plural morpheme is schematic for the class of plural nouns (and that the so-called 'NP' is schematic for the class of type specifications).

4.5 CASE

The possessive morpheme in English is sometimes referred to as a case marker. A topic of special interest to us, therefore, will be the status and proper characterization of case morphemes. This chapter concludes with some remarks on this topic. In the next chapter, we examine in greater depth the claim that POSS is a marker of genitive case.

It goes without saying that in cognitive grammar, case morphemes, like all other components of a linguistic expression, are inherently symbolic, and hence inherently meaningful. The thrust of the preceding discussion suggests that a case morpheme will head the nominal expression which it case-marks; alternatively: a case morpheme is schematic for the set of case-marked expressions that it defines.

Discussion of case is hampered by uncertainties as to what the term should cover. In this book, I adopt a rather narrow view of case, recognizing as prototypical case markers the inflectional affixes characteristic of many of the Indo-European languages, such as Latin and Russian. Since the possessive morpheme in English is defintely not an inflectional affix, POSS, on this understanding of case, does not count as a case marker. On a broader understanding of case, however, all manner of grammatical devices which have semantic values similar to those of the inflectional case morphemes could be assimilated to the category of case markers. Assorted particles, not to mention prepositions and postpositions, could be regarded as case-marking morphemes. On this broader understanding of the notion, POSS might well count as a case marker. On the other hand, by construing the category so broadly, the notion of case could well be emptied of any distinctive content, with case markers being absorbed into the broader category of atemporal relational predicates. Even facts of constituent order, such as the fact that in English the subject of a clause (usually) occurs before the verb,

while the direct object (usually) occurs post-verbally, might be considered manifestations of case.

In order to arrive at a workable understanding of case, we will need to consider two issues: (*a*) The category of item to which the putative case marker
attaches. Intuitively, case is a property of noun phrases. However, a remarkable
fact about the Indo-European case markers is that they attach, not to the noun
phrase *per se*, but to the various components of a noun phrase—to the noun in
the first instance, and then, by agreement, to other components, such as adjectives, demonstratives, and (if the language has them) determiners. (*b*) The profile
of the putative case marker. A crucial question is whether the profile of the case
morpheme is nominal or relational.

Let us focus first on the second of these issues. Consider the following Latin
sentences.

(21) *a*. Puella   amat puerum.
          girl-NOM-SG-F loves boy-ACC-SG-M
      b. Puer   amat puellam.
          boy-NOM-SG-M loves girl-ACC-SG-F

The choice of nominative vs. accusative case communicates the role of the
associated nominal within a transitive clause, specifically, that the nominal functions as the trajector, alternatively, as the landmark of the temporal relation
profiled by the verb. We may say, therefore, that the case morphemes profile a
highly schematic thing, construed, within its scope of predication, as the trajector
or, respectively, the landmark, of an equally schematically characterized process. The schematic trajector of the case morpheme receives conceptual substance through unification with the profile of the host; the host is therefore the
complement of the case marker (and in apposition to it, since both case marker
and host designate the same entity). At the same time, the schematic process
within the scope of predication of the case marker gets elaborated by the process
designated by the verb, *amat*.

The next example, from Russian, is a little more problematic.

(22) Anna   edet v gorod   avtobusom.
      Anna-NOM goes to town-ACC bus-INST
      "Anna goes to town by bus"

In terms of its phonological structure, *avtobusom* looks exactly like Latin *puellam*; the word consists of a case-marking affix, *-om*, attached to a nominal
root, *avtobus*. But whereas *puellam* uncontroversially profiles a thing (*puellam*
functions as the direct object of a verb, and the direct object of a verb is
uncontroversially a nominal), it is by no means obvious that *avtobusom* likewise
has a nominal profile. Especially in view of its English translation, we might
want to say that *avtobusom* has a relational profile, whose trajector is the process
designated by *Anna edet v gorod*, and whose landmark is the nominal *avtobus*.
On this view, *-om* still heads *avtobusom*. The case marker, however, would have

a relational profile, comparable, in all essential respects, to the profile of an English proposition. This reasoning would lead us to the conclusion that there are two categories of case markers—those, like nominative and accusative, which are nominal in character, and those, like instrumental (as well as dative, ablative, etc., and possibly also the genitive) that are relational in character. The distinction would correspond by and large to the traditional distinction between the 'structural', or 'grammatical' cases, and the 'semantic', or 'concrete' cases (Kuryłowicz 1964: 31–2).

This dichotomy is problematic. First, one encounters, in languages such as Latin and Russian, prepositions which select, as their complement, a nominal marked with one of the so-called semantic cases. In (23), Russian *s* "together with" and *za* "behind" select as their complement a nominal marked for instrumental case.

(23) *a.* Anna   edet v gorod   s   podrugoj.
        Anna-NOM goes to town-ACC with friend-INST
      b. Anna   stoit za   domom.
        Anna-NOM stands behind house-INST

Here, we should presumably want to say that the case-marked nominals *podrugoj* and *domom* designate things, not relations; after all, *podrugoj* and *domom* function as the complements of prepositions, and these complements are typically nominal in character. To claim otherwise would lead to some very bizarre conclusions. In the first place, we should have to say that the Russian prepositions *s* and *za* differ fundamentally in their semantic structure from their English equivalents, *with* and *behind*, in that the landmark of the Russian prepositions is obligatorily a relation, whilst the landmark of the English prepositions is obligatorily a thing. Such a distinction is conceptually totally unfounded. (What, concretely, would be the relation profiled by the complements of the Russian prepositions?) Not only this. Assuming that accusative-marked nominals in Russian (as in Latin) uncontroversially designate things, we would have to draw a distinction between those Russian prepositions, such as *v* in (23*a*), that have nominal (accusative) landmarks, and other prepositions, such as *s* and *za* in (23), which have relational (e.g. instrumental) landmarks. Again, this is a distinction that is conceptually without any foundation.

Still keeping to Russian, consider now (24).

(24) Anna   edet v gorod   poslednim avtobusom.
        Anna-NOM goes to town-ACC last-INST   bus-INST
        "Anna goes to town with the last bus"

Here, we see that instrumental case is marked both on the noun *avtobus* and on the modifying adjective *posledn-*.

Two questions arise. One has to do with whether instrumental case-marking, when it appears on the adjective, has the same semantic structure as instrumental case-marking on a noun. The most economical solution (Occam's razor!) is that the semantic structure is exactly the same in both instances.

A second question concerns the semantic structure of the case-marked adjective *poslednim*. We already mentioned some aspects of the semantic structure of adjectives (section 4.2). An adjective profiles a relation between its trajector and a region in some domain. With respect to the expression *last bus*, the trajector of *last* is *bus*, and the landmark is a region in the domain of 'temporal sequence'. Instrumental case marking on the Russian adjective does not affect the adjective's profile. Instrumental *poslednim*, in *poslednim avtobusom*, is no less of an adjective than nominative *poslednij* in *poslednij avtobus*. What then of the case marker, and its integration with the adjectival stem? We need to postulate a valence relation between them, in virtue of some aspect of the semantic structure of the case morpheme being identified with some component in the semantic structure of the adjectival stem. The identity, I suggest, is between the profile of the case marker and the schematic trajector of the adjective. The semantic structure of *poslednim* turns out to be such that the adjective can enter into a valence relation only with a noun that is marked for instrumental case (and that is also masculine and singular). This is precisely the kind of analysis that Langacker (1991: 187–8) presents for number and gender marking of adjectives in Spanish, and is one that perfectly captures the mechanics of agreement patterns. Note that the analysis attributes a nominal profile to the case marker; indeed, it is obscure how conceptual integration between case marker and adjective could take place at all, if the case marker were to be attributed a relational profile.

There are compelling grounds, therefore, for regarding case-marked nominals such as *avtobusom*, *podrugoj*, and *domom* as nominals, not as relational predicates. Their profile is a thing, construed in its scope of predication as a participant in a relation. In (22), case-marked *avtobusom* "by bus" designates the bus, construed as a participant in the relation designated by *Anna edet v gorod* "Anna goes to town". In (23) case-marked *podrugoj* in *s podrugoj* "with friend", and case-marked *domom* in *za domom* "behind house", designate, respectively, the friend and the house, which are construed as the landmark of the associated preposition, whilst the relation in the scope of predication of the case-marker is identified with the relation profiled by the preposition. In (24), the case-marked nominal and the case-marked adjective are integrated in that the case marker on the adjective is schematic for the case-marked nominal with which the adjective combines. To the extent that we may want to maintain the distinction between 'structural' and 'semantic' case, the distinction will have to do with the nature of the unprofiled relation within the semantic structure of the case morpheme.

Case marked *poslednim avtobusom* in (24) differs substantially in its semantic structure from its English translation, *with (the) last bus*. The case markers, on both the adjective and the noun in Russian, have a nominal profile, whereas

English *with* is relational. Secondly, the Russian case markers attach to components of the noun phrase, whereas *with* combines externally with a noun phrase. A third difference is that the case markers are affixes, phonologically integrated with their hosts; *with*, on the other hand, is a phonologically autonomous word.

Exactly the same considerations apply to genitive-marked nominals in Russian, and the other case-marking languages of Indo-European. In spite of the possibility of an English translation with the relational preposition *of*, we will want to say that in *dni nedeli* "days week-GEN", i.e. "days of the week", genitive-marked *nedeli* has a nominal profile, which construes 'week' as a participant in an unprofiled relation to another entity; *nedeli*, in other words, does not profile the relation itself.

The distinction between case markers and items such as prepositions will not always be so clear-cut, however. Consider the so-called case markers of Hungarian and Finnish. In some respects, the Hungarian case morphemes are closer to postpositions than to the case markers of Latin and Russian.

(25)   *a.* könyv-em-ben.
       book-my-in
       "in my book"
       b. ház-am-ban.
       house-my-in
       "in my house"

The case marker is phonologically integrated with its host, as shown by facts of vowel harmony. To this extent, the case markers are nominal affixes. On the other hand, the case marker occurs external to the grounded noun phrases *könyvem* "my book" and *házam* "my house". There could be grounds, therefore, to say that the phrases in (25) have relational profiles, inherited from the relation profile of *-ben*, *-ban*. (At any rate, the arguments which led us to attribute a nominal profile to Russian *avtombusom* do not apply to the Hungarian examples.) But we should still, presumably, want to say that the accusative marked *könyvemet* "my book (ACC)", *házamat* "my house (ACC)" have a nominal profile.

The Finnish equivalents of (25) differ significantly, in that case marking is internal to grounding by the possessor.

(26)   *a.* talo-ssa-ni.
       house-in-my
       "in my house"
       b. kirja-ssa-ni.
       book-in-my
       "in my book"

The fact that grounding (by the possessive morpheme) is external to case marking, suggests that case-marked *talossa* and *kirjassa* do indeed have a nominal, not a relational profile. What is 'mine', in (26a), is not the *in*-relation, but the house, construed as the landmark of an *in*-relation. To this extent, therefore, the Finnish case markers are closer to the Indo-European case markers than they are to postpositions.[13]

Or consider the topic, subject, and object markers of Japanese, i.e. *wa*, *ga*, and *o*. These morphemes mark a phrasal element as, respectively, a sentence topic, subject, or object. The markers attach externally to the phrase that they mark.

(27) Kono ki wa   eda   ga   sukunai.
      this   tree TOPIC branch SUB few
      As for this tree, its branches are few
      "This tree doesn't have many branches"

Here, we could say that *wa* and *ga* each profiles a schematic thing, construed with respect to its role in the larger predication; the schematic profile is both in apposition with and is elaborated by its complement, *kono ki* "this tree" and *eda* "branch", respectively. To this extent, *wa* and *ga* are fairly representative case markers. However, *wa* can mark, not only what is uncontroversially a nominal, but also what looks to be a relational phrase.

(28) John ni wa   okane ga arimasu
      John LOC TOPIC money SUB exist
      "John has money"

We could still say that the sentence topic, i.e. *John ni wa*, is nominal in character, having inherited the nominal profile of *wa*. But this begs the question of the status of *John ni*, and, hence, of *ni*. The question boils down to whether *John ni* is indeed relational, in which case *ni* counts as a relational predicate, i.e. as a postposition, analogous in its semantic structure to the English prepositions, or whether *John ni* is nominal in character, in which case *ni* is a case marker, analogous to the case markers of Indo-European.

Ultimately, we may need to regard the categories of case markers and prepositions (postpositions) as gradient, rather than clear-cut. The fact of gradience, however, does not mean that we should give up on attempts to characterize salient regions of the continuum. I propose, therefore, to restrict case markers to elements with a nominal profile. Case markers (or, at least, prototypical case markers) are morphemes which profile a highly schematic thing, construed in terms of a relation with some other participant(s) in a situation. To relax the condition on the nominal profile, and to allow into the category elements with a relational profile, would mean, *inter alia*, that prepositions, in many of their uses, would have to be regarded as case markers. We would have to say that *by*, in *by bus*, is no less of a case marker than *-om* in *avtobusom*. To obliterate the

---

[13] The Hungarian–Finnish contrast was suggested by Spencer (1992). Spencer cited the contrast as evidence against the notion that case markers head a case-marked phrase; rather, in the spirit of Chomsky (1965), he argued that case should be regarded as a feature on a noun phrase. Spencer's conclusions do not follow, given a proper characterization of the profile of a case-marked nominal.

distinction between prepositions and case markers (narrowly construed) would render the notion of case marker quite vacuous.

Where the possessive morpheme fits into this picture, will be one of the topics of the next chapter.

5 The Constituent Structure of Prenominal Possessives

IN approaching any linguistic expression, one of the first questions that a linguist is trained to ask concerns the constituent structure of the expression. What is the syntactic category of the expression? What heads the expression? To which lexical category does the head belong? What are the constituent parts of the expression, and to which syntactic categories do they belong? What are the relations between the constituent parts?

In this chapter I discuss the constituent structure of prenominal possessives, focusing on some of the more controversial issues that arise within mainstream phrase structure and GB theories, and concluding with a cognitive grammar account of its constituency.

I begin by reviewing some basic facts about the construction. This first section presupposes a conservative version of X-bar syntax, as outlined in Section 2.4. I go on to interpret these facts within a cognitive grammar framework.

5.1 SOME BASIC FACTS

The internal structure of prenominal possessives appears, at first glance, to be quite unproblematic. At issue are the kinds of expressions cited at the beginning of Chapter 1.

(1) *a.* John's wife.
    b. the neighbour's car.
    c. the country's population.
    d. yesterday's news.
    e. the train's arrival.
    f. Rome's destruction.

These all have the schematic structure [X-POSS-Y], where X denotes the possessor, Y the possessee, and POSS is the possessive morpheme. The following observations capture some (relatively) uncontroversial aspects of these expressions.

(*a*) *A prenominal possessive consitutes an NP.* This proposition, I take it, is uncontroversial (at least in traditional syntactic theories), and is not in need of demonstration.

(*b*) *The Y constituent constitutes an N′.* That Y is an N′, rather than an N, is shown by the fact that Y may contain both prenominal and postnominal modifiers, as well as a postnominal complement.

(2)   *a.* Russia's [$_N$recent invasion of Chechnya].
       b. my [$_N$new summer house by the sea].

That Y is an N′ rather than an NP is shown by the fact that items normally regarded as NP specifiers—articles, demonstratives, some quantifiers—are excluded from the Y constituent.

(3)   *a.* *my [$_{NP}$a child].
       b. *his [$_{NP}$that car].
       c. *John's [$_{NP}${all/some/no} children].

There are, however, some wrinkles.

   (i) Numerals, and some of the quantifiers, such as *every, each and every* (though not *each*), and *many* (though not *much*), are permitted in the Y constituent.

(4)   *a.* John's three children.
       b. my one (and only) friend.
       c. (?)John's several friends.
       d. his (each and) every move.
       e. *his each move.
       f. John's many friends.
       g. *John's much money.

Here, we could claim that the numerals, and some of the quantifiers, function as modifiers (and are thus included in N′), not as specifiers. Still, we would have to acknowledge some idiosyncratic behaviours, concerning, for example, the difference between *every* and *each*, and between *many* and *much*.

   (ii) Some curious restrictions on the possibility of modifying the possessee have been noted. Lyons (1986*b*: 124) observes that defining relative clauses on the possessee tend to be infelicitous.

(5)   *John's book that you borrowed.
       [asterisked by Lyons]

The contrast in (6) is due to Chomsky (1970: 197), who observes that the less felicitous example contains a 'true reduced relative'. The contrast in (7) is due to Giorgi and Longobardi (1991: 132).

(6)   *a.* John's house in the woods.
       b. ?John's book on the table.   — OK
(7)   *a.* John's books by my favourite author.
       b. *John's books of my favourite author.

We return to these examples in a later chapter.

   (*c*) *The X constituent is an NP.* Structurally quite complex NPs can occupy the X position.

(8) *a.* [_{NP}the people who live across the road]'s new car.

    b. [_{NP}The house of a friend of mine]'s roof blew off.[1] ——— *see Halliday FN*

Given that the X constituent is an NP, and that a prenominal possessive is itself an NP, we expect a prenominal possessive to be able to occupy the X position. This kind of recursion is indeed possible.

(9) [John]'s wife.

    [John's wife]'s mother.

    [John's wife's mother]'s friend.

    [John's wife's mother's friend]'s baby.

Again, there are some restrictions on the kinds of NPs that can occur as possessors.

  (i) Not all possessive expressions are equally felicitous as possessors. Halitsky (1975: 291) cites the following (in his judgement ungrammatical) examples, which contrast with the fully acceptable expressions in (9).

(10) *a.* *[the peasant's rebellion]'s outcome.

    b. *[Kennedy's assassination]'s effect on the country.

    c. *[America's invasion of Cambodia]'s failure.

  (ii) As (8a) shows, an NP containing a defining relative clause can function as the X constituent. NPs containing a non-defining relative, however, are excluded.

(11) ??Our neighbours, who moved in last week's new car.   *Our neighbours across the road's new car is OK*

Somewhat marginal as possessors are NPs containing an appositional phrase.

(12) ?Our neighbour the butcher's new car.   *John Smith, our GP's, new car*

  (iii) Demonstrative and quantifying pronouns are not able to function as possessors. While *the plane's arrival* is normal, I cannot point to a plane and say **that's arrival* (although I could point to a plane and say *That arrived*). In some of their uses, *any*, *two*, *many*, constitute full NPs (*Any will do*, *Two arrived*, *Many left*). These items cannot, however, function as possessors: **any's use*, **two's arrival*, **many's departure*.

  (iv) In the examples so far cited, the X constituent has been an NP with definite reference. Indefinites and generics, and even negatives, may also function as possessors.

(13) *a.* I've been reading a student's essays.

    b. Somebody's car is occupying my parking bay.

    c. The elephant's brain is larger than man's brain.

    d. He was nobody's friend.

    e. No country's economy can sustain such high growth rates over a prolonged period of time.

But while *nobody's friend* is acceptable (13d), *nowhere* and *nothing* appear to be prohibited as possessors: **nowhere's population* (cf. *the country's population*), **nothing's value* (cf. *the car's value*).

---

[1] Authentic example, cited from Halliday (1985b: 114).

??? Our neighbours, who had a party last night's, car

(*d*) *X-POSS-Y expressions have the structure [X POSS] [Y]*; that is, X and POSS together form a constituent, whereas POSS and Y do not. This constituency is suggested by the fact that X-POSS constituents may be coordinated, as may Y constituents. Coordination of POSS-Y, however, is not possible. Also suggestive of the proposed constituency is the fact that many speakers accept pronominal *one*(*s*) as the Y constituent.

(14)   *a.*   John's and Mary's books are on the table.
              (= John's books and Mary's books)   *Y IS ZERO*
        b.   John's books and notes are on the table.
              (= John's books and John's notes)
        c.   *John's books and 's notes are on the table.
        d.   John's ones are on the table.   (or John's are on the table) OK

In earlier forms of English, however, the constituency of possessives was by no means so obvious. Between the fifteenth and seventeenth centuries, and even later, expressions of the following kind (from Wyld 1936: 315–16) were common. (The year of attested usage is given in parentheses.)

(15)   *a.*   the Kinge his wisdome. (1545)
        b.   Mr Careless his letter. (1693)
        c.   Mrs. Francis her mariage. (1647)
        d.   Canterbury and Chillingworth their books. (1645)

(The construction still survives in the prayer-book phrase *for Jesus Christ his sake*.) Wyld suggests that initially, *the kyng hys sonne* was simply an orthographic variant of *the kyngys sonne*, unstressed *hys* being homonymous with the genitive suffix -*ys*. This view is supported by the fact that *hys*, or *ys*, were initially used for feminine as well as for masculine possessors.

(16)   *a.*   the quene ys modýr. (before 1467)   — mother
        b.   Margaret ys doughter. (c.1480)
        c.   my moder ys sake. (1440–70)

The later use of *her* and *their* with feminines and plurals suggests that the construction underwent substantial reanalysis, with *his*, *her*, and *their* being construed as possessive adjectives to the possessee nominal. Presumably, such expressions had the structure [X] [Z Y], where Z stands for the possessive adjective.[2]

----

[2] The validity of the structure [X] [Z Y] in earlier forms of English is also suggested by the now archaic oaths *zounds* < *God's wounds*, *'sblood*, *'sfoot*, *'sdeath*, etc., as well as the still current *strewth* < *God's truth* (Jespersen 1909–49 vii: 313). These expressions were derived from full possessives by omission of the initial X constituent, i.e. *God*.
   The structure [X] [Z Y] is attested in Afrikaans, which employs the morpheme *se* for all possessors, irrespective of gender and number. Not unexpectedly, coordination of *se*-Y is possible in Afrikaans: *Ek het nie die kind se trui of se skoene gesien nie* I have NEG the child POSS jersey or POSS shoes seen NEG, i.e. "I haven't see the child's jersey or shoes"; *Jan se ma, se pa en se oom kom vandag kuier* "John's mum, dad, and uncle will be visiting today" (Oosthuizen and Waher 1994: 31).

Since our topic in this chapter is constituent structure, let us make a brief excursus and consider the syntax of the now archaic *the Kinge his wisdome* and *Mr Careless his letter*. We have suggested the structure [X] [Z Y]. The question arises of the status of [X] within the syntagma as a whole. [X] seems not to bear any direct syntactic relation to the [Z Y] constituent, at least, not in terms of the standard relations (of complement, modifier, and specifier) that are sanctioned by X-bar syntax.

One approach is to regard the initial NP as a left-dislocated element, analogous to the initial NPs in (17).

(17)   *a.* [That kind of pen], what can you use it for?
        b. [Politicians], I've never met one I could trust.[3]

Dislocation is discussed in Radford (1988: 530–3) and Haegeman (1991: 368–70), who advance a number of reasons why dislocated elements need to be generated by phrase structure rules (that is to say, dislocation is not the product of movement). They suggest that the X-bar framework needs to be extended by a general rule of the following form.

(18) $XP_1 \longrightarrow YP\ XP_2$

The rule permits a phrasal constituent YP to be adjoined as sister to a phrasal constituent XP under an XP node.

(19)

$$XP_1$$
$$\diagup\ \diagdown$$
$$YP\quad XP_2$$

The possessives under consideration would be generated by a special instance of (18).

(20) $NP_1 \longrightarrow NP\ NP_2$

The expressions in (15) thus have the following structure.

(21)

$$NP_1$$
$$\diagup\ \diagdown$$
$$NP\qquad NP_2$$
the Kinge   his wisdome

The examples of left dislocation discussed by Radford and Haegeman involve dislocation from finite clauses (IP, i.e. inflection phrase, or CP, i.e. complementizer phrase), as in (17). The adjunction account of the possessives could be of interest in that it shows that XP in (18) can stand for NP, as well as for IP and CP. The analysis will be highly valued in that it documents the generality of (18).

From a cognitive grammar perspective, however, the adjunction account is rather unsatisfactory, in that it is not at all clear what the conceptual import of

---

[3] (17*a*) is from Radford (1988: 532), (17*b*) is from Givón (1990: 758).

adjunction, as formulated in (18), might be. In fact, in terms of the syntagmatic relations sanctioned by cognitive grammar, the relation of the dislocated element to its host turns out to be one of complementation.[4] Recall our definition of complement in section 4.5.

(22)   A complement elaborates a schematic entity within the semantic structure of the profile determinant

In *the Kinge his wisdome*, *the Kinge* provides additional conceptual substance to the schematically characterized 'he' in the semantic structure of the profile determinant, *his wisdome*. *The Kinge* is not, perhaps, a typical complement, in that the schematic entity which it elaborates is not profiled by the profile determinant. Neither is the presence of the complement necessary, either conceptually or syntactically. (*His wisdome* is a perfectly coherent noun phrase.) The relation between *the Kinge* and *his wisdome* is therefore felt to be somewhat 'looser' than with the canonical head–complement relation discussed in section 4.5.

The configurational account of (15) also fails to provide an ultimate motivation for the dislocated possessive. Why *should* a language have left dislocation, and why should the phenomenon turn up in possessives? Consider the function of the initial phrase. Givón (1990: 757–8) discusses dislocation under topicalization; he takes it to be a device for rendering a concept more accessible. In the examples in (17), the dislocated element thus provides a framework for a proper understanding of the adjoined clause. *What can you use it for?* only makes sense if the hearer knows what *it* refers to. Likewise, talk of *his wisdom* would be incoherent unless the person to whom wisdom is being attributed has been identified. Again, the topicalized possessor provides the context for the proper understanding of the following phrase.

(*e*) *The X-POSS constituent functions as a kind of determiner, or specifier, to Y.* To the extent that the possessor phrase X-POSS occurs in much the same range of environments as the articles and demonstratives, this aspect of the construction is uncontroversial. (Other aspects, however, such as the proper status of determiners, and the referential properties of a possessive, are less clear; these will be addressed in due course.)

Observe that determiners and possessor phrases are subject to much the same distributional restrictions.

(23)   *a.*   *my a car. [cf. (3)]
             *the a car.
       b.   *his the child.
             *that the child.
       c.   *John's {all/some/no} children.
             *those {all/some/no} children.

John's car
the car
this

---

[4]   (17*a*) also has features of apposition, in that *that kind of pen* and *it* designate the same entity. However, the complementation relation still holds, in that *that kind of pen* adds conceptual substance to the highly schematic profile of *it*.

(24) *a.* John's three children. [cf. (4)]
        those three children.
      b. my one (and only) friend.
        this one (and only) friend (that I have).
      c. ?John's several friends.
        ?the several friends (that John has).
      d. John's many friends.
        the many friends (that John has).
      e. *John's much money.
        *the much money (that John has).

The parallels, though, are not perfect. Alongside (4*d*) *his (each and) every move*, we do not have **the (each and) every move (that he made)*.

A further similarity is that both possessors and definite determiners may be preceded by quantifying expressions such as *all*, *half*, *twice*, and *three times* (though not by *some* and *no*).

(25) *a.* {all/*some/*no} John's friends.
        {all/*some/*no} those people.
      b. {half/twice/three times} my salary.
        {half/twice/three times} the amount.

The possessor may also be preceded by a demonstrative.

(26) In this his first novel.

The construction appears to have been more common in older forms of English;[5] in modern English it has a distinctly formal, literary status. The same possibility exists for the definite determiner *the*, a usage which also has a formal, literary flavour.

(27) On this the first day of the year.

Given the possibility of an intonation break after the demonstrative in (26) and (27), it would be plausible to claim that the determiners *this* and *his* in (26), *this* and *the* in (27), are in apposition. Each serves to ground the noun expression with which it is associated, but they do so in different, and complementary ways.

Let us summarize so far. We have presupposed a conservative version of X-bar theory. In terms of this theory, the evidence from (*a*) to (*e*) points unambiguously to the following structure.

(28) [$_{NP}$[$_{DET}$NP POSS] [N']]

---

[5] Some examples from Shakespeare's *Antony and Cleopatra*: 'Those his goodly eyes' (i. i. 2); 'And threats the throat of that his officer I that murder'd Pompey' (ii. iv. 18); 'Draw that thy honest sword' (iv. xiv. 78). Plank (1992) cites the following examples: 'Both of them used to talk pleasantly of *this their first journey* to London' (Boswell, *Life of Johnson*, 1791); 'Granting that the White Whale fully incites the hearts of *this my savage crew*' (Melville, *Moby Dick*, 1851); 'He told them that the house of theirs to which he alluded was *this their church* in which he now addressed them for the first time' (Trollope, *Barchester Towers*, 1857). Plank (p. 455) states that the construction is only possible with a pronominal possessive. To my ears, however, the following seems quite acceptable: *In this the author's first novel.*

According to this formula, a prenominal possessive constitutes a noun phrase that is headed by the possessee, and to which the possessor phrase, consisting of the possessor nominal in association with the possessive morpheme, functions as a determiner.

Some crucial questions remain, however. These centre on the nature of the possessor phrase [NP POSS]. Even in terms of the X-bar theory we have presupposed, this constituent is highly anomalous, in that the possessor phrase is not an XP. We will therefore need to enquire more closely into its internal structure and its syntactic category.

Also on conceptual grounds, the formula in (28) is unsatisfactory as it stands. The formula gives no clue as to how a phrase of the form [NP POSS] could function as a determiner, i.e. how it could ground the possessee. Even less does it explain why an [NP POSS] constituent normally functions as a specific (and usually also as a definite) determiner, rather than as, say, an indefinite determiner.

In the remaining part of this chapter, I discuss these issues by focusing on the nature of the possessive morpheme. We can identify three main approaches. On one analysis, POSS is a marker of genitive case, and the possessor phrase [NP POSS] is a case-marked nominal. This is the traditional approach, it is also one that has been assumed in much of the generative literature. A second approach has been to treat POSS as a kind of preposition (more accurately, as a postposition). On this approach, [NP POSS] turns out to be a kind of prepositional phrase, headed by POSS, and in which the possessor nominal is a complement to POSS. This analysis underlies Langacker's account of the construction; it has also been assumed by some generativists. A more radical analysis is to regard POSS as a determiner. In X-bar terms, a prenominal possessive is a determiner phrase (DP), which is headed by POSS, and in which the possessee is a complement to POSS, and the possessor is its specifier. Although I have severe conceptual problems with the DP analysis, to the extent that I also take POSS to be a determiner, which in association with the possessor nominal serves to ground the possessee, the account that I shall propose is partially compatible with it.

5.2 POSS AS A CASE MARKER

The majority opinion, probably, is that the possessive morpheme is a marker of genitive case, and that, consequently, possessor nominals inflect for genitive case. This, certainly, was the approach of older grammatical traditions. It has been adopted in more recent times in the descriptive grammars of Quirk *et al.* (1972; 1985), as well as in pedagogically oriented works, such as Thomson and Martinet (1960). The notion that possessor nominals are marked for genitive case has also been taken up by GB theorists (although case, in GB theory, is a rather different concept from traditional case).

In this section I examine the traditional view of POSS as a case marker, postponing until section 5.4 a discussion of the GB approach.

A typical exponent of the traditional approach was Otto Jespersen. For Jespersen, morphology was the main criterion for the identification of case. Case is marked by affixes which, when attached to word stems, convey the relation of the item to other constituents in a clause. Jespersen (1924: ch. 13) argued against the practice of forcing English into the descriptive framework of the European case-marking languages. It is simply nonsense, he said, to apply the categories of nominative, accusative, dative, etc. to an English noun like *book*, since these categories receive no overt marking whatsoever. Jespersen did, however, recognize a genitive case in English. Just as, in the Latin sentence *Petrus filio Pauli librum dat*, there can be no doubt, he writes, that *Petrus* is a nominative, *filio* a dative, *Pauli* a genitive, *librum* an accusative, so, in the English sentence *Peter gives Paul's son a book*, 'there can be no doubt that the English word *Paul's* is in the genitive' (p. 173).

For Jespersen, therefore, English nouns have two cases: genitive case, marked by *'s* (or by the apostrophe alone), and 'common case' (with zero marking). For pronouns he recognized a different system, with 'nominative' *I*, *he*, *we*, etc. contrasting with 'oblique' *me*, *him*, *us*, etc. (Oblique therefore neutralizes the accusative–dative distinction of other languages.) Curiously, Jespersen did not regard *my*, *his*, *our*, etc. as genitives. These he consistently refers to as 'possessives', categorizing them as a type of adjective, not as inflected pronouns.

Whether it is correct to analyse the possessive morpheme of modern English as a marker of genitive case will obviously depend on how we construe the notion of case marker. In section 4.5 I argued for a rather restricted view of case marking. On this view, a crucial feature of case markers is their nominal profile. Case markers profile a schematically characterized thing in terms of its relation to some other constituent(s) of a predication. As far as the 'structural' cases are concerned—nominative and accusative (and ergative and absolutive)—the nominal character of case markers is, I take it, self-evident. For the 'semantic' cases (such as instrumental and presumably also genitive), the nominal character is suggested by the possibility of the case-marked nominal to function as the complement of a relational predicate, such as a preposition. I also argued that the mechanics of case agreement within the noun phrase fall out naturally from the assumption that case markers have a nominal profile.

It would be futile to deny that there are some obvious affinities between the possessive morpheme of modern English and genitive case markers of other languages. The affinities are shown, first and foremost, by translation equivalences: *filius Pauli* = *Paul's son*. There is, in addition, the fact that the possessive morpheme of modern English is related, diachronically, to one of the Old English genitive markers. (But as we shall see in section 5.3, the parentage is not direct.) In spite of these affinities, the balance of the evidence is against the case-marker analysis. I review the evidence below.

(*a*) Leaving aside some relics in the pronoun system, modern English is definitely not a case-marking language! A genitive case in modern English would be an anomaly, out of step with the way in which syntagmatic relations are symbolized in the language. Moreover, of the various case categories that receive morphological marking cross-linguistically, genitive is also something of an anomaly. Nominative, accusative, dative, and the rest (prototypically) construe the case-marked nominal with respect to its participation in a process. A principle use of the genitive case (in English, it would be the *only* use) is to symbolize a relation between nominals.

(*b*) To attribute to the possessive morpheme the status of case marker would fail to throw light on a crucial facet of the possessive construction, namely, the fact that the possessor phrase serves to ground the possessee, by conferring (in the majority of instances) specific reference on it. Genitive-marked nominals do not (normally) have this property. In the German expression *die Zerstörung der Stadt* "the destruction the-GEN city", the genitive nominal may serve to restrict the referential possibilities of *Zerstörung*, but it does not ground it. (*Zerstörung*, and *Zerstörung der Stadt* are both type specifications; grounding is effected in both cases by the determiner *die*.) To say that *the city's*, in *the city's destruction*, is a genitive-marked nominal, begs the question of its grounding function.

(*c*) The status of POSS as a case marker or as some other kind of entity, will depend crucially on the nature of the morpheme's profile. On the assumption that POSS, like case markers and other functional morphemes, heads the phrase to which it attaches (section 4.4), we may compare the profiles of possessive-marked nominals (i.e. expressions of the structure [NP POSS]) and genitive-marked nominals for evidence of their similarity, or, as the case may be, their dissimilarity.

Evidence that possessive-marked nominals and genitive-marked nominals differ significantly in their semantic structure comes from some important differences in their distribution. In the case-marking languages, verbs, adjectives, and prepositions require that their complements be marked for a specific case—accusative, dative, instrumental, and, sometimes, genitive. The genitive marking of complements has no parallel at all in modern English.

There is, though, the possibility in English for possessive-marked nominals to occur in environments normally reserved for noun phrases. [NP POSS] can occur as a sentence subject (29), and even as the complement of a verb or preposition (30). But there is a crucial difference between these examples and genitive complements in a case-marking language. Consider the German examples in (31).

(29)   John's has broken down.

(30)   *a.* I need John's.

     b. because of John's.

(31)   *a.* Dies bedarf einer   Erklärung.

       This needs an-GEN explanation

    b. wegen   des   Regens.
      because-of the-GEN rain-GEN

English *need* and *because of* do not select a possessive complement; *I need John* and *because of John* are perfectly acceptable. German *bedürfen* and *wegen* do select a genitive complement. But there is a crucial semantic difference. What is needed, in (31*a*), is an explanation. What is needed, in (30*a*), is not John, but some entity(ies) construed as bearing a relation to John.

While, therefore, the genitive-marked nominals in German and the possessive-marked nominals in English both have a nominal profile, genitive *einer Erklärung* designates the same entity as nominative *eine Erklärung*, whereas *John's* does not designate 'John', but something that 'is John's'. With regard to the German examples, and in line with our discussion in section 4.5, we can say that the profile of the German case marker coincides with the profile of the noun to which it attaches (they are, in other words in apposition), whereas the possessive morpheme profiles a schematic possessee, with the possessor elaborating a nominal entity in the unprofiled base of the possessive morpheme.

That *John's* in (30) designates the (schematically characterized) possessee, does not entail that *John's*, in *John's car*, has exactly the same semantic value. Some evidence for the need to make a distinction comes from the fact that some possessor phrases, namely *my*, *your*, *her*, etc., have special forms for the environment in (30): *mine*, *yours*, *hers*, etc. A unitary account, though, would have descriptive economy on its side, and it is this approach that I shall, in fact, take in Chapter 12.

(*d*) Further support for the view that the possessive marker is a different kind of animal than the genitive case markers comes from an examination of their phonological properties, in particular, their phonological stability. By this I refer to the degree of variability in the morpheme's phonological expression.

In the Indo-European case-marking languages, it is very rare for a case category to have an invariant phonological realization. Typically, each case category is associated with a set of phonological forms, which might bear little or no phonetic resemblance amongst themselves. Amongst the exponents of genitive in Russian, for example, are such diverse forms as *-a, -j, -ov, -ei, -ev*, and zero. It is true that these forms convey, not only case, but also number and gender. Nevertheless, it is clearly not possible to extract from them a common phonological denominator, identifiable as the exponent of genitive case. Furthermore, the choice between these forms does not depend (or does not depend primarily) on the phonological properties of the host item, but on its gender and declension. Sometimes, even, there is an interaction between case marker and stem, in that the case marker influences the phonological shape of the stem. Indeed, stem and the case marker may sometimes fuse together to such an extent that it is impossible to segment the case-marked form into stem and case marker.

In comparison, POSS displays a rather high degree of phonological stability.

Leaving aside the fused pronominal forms *my*, *your*, *his*, and so on (where it is indeed impossible to identify a common phonological exponent of POSS), there are four realizations of the possessive morpheme: /s/, /z/, /əz/, and zero. The first three clearly share a common phonological element. Furthermore, the choice of one of these variants is determined, by and large, by purely phonological properties of the host.

(i) POSS is realized as /s/ if the host terminates in a voiceless segment.

(ii) POSS is realized as /z/ if the host terminates in a voiced segment, i.e. a voiced consonant or a vowel.

These two conditions are cases of an automatic (cf. Bloomfield 1933: 211–13) phonological process, i.e. voice assimilation.

(iii) Overriding the above conditions, POSS is realized as /əz/ if the host terminates in an *s*-like segment, more precisely, in a segment with the features [+STRIDENT] and [+CORONAL], i.e. /s, z, ʃ, ʒ, tʃ, dʒ/.

This condition appears to be motivated by a desire to avoid adjacent segments which are similar, or even identical to each other, i.e. sequences such as /zs/ or /dʒz/. Exactly the same condition applies to the (regular) realization of the plural morpheme in English.

(iv) Condition (iii) may be overridden if the host terminates in an unstressed syllable which phonetically resembles /əz/. A template for such syllables could be /V(L)C/, where V is an unstressed non-low and non-back vowel, (L) is an optional liquid or nasal, and C is /s,z/.

This condition appears to be motivated by a desire to avoid what Bolinger (1979), in another context, called 'jingles', that is, sequences of identical, or very similar-sounding syllables. This condition, not surprisingly, is variable in its application, since it has to do with judgements of euphony, and these are inherently subjective. Some speakers might reject *Dickens's novels* in favour of the more euphonic (less 'jingling') *Dickens' novels*. A similar euphony condition applies to plural formation. Singular nouns terminating in an /əz/-like syllable sometimes fail to form their plurals by addition of /əz/, e.g. *axis*, *thesis*, *series*. The jingling forms */æksɪsəz/, */θiːsɪsəz/, */siːriːzəz/ are thereby avoided.

The above conditions make reference only to the phonological properties of the host. Grammatical properties, though, are sometimes relevant.

(v) Condition (iii) is overridden if the final /s/, /z/, or /əz/ of the host is a marker of plural number. In this case, POSS is not phonologically realized. Although this condition appeals to a grammatical aspect of the host, its motivation again appears to be a dispreference for sequences of items, in this case, exponents of PLURAL and POSS, which are phonetically similar.

A further point of contrast with (Indo-European) case markers (and, indeed, Indo-European affixes in general) is the absence of lexically conditioned exceptions to the above conditions. One need only compare the possessive morpheme with the plural morpheme in English. A number of nouns idiosyncratically form their plurals other than by addition of /s/, /z/, or /əz/. The possessive morpheme is *absolutely regular* in its phonological expression. Apart from the pronominal possessors, there are absolutely no exceptions to the realization of the possessive morpheme.

(*e*) Related to the last point is a further difference between the possessive morpheme of modern English and the case markers of Indo-European (including Old English). This concerns the kind of item to which the morphemes attach.

The Indo-European case markers attach internally to a grounded noun phrase. The nouns, adjectives, and demonstratives (and, if the language has them, the determiners) of these languages are associated with a paradigm of inflected forms. Each of these forms is a phonologically autonomous word, of which the case marker is a part. The possessive marker, in contrast, attaches to a fully grounded noun phrase, and is phonologically integrated with whatever word happens to stand at the end of the noun phrase.

Possessor nominals in English do tend to be structurally rather simple (Taylor 1991a). If, as is often the case, the possessor nominal lacks post-modification, POSS will attach to the possessor noun, creating the impression that English nouns also inflect for genitive case. We might want to say, with Jespersen, that *Paul's son*, like Latin *filius Pauli*, consists of two words, *Paul's* and *son*, *Paul's* being an inflected form of *Paul*.

But with structurally more complex possessor nominals, namely those which contain post-modifying elements, POSS does not attach to the possessor noun, it occurs to the right of the nominal, and attaches to the word that happens to be at the end, be it a verb, a preposition, a noun in complement position, or whatever.

(32) *a*. The man I met's children.
      b. The people we live next to's car.
      c. The people across the road's new car.

And with one possessive form, namely *whose*, there is the possibility of intercalating a parenthetical phrase between the possessor (i.e. *who*, whether an interrogative or a relative pronoun) and POSS.

(33) *a*. Whose car is that?
         Who the hell's car is that?
      b. That's the guy whose sister is the lead singer.
         That's the guy who I think's sister is the lead singer.
         [authentic example, from Radford 1988: 526[6]]

---

[6] A reader points out that this example could have a different interpretation, in that the element attached to *think* could be a phonetically reduced form of resumptive *his*: *That's the guy who I think his sister is the lead singer.* The sentence would exemplify the dislocated possessive construction, as in (15) and (16).

We should certainly not want to say that the verb *met*, the preposition *to*, or even the noun *road*, are case-marked. *Met's*, or *think's*, can scarcely be categorized as words, and we should certainly not want to propose an inflectional paradigm of *met* which includes, as one of its members, the form *met's*!

To accommodate cases like these, traditional and pedagogical grammars set up a distinct category in addition to the 'inflectional genitive', namely, the 'group genitive', in which POSS attaches to a 'word group', not to a noun (see e.g. Quirk *et al.* 1985: 328). But this multiplication of categories misses the obvious generalization that POSS *always* attaches to the final word of the possessor nominal. Usually, the final word will designate the possessor, but it need not do so. Occam's razor requires us to conflate the inflectional genitive and the group genitive, and to treat all instances of the genitive as instances of the group genitive, as it were. Even in apparently straightforward cases, like *the man's car*, we will want to say that POSS is construed, not with the noun *man*, but with the noun phrase *the man*.

Admittedly, on a wider cross-linguistic perspective, the group genitive does not of itself exclude the possibility that the possessive morpheme is a case marker. It should, however, make us wary of a too-facile identification of the possessive marker with the genitive markers of Indo-European. Moreover, the group genitive does raise some special problems, which are worth reviewing here.

The problems are especially acute for those structuralist approaches that assume that every utterance can be exhaustively analysed into 'words', 'groups of words', and 'parts of words' (Householder 1988: 384). The possessive morpheme turns out to be neither a word, nor a word part. Lacking the phonological autonomy of a word, it must attach itself, phonologically, to another word. Yet the resultant form, such as *met's* in (32a), need not itself be a word, hence the possessive morpheme cannot be a word part.

Various solutions present themselves. One has been to say that, appearances notwithstanding, the possessive morpheme is indeed a word—not a prototypical word, but a phonologically dependent word, or clitic.[7] The other has been to retain the affix status of POSS, but to incorporate into the grammar the possibility that an affix can attach, not only to words, but also to phrases. Both solutions involve fudging the distinction between, on the one hand, words and affixes, and, on the other, between words and phrases. And, indeed, POSS will be problematic only on the assumption that affix, word, and phrase are clearly demarcated categories.

Let us look at Lieber's (1988) proposals. As noted, the problem of the group genitive is closely tied up with the distinction between words and phrases, between morphology (the structure of words) and syntax (the structure of phrases). As an affix, POSS appears to belong to the domain of morphology. To the extent that it attaches to full noun phrases, we are in the domain of syntax.

---

[7] On the nature of clitics, see Zwicky (1985) and Klavens (1985). For discussion of POSS as a clitic, see Taylor (1995b: 181).

The distinction between morphology and syntax, however, is not always clear-cut, as evidenced by the extremely productive phenomenon of phrasal compounding in English. The following examples are from Lieber (1988: 204–5).

(34)   *a.* the [~NP~Charles and Di] syndrome.
      b. an [~PP~off the rack] dress.
      c. this [~AP~pleasant to read] book.
      d. my [~VP~ate too much] headache.
      e. that [~CP~win a Mazda] competition.

These all contain a nominal compound whose first element is a phrasal category (the bracketed NP, PP, AP, VP, and CP). Expressions of the kind *Charles and Di syndrome* thus show that compounding (a morphological, or word-formation process) can operate over phrases (the product of syntactic processes).

To account for phrasal compounds like those in (34), Lieber (p. 206) proposes (35) as a schematic lexical structure.

(35)

We might note, though, that in spite of its claim to cross-category generality, (35) is attested in English only with X = N; there are no compound verbs, adjectives, or prepositions that are formed in the manner of (35).

Lieber suggests that the group genitive might instantiate (35). She makes two alternative proposals. The first rests on the assumption that the possessive morpheme is categoryless. This assumption is based on the observation that 'in general, inflection does not change category' (p. 220). (A plural noun is still a noun, a case-marked adjective remains an adjective.) The head node in (35) acquires a category by 'upward percolation' of the category features of YP. Hence, the structure of a group genitive is as follows.

(36)

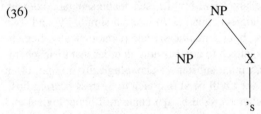

It is not at all clear what we should make of (36), at least in terms of cognitive grammar.[8] Whilst the notion of 'upward percolation' could perhaps be equated with profile inheritance—it is the nominal profile of the lower NP in (36) that

---

[8] A structure which is superficially similar to (36) was proposed by Anderson (1984). She suggests that in some instances the possessive morpheme (whose categorial status is not discussed) is adjoined to the possessor NP, i.e. NP → NP POSS. My comments on the obscurity of the structural/semantic relation that adjunction is meant to represent carry over to Anderson's proposal.

is inherited by the upper node—the structure postulated in (36) gives no clue as to how the semantic structures of the component elements are to be integrated. Especially problematic is the notion of a 'categoryless' morpheme. In cognitive grammar, a categoryless morpheme would be one whose semantic structure lacks a profile, and which therefore fails to designate. Such entities are ruled out in principle.

Lieber suggests another possibility, analogous to the structure of phrasal nominal compounds. She suggests, namely, that POSS bears the category N, and that possessor phrases likewise are nouns.

(37)

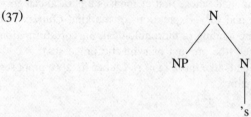

Lieber (p. 220) states that she has 'no way of deciding between' (37) and (36). But (37) cannot be correct, either. Whatever else [NP POSS] might be, it is certainly not a noun, even less a kind of compound noun!

Whilst the technical details of Lieber's proposals must be rejected, the thrust of her paper—that morphology cannot be cleanly separated from syntax—is certainly congenial to cognitive grammar.

Recall the basic assumption that a language is a set of symbolic units. The symbolic units will differ along various parameters: the schematicity of their semantic and phonological poles; their internal complexity; their semantic and phonological independence; and their degree of entrenchment. We can think of these various aspects as defining a multi-dimensional space. Different kinds of symbolic unit will cluster in different regions in this space.

- *Affixes* cluster in a region characterized by (*a*) schematic semantic content, but possibly specific phonological content; (*b*) internal simplicity; and (*c*) a low degree of independence, both semantically and phonologically. Semantically, the units will need to attach to another unit, in order that their schematic profile can receive conceptual substance; phonologically, in that, often being inherently stressless, they will need to attach to a stress-bearing host.
- *Words* cluster in a region characterized by (*a*) contentful phonological and semantic representations; (*b*) a high degree of independence with respect to the items to which they can attach; and (*c*) a high degree of entrenchment. Internal complexity *per se* will not be an issue. However, for words that are internally complex, one of the constituent units will typically be an affix.
- *Phrases* differ from words principally with regard to their constituents. These will typically be words, or phrases, not affixes. Entrenchment, however, will not be an issue. Some phrases may be highly entrenched, and will

have the status of fully established symbolic units, whilst others (the majority, perhaps) will be *ad hoc* creations.
* *Construction schemas* will be highly schematic, both with regard to their semantic representation and their phonological representation. By definition, they are internally complex.

Since the parameters of schematicity, complexity, independence, and entrenchment are inherently gradable, the regions characterized above will necessarily be diffuse, and fuzzy, and the unambiguous categorization of many symbolic units may be difficult. (Compounds, for example, have features both of words and of phrases.) This need not be regarded as in the least problematic, or unexpected.

Consider, again, the examples in (34). In cognitive grammar, the formation of internally complex words (morphology) and the formation of internally complex phrases (syntax) are both handled by exactly the same mechanism, viz. by the establishment of valence relations between the component parts, as sanctioned by construction schemas. Where word-formation and phrase-formation differ is with respect to the kinds of items that are combined. Generally, morphology will involve the combination of items that are internally non-complex, and at least one of which is an affix, i.e. has a schematic profile, which requires a host item in order to acquire conceptual content. Generally, syntax will involve the integration of units that themselves have the status of words. The distinction, however, will in many cases be far from clear-cut. Nominal compounding, for example, is a syntactic-like process, in that it involves the combination of words, and even phrases, although we might want to say that the product of nominal compounding is a word, rather than a phrase. The affixing of the possessive morpheme looks like a typical word-formation process. Yet the host could be an internally complex phrase, not a word, or even a word stem.

We have reviewed various kinds of evidence which all point to the distinctiveness of the possessive morpheme *vis-à-vis* the case markers of Indo-European. The most crucial evidence was that cited under (*c*), concerning the semantic value of a [NP POSS] constituent. Other evidence, pertaining to the relative phonological stability of the possessive morpheme, and to the fact that the morpheme attaches to phrases, not to words, is not, of itself, decisive. Taken together, however, the points covered in (*a*)–(*e*) above strongly suggest that the possessive morpheme is *not* a case marker.

But if POSS is not a case marker, what is it? Cognitive grammar allows for only two possibilities. One is that the possessive morpheme profiles the relation between possessor and possessee. On this view, POSS would be akin to the prepositions. The other possibility is that POSS profiles, not a schematic possessor (this would be the profile of a genitive case marker), but a schematic possessee. More specifically, given the grounding function of the possessor phrase, we could say that POSS profiles a grounded instance of the possessee. On this view, POSS would turn out to be akin to the definite determiners.

Interestingly, both possibilities have been entertained within the generative tradition. We shall consider them in sections 5.5 and 5.6. First, however, I want to glance at the diachronic development of POSS from the case markers of Old English, and then to review the GB account of POSS as a marker of genitive case.

5.3 FROM GENITIVE TO POSSESSIVE

Having emphasized the differences between POSS and the case markers, I would like, in this section, to examine their continuity from a historical perspective.

Old English was a typical case-marking language, with a rich array of noun inflections, and agreement patterns between case-marked nouns, adjectives, and demonstratives. Consider the following example, from Jespersen (1909–49: vi. 283).

(38) Æðelwulfes   dohtor   West Seaxna   cininges.
     Aethelwulf-GEN-SG daughter West Saxon-GEN-PL king-GEN-SG
     "Aethelwulf, the king of the West Saxons' daughter"
     i.e. "the daughter of Aethelwulf, the king of the West Saxons"

Here, 'Aethelwulf' and 'king' are in apposition, and both are marked with genitive case; the superficial complexity of the example is due to the fact that the nominals in apposition have been separated, first by *dohtor*, and then by *West Seaxna*, itself a genitive modifier of *cining*.

With the decay of inflections on demonstratives and adjectives, the possibility arose, in the early middle English period, of case markers attaching only to the nominal head of the possessor phrase. Jespersen (1909–49: vi. 282) cites the following example, from as early as the thirteenth century. The example contrasts with the more conservative *þisses deofles bearn*, where *þisses* is in the genitive singular, in agreement with *deofles*.

(39) þes   deofles   bearn.
     this-NOM devil-GEN child-NOM
     this devil's child

(39) clearly contains the seeds of the modern English construction, to the extent that case marking is attached only to the final element of the possessor nominal.

Crucial evidence for the emergence of the modern English construction comes from expressions in which the possessor nominal is internally complex, especially when the complexity is due to post-modification. At issue is the location of genitive/possessive marking, i.e. whether it occurs on the head noun, or on the final word of the possessor nominal.

The following example from the middle English period is also from Jespersen (p. 282); the absence of genitive marking on *god* clearly foreshadows the group genitive of modern English.

(40) for god almiȝtties drede.

The following examples, from the end of the middle English period (cited from Wyld 1936: 318), also show that the group genitive was current by this time.

(41)   a. þe erle of Wyltones wyf. (1420)
      b. the Archebishoppe of Cantreburys barge. (1501)
      c. the Erle of Kyldares sonnes. (1515)

With postmodified possessors, the usual construction in middle English is exemplified by the title of the song *The bailiff's daughter of Islington*. Wyld (p. 318) cites the following examples, which are contemporary with those of (41).

(42)   a. a man of the Ducs of Orliance. (1418)
      b. the Lordys wyffe Nevyle. (= "Lord Neville's wife") (before 1467)
      c. the kynges doughter of Englande. (1520)

Here, the possessive morpheme still retains something of the inflectional character it had inherited from Old English, in that it attaches to the head of the possessor phrase. These expressions therefore stand midway between the group genitive of modern English (cf. *the bailiff of Islington's daughter*), where POSS attaches to the final element of a post-modified possessor NP, and a hypothetical inflectional genitive (**the bailiff's of Islington daughter*), where POSS occurs medially and attaches to the head noun of the possessor NP.

Structurally, expressions of the kind *the bailiff's daughter of Islington* are highly anomalous. The anomaly resides in the fact that head and complement of the possessor phrase (*bailiff of Islington*) have been separated, not only by a phonologically autonomous word (*daughter*), but also by a phonologically dependent morpheme, *'s*. Not only this, but *daughter of Islington* is a potentially meaningful expression in itself. This state of affairs presents the hearer with a serious processing problem. Instead of construing *of Islington* as the complement of the noun to which it is adjacent (i.e. *daughter*)—the simplest and most natural interpretation—the hearer has to search backwards, over intervening material, for the appropriate head.

The anomalous syntax of the construction was no doubt a cogent reason for its subsequent demise from the language, and for the consolidation of the group genitive. Echoes of the construction, though, can still be found as late as the Elizabethan period. Jespersen (1909–49: vi. 282) cites the following examples, the first from Marlowe, the second from Shakespeare.

(43)   a. You will needs haue ten years tribute past.
        (= "the tribute of ten years past")
      b. With them a bastard of the kings deceast.
        (= "a bastard of the deceased king's")

Interestingly, Jespersen notes that (43*b*) (from *King John* II. i. 65) was changed in later folios to *the king deceased*, commenting that the type-setters 'evidently no longer [understood] the construction'.

A further fact conspiring towards the consolidation of the group genitive was the currency, over many centuries, of the dislocated construction that we discussed earlier. In expressions of the kind *the Kinge his wisdome*, the possessive adjective takes up the entire possessor NP, not its head. The construction was therefore particularly suited to expressions whose possessor nominal was syntactically complex.

(44) *a.* my lord of Excetre is tenants. (*c.*1450)
       b. the Busshoppe of Rome his lawes. (*c.*1530)
       c. the Bishop of London and Coventre ys wiff. (*c.*1550)
          (Wyld 1936: 315)

The special importance of this construction in the evolution of the modern English possessive is suggested also by the orthographic device of the apostrophe. The use of the possessive apostrophe dates from the late sixteenth century, although it was only by the middle of the eighteenth century that the apostrophe (with singular possessors) became fully established (Sklar 1976). (The use of the apostrophe with plural possessors developed later, and was standardized only towards the end of the nineteenth century.)

The general function of the apostrophe has always been to signal the omission of a letter, or sound. What, then, motivated the use of the apostrophe in possessives, e.g. *the man's hat*, from the late sixteenth century onwards? It could hardly have been the memory of the syllabic genitive inflection of old English *mannes*. More likely, the apostrophe was felt to signal the omission of the vowel in the possessive adjective *his* (Baugh and Cable 1978: 241).

The evolution of the genitive case marker of Old English into the modern English possessive morpheme was by and large complete by the end of the middle English period. Various factors conspired to facilitate the evolution. First, the loss of case and other inflections on adjectives and determiners resulted in genitive marking being restricted to the head of the possessor phrase. The chance homonymy of one of the genitive case markers and the unstressed possessive adjective *his* gave rise to the possibility of construing the possessor nominal as a dislocated element, whose internal structure could become quite complex. Another factor was the possibility of the genitive-marked nominal to occur before the nominal head which it modified. In this way, the possessor phrase could acquire the function of a determiner. This process presupposes a semantic continuity between a preposed genitive nominal and the possessor phrase of modern English. A genitive modifier serves to restrict the referential possibilities of the head noun. In the limiting case, we may suppose, it restricts the reference down to just one possibility. This is, precisely, the function of the possessor phrase in modern English, in its status as a kind of definite determiner.

5.4 POSS AS A CASE MARKER: GENERATIVE ACCOUNTS

So far, I have considered case as a morphophonological category. Like Jespersen, I take it that case categories such as nominative, accusative, dative, etc., are simply inapplicable to the nouns of modern English, since these categories receive no phonological marking whatsoever.

There are at least two other approaches to case that we need to consider. On one approach, case—sometimes called 'deep case'—refers to the semantic relations, however they may be expressed, that hold between nominals and other constituents of a clause, in the first instance, a verb. This understanding of case underlies Fillmore's (1968) case grammar, and it has much in common with the 'actant' relations of dependency grammar (Tesnière 1959), and with the thematic relations of GB theory.

Government and binding theory draws a distinction between thematic relations and 'abstract case'. Whereas thematic relations are semantically based, abstract case is construed as a structural relation between constituents. How, or whether, the relation is phonologically expressed, is not an issue. The crucial point is merely that each nominal constituent—or, to be more precise (since GB postulates invisible constituents), each phonetically realized nominal constituent—must be assigned some case, i.e. must appear in an appropriate structural configuration. The 'case filter' rules out as ungrammatical a sentence with a caseless nominal.

The conditions under which case, in the GB sense, is assigned, are the following (from Chomsky 1981: 170).

(i) An NP has nominative case if it is governed[9] by INFL, i.e. that feature of a verb which shows person and number agreement with its subject.
(ii) Accusative case is assigned to an NP if the NP is governed by a verb.
(iii) An NP is in oblique case if governed by a preposition.
(iv) An NP is in genitive case if it occurs in the environment $[_{NP}\_\_\_X']$.

Here, I offer some general remarks about the GB concept of case, followed by some observations on genitive case in particular.

(*a*) GB theory, we have said, makes a distinction between thematic relations (based in semantics) and case relations, which are purely structural. In cognitive grammar, such a distinction can have no legitimization. If an NP bears a structural relation to another constituent (if the NP, say, functions as subject or direct object of a verb), then necessarily that NP bears a semantic relation to the verb, in that it elaborates the schematic tr or lm of the process designated by the verb. To this extent, the case filter is conceptually motivated. A caseless nominal would be a nominal which failed to enter a valence relation with any other constituent in an expression.

(*b*) According to the above four conditions, case is assigned to an NP as a whole. It is, namely, a full NP which functions as direct object of a verb, not some component of the NP. Yet in many languages with overt morphological case marking, especially in Indo-European, case is marked, not on the NP, but on the nominal head of the NP. To account for this state of affairs, Chomsky

---

[9] For a definition of government, see section 2.4.

(1981: 49) proposes that case, having been assigned to an NP, 'percolates down' to the head constituent, where it may be marked by the appropriate affix. Presumably (to continue the hydrological metaphor), case then 'seeps through' to other constituents of the noun phrase, such as the adjectival modifiers, where it is likewise marked by the appropriate desinence.

(45)

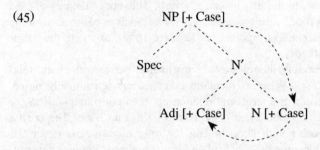

In discusssing (35) we already encountered the metaphor of 'upward percolation'. In cognitive grammar terms, upward percolation might be construed as an instance of profile inheritance. It is obscure, however, what 'downward percolation' might be.

The root of the problem is the initial metaphor of case 'assignment'. The underlying idea seems to be that at some stage in the generation of a sentence, NPs are caseless, and that they 'receive' case in virtue of the configuration in which they occur. Cognitive grammar offers an alternative metaphor, according to which complex expressions are assembled from their component parts, by the establishment of valence relations between them, as sanctioned by construction schemas. Amongst the constituent elements are the case morphemes, which, like all other morphemes, are inherently meaningful (even though their meanings might be highly schematic), and which also contract valence relations with their neighbours.

(*c*) Since genitive case in English is marked on the possessor NP, not on the noun head, genitive case assignment does not require the curious device of downward percolation. This prompts the further observation that even within the GB framework, genitive case turns out to be something of an anomaly in comparison with the other three cases. In the first place, it is the only case which is assigned, not under the structural relation of government, but in an arbitrarily stated environment. Moreover, the environment, as stated in condition (iv) above, is peculiar to modern English. A further parochial fact about case in modern English is that it is the only one of the four cases that obligatorily receives overt phonological marking.

More curious still is the fact that, given Chomsky's definition of government, and assuming *John's book* to have the base structure in (46)—this is the structure which, it is claimed, triggers genitive insertion—*John* is indeed governed by *book*, permitting the statement that an NP is genitive if governed by a noun.

(46)

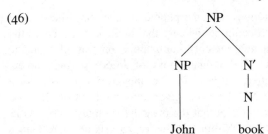

The reason for this asymmetry in case-assigning mechanisms appears to be Chomsky's (1981: 50) desire to maintain that in English, only the [−N] categories of verb and preposition can be governers.[10] This claim is motivated by the inability of nouns and adjectives to assign case to an NP complement, whence the unacceptability of (47) in contrast with (48):

(47)   *a.* *the [$_{N'}$destruction [$_{NP}$the city]]
       b. *[$_{AdjP}$proud [$_{NP}$John]]
(48)   *a.* [$_{V'}$destroy [$_{NP}$the city]]
       b. [$_{PP}$to [$_{NP}$the city]]

Subsequently, Chomsky (1986: 194; 1988: 112) changed his position on this issue, and proposed that nouns, too, may be case assigners, more specifically, that nouns assign genitive case to their NP complements. Genitive case receives different phonological expression according to whether the complement appears to the right or to the left of the noun. If the complement appears to the right, genitive case is marked by the preposition *of*; (47) thus surface as *the destruction of the city* and *proud of John*. If the complement appears to the left, case is marked by the possessive morpheme, giving *the city's destruction*. POSS and *of* are therefore in complementary distribution, and are inserted merely in order to guarantee proper case assignment. To the extent that abstract case is a purely structural relation, of no inherent semantic import, both POSS and *of* are taken to be semantically empty.

This is a view which, needless to say, is incompatible with the symbolic thesis which motivates cognitive grammar. It is also incompatible with the linguistic data. As noted in Chapter 1, *the enemy's fear* and *fear of the enemy* are not the same thing! If POSS and *of* are each inserted merely to guarantee case assignment to *the enemy*, these two morphemes ought to make exactly the same semantic contribution to the complex expressions in which they occur, that it is to say, they ought to make no semantic contribution at all. Yet *of*-expressions are not always synonymous with their prenominal possessive equivalents.

Note, incidentally, that one cannot motivate the meaninglessness of POSS and *of* merely on the grounds that these morphemes are obligatory in the contexts in

---

[10] In GB theory, the lexical categories noun, verb, adjective, and preposition are defined in terms of the features [±N] and [±V], nouns and adjectives being [+N], verbs and prepositions [−N].

which they occur.[11] The obligatoriness of a morpheme, in a certain context, does not entail its meaninglessness. It could be the case that in the circumstances the symbolization of a certain semantic content is obligatory, on pain of syntactic (and semantic) ill-formedness. The obligatoriness of POSS in the context [NP____N′] could therefore reflect the need for the obligatory expression of a semantic link between NP and N′. However, given the premises of GB case theory, it would be of little use to claim that the meaning symbolized by POSS is, let us say, the genitive relation. Within GB theory, case is no more than a condition on syntactic well-formedness, with no semantic implications.

5.5 POSS AS A RELATIONAL PREDICATE

A number of linguists working within the generative tradition have analysed the possessive morpheme as a preposition-like element. An analysis of POSS as a relational predicate, akin to the prepositions, has also been proposed within cognitive grammar.

Let us first consider the plausibility of this analysis within the framework of a conservative version of X-bar theory.

A fundamental assumption of X-bar theory is that a phrasal category XP is headed by a lexical item of category X. A further assumption has been been that complements, modifiers, and specifiers themselves have the status of phrasal categories.

We saw in Section 5.1 that there are good reasons to claim that NP-POSS functions as a kind of determiner to the possessee nominal. The possessor phrase thus occupies the specifier position of the containing NP. Given the above assumptions of X-bar theory, the possessor phrase must be analysed as a phrasal category. Let us provisionally call this phrasal category PossP (possessive phrase). PossP cannot be headed by NP, since phrases must have lexical categories as their heads. The only candidate for head, therefore, is POSS. On this approach, the structure of NP-POSS is the following.

(49)

POSS, of course, does not constitute one of the generally recognized lexical categories. We need to ask, therefore, whether it is possible to assimilate POSS to one of the more familiar categories.

---

[11] In point of fact, it is not even true that POSS and *of* are always obligatory. *Fear of the enemy* contrasts with *fear towards the enemy, fear when confronted by the enemy*, and so on. In compound nouns, the possessive morpheme may be in paradigmatic contrast with its absence (*collector's items* vs. *collector items*), a phenomenon discussed in Ch. 11.

An obligatory component of PossP is the NP constituent. The very obligatoriness of the NP constituent suggests that this constituent may be plausibly analysed as a complement of POSS; a typical diagnostic of a complement in contrast to a modifier, or specifier, is that a complement may be obligatory, while modifiers and specifiers never are (Radford 1988: 243). There are only two lexical categories in English which take an NP complement, verbs and prepositions. POSS is clearly not a verb; it cannot, for example, carry expressions of tense, person, or aspect. The alternative is to regard it as a kind of preposition, and NP-POSS phrases as a kind of prepositional phrase.

Admittedly, POSS would be a rather untypical preposition. First, it obligatorily follows its complement. (Strictly speaking, therefore, POSS is a postposition, prepositions and postpositions being subsumed under the general term adposition.) In this respect, phrases headed by POSS represent a significant departure from the head–complement pattern, characteristic not only of prepositional phrases, but of all kinds of syntactic phrases in English. Even so, there are already in English one or two lexical items which idiosyncratically have preceding complements. *Ago* is invariably phrase-final (*a month ago*), and is plausibly categorized as a postposition, while *notwithstanding* can be used both as a preposition (*notwithstanding my protestations*) and as a postposition (*my protestations notwithstanding*).[12]

A second respect in which POSS differs from other members of the preposition class is that it is always phonologically dependent on its host, that is, on its obligatory complement. Again, this characteristic need not be problematic. When they occur in non-phrase-final position, most of the shorter prepositions of English (*of*, *at*, *to*, etc.) are typically unstressed, and are thus phonologically dependent on an adjacent item. What distinguishes POSS is the impossibility of its appearing with stress, in any context. But if we look beyond English, to Russian, for example, we will find examples of prepositions whose phonological behaviour matches that of POSS rather closely. Consider the monophonemic prepositions *v* "to, at" and *s* "with". These prepositions are phonologically integrated with a following word. Just as POSS is realized as /s/ or /z/ according to the voicing of the preceding segment, so these prepositions exhibit voicing assimilation to a following obstruent: /s tovoj/ "with you", /z Galej/ "with Galja". There is even a parallel in the insertion of an epenthetic vowel. When the possessive morpheme is attached to a word terminating in an *s*-like consonant an epenthetic schwa vowel is inserted. Likewise an epenthetic unstressed /o/ is inserted when *v* and *s* precede certain consonant clusters: /so mnoi/ "with me". In brief, the phonological characteristics of the Russian prepositions are exact mirror images of the phonological characteristics of POSS.

The postposition analysis of POSS has been proposed by traditionally oriented

---

[12] The categorial status of *ago* and *notwithstanding* is open to dispute. I regard them as prepositions (postpositions) in line with the characterization given in section 4.2.

grammarians, including Huddleston (1984: 46–7) and Quirk *et al.* (1985: 328), as well as by some linguists working within the generative paradigm, e.g. Giorgi and Longobardi (1991: 99). Anderson (1984) proposes a hybrid account, with some instances of POSS being analysed as a postposition, other instances being regarded as a semantically empty case marker. (I discuss Anderson's account in more detail in the next chapter.)

The postposition analysis has several things going for it. In the first place, it makes sense semantically. The possessee bears a semantic relation to the possessor. Being a relational predicate, the possessive morpheme is able to profile this relation.

Like the prepositions, POSS takes a fully grounded NP as its complement. The postpositional analysis thus readily accommodates the fact that we found troublesome for the case-marker analysis of POSS, i.e. that POSS attaches externally to the possessor nominal.

Moreover, the postposition analysis nicely captures the affinity between prenominal possessives and postnominal *of*-expressions, between, for example, *the king's daughter* and *the daughter of the king*. The one expression turns out, in fact, to be an almost exact mirror image of the other. In *the king's daughter*, *daughter* is preceded by a postpositional phrase [NP POSS]; in *the daughter of the king*, *daughter* is followed by a prepositional phrase [P NP].

The mirror-image relationship can be elegantly depicted in cognitive grammar. Figure 5.1 diagrams the integration of the two phrases. Note that Figure 5.1(*a*), which diagrams the assembly of the *of*-phrase, exactly matches Figure 4.4. Here, *the king* is a complement of *of*, while *of the king* is a modifier of *daughter*. Concerning the assembly of the possessor phrase, I assume that the landmark of POSS is the possessor nominal, thereby construing the possessor nominal as the complement of POSS. The possessee elaborates the trajector of POSS, thereby construing the possessor phrase as a modifier to the head.

This analysis was entertained in Taylor (1992). As it stands, however, it is not fully adequate, to the extent that *the daughter of the king* and *the king's daughter* are not *exact* mirror images of each other. In the former, *daughter* (or, more accurately, *daughter of the king*) is grounded by the initial article *the*, whereas in the latter, it is the possessor phrase itself which serves to ground *daughter*. The phrase structures are as follows.

(50)   *a.* [$_{NP}$ [$_{DET}$ the] [$_{N'}$ [N [$_{PP}$of NP]]]]
       b. [$_{NP}$ [$_{DET}$NP POSS] [N']]

That, in Figure 5.1, the one expression can be represented as the exact mirror image of the other results from the fact that Figure 5.1 ignores the role of the grounding elements.

To this extent, the postpositional account fails to capture the traditional insight that the possessor phrase functions as a kind of determiner to the possessee. We therefore need to elaborate the semantic representation of POSS, by

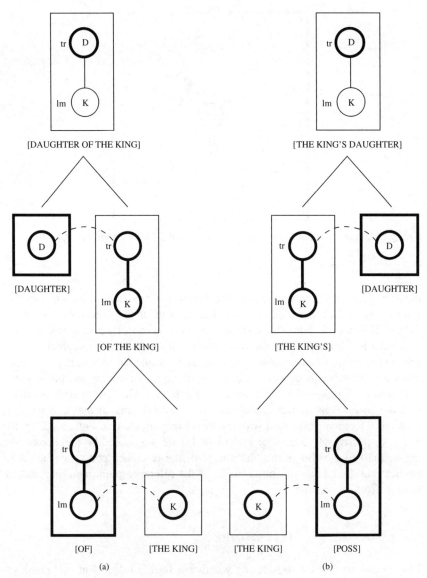

FIG. 5.1. Prepositional *of* vs. postpositional POSS
Source: After Langacker 1991: 172.

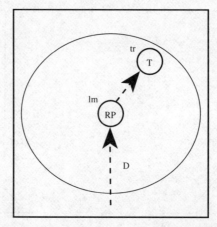

FIG. 5.2. Langacker's reference point analysis of POSS (After Langacker 1991:172)

incorporating into it some aspects of a grounding predication. In this way, we shall arrive at Langacker's more detailed account of the semantic structure of POSS. This incorporates the reference point analysis of possessives, which I presented in Chapter 1. On the reference point analysis, a conceptualizer first establishes mental contact with the possessor entity; this serves as a reference point for the subsequent identification of the target entity, i.e. the possessee.

Langacker's proposal is diagrammed in Figure 5.2. The broken arrow symbolizes the path taken by the conceptualizer in establishing mental contact, first with the reference point, then with the target (represented, in Figure 5.2, by RP and T respectively). One other feature of Figure 5.2 should be mentioned, the region marked D. This is the 'dominion' of the reference point, i.e. the set of entities that are in the 'neighbourhood' of the reference point, and that may be located from its vantage.

5.6 POSS AS A DETERMINER

I begin this section by considering whether a further refinement of Figure 5.2 might not be indicated.

In section 4.5 I addressed the question of the profile of the definite determiner, that is, whether the determiner profiles the grounding *relation*, or whether it profiles the *grounded entity*. For various reasons, I opted for the second analysis. Given that the possessor phrase functions as a kind of determiner, an analogous account of the possessive morpheme suggests itself. On this account, the possessive morpheme profiles, not the relation between reference point and target, but

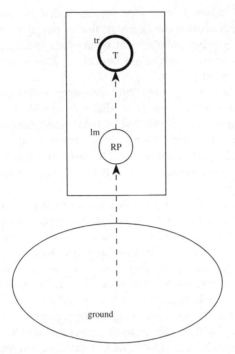

FIG. 5.3. POSS as a determiner

the schematic target, that is, the possessee.[13] We have, in fact, already entertained this analysis, when we noted in discussing (30a) that *John's*, in *I need
John's*, denotes the possessee, i.e. a schematic entity that 'is John's'. This alternative is sketched in Figure 5.3.

This analysis would be consistent with Langacker's (1991: 220) generalization
that grounding predications profile the grounded entity, not the grounding relation.
Langacker, however, seems reluctant to accept this analysis of the possessive
morpheme. He mentions 'certain difficulties' (p. 168) associated with the idea that
possessives might be inherently grounding predications. Let us consider them.

(*a*) First, Langacker writes that a 'grounding predication must establish some
relationship between the designated entity and the speech-act participants, but it
is not obvious that a third-person possessive (e.g. *Tom's* [in *Tom's hat*: JRT])
accomplishes this' (p. 168). It is true that there is no *overt* reference to the
speech-act participants in talk of *Tom's hat*—but neither is there overt mention
of the speech-act participants in talk of *the hat*, or of *the hat that Tom shredded*.

---

[13] My analysis of POSS shares affinities with its treatment in Hudson's word grammar. Thus,
Hudson (1990: 276–8) argues that the possessive morpheme is a determiner which heads the possessive expression, furthermore, that the possessive morpheme refers to the same entity as the
possessee nominal. Thus, in *the King's hat*, both POSS and *hat* refer to the hat, according to Hudson.

There is, though, implied reference, to the extent that the speaker, in talking of *Tom's hat*, presupposes that the hearer is able to uniquely identify the referent of *Tom*. And the implied involvement of the speech-act participants may be made explicit, as when a person, on hearing of *Tom's hat*, remarks: 'Who's Tom? I've never heard of him.'

(*b*) Langacker observes (p. 168) that in some languages, possessives may co-occur with a definite determiner, as in Malagasy *ni alika-ko* "the dog-my", i.e. "my dog". Here, grounding is effected by the definite determiner, with *-ko* as a possessive modifier. Examples such as these, however, are surely irrelevant to an analysis of the English construction. The distinctive character of the English construction—its 'parochialism'—stems largely from the grounding function of the possessor phrase.

(*c*) Finally, there is the point that the possessor phrase in English does not always confer definiteness, or even specificity, on the possessee. However, as Langacker himself notes (p. 168), grounding can confer either definiteness or indefiniteness. (*A dog* is no less grounded for being indefinite than *the dog*.) The admittedly somewhat rare possibility that a prenominal possessive may have indefinite, and even non-specific reference, is therefore also not relevant.

The difficulties that Langacker mentions, therefore, are not insuperable. On the contrary, there is every reason to regard the prenominal possessor phrase as a regular grounding device. This analysis entails that the possessive morpheme is a species of determiner. It is interesting to observe that recent developments in X-bar theory have led to essentially the same conclusion. It is to these that I now turn.

One locus of these developments in X-bar theory has been the proper treatment of determiners. We have already observed that the category of determiner creates some problems for conservative versions of the theory (section 2.4). One of the axioms of the theory is that specifier, modifier, and complement are phrasal categories of the kind XP. The problem is that determiners, such as *the*, *this*, etc. do not seem to head phrasal categories. If the specifier position were occupied by a phrasal category, we would expect that a determiner, like other lexical heads, could be associated with its own complement and modifier, and even with its own specifier.

Radford argues that what are traditionally regarded as determiners can indeed be preceded by items that might plausibly be analysed as specifiers to determiner. He (1988: 264) cites such expressions as *along [essentially these] lines*, *[so few] people*, *[quite some] time*, pointing out that *essentially*, *so*, and *quite* might be taken to be specifiers to the determiners *these*, *few*, and *some*. Another item that might qualify is *all*: *[all the] time*, *[all those] people*. Interestingly, *all* is one of the items that can precede a possessor phrase: *[all my] chocolates*, *[all John's] friends*—a fact which further strengthens the supposition that the possessor phrase functions as a determiner.

Pursuing this line of argument, we may postulate that the specifier to an NP is filled, not by a determiner, but by a determiner phrase (DP). *So few people* thus has the structure shown in (51). (I leave open the question of the phrasal category to which *so*, the specifier to the determiner, belongs.)

(51)

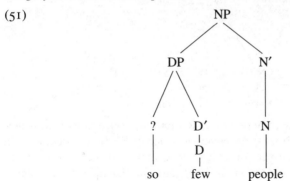

The following analysis of NP-POSS-N′ now becomes possible. In (52), POSS heads the determiner phrase, and the possessor functions as its specifier.

(52)

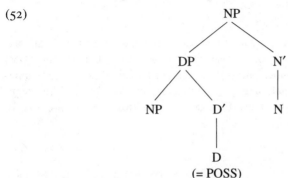

In recent years, even more radical revisions have been proposed. The idea is that what has traditionally been called a noun phrase is headed, not by a noun, but by its determiner. The traditional noun phrase thus becomes a determiner phrase (DP). DP is headed by a determiner, and the erstwhile N′ becomes an NP complement of the determiner. *The car* thus has the structure:

(53)

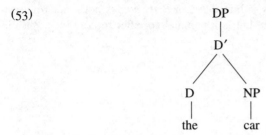

On the assumption that POSS is a determiner, and therefore the head of a possessive expression, *Betty's car* might have the following structure, with *Betty* an NP specifier of DP.

(54)

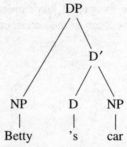

This is the phrase structure presupposed in Radford's (1990) study of the acquisition of English syntax. It is worth mentioning one of Radford's arguments in its favour. A well-known aspect of early child grammars of English is the absence of determiners. Radford (p. 84) cites the following examples from children aged 18–20 months:

(55) *a.* Paula good girl.
      b. Open door.
      c. Blanket gone.

Radford is keen to establish the thesis that early grammars of English make use only of lexical categories (noun phrase, verb phrase, etc.), but not functional categories (such as determiner phrase). A problem for this thesis is that alongside determiner-less nominals like *good girl*, *door*, and *blanket*, children regularly use prenominal possessives. Examples, again from 18–20-month-olds, include the following.

(56) *a.* Betty car.
      b. Mommy coat.
      c. Hayley book.

If the possessor nominals (*Betty, Mommy, Hayley*) were here taken to be determiners, the occurrence of (56) would threaten the thesis that early child grammars lack the category of determiner. Significantly, however, early possessives regularly lack the possessive morpheme, the very item that, it is claimed, would constitute the head of the determiner phrase. An alternative analysis thus becomes possible. The claim now is that *Betty*, in *Betty car*, is not a determiner, nor even in determiner position, but is a nominal specifier to *car*.

(57)

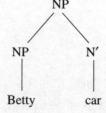

Radford further claims that (57) plays a role in the derivation of adult possessives. He proposes (58) as the deep structure of *Betty's car*. The surface structure is formed through movement of *Betty* from specifier of NP into specifier of DP:

(58)

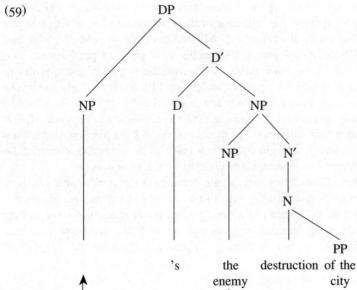

One argument presented by Radford in support of this analysis is that in *the enemy's destruction of the city*, *the enemy* must originate within the NP headed by *destruction* (namely, as specifier) in order to be assigned its proper θ-role (that of Agent). Its movement is 'forced' by the requirement that *the enemy* also be assigned case. The claim is that *the enemy*, in its new position, is assigned genitive case by POSS.

(59)

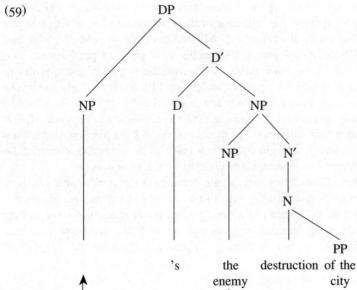

The relentless logic of X-bar syntax has given us an analysis of prenominal possessives which rejects most of those aspects of the construction that at the beginning of this chapter we had supposed to be uncontroversial. For example, *Betty's* and *the enemy's*, in (58) and (59), do not even have the status of constituents, either at deep structure, or on the surface!

The thesis that not only determiners, but other functional morphemes such as markers of number and case, are phrasal heads is now widely accepted in generative syntactic theory. There is an obvious convergence with the cognitive grammar account that I have presented in this and the preceding chapter. However, I would hate to give the impression that the X-bar accounts and the cognitive grammar accounts are mere notational variants. There are, on the contrary, some crucial conceptual differences between the two approaches, which are worth a brief discussion.

The revisions of X-bar theory that we have reviewed were motivated by problems with the category of specifier to XP. The category is indeed problematic —but for reasons over and above the theory-internal reasons that we have mentioned. The category is problematic because it is by no means obvious what its conceptual foundation might be.

We saw in section 4.3 that the structural notions of head, complement, and modifier can be given insightful characterizations in cognitive grammar. What are we to say about specifiers? If we restrict our attention only to noun phrases, the specifier, as this notion was used in conservative X-bar theory, would appear to comprise the grounding elements of the noun phrase, i.e. those elements which 'specify', or 'fix', the reference of the head noun. Possibly, the notion could also be extended to the verb phrase. The analogous constituent of a verb phrase would comprise markers of tense and modality—elements which likewise ground, or 'specify' the reference of the verb phrase. The situation is less clear with other kinds of phrase, e.g. AP (adjective phrase), AdvP (Adverbial phrase), PP (Prepositional phrase). Although these kinds of phrase were supposed also to have a specifier position, the semantic import of the specifier in no way parallels that of the specifier to NP (or VP). *Right*, in *right out of the window*, or *very*, in *very proud of her son* (Radford 1988: 228) do not 'ground', 'fix', or 'specify' the reference of the respective phrases at all. They are, if anything, straightforward modifiers! For these reasons, at least one linguist working within the generative paradigm (Bierwisch 1988: 3) has proposed to restrict the notion of specifier to the determiner element of the noun phrase.

The creation of the determiner phrase reanalysed the problematic category 'specifier to noun phrase'. To the extent that there are sound reasons for regarding the determiner as the head of a noun phrase, the analysis of *the car* in (53) is conceptually well founded and compatible with the cognitive grammar account. Unfortunately, the creation of DP did not eliminate the category of specifier. On the contrary, as we see in (54), (58), and (59), determiner phrases also get lumbered with specifiers. If the notions of specifier to PP, specifier to AP, and specifier to AdjP make little sense, conceptually, the notion of specifier to DP is even more obscure.

Such considerations seem not to have restrained some recent developments in government and binding theory. Here we witness a proliferation of functional heads, each with its own specifier. For a not untypical example, consider Oosthuizen and Waher's (1994) analysis of the Afrikaans possessive construction. The possessive morpheme in Afrikaans is *se*, which behaves very much like its English counterpart.

(60)   *a.* die kind se   trui.
             the child POSS jersey
             "the child's jersey"
       b. dosente se   salarisse.
             lecturers POSS salaries
             "lecturers' salaries"

(In point of fact, as remarked in n. 2 of this chapter, the Afrikaans construction is probably closer to the now obsolete dislocated possessive of English—cf. *the child his jersey*—than it is to the modern English construction, in that *se* appears to attach rhythmically to the possessee, not to the possessor; consequently, *se*-NP constituents can be readily coordinated in Afrikaans, a possibility not available in English.)

Oosthuizen and Waher propose (61) as the structure of (60*a*). There are three layers of functional constituents, labelled DP_1, DP_2, and DP_3. Overall, the expression is a DP (DP_1), which is headed by a phonologically vacuous determiner bearing the feature [Definite]. This determiner element takes as its complement another DP (DP_2), which is headed by the exponent of genitive case, *se*, which is, however, unmarked for definiteness. *Se* takes an NP complement (NP_1), which is headed by the possessee *trui*, and which has the possessor *die kind* as its specifier. Finally, *die kind* is analysed as a DP (DP_3), headed by the definite determiner *die*, with *kind* as its NP complement (NP_2).

(61), of course, has the overt constituents *se*, *die kind*, and *trui* in the wrong order. It is necessary to 'raise' the possessor phrase *die kind* from embedded NP_1 to specifier positions of DP_1. This proceeds in two stages. First, *die kind* raises to specifier of DP_2 (i.e. to specifier of *se*), where by the curious device of Spec–head agreement it acquires genitive case. In its position in DP_2, however, it remains unmarked for definiteness. *Die kind* (along with its newly acquired genitive feature) raises once again to specifier of DP_1, where it acquires the feature of definiteness, again by the mechanism of Spec–head agreement.

(61)

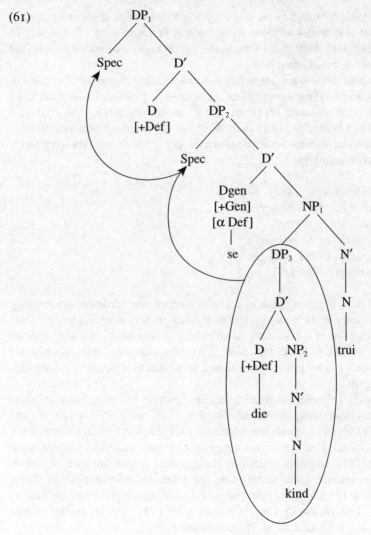

The overall expression is therefore headed by an invisible determiner — the feature [Definite]—whose specifier, *die kind*, bears the invisible feature [Genitive], whereby the phonological exponent of genitive case—*se*—heads the complement of this invisible element [Definite]. Here, I submit, we have reached a situation where the notions of 'determiner', 'specifier', 'head', and 'complement' have been emptied of any conceptual content they once might have had. The example (and it is by no means untypical of the kinds of analyses currently being proposed in the GB literature) vividly illustrates how failure to give conceptual foundation to the categories that one postulates, effectively deprives linguistic theory of all constraints on the possible, thus opening the way to analyses that defy rational evaluation, and which violate both intuition and common sense.

6 Prenominal Possessives: Some Generative Approaches

THE prenominal possessive construction in English has a number of distinctive properties, concerning both its internal structure and its usage range, which set it apart from possessive constructions in many other languages (section 1.1.3). In spite of (or perhaps because of) its parochial character, the construction has figured quite prominently in the transformational-generative literature of the past two and a half decades or so. In this chapter, I undertake a critical review of some of these analyses.

I believe this kind of historical review is important, for several reasons.

First, even though I shall have much to criticize in the generative accounts (indeed, many of the analyses put forward in the earlier days of generative grammar were subsequently rejected even by their proponents), many of the problems that were addressed still remain. In fact, some of the issues that were raised in the 1970s still await a satisfactory solution.

Secondly, even though the theoretical framework of cognitive grammar diverges radically from that of the generative paradigm, it would be foolish to reject all aspects of generative analyses just for this reason. On the contrary, we will want to preserve and enlarge upon the sometimes valuable insights of generative analyses. The challenge will be to reinterpret these insights within the restricted conceptual framework of cognitive grammar.

A more general issue is also at stake. This has to do with the internal dynamics of linguistic theorizing. Consider an account of a subset of possessives that was current in the earliest days of generative grammar. An introductory textbook of the time (Jacobs and Rosenbaum 1968: 231) proposed that *Eric's dictionary* could be transformationally derived from the same deep structure that gives the relative clause construction *the dictionary that Eric has*—an analysis also entertained in Chomsky (1970). Nowadays, of course, no one would dream of deriving a possessive in this way. Amongst the most transparent shortcomings of Jacob and Rosenbaum's proposal are (*a*) the possessive expression can have meanings which the relative clause expression does not have (*Eric's dictionary* could mean, *inter alia*, 'the dictionary that Eric compiled', 'the dictionary that Eric published', etc.); (*b*) the possessive expression is tenseless, whereas the relative clause is necessarily marked for tense; and (*c*) not every prenominal possessive has a corresponding relative clause transform (corresponding to *the* *train's arrival* there is no **the arrival that the train has*). In brief, *the dictionary that Eric has* turns out to be nothing other than a rough paraphrase of one of the many possible readings of *Eric's dictionary*—and even this paraphrase relation fails to hold for the full spectrum of prenominal possessives.

In considering the transformational analysis, we need to ask ourselves, not only what is wrong with the analysis, and why it was subsequently abandoned even by the generative community, but also the more basic question of why this clearly inadequate account could be entertained in the first place, even by eminent linguists of the day.

The answer to this last question, I think, is fairly transparent (at least with hindsight). The prevailing theory of the day had made the notion of deep structure, and the device of transformations operating on deep structures, available to linguists, as resources they could draw on in order to account for paraphrase relations between sentences. Yet little thought had been given to the conceptual foundation of 'deep structure' and 'transformation'. The content and scope of any specific proposal could not therefore be evaluated from the perspective of an insightful characterization of the devices that were invoked. In fact, since deep structures cannot be observed, either directly, in the linguistic data itself, nor indeed indirectly, by introspection, the only constraints on the content of deep structures, and on the scope of transformations, were those that were imposed by the theory, as formulated at any given time. As the theory mutated, so did the possible configurations of deep structures, and the scope of transformations. Since the theory itself was constructed around devices whose conceptual foundation had not been established, the theory was in fact prone to rather rapid mutation. Whilst subsequent versions of the theory might attempt to impose rather severe constraints on the content of deep structures and on the scope of transformations, these basic theoretical constructs continued to lack an insightful conceptual clarification. In the long run, subsequent generative accounts are likely to turn out to be no less ephemeral than the transformational analysis of *Eric's dictionary*.

Having said this, we should not lose sight of the basic insight which motivated the transformational analysis in the first place. This is that *Eric's dictionary* does have, as one of its highly salient readings, "the dictionary that Eric has". Whilst we must reject the mechanics of the transformational account of this relation, we still have to explain the very strong intuition that many possessives do invoke, as one of their highly salient readings, a *have*-relation.

6.1 CHOMSKY'S 'REMARKS ON NOMINALIZATION' (1970)

The first substantial treatment of prenominal possessives within the generative-transformational tradition is to be found in Chomsky's 'Remarks on nominalization' (1970).

The import of this seminal paper was to greatly restrict the power of the transformational component of the grammar.[1] Consider the rather striking semantic and syntactic parallels between the sentences in (1) and the noun phrases in (2).

(1) *a.* John is eager to please.
     b. John has refused the offer.
     c. John criticized the book.
(2) *a.* John's eagerness to please.
     b. John's refusal of the offer.
     c. John's criticism of the book.

Before the appearance of Chomsky's paper, it had been generally assumed by the generative community that the parallels between (1) and (2) could be captured by positing a common deep structure. Essentially, the noun phrases in (2) were to be derived from underlying sentences by means of a nominalizing transformation. This, certainly, was the approach that Chomsky had taken five years earlier (Chomsky 1965: 184–6).

Whereas Chomsky (1965: 186) had asserted that nouns like *sincerity* and *refusal* 'would surely not be entered into the lexicon', now, in his 1970 paper, Chomsky was arguing that nouns like *eagerness*, *refusal*, and *criticism* are fully independent lexical items, largely on the grounds of their distribution and their idiosyncratic semantic values. As such, they must indeed be listed in the lexicon. Consequently, the expressions in (2) are not derived by transformation, but need to be 'base-generated'. To this end, Chomsky proposed phrase structure rules as in (3).

(3) NP → DET N′
     DET → NP POSS

The commonalities between (1) and (2) were captured, not by means of a nominalizing transformation, but by means of shared subcategorization features. Just as (*to*) *destroy* selected, as its complement, the names of 'destructable' entities, so too did the derived noun *destruction*. In the ideal case, the noun simply 'inherited' the subcategorization features of its base verb.

It would, no doubt, have been consistent with the general thrust of 'Remarks' if Chomsky had proposed to base-generate the full range of prenominal possessives by (3). But alongside base-generated possessives, he recognized two further kinds, which were transformationally derived. These were expressions of 'alienable

[1] Chomsky (1970) is especially significant as it marks the parting of the ways between mainstream generative linguistics, centred around Chomsky and his teachings, and the breakaway 'generative semantics' movement. The latter proposed underlying structures of ever greater depth, and transformations of ever increasing scope, in order to capture the semantic relatedness of sentences of very different surface structure, and even of different lexical content. The mainstream, in contrast, sought to restrict the power and scope of transformations and favoured an increasingly 'shallow' deep structure. On the polemical background of Chomsky's paper, see Randy Harris (1993).

possession', and expressions involving NP-preposing. In all, then, we have three kinds of prenominal possessives.

(*a*) Expressions denoting 'alienable possession', e.g. *John's car*. These were derived from a relative clause structure containing the verb *have*. Thus, *John's car* derives from the same deep structure as *the car that John has*.

(*b*) Expressions of 'inalienable possession'. The notion of inalienable possession (traditionally understood as involving whole–part relations) generalizes to encompass what Chomsky calls a relation of 'intrinsic connection'. Expressions involving intrinsic connection are base-generated by (3). The expressions in (2) are examples; others include *John's picture* "the picture that John painted" and *John's proof* (*of the theorem*), as well as whole–part possessives (*John's leg*). Note that an alternative reading of *John's leg* corresponds to a different source. In the sense "the leg that is part of John's body" the expression is base-generated. In the sense "the leg (e.g. the leg of lamb) that John has in his possession" the expression denotes alienable possession, and is derived from an underlying relative clause.

(*c*) Expressions derived by NP-preposing. NP-preposing is invoked for possessor nominals with an 'objective' reading.[2] By analogy to the transformation deriving a passive sentence from an active, by movement of the direct object into subject position, the 'direct object' of the possessee noun gets moved from the right of the noun to the determiner position to its left. Thus *the city's destruction* (*by the enemy*) is derived from *the destruction of the city* (*by the enemy*), by leftward movement of *the city*. In contrast, possessors with a 'subjective' reading (as in *the enemy's destruction of the city*) exemplify a relation of inherent connection, and are base-generated by (3).

Given three different sources of prenominal possessives, one might expect to find at least some expressions that are three ways ambiguous. This, Chomsky claims, is indeed the case. Consider the three readings of *John's picture*:

(*a*) "The picture that John has in his possession". This is a relation of 'alienable possession', and is derived from an underlying *have*-clause.

(*b*) "The picture that John created". This is a relation of 'intrinsic connection', and is generated by (3).

(*c*) "The picture that depicts John". This is derived, by NP-preposing, from *the picture of John*.

---

[2] The terms 'subjective genitive' and 'objective genitive' were standard in traditional grammar. I shall say that a possessor has a subjective reading if the semantic relation between possessee and possessor is analogous to that between an active verb and its subject. Likewise, an objective reading obtains if the semantic relation is analogous to that between an active verb and its direct object. Hence, *John*, in *John's proof of the theorem* has a subjective reading (cf. *John proved the theorem*), whilst *the theorem*, in *the theorem's proof*, has an objective reading.

I must stress that in speaking of subjective and objective readings I do not wish to imply that nouns (such as *proof*) take subjects and direct objects.

As further evidence for the distinctness of the three categories, Chomsky invokes a transformation of NP-postposing. NP-postposing derives *that picture of John's* from *John's picture*. NP-postposing applies only to expressions of alienable possession. *That picture of John's* can only mean "that picture in John's possession", not "that picture that John created", or "that picture that depicts John". This latter reading is associated with *that picture of John*.

Such, in brief, was Chomsky's 1970 analysis of prenominal possessives. The account was anything but the last word on the topic. In the following two and a half decades, Chomsky's analysis was subject to extensive revision and counter-revision.[3] Indeed, the proper treatment of prenominal possessives has been a recurring theme in the generative literature, as evidenced by a steady stream of papers and monographs, some focusing specifically on possessives, others dealing with issues which touch, directly or indirectly, on their analysis. It would probably not be too much of an exaggeration to say that a comprehensive review would, in a very real sense, constitute a full history of generative linguistics from 1970 to the present day. In this chapter, I will have to limit my attention to some of the more salient landmarks of the territory.

Before discussing these subsequent developments, I would like to mention

---

[3] The years immediately following the appearance of 'Remarks' saw some quite extensive tinkering with Chomsky's three categories, and the mechanics of their derivation.

The derivation from *have*-sentences was quickly abandoned. The derivation of *Eric's dictionary* from *the dictionary that Eric has* involves a very considerable structural change, moving the subject NP of the *have*-clause into prenominal position, and then deleting what is left of the *have*-clause. The Extended Standard Theory that was adumbrated in 'Remarks' severely restricted the power of transformations; in particular, transformations which deleted, or which changed the category of nodes in deep structure, were no longer permitted.

Transformations which moved NP enjoyed a better fate. Indeed, the years following Chomsky's 'Remarks' saw NP movement rules run riot, with NPs within nominalizations bouncing back and forth like tennis balls. Chomsky's original rule of NP-preposing had applied only within passive nominalizations, moving an NP out of the 'object' position to the right of the head noun into the 'subject' position before the noun. Fiengo (1977) went further and postulated two NP movements in the derivation of *Carthage's destruction by Rome*. Given the underlying structure *Rome's destruction of Carthage*, NP-postposing first moves *Rome* from the subject position into a postnominal *by*-phrase, while NP-preposing moves *Carthage* into prenominal position. Emonds (1976: 102) appealed to NP-preposing to derive both active and passive nominalizations. *Rome's destruction of Carthage* and *Carthage's destruction by Rome*, he claimed, both derive from: $[_{NP} \Delta]$ destruction $[_{PP}(by)$ Rome]— Carthage. The active nominalization involves preposing *Rome* (with deletion of *by* and insertion of *of*), while the passive nominalization is derived by preposing *Carthage*. Emonds (1976: 98) also has a rule of NP-postposing deriving *the stupidity of John* from the 'more basic' *John's stupidity*. Presumably, though, this rule would not apply to *John's book* (cf. *the book of John). The structure of this kind of possessive is not discussed by Emonds.

The bewildering variety of (often mutually incompatible) NP-movement rules that proliferated in the 70s (and not only in the the 70s—consider the movements postulated by DP accounts of possessives, discussed at the end of the last chapter) raises the fundamental theoretical question of the status and function of movement rules in the first place. Presumably, the initial motivation for a movement rule is that the postulated underlying structure is in some sense 'closer' to semantic form than the surface expression. The need for underlying structures is thus conditional upon the supposed difficulty of accessing semantic structure from the surface arrangement of the constituents. If it can be shown that surface structure is semantically transparent, then underlying structures, along with movement rules which transform them, become redundant.

one aspect of Chomsky's 1970 account that has survived virtually intact up to the present. This is the recognition of different kinds of possessive expressions. For Chomsky, as we have seen, these were distinguished both semantically and derivationally. Subsequent accounts did not all draw the boundaries between different kinds in the same places as Chomsky did in 'Remarks', and some reduced Chomsky's three categories to two. Nevertheless, a feature of just about all subsequent generative treatments has been a reluctance to offer a unified account of expressions with the schematic structure [NP POSS N']. A major division has been between possessives that are headed by derived nouns (which are presumed to have an argument structure), such as *destruction*, and those that are headed by nouns which lack an argument structure (such as *car*). Of the expressions headed by derived nouns, 'passive' nominalizations (in which the possessor has an objective reading), of the kind *the city's destruction (by the enemy)*, have in general been accorded a different treatment from those in which the possessor stands in a subjective relation (as in *the enemy's destruction of the city*).

Rarely addressed, however, has been the relation amongst these different kinds of possessives. Prima facie, one might suppose that expressions which share a common (surface) structure would share a common semantics. Chomsky (1970), however, excludes in principle the possibility that expressions with the surface structure [NP POSS N'] could share a common essence. The account leaves us with the impression that it is pure coincidence that the very same surface structure should be used, in English, to express a *have*-relation (*Eric's dictionary*), a subjective relation (*John's proof*), and an objective relation (*the theorem's proof*). On Chomsky's account, the possessive construction turns out to be akin to a homonymous word, whose different senses bear no relation whatsoever to each other.

6.2 CONSTRAINTS ON POSSESSIVE NOMINALIZATIONS

One subcategory of possessives has been the object of particular interest over the years. This is the category of *possessive nominalizations*, that is, possessives in which the possessee is a derived,[4] usually deverbal noun, and in which the possessor stands in some kind of argument relation to the possessee.

Possessive nominalizations raise a number of special problems, especially with regard to the interpretation of the possessor nominal. At issue, essentially, is the possibility that the possessor can stand in a subjective and/or objective relation to the possessee.

---

[4] The term 'derived' is potentially misleading, in that it could suggest that a derived noun is somehow secondary, in some psychologically real sense, to the base form. I use the term in a purely descriptive way, to express a relation between a noun and a word of some other class.

I shall first present the facts, in a fairly theory-neutral manner. Then I shall discuss some accounts of the data that have been proposed.

We can distinguish two broad paradigms of possessive nominalizations in English. The first is exemplified by *destruction*.

(4) *a.* the enemy's destruction of the city.
     b. the city's destruction by the enemy.
     c. the city's destruction. [objective reading only]

Salient aspects of (4) are: (i) the possessor can in principle have both a subjective and an objective reading; (ii) the subjective reading is possible only if the notional object is expressed in an *of*-phrase; (iii) in the absence of an *of*-phrase, the possessor only has an objective reading.

A large number of derived nouns pattern like *destruction*.

(5) *a.* Iraq's invasion of Kuwait.
     b. Kuwait's invasion by Iraq.
     c. Kuwait's invasion. [objective reading only]
(6) *a.* Oswald's assassination of Kennedy.
     b. Kennedy's assassination by Oswald.
     c. Kennedy's assassination. [objective reading only]
(7) *a.* the minister's dismissal of the ambassador.
     b. the ambassador's dismissal by the minister.
     c. the ambassador's dismissal. [objective reading only]

What these nouns (*destruction, invasion, assassination, dismissal*) have in common, is that they derive from verbs which denote situations in which one entity (the Agent, encoded by the subject of the verb) performs some act which results in a substantial change in state of another entity (the Patient, denoted by the direct object of the verb). We may refer to these nouns, therefore, as *action nouns*.

A very different paradigm holds for nouns which derive from what we might call *cognitive verbs*. Cognitive verbs denote a situation in which a cognizing entity, prototypically a human being (the Experiencer, expressed usually by the subject of the verb), experiences a cognitive or emotional state with respect to a Stimulus entity (usually denoted by the verb's direct object). Examples include (*to*) *love, admire, fear, know, distrust*, and many more. Nouns derived from these verbs pattern as follows.

(8) *a.* John's knowledge of the facts.
     b. *the facts' knowledge by John.
     c. John's knowledge. [subjective reading only]

Note that in (8*a*) the notional direct object of *knowledge* is expressed in an *of*-phrase. Some cognitive nouns can select a preposition other than *of* for the expression of their 'object'.

(9) *a.* John's love {of/for} Mary.
     b. the voters' admiration {of/for} the politician.

A salient aspect of cognitive nouns is that the possessor can have only a subjective reading,[5] corresponding to the Experiencer, irrespective of whether or not the notional object is expressed in a postnominal prepositional phrase. This fact is all the more remarkable in that the base verbs readily passivize.

(10) *a.* The facts are known by everyone.
      b. *the facts' knowledge.
(11) *a.* The politician is admired by the people.
      b. *the politician's admiration. [unacceptable on objective reading]
(12) *a.* The enemy is feared by the soldiers.
      b. *the enemy's fear. [unacceptable on objective reading]

Many nouns, while conforming in the main with one or the other of these two paradigms, nevertheless exhibit some significant discrepancies.

(*a*) First, there are nouns which pattern in the main like action nouns, but which readily permit a subjective reading of the possessor, even in the absence of a postnominal phrase. Compare (13) with (14)–(16).

(13) *a.* the enemy's destruction *(of the city).
      b. the city's destruction (by the enemy).
(14) *a.* the company's donation (of the money).
      b. the money's donation (by the company).
(15) *a.* the critic's review (of the book).
      b. the book's review (by the critic).
(16) *a.* the doctor's examination (of the patient).
      b. the patient's examination (by the doctor).

(*b*) Some derived nouns, while they clearly denote actions rather than cognitive attitudes, nevertheless fail to permit an objective reading of the possessor. Compare (17) with (18) and (19).

(17) *a.* the destruction of the city (by the enemy).
      b. the city's destruction (by the enemy).
(18) *a.* the hikers' avoidance of the cliff.
      b. *the cliff's avoidance (by the hikers).
(19) *a.* John's expression of relief.
      b. *relief's expression (by John).

(*c*) Some cognitive nouns permit only objective readings of the possessor. Compare, in this respect, *fear* and *fright*.

---

[5] There is a striking contrast here with genitive case nominals in some other languages. Whereas *God's love* can only have a subjective reading, Latin *amor Dei* could mean either God's love (for mankind), or the love (of mankind) for God. On the meaning of *metus hostium* "the fear of the enemy", Seiler (1983: 53) quotes the Latin rhetorician Gellius: 'metus hostium recte dicitur, et cum timent hostes et cum timentur' "*metus hostium* is an appropriate expression both when the enemy is in fear and when they are being feared". In English, of course, *the enemy's fear* can only have the former reading.

(20) *a.* Amy feared the scarecrow.
      b. Amy's fear of the scarecrow.
(21) *a.* The scarecrow frightened Amy.
      b. *the scarecrow's fright of Amy.
      c. Amy's fright at the scarecrow.

Similarly, nouns derived from *interest, bore, horrify* take as their possessor the person who is interested, bored, or horrified, corresponding to the direct object of the verb, not the thing that interests, bores, or horrifies.

(22) *a.* The story interested the child.
      b. the child's interest in the story.
(23) *a.* The lecture bored the students.
      b. the students' boredom {at/with} the lecture.
(24) *a.* The news horrified me.
      b. my horror at the news.

Note, again, that these cognitive nouns select a preposition other than *of* in the postnominal phrase.

(*d*) Finally, some nouns, while patently related to transitive verbs, seem to permit neither subjective nor objective readings. Consider *sight* and *speech*.

(25) *a.* I saw John.
      b. ??my sight of John.
      c. John was seen by the neighbours.
      d. *John's sight (by the neighbours).
(26) *a.* I spoke those words.
      b. *my speech of those words.
      c. Those words were spoken by me.
      d. *those words' speech (by me).

(*John's sight*, is, of course, acceptable; it does not, however, refer to an act of seeing, but rather to John's ability to see, or to his visual acuity. Likewise, *my speech* refers to the product of my speaking activity, or to my speaking ability, not to an act of speaking on my part.)

At first sight, therefore, we appear to be faced with a good deal of lexically conditioned idiosyncrasy. A number of proposals have been put forward in an attempt to bring some order to the data. One of the earliest is the *Affectedness Constraint*,[6] proposed by Anderson (1978), and taken up by Fiengo (1980) and many others. As we shall see, the Affectedness Constraint continues to inform discussion of prenominal possessives to this day.

Anderson focused on possessives with an objective reading; these, following Chomsky (1970), she derived by a rule of NP-preposing. She observed that only NPs which designate entities that are 'affected' by the activity denoted by the deverbal noun can function as prenominal possessors; entities that are not affected

---

[6] The term itself is due to Jaeggli (1986).

are banned from prenominal position. Admittedly, Anderson needed to characterize 'affectedness' rather broadly, to encompass not only change in physical condition (*the city's destruction*) and change in status (*the criminal's rehabilitation*), but also change in accessibility (*the knife's concealment, the corruption's exposure*), and change in existential status. Thus, in *the book's translation*, the activity of translating the book brings the translation into existence. Somewhat less plausibly, perhaps, Anderson argues that *the play's performance* is sanctioned by the fact that, while the play, as an abstract object, is not affected by its being performed, nevertheless a specific instance of the play is created by its performance. Likewise with *Canada's history, the word's definition, Truman's biography*. On the other hand, a fact is in no way affected by its being known, or indeed by its not being known, neither is an object affected by its being scrutinized, avoided, or evaded. Whence, according to Anderson, the ungrammaticality of **the fact's knowledge, *the bird's scrutiny, *the cliff's avoidance, *the police's evasion*, and so on.

There is little doubt that Anderson put her finger on an important generalization on the distribution of possessor nominals. Consideration of some borderline cases only confirms its validity.[7] Is a child 'affected' through being neglected by her parents? Uncertainty on this issue correlates with wavering intuitions on the passive nominalization (27*a*). And while we might agree that a cliff is in no way affected by its being avoided by the hikers, we might be in two minds as to whether a person is affected by being avoided by her colleagues. Again, the passive nominalization is of uncertain acceptability (27*b*).

(27) *a.* ?the child's neglect (by her parents).
      b. ?Debby's avoidance (by her colleagues).

Anderson's account of objective possessives presupposes the movement analysis of Chomsky (1970). Rappaport (1983), developing some observations by Amritavalli (1980), dealt with nominalizations within the framework of lexical functional grammar. In LFG, relational predicates (verbs in the first instance, but also deverbal nouns) are specified for the grammatical functions (subject, object, possessor, oblique, etc.) with which they are associated. Rappaport proposed to capture the relation of nouns to the verbs from which they derive by means of rules which map the grammatical functions of the verbs onto those of the nouns. The data addressed by Anderson were covered by the following rules.

(28) OBJ $\Rightarrow$ POSS (condition: OBJ = +affected)
      SUBJ $\Rightarrow$ OBL$_{AG}$

---

[7] Fiengo (1980: 46) points to the role of 'extragrammatical knowledge' in determining whether an entity is 'affected' or not. He cites the contrast between *Cuba's recognition by the U.S.* and **John's recognition by Fred*, and between *John's possession (by the devil)* and **a lot of money's possession*, observing, in connection with the first pair, that 'a country can change another country's status by recognizing it, whereas the same is not true of persons'. These observations, again, confirm the general validity of Anderson's generalization.

The direct object of a verb corresponds to the possessor, on condition that the direct object is affected. Contemporaneously, the subject of the verb corresponds to the oblique Agent (expressed in a *by*-phrase) of the noun.

Rappaport drew attention to a further constraint on prenominal possessors. This we may refer to as the *Experiencer Constraint*. Cognitive verbs, like *fear*, *frighten*, *shock*, *bore*, *love*, *know*, denote a relation between two entities, one of which is an animate and sentient Experiencer of a cognitive state, the other is the source, cause, or object of the experience ('Experienced', in Rappaport's terminology). Rappaport noted that derived cognitive nouns only permit the Experiencer, never the Experienced, to function as possessor. This holds, irrespective of whether the base verb takes Experiencer as its subject or direct object. *(To) fear* takes Experiencer as its subject, whereas *frighten* has Experiencer as its direct object. *The scarecrow's fear* (*by Amy*) and *The scarecrow's fright* (*of Amy*) are equally impossible. Likewise, *Louise's love* can only convey that Louise loved (someone or something), i.e. Louise is Experiencer, not that Louise engendered, or was the object of, feelings of love in someone.

Rappaport (1983: 134) proposed to handle the Experiencer Constraint by means of 'linking conventions'. The deverbal noun shares the argument structure of the base verb. For the noun, however, the semantic role of Experiencer is always mapped on to the grammatical function of possessor, while Experienced is mapped on to a prepositional phrase. This is precisely the generalization that is needed to capture the facts presented earlier, in (20)–(24).

Whatever the formalism adopted, there can again be little question that the Experiencer Constraint captures an important generalization over possessive nominalizations denoting cognitive states and attitudes. In fact, we could even see the Experiencer Constraint as a special instance of the Affectedness Constraint. Arguably, the Experiencer of a cognitive state is 'affected' by the experience, to the extent that the Experiencer is in a cognitive state different from that in which he would find himself if he had not experienced the state. On the other hand, the object of the cognitive state (the Experienced) is in no way affected through being the object of a person's cognitive state.

The possibility therefore arises of collapsing the two constraints. This is the import of Rozwadowska's (1988) *Neutral Constraint*. Rozwadowska (p. 151) construes 'neutral' as a thematic role, which she defines as follows.

(29)   An entity X holds a thematic relation NEUTRAL (N-role) with respect to a predicate Y if
   (i) X is in no way affected by the action, process, or state described by Y,
   (ii) X does not have any control over the action, process, or state described by Y.

She goes on (p. 152) to propose the following rule.

(30)   Neutral cannot appear in specifier position of a nominal.

This rule correctly predicts the ungrammaticality of *the news's disappointment of the audience* and *the book's amusement of the children*, since *the news* and *the book* are neither affected, nor conscious controllers of the states of affairs described. By the same token, *John's knowledge of history* is sanctioned, since, presumably, knowing history causes a change in state in John, i.e. John passes from a state of ignorance to a state of knowing. On the other hand, the grammaticality of *John's ignorance (of history)* could be problematic, since John is presumably not 'affected' by his ignorance, nor does he 'control' this state of affairs. Rozwadowska herself (p. 160) notes the problem of the acceptability of *John's resemblance to Bill*. She speculates that the notion of 'neutral' might have no validity for symmetrical predicates, like *resemble*. Even so, the general validity of the Neutral Constraint seems to be empirically well founded.

We might also mention that the constraints we have discussed could have even wider scope, in that, as pointed out by Zubizarreta (1987: 44), they can plausibly account for some further restrictions on possessor nominals. For example, raised NPs are barred from functioning as possessors.

(31)   *a.* The Earth appears to be flat.
       b. *the Earth's appearance to be flat.

On standard generativist accounts of (31), *the Earth* originates as an argument of *be flat*, and so bears no direct thematic relation to *appear/appearance*; the question of affectedness cannot therefore arise. Also on Langacker's (1991: 453–7) 'active zone' account of raising, the Earth cannot be said to be 'affected' by how it appears. Consider also the 'dummy' NPs *there* and *it*. Langacker (1991: 351–5) takes these to be semantically contentful expressions, designating the 'abstract setting'. Again, the situations described in (32) and (33) in no way 'affect' the setting. And on standard generative accounts, of course, *there* and *it*, being semantically empty, are not arguments at all, so again cannot be construed as affected.

(32)   *a.* There appeared a man on the horizon.
       b. *there's appearance of a man on the horizon.
(33)   *a.* It appears that a mistake has been made.
       b. *its appearance that a mistake has been made.

6.3 EXPLAINING THE CONSTRAINTS

As I have emphasized, there can be little doubt about the descriptive adequacy of the Affectedness and the Experiencer Constraints. (This is not to say that there are not some striking counterexamples to the constraints. These will be discussed in section 8.3.1) The constraints, however, give rise to a nagging question. Why *should* non-affected and experienced entities be banned from the possessor role? After all, there is no general ban on the construal of non-affected and experienced entities with a deverbal noun, as shown by the (*b*) expressions below. Moreover, the base verbs readily passivize, and can take non-affected and experienced entities as their subjects, as shown by the (c) expressions.

(34)   *a.* *the cliff's avoidance (by the hikers).
     b. the avoidance of the cliff.
     c. The cliff was avoided (by the hikers).
(35)   *a.* *the enemy's fear (by the soldiers).
     b. the fear of the enemy (on the part of the soldiers).
     c. The enemy is feared by the soldiers.

In section 2.10 we already touched on the learnability problem, as raised by possessive nominalizations. Why does a speaker of English not generalize from the known possibility of an objective reading of *the city's destruction* to an objective reading of *the cliff's avoidance* or *the enemy's fear*? We cannot answer this question merely by appealing to the Affectedness and Experiencer Constraints. The constraints merely describe the facts of usage, they do not explain them. But with the constraints in hand, the focus of investigation can shift. Essentially, we will need to derive the constraints from more general syntactic and/or semantic principles, which are operative in constructions other than prenominal possessives. Failing such an explanation, the Affectedness and Experiencer Constraints will be nothing more than arbitrary stipulations on grammaticality.

It is probably not too much of an exaggeration to say that a truly insightful explanation of the Affectedness and Experiencer Constraints is outstanding to this day. As we shall see, attempts to explain the constraints have, all too often, invoked principles whose empirical foundation is extremely shaky, and which are perhaps even more obscure than the constraints themselves. Consider, for example, Anderson's (1978) own explanation of the Affectedness Constraint. Recall that for Anderson an objective possessor is derived by NP-preposing, that is, the possessor nominal originates to the right of the possessee. Since not all NPs may be preposed, the question becomes, how to delimit the class of preposable NPs from those NPs which may not be preposed.

Anderson observes that postnominal NPs introduced by prepositions other than *of* cannot be extracted out of their prepositional phrases, neither can the stranded preposition be deleted.

(36)   *a.* admiration for the president ⇒ *the president's admiration for/*the president's admiration
     b. accord with Panama ⇒ *Panama's accord with/*Panama's accord
     c. reliance on this leader ⇒ *this leader's reliance on/*this leader's reliance

Preposing is, however, possible in (37). In this case, the preposition *of* does get deleted.

(37)   *a.* exposure of the corruption ⇒ the corruption's exposure
     b. concealment of the knife ⇒ the knife's concealment

This contrasting behaviour suggested to Anderson a distinction between two kinds of preposition. The prepositions in (36) are 'genuine' prepositions, which are subcategorized by the head noun. As such, they are introduced in deep structure, and may not be deleted. In contrast, the head nouns in (37)—*exposure, concealment*—take in deep structure a bare NP complement, and *of* is a 'dummy' element of surface structure, introduced solely to satisfy surface structure constraints. (In subsequent versions of GB theory, the constraint in question is the requirement that the NP complement be assigned case. Since nouns cannot assign case, the case-assigning preposition *of* must be introduced.) Anderson's claim is that NPs in genuine prepositional phrases may not be preposed. On the other hand, bare NP complements can be preposed, in which case, of course, the dummy preposition fails to materialize.

Given the assumptions of cognitive grammar, we must, of course, resist the notion of a dummy (i.e. semantically vacuous) preposition. Even so, we might still be able to maintain a distinction between Anderson's 'genuine' prepositions (*for, with, on, to*, etc.) and the preposition *of*, to the extent that the former do have a more clearly defined semantic content, whilst *of* is semantically much more vague.

The real problem with Anderson's analysis is that not all NP complements introduced by *of* may be preposed. The inability of *the cliff* and *the fact* in (38) to prepose suggests that here, *of* is a genuine preposition.

(38) *a.* avoidance of the cliff ⇒ *the cliff's avoidance
      b. knowledge of the fact ⇒ *the fact's knowledge

Anderson is therefore forced to make a distinction between two kinds of *of*. Some *of*s, like those in (38), are genuine prepositions, which are subcategorized by the head noun and may not be deleted, whilst other *of*s, like those in (37), are dummies. Unfortunately, the only evidence for the existence of these two kinds of *of* is the very phenomenon that the distinction is meant to explain, namely the ability or inability of an *of*-complement to prepose.

An explanation for the constraints on possessor nominals might be more readily forthcoming if the notion of affectedness, as it applies to possessives, were to figure in the statement of other grammatical phenomena in English. As we shall see, attempts to find reflexes of affectedness outside prenominal possessives have not been very successful. The net result must be to render the Affectedness Constraint a highly mysterious phenomenon.

6.4 POSSESSIVES AND THEMATIC ROLES

One of the major innovations introduced by Chomsky in the early 1980s was the theta criterion, which stipulates that each NP in a sentence be assigned one, and only one thematic role. Here we review some implications of θ-theory for prenominal possessives. A central question concerns the θ-role assigned to the possessor. Another important issue is the mechanism by which the possessor nominal gets its θ-role. Our discussion will also require us to examine more closely the alleged distinction between thematic relations on the one hand, and the supposedly non-thematic relations that some NPs may bear.

Chomsky (1981, 1986) by and large retains the tripartite analysis of possessives he proposed in 'Remarks'. One subset, exemplified by *the city's destruction*, is derived by NP-preposing. The possessor nominal (*the city*) originates in deep structure as the complement of the possessee, *destruction*. It is assumed that the noun *destruction*, like the verb *destroy*, assigns the role of Theme to its complement. *The city* then moves into prenominal position, taking its θ-role along with it. Other kinds of possessor nominals are base-generated in prenominal position. In the case of possessors with a subjective reading, as in *John's proof* (*of the theorem*) and *the enemy's destruction of the city*, it is again the possessee which assigns the θ-role. Just as the verbs *prove* and *destroy* assign the role of Agent to their subject, so the derived nouns *proof* and *destruction* assign the role of Agent to the possessor.

Problematic, on this account, are run-of-the-mill possessives like *John's book* and *John's car*. What is the θ-role of *John* in these expressions? Chomsky (1986: 195), following Gruber (1976), suggests the thematic role of Possessor. The question, now, concerns the mechanism by which the possessor nominal acquires this thematic role. We can scarcely claim that the nouns *book* and *car* assign the θ-role of Possessor to *John*, since *book* and *car* hardly qualify as relational nouns, associated with a thematic grid.[8] A second possibility—assuming the derivation of alienable possessives from underlying *have*-clauses—would be to say that *John* gets the θ-role of Possessor from its position as subject of *have*. This account we must also reject, given the dubious status of the *have*-transformation; and indeed, restrictions on the power of transformations associated with the GB framework rule out the *have*-transformation as illegitimate. Chomsky (1986: 195) suggests a third possibility, namely that the role of Possessor is assigned by the structural configuration of a possessive expression, namely $[_{NP}\underline{\quad} X']$.

This proposal quickly runs into difficulties. As already indicated, a general thrust of GB theory was to place severe restrictions on the power of transformations. Concerning NP movement, one restriction (Chomsky 1981: 46) was that only NPs in argument positions can move; that is to say, prior to movement, the NP must already have been assigned a θ-role. This restriction reflects the general requirement that NPs in deep structure directly encode thematic relations. The moved NP then takes its already assigned θ-role along with it. Since by the theta

---

[8] Stowell (1989: 240), though, is led to the conclusion that 'nouns like *shoe* have no true θ-roles other than [the Possessor role] to assign'. This statement begs the question of what 'true' θ-roles (in contrast, presumably, to 'fake' θ-roles?) might be, and why Possessor should count as one of them.

criterion an NP cannot bear two θ-roles, it follows that an NP can only move into a position that is not θ-marked. A further consideration is the requirement that each NP in surface structure be assigned case. It is in fact the case requirement that triggers NP movement in the first place, in that a base-generated NP lacking case must move into a position where it can be case-marked. The following conditions on NP movement therefore apply: (*a*) The only NPs that can move are those that, in deep structure, receive a θ-role but no case; and (*b*) NPs must move into a position which assigns case, but no θ-role.

Consider again the derivation of (39*a*) from (39*b*).

(39)   *a.* the city's destruction.

      b. [$_{NP}$the destruction [$_{NP}$the city]]

The movement analysis entails that the prenominal position is not θ-marked; *the city* gets its θ-role from its original site as the complement of *destruction*. But, now, what about *John's proof of the theorem*? How does *John* get the θ-role of Agent, if it originates in the non-θ-marked prenominal position? (One escape route here could be to say that assignment of the Agent role is optional, and only occurs in default, as it were, of the prenominal possessor having already received a θ-role by some other mechanism.) The same problem arises with *John's book*. The claim that *John* gets its θ-role from the structural configuration in which it occurs is inconsistent with the derivation of *the city's destruction*, in which *the city* moves into what is required to be a non-θ-marked position.

One way out of these inherent contradictions could be to propose the co-existence of at least two kinds of prenominal possessives, with radically different syntactic properties. This was the solution adopted by Anderson, in her second important contribution to the possessives literature. Just as, in Anderson (1978), she distinguished between 'genuine', i.e. base-generated prepositions, and 'dummy' (i.e. transformationally inserted) *of*, now, in Anderson (1984), she distinguishes between a base-generated, and semantically contentful possessive morpheme, and a homophonous, semantically empty case-marker, inserted by a transformational rule.

Consider, first, her account of *John's book*. She analyses the possessive morpheme as a kind of adposition, with syntactic and semantic properties akin to those of a genuine preposition. *John's* has the status of a 'possessive phrase', which is headed by the possessive morpheme, POSS, and in which *John* is the complement of POSS. Given this analysis, it becomes possible to attach some semantic content to the possessive morpheme (say, 'relation to possessor'), and to claim that, just as prepositions (in their spatial senses) assign the θ-role Location to their complements, so POSS assigns the θ-role Possessor to its complement. Likewise, just as a preposition can assign case to its complement, so POSS can assign case to the possessor nominal, thus satisfying the requirement that the possessor NP be case-marked.

Anderson recognizes the need to characterize the notion of possession sufficiently broadly so as to accommodate the range of interpretations available for *John's book*, *John's train*, and so on. At the same time, she insists that possession needs to be understood sufficiently narrowly so as to exclude, as possible instances of possession, the kinds of semantic relation encoded by *the city's destruction* and *John's proof of the theorem*. For expressions of this latter type she proposes a different structural analysis. These expressions, she claims, instantiate the structural configuration [$_{NP}$NP N']. Chomsky's (1980: 50) 'genitive rule' inserts the possessive morpheme into this configuration, with the morpheme then getting 'adjoined' to the possessor NP. Whilst transformationally inserted POSS is semantically vacuous, it must, like adpositional POSS, be able to assign case to the possessor nominal, thereby satisfying the case requirement. It fails, however, to assign a θ-role, for the possessor nominals in question have already been assigned a θ-role, Theme in the case of *the city's destruction*, Agent in the case of *John's proof of the theorem*, and double θ-role assignment is ruled out by the theory.

Given these assumptions about the properties of the two kinds of possessive morpheme (observe how their properties are motivated solely by the requirements of the syntactic theory, not by any general conceptual considerations), expressions that might appear to be structurally identical are assigned different syntactic analyses; (40) exemplifies the adpositional morpheme, (41) the semantically vacuous, transformationally inserted morpheme.

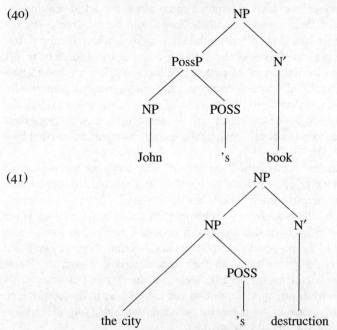

In support of these different analyses, Anderson points out that only expressions of the first kind have postnominal and predicative analogues.

(42)   *a.* John's book.
       b. a book of John's.
       c. This book is John's.
(43)   *a.* Rome's destruction.
       b. *a destruction of Rome's.
       c. *This destruction is Rome's.

In each of the expressions in (42), POSS has genuine semantic content and assigns the θ-role Possessor to its complement, i.e. *John*. *A book of John's* Anderson takes to be an instance of 'attributive *of*', similar to *a book of fifty pages*, *that house of straw*. The expression attributes possession by John to the book. In *This book is John's*, possession of the book by John is predicated of the book. The sentence is analogous to *The book is on the table*, which predicates a location of the book. In (43), these kinds of interpretations fail, due to violations of a selection restriction; a 'destruction' is not a possessible entity, and cannot therefore feature as the complement of adpositional POSS. Neither can POSS, in (42*b*) and (42*c*), be analysed as a dummy element, since the structural environment for the insertion of this element, viz. [$_{NP}$NP N′], is not present.

While the contrast between (42) and (43) is compelling, it is not unproblematic. On my intuition, postnominal and especially pronominal possessives have a somewhat more restricted range of interpretations than the prenominal construction. *This book is John's* strongly suggests that the book is one that John owns, not one that he has written, that he is always talking about, that he happens to be carrying, etc. (interpretations that could be appropriate for *John's book*). If this is the case, then either the meaning of the possessive morpheme is different in prenominal and other contexts, or, more reasonably, the predicative and attributive constructions somehow restrict the ways in which the relation between the book and John is to be construed.

Anderson makes a further generalization about the distribution of the two kinds of possessive morpheme. She suggests that, in general, non-count abstract nouns designate non-possessible entities. These nouns assign θ-roles in their own right, a possessive nominal stands in an argument relation to these nouns, and the possessive morpheme is inserted by the genitive rule; hence, for these kinds of nouns, structure (41) is indicated. In contrast, concrete nouns, and those abstract nouns that are [+Count], designate 'possessible' entities. A possessor nominal cannot stand in an argument relation to these nouns, since the nouns do not assign θ-roles. Consequently, the possessive morpheme must be a meaningful element of deep structure, and structure (40) is indicated. To illustrate the contrast, she cites (p. 5) the following minimal pair.

(44)   *a.* John's reconstruction of an 18th-century French village was damaged in the fire. ['concrete' reading of *reconstruction*]
       b. John's reconstruction of the crime required deductive skills. ['abstract' reading of *reconstruction*]

In (44a), *reconstruction* is [+Count] and [+Concrete], and cannot assign a θ-role to *John*. Rather, the noun designates a particular kind of artefact, which may stand in a possession relation to John. In (44b), *reconstruction* is [–Count] and [+Abstract], and assigns a θ-role (that of Agent) to *John*. Accordingly, we find that the possession relation may be predicated of the concrete noun, but not of the abstract noun:

(45)   a. This reconstruction of an 18th-century French village is John's.
       b. *This reconstruction of the crime is John's.

Again, there are problems. Consider kinship terms (*father*, *sister*, etc.), and the large number of nouns which designate a person by invoking some kind of relation to another person or to an institution (*friend*, *enemy*, *president*, *chairman*). These nouns are [+Count], [+Concrete], and therefore ought to designate 'possessible' entities, and at the same time be incapable of assigning thematic roles. The acceptability of the postnominal possessive (*a sister of John's*, *a friend of mine*) does indeed suggest that these nouns should be grouped with concrete nouns like *book*—cf. (42b). On the other hand, with respect to the predicative possessive (**This sister is John's*, **This friend is mine*), the nouns pattern like *destruction*—cf. (43c)—suggesting that the nouns should be grouped with the θ-role assigning nouns.

Part-terms give rise to the same kinds of problem. Anderson conflates the alienable and inalienable readings of *the pig's tail*, claiming that part-terms are 'strictly concrete nouns with no power to assign thematic roles' (p. 16). That on the normal interpretation of *the pig's tail*, the tail is taken to be a part of the pig, is, for Anderson, 'not a grammatical fact' (p. 16). (One wonders, though, whether the unacceptability of **This tail is the pig's* is also not a grammatical fact?) Even *reconstruction*, in its concrete sense (44a), is not quite as straightforward as Anderson would have us believe. If *crime*, in *reconstruction of the crime*, stands in a thematic relation to *reconstruction* (in its abstract sense), then does not *an 18th-century French village*, in *reconstruction of an 18th-century French village*, also bear a thematic relation to the concrete sense of *reconstruction*? (A 'concrete' reconstruction is necessarily a reconstruction of something.) If this is accepted, we shall have to say that even on its concrete reading, *reconstruction* is able to assign θ-roles. Anderson's distinction between concrete countables and abstract non-countables is thereby called into question.

Consider also the fact that John, in (44a), may be either the owner of the reconstruction or its creator, whilst (45a) seems only to convey that John is the owner. Prima facie, this suggests that only the owner role is assigned by POSS, whereas the creator role is assigned by *reconstruction*, a noun which, in its concrete sense, is claimed not to be able to assign θ-roles at all.

The basic issue here is the distinction between thematic relations which are assigned by the possessee, and those which are assigned by the possessive morpheme. The absence of unambiguous criteria for the distinction will inevitably

blur the line between prenominal possessives which invoke a relation of possession (assigned by POSS), and those which invoke some other thematic relation
(assigned by the possessee). A related issue is the nature of the θ-role of Possession, and the kinds of semantic relation that are implicated by it. In *John's
sister*, does POSS assign the role of Possessor to John, or is John assigned a
θ-role by *sister*? We have seen that the syntactic tests in (42) and (43) give
ambiguous results. Without a clear answer, we have no means for deciding
whether *John's sister* has the syntax of (40), or the syntax of (41).

The problematic nature of θ-roles, especially their status as a special subcategory of semantic relations in general, emerges from another account of possessives, that proposed by Safir (1987).

6.5 SAFIR (1987)

Safir distinguishes two broad classes of prenominal possessives: those in which
the possessor nominal is assigned a thematic role by the head noun, and those
in which the possessor nominal is subject to 'free thematic interpretation'.

Safir presupposes the distinction—introduced by Williams (1981)—between
internal arguments and external arguments. The internal argument of a verb is
the argument that is assigned a θ-role within the VP, while the external argument is assigned a θ-role outside the VP. This amounts to equating the internal
argument with the direct object of a verb (this, in most cases, will bear the θ-
role of Theme), while the external argument (mostly, the Agent) is expressed by
the subject. Safir tacitly assumes that the distinction between internal and external argument is inherited by a deverbal noun. He makes two specific claims: (*a*)
a possessor NP is thematically marked only if the head noun's full thematic
array is satisfied, and (*b*) the external argument can only be expressed if the
internal argument is expressed. Otherwise, a prenominal possessor is subject to
'free thematic interpretation'.

It follows that the possessor NPs in (46) are thematically marked, since the
full thematic array of the head noun is satisfied, i.e. both Agent and Theme are
assigned.

(46) *a*. the enemy's destruction of the city.
         [AGENT]   [THEME]
      b. John's discussion of the issue.
         [AGENT]   [THEME]

In contrast, the possessors in (47) are subject to free thematic interpretation.
Discussion cannot assign the role of Agent to *John*, since the role of Theme has
not been assigned, while *destruction* cannot assign the role of Theme to *the city*
since the full thematic array of *destruction* is not satisfied.

(47)   *a.* John's discussion
     b. the city's destruction.
     [Free thematic interpretation]

Safir next considers nominals derived from intransitive verbs. Following Burzio (1986), he distinguishes between 'unaccusatives' and 'unergatives'. Unaccusatives (*arrive, enter, appear*, etc.) take only an internal argument (i.e. Theme), unergatives (*run, walk, work*, etc.) take only an external argument (Agent). Hence, in (48*a*), *John* is assigned the role of Theme by *arrival*, the full thematic array of *arrival* being thereby satisfied. In contrast, in (48*b*), *John* is subject to free thematic interpretation; since an internal argument has not been assigned, *walk* cannot assign an external argument.

(48)   *a.* John's arrival.
     [THEME]
     b. John's walk.
     [Free thematic interpretation]

Finally, Safir turns to possessives containing an explicit *by*-phrase. In (49) both Agent and Theme are assigned.

(49)   the examination of the patient by the doctor.
                [THEME]   [AGENT]

NP-preposing may move *the patient* (along with its θ-role) into prenominal position. Hence, (50*a*) contrasts with (50*b*) in regard to thematic interpretation.

(50)   *a.* the patient's examination by the doctor.
     [THEME]   [AGENT]
     b. the patient's examination.
     [Free thematic interpretation]

Safir emphasizes that free thematic interpretation does not of itself exclude the possibility that the nominal in question may come to be interpreted as Theme or Agent. However, other thematic roles, such as Possessor or Author, or indeed 'any other pragmatically accessible role' (p. 568), may be assigned. The mechanism of free thematic interpretation is touched on only briefly. It appears to have to do with 'entailments' of the lexical conceptual structure of the possessee noun (pp. 592–3). In other words, the various possibilities of free thematic interpretation of *John's photograph* emerge as a consequence of one's knowledge of what a photograph is.

At this point, the basis of the distinction between assigned roles and interpreted roles comes to the fore. Could we not say, for example, that the assignment of Theme to the possessor in *John's arrival* is also a function of the entailments of the semantic structure of *arrival*; the fact that an 'arrival' takes places entails a person or thing that arrives. An arrival entails much else as well, of course, such as a particular time at which, or during which, the arrival takes place. A possessor NP can indeed express a temporal role: *yesterday's arrivals*. According to Safir, however, the temporal role comes about by free interpretation, while the Theme role is by assignment.

Can this distinction be upheld? To justify it, it will be necessary to show that nominals with an assigned thematic role have semantic and/or syntactic properties not shared by nominals which acquire their thematic role by free interpretation. Safir's main evidence, here, concerns a 'curious restriction' (p. 565) on predicative adjectival adjuncts. He claims that these adjuncts can only modify a thematically-assigned nominal.

(51) *a.* [John's]$_i$ treatment of [Bill]$_j$ [naked]$_{i/j}$.
    [= Safir's (7*a*)]
  b. [Bill's]$_i$ treatment by [John]$_j$ [naked]$_{i/j}$.
    [cf. Safir's (44*a*)]

(52) *[Bill's]$_i$ treatment [naked]$_i$.
    [= Safir's (9*a*)]

In (51), *John* and *Bill* are assigned the thematic roles of Agent and Theme, respectively; *naked* can therefore modify either *John* or *Bill*. (Safir, p. 587, observes, though, that intuitions on the passive nominalization are somewhat less clear than for the active nominalization.) In contrast, in (52), *Bill* is subject to free thematic interpretation; it is not possible, Safir claims, for *naked* to modify *Bill*, irrespective of whether Bill is interpreted as the one doing the treating, or as the one being treated. (As a matter of fact, on my intuition, this second interpretation does seem marginally possible.) Similarly with intransitive nominalizations.

(53) *a.* Andy's arrival drunk. [= Safir's (13*a*)]
  b. *John's walk drunk. [= Safir's (14*a*)]
    [Safir's grammaticality judgements]

The effect, though, only shows up with action nominalizations. With *sick* modifying *Bill*, (54) is unacceptable, even though *Bill* is thematically marked.

(54) *[Bill's]$_i$ photograph of John [sick]$_i$.
    [= Safir's (5*b*)]

The evidence of the adjectival adjuncts is difficult to evaluate. In the first place, it is anything but obvious why thematic role assignment should have repercussions at all on the distribution of predicative adjectival adjuncts. But there is also a question of the data itself. Intuitions on the acceptability of the adjuncts are not only variable, they seem to depend more on the identity of the lexical items concerned, than on the syntactic configurations in which they occur. (55) ought to be fully acceptable, since *John* has been assigned a thematic role. But on my intuition, (55) fares no better, in fact it is rather worse, than the expressions in (56), both of which ought to be impossible.

(55) [John's]$_i$ persuasion of [Mary] [drunk]$_i$.

(56) *a.* [John's]$_i$ advice [drunk]$_i$ is not worth a cent.
  b. [Professor Smith's]$_i$ lecture [drunk]$_i$ was a scandal.

Or consider (57).

(57)   *a.* [John's]ᵢ arrival [dead]ⱼ.
       b. the arrival of [John]ᵢ [dead]ⱼ.

On Safir's thesis, both of these have to be fully grammatical. Yet Williams (1982: 278), arguing a different theoretical point, had asterisked these very two expressions! And Williams is not alone in his judgement. Hornstein and Lightfoot (1987: 29) also cite (57*a*) as ungrammatical.[9]

The flexibility of intuitions on the adjectival adjuncts possibly reflects the extreme rarity of the adjunct construction, especially in association with a possessive nominalization. There are, in any case, only a handful of adjectives which can occur in predicative adjunct position; Safir's examples all play on the same three items *sick*, *naked*, and *drunk* (and their synonyms). Be that as it may, such flimsy data hardly constitute a solid basis for drawing what is presented as a fundamental theoretical distinction.

Safir (1987: 591) mentions a second way in which thematically marked nominals differ from those subject to free thematic interpretation. His claim is that extraction across a prenominal possessor is possible only if the prenominal possessor is thematically marked. On the assumption that *play* (in the sense "drama") does not assign θ-roles, *Bill* in (58*a*) is subject to free thematic intepretation, hence extraction over the possessor is impossible. On the other hand, in *Bill's comments on X*, the full thematic array of *comment(s)* is satisfied. *Bill* is assigned a θ-role, and extraction over *Bill* is permitted.

(58)   *a.* *What is John reading Bill's play about?
           [= Safir's (52*c*)]
       b. Whose book did you read Bill's comments on?
           [= Safir's (53*b*); Safir's acceptability judgements]

Again, the alleged difference turns out to be less than fully convincing. Deane (1988, 1992) argues at length that what makes extraction possible, is not so much the syntactic configuration of a sentence, as pragmatic considerations of focus and topicality. (See the brief discussion of these issues in section 2.2.) Given a context in which *Bill's play about X* is topical (i.e. already has 'given' status in the discourse), and in which the subject matter of the play is in focus (i.e. constitutes the 'point' of an utterance), (58*a*) can become much more acceptable.

(59)   A. I'm reading Bill's play about an English king.
       B. Which English king did you say you were reading Bill's play about?

---

[9] Hornstein and Lightfoot's rejection of (57*a*) concerns not just the pragmatic oddity of claiming of a dead person that he arrives. They (1987: 29) also asterisk the following, where the issue of pragmatic oddity does not arise: **John's acceptance of the gift happy*. Note again that Safir's thesis requires this expression to be fully grammatical.

Safir (his n. 6) acknowledges the problem of alternative judgements, claiming that they can be put down to 'the wrong interpretation of the data'(!).

Similarly with (58*b*). Increase the information content of the extraction site, thereby reducing its topicality, and the sentence becomes rather less acceptable.

(60)   ?What did you read the most famous living philospher's comments on?

Of course, it might still be possible to defend Safir's claim that the data in (58) do point to a real difference between assigned and interpreted roles. But to do this, it would be necessary to determine that possessors which are assigned thematic roles tend to be higher in topicality than possessors with freely interpreted thematic roles, and that complements of θ-role-assigning nouns tend to be more in focus than the complements of non-θ-role-assigning nominals. But since topicality and focus are quintessentially discourse notions, and therefore subject to contextual variation, I doubt whether such correlations could be reliably established. In the meantime, I think we can safely conclude that Safir has failed to offer any substantive justification for the distinction between two kinds of thematic roles.

6.6 GIORGI AND LONGOBARDI (1991)

The accounts of possessives discussed so far have been very much oriented towards syntactic explanations. In this section I discuss another syntactically oriented account, that of Giorgi and Longobardi (1991, henceforth G&L).

G&L, working within the more or less standard GB mainstream, are intent on establishing a typological difference between English and Italian (and, more generally, between Germanic and Romance). A basic assumption is that derived nouns in both languages inherit the argument structure of their base forms. Both derived and underived nouns may also be associated with what they call possessors, i.e. elements that are 'semantically connected with the head in a looser way than through a specific θ-role' (p. 117). The crucial distinction for G&L, however, is not between 'arguments' and 'looser semantic connections', but between internal arguments and all other semantic relations.

Their claim, essentially, is that in Italian (and in Romance in general), all the arguments of a noun (internal and external, as well as possessors) are base-generated to the right of the noun, whereas in English (and some other Germanic languages), only the internal argument is generated to the right, all other arguments (possessors and the external argument) being base-generated to the left, namely in specifier position.

Discrepancies from the underlying order are the result of movement transformations. 'Heavy' prenominal NPs in English may optionally move into postnominal position, leaving behind a trace in Spec, whereby the moved NP is associated, in its new position, with the preposition *of*. Hence *the book of the man I met yesterday*, with a heavy possessor, derives from *the man I met yesterday's book*. The internal argument can also move, by the now familiar rule of NP-preposing, into specifier position. Hence, *the city's destruction* derives from *the destruction of the city*. In Italian, of course, only pronominalized possessors and arguments can appear in prenominal position, in which case they appear as possessive adjectives.

The theory neatly accounts for the difference between the following sentences, which, superficially, share the same syntactic structure.

(61)   *a.* The description of Mary was inaccurate.
       b. La descrizione di Maria non era accurata.

In (61*a*), *Mary*, not being a heavy NP, could not have originated in prenominal position. It is therefore understood as the internal argument, that is, as the person described. In (61*b*), on the other hand, *Maria* could be either the internal or external argument, or even the 'possessor', or 'owner' of the description. The sentence, therefore, is genuinely ambiguous.

G&L present a number of subtle arguments in support of their theory. Here there is space to review only some of them. Consider, for example, the curious restriction in (62*a*).

(62)   *a.* {*his/*John's} books of my favourite writer.
       b. {his/John's} books by my favourite writer.
(63)   *a.* i libri di Gianni del mio autore preferito.
       b. i suoi libri del mio autore preferito.

G&L (p. 133) propose the 'Argument Uniqueness in Spec Constraint', according to which only one argument may be present in specifier position. *My favourite writer* in (62*a*) originates in Spec, where it leaves a trace. But by the Argument Uniqueness Constraint, Spec cannot be simultaneously occupied by the trace of *my favourite writer* and by the possessor *he/John*. Whence the unacceptability of (62*a*). In (62*b*), *by my favourite writer* is an independent, base-generated adjunct phrase, so the possessor is the only occupant of Spec. In Italian, neither the possessor nor the author argument originates in Spec. There is no question, therefore, of Spec being doubly occupied, hence both phrases in (63) are acceptable.

Consider next the control phenomenon, briefly alluded to in 2.10. Drawing on Roeper (1987) and Williams (1985), G&L (p. 135) claim that *destruction* in (64*a*) is associated with an unexpressed Agent argument in Spec. This 'implicit argument' is able to 'control', i.e. is construed as identical with, the implied subject of the infinitival clause *to collect the insurance*. The sentence is therefore interpreted to mean that whoever destroyed the ship, did so to collect the insurance. The (*b*) sentences, however, are much less acceptable. The reason, according to G&L, is that the internal argument *the ship* has been preposed into Spec, thereby obliterating the Agent argument. There is therefore no implicit argument which is able to control the infinitival clause.

(64) *a.* I disapprove of the destruction of the ship to collect the insurance.
      b. *I disapprove of {its/the ship's} destruction to collect the insurance.

G&L note that this grammaticality contrast does not obtain in Italian. This falls out from their claim that in Italian the implied Agent does not originate in Spec, and so does not get obliterated by the possessive adjective *sua*.

(65) *a.* Disapprovo la destruzione della nave per riscuotere l'assicurazione.
      b. A proposito di questa nave, disapprovo la sua destruzione per riscuotere l'assicurazione.

Of special interest to us here is G&L's account of the Affectedness Constraint. Again, they point to what they see as a major difference between English and Italian. Cinque (1980: 96) had noted that the Affectedness Constraint does not hold in Italian, to the extent that a possessive adjective may unproblematically denote an unaffected entity. Whereas (66a) is ungrammatical, due to the unaffected status of *this discussion*, the Italian phrase in (66b) is genuinely ambiguous between a subjective and an objective reading, i.e. *sua* can denote either the person who discussed, or the matter that was discussed. The same goes for *la sua comprensione* "his/her/its understanding", *il suo ricordo* "his/her/its recollection", *la sua conoscenza* "his/her/its knowledge".

(66) *a.* *this problem's discussion.
      b. la sua discussione.
      "his/her/its discussion"

On the other hand, the Experiencer Constraint seems to hold in both languages. The prenominal possessor to a cognitive noun, such as Italian *desiderio* "desire", *amore* "love", *odio* "hatred", can only be the Experiencer; as in English, the Stimulus must be expressed in a prepositional phrase.

(67) *a.* il tuo desiderio.
      "your desire" [you = Experiencer]
      b. il desiderio di te.
      "the desire of/for you" [you = Stimulus]

Let us consider first the Affectedness Constraint. G&L (pp. 140–5) propose that, for a certain class of deverbal nouns in English, namely, those with unaffected internal arguments, Spec position is obligatorily occupied by the external θ-role (even if the role receives no overt lexical expression); the external θ-role may not be 'obliterated', as it would be if it were overwritten by a moved internal argument. Whence the impossibility, in English, of moving the internal argument into Spec, as in *the book's discussion, *the problem's understanding, *the event's recollection. In Italian, of course, the situation does not arise, since the external argument is generated to the right of the head noun, not in Spec; hence, in Italian, any internal argument (if pronominalized) can move into Spec.

For G&L (p. 143), therefore, the Affectedness Constraint reduces to (68).

(68) If a complement of X is unaffected, it is impossible to eliminate the external θ-role of X.

Of course, (68) does not *explain* the Affectedness Constraint, it merely restates it in the language of GB theory. G&L do, however, claim that (68) is 'independently motivated' (p. 143) by the evidence of the middle construction in English. In middles, a normally transitive verb is used as intransitive, whereby the subject of the intransitive designates the internal argument. Examples include *This car drives smoothly, The bread slices easily, The book won't sell*. As noted by Jaeggli (1986), verbs with non-affected internal arguments are especially infelicitous as middles. The reason, according to G&L, is that putting the internal argument in subject position would obliterate the obligatory external argument. For G&L, therefore, the middles in (69) and the possessives in (70) are ungrammatical for exactly the same reason.

(69) *a.* *The situation discusses with embarrassment.
      b. *Such events recollect easily.
      c. *The novel understands with difficulty.
(70) *a.* *the situation's discussion.
      b. *the events' recollection.
      c. *the novel's understanding.

While the correlation between the (un)acceptability of possessives and middles is quite compelling, in many cases, it has to be recognized that the correlation is far from perfect.[10] To my ears, the middles in (71) are decidedly odd, in contrast to the easy acceptability of the possessives in (72).

(71) *a.* ?The city won't destroy.
      b. ?Dictators don't assassinate easily.
      c. ?These politicians won't remove from office.
(72) *a.* the city's destruction.
      b. the dictator's assassination.
      c. the politician's removal from office.

Or consider a perfectly good middle such as *Bert doesn't interview very well*. That Bert could be 'affected' by being interviewed seems to be of little relevance to the semantics of this sentence. The crucial aspect is surely the extent to which Bert is 'responsible' (possibly in some extended, metaphorical sense) for the outcome of the interview, for example, in virtue of his personality, characteristic behaviour, appearance, and so on.[11] The most reasonable conclusion would be

---

[10] Testing for the alleged correlation between objective possessives and middles is rendered difficult by the fact that not every verb that is a candidate for the middle construction has a derived noun (of the appropriate semantic type) associated with it. One would like to be able to test whether the well-known contrast between *This book sells well*; **This book buys well* carries over to possessives. While *the book's sale* does seem possible, there is unfortunately no derived noun from *buy*, analogous to *sale*, on which one could ascertain the impossibility of the objective possessive. (Of course, *the book's buy* is unacceptable, but so is **the buy of the book*; this is because *buy* is not an episodic nominalization, of the same semantic type as *sale*.)

[11] For discussion along these lines, see Van Oosten (1986).

that while the affectedness of the internal argument could well be one parameter bearing on the acceptability of a middle, the middle construction needs to be recognized as an independent construction in English, with its own unique semantic properties.

We are left, then, with the need to explain (68), as it applies to possessives. The crucial question, of course, is why verbs with unaffected internal arguments should have an external θ-role with just the requisite property, viz. non-erasability. Although they do raise the matter (pp. 143, 251), G&L fail to offer any proposals for independently identifying the relevant class of verbs.

G&L's account of the Experiencer Constraint can be dealt with more briefly. They (pp. 144–5) adopt, virtually unaltered, Anderson's (1978) distinction between 'genuine' and 'dummy' prepositions. They claim that only arguments introduced by the dummy genitive preposition *of/di* are candidates for preposing. Stimulus, on the other hand, is always introduced by a genuine preposition. Whence the general impossibility, in Romance and Germanic alike, of Stimulus appearing in prenominal position, cf. (67). My earlier comments, in section 6.2, on the inadequacy of Anderson's explanation of restrictions on NP-preposing, thus carry over to G&L's account.

G&L present the evidence from noun phrases in English and Italian in support of their particular conception of government and binding theory. It cannot be denied that, given their theoretical assumptions, G&L do offer a remarkably elegant account of a wide range of phenomena. We have seen, however, that G&L actually fail to explain either the Affectedness Constraint or the Experiencer Constraint. Their account of the Affectedness Constraint merely paraphrases the constraint, while their account of the Experiencer Constraint invokes an *ad hoc* distinction whose sole justification is, precisely, the constraint at issue. Concerning other aspects of noun phrases which they cite, e.g. those in (62)–(65), the force of their argumentation will crucially depend on the availability of alternative explantions of the data. We shall, in fact, have occasion to return to these data later in this book, and attempt to show that alternative explanations are indeed available.

6.7 ASPECTUAL ACCOUNTS

I now turn to some accounts of possessive nominalizations that are more semantics-based. These accounts share a concern with aspectual properties of the situation denoted by the nominalization, in particular, its temporal properties.

Fellbaum (1987), addressing possessives with preposed themes (or, to put it more neutrally, possessives with an objective reading), doubts whether the crucial determinant of acceptability is the semantic relation between possessor and possessee. She is particularly sceptical of the notion of affectedness. To claim that the possessor in (73*a*) is 'affected' could stretch the notion unreasonably. Furthermore, the ungrammaticality of (73*b*) suggests that this extended notion of affectedness, as it applies to possessives, fails to coincide with the notion of affectedness as it applies to middles.

(73)   *a.* the sermon's delivery
       b. *Sermons deliver on Sundays.

Rather, for Fellbaum, the crucial parameter in the acceptability of a possessive nominalization is the aspectual character of the situation it denotes, in that the situation must be construable as accomplished and perfective (in the sense of Vendler 1967), rather than as an activity in progress.

As evidence, she notes that possessive nominalizations may co-occur with expressions of the kind *in X amount of time* (a diagnostic for a perfective interpretation), but not with *for X amount of time* (indicative of a non-perfective interpretation).

(74)   *a.* The city's destruction occurred {*for/in} three days.
       b. The proposal's defeat happened {*for/in} two voting rounds.

Nominalizations of unaccusative verbs exhibit the same property.

(75)   *a.* The body's disintegration occurred {*for/in} a few days.
       b. The patient's recovery occurred {*for/in} less than two weeks.

On the other hand, nouns derived from inherently activity verbs do not permit objective readings of a possessor.

(76)   *a.* Great relief was expressed {for/??in} the entire evening.
       b. *Great relief's expression took place {for/in} the entire evening.
(77)   *a.* *The book was understood for the whole evening.
       b. *the book's understanding.

Further support for Fellbaum's thesis comes from the fact that many prenominal possessives can be rendered unacceptable if a definite possessor is replaced by an indefinite plural.

(78)   *a.* the city's destruction/*cities' destruction.
       b. the proposal's alteration/*proposals' alteration.

The point here is that, whereas 'the destruction of the city' may constitute a completed event, 'the destruction of cities' constitutes an imperfective activity.

As a matter of fact, the referential properties of the possessor have wider implications than Fellbaum acknowledges. *Twins' parents* (in the sense "the parents of twins") is decidedly less acceptable than *the twins' parents* "the parents of the twins", even though perfectivity is quite irrelevant to these examples. There are other respects in which Fellbaum's data might be questioned. (79) seem quite acceptable to me, even though they demand an imperfective, activity reading.

(79)   *a.* The city's bombardment continued for several weeks.
       b. {Sarajevo's destruction/Bosnia's dismemberment} continues in spite of the ceasefires.

A further point is that Fellbaum ignores the possibility that a derived noun may actually be ambiguous between a number of aspectually distinct readings. This is one of the issues addressed in Grimshaw's (1990) major study, which we turn to next.

Anderson (1984) had noted that some deverbal nouns, like *reconstruction*, can be used in both an abstract and a concrete sense. In its concrete sense, *reconstruction* denotes the result, or the product, of the kind of process denoted by the base verb, or by the noun in its abstract sense. A 'reconstruction' comes into existence as the result of the activity of 'reconstruction'. A large number of deverbal nouns exhibit a similar ambiguity: *announcement, assignment, creation, criticism, examination, expression, proposal*, and countless more. Thus, *announcement* may denote the process of announcing, as in *the announcement of the news*, or it may denote the message that is announced, as in *We heard the announcement*.

For Grimshaw, however, the crucial distinction is not so much between process and result readings of a nominal (or even between abstract and concrete readings), but between what she calls 'complex event nominals' and 'simple event nominals'.

The framework for Grimshaw's analysis is a three-way distinction between arguments, complements, and modifiers. Complements have to do with the 'lexical conceptual structure' (roughly, the 'meaning') of a predicate. The representation of lexical conceptual structure includes, amongst other things, a statement of the participants in the activities or states denoted by the predicate (1990: 5). These participants can be (optionally) expressed in complements. Some complements, however, have a privileged status, namely, as arguments of the predicate. Arguments are licensed by the 'argument structure' of the predicate, they are often obligatory, they occur in 'argument positions', and are thematically marked. Argument structure, though based in lexical conceptual structure, is an essentially grammatical property of a predicate. A modifier, on the other hand, is a more peripheral element, which gives additional information about the reference of the modified term. Modifiers are typically paraphrasable by means of a copulative (*a book by Chomsky* ⇒ *a book which is by Chomsky*), and have to do with 'real-world knowledge' (p. 93) of the referent. Grimshaw motivates these distinctions—especially the distinction between a semantics-based lexical conceptual structure and an essentially grammatical level of argument structure—by pointing out that the meaning of a predicate does not necessarily predict its grammatical properties. *Trip* denotes a perfective event, and perfective events take place in a certain amount of time; these 'conceptual' facts, however, do not legitimize the grammaticality of (80a), although (80b) is unproblematic. The difference, according to Grimshaw (p. 59), is due to the fact that *trip* does not have an argument structure (it is a simple event nominal), while *destruction* (a complex event nominal) in (80b) does.

(80) a. *Jack's trip in five hours was interesting.
      b. The total destruction of the city in only two days appalled everyone.

Complex event nominals preserve, in their semantic structure, the aspectual properties of the verb from which they derive, the event, in other words, is construed with respect to its successive temporal stages. It is in virtue of this property, according to Grimshaw, that complex event nominals, like verbs, have an argument structure. This entails the obligatory expression of the internal argument (in an *of*-phrase), whilst the expression of the external argument (in a possessor phrase) is optional. She draws attention to some further syntactic properties of complex event nominals, including the fact that they do not pluralize, and tolerate only a limited class of determiners, namely *the*, a possessor phrase, or (more marginally) zero. She (p. 58) also points out that complex event nominals may inherit the perfectivity of the base verb (the phenomenon noted by Fellbaum), as shown by their ability to combine with phrases of the kind *in an hour, for six weeks*.

Simple event nominals, in contrast, do not have an argument structure. Possessors and prepositional phrases therefore do not satisfy argument positions, they have the status of optional complements or modifiers. Simple event nominals may have either mass or count status (and, if count, may pluralize), and they take the full range of determiners appropriate to their mass/count status.

Grimshaw points out that the distinction between the two kinds of nominals tends to be obscured by the fact that many derived nouns are regularly ambiguous between a complex event and a simple event reading. Furthermore, complex event and simple event nominals may well evoke the very same conceptual scene, involving the same kinds of participants. A vague appeal to the 'meanings' of the nominals is therefore not a good basis for drawing the distinction. The distinction, rather, is essentially a grammatical one. In the one case, the participants in a scene function as arguments of the head noun, in the other case they have the status of (optional) complements or of even more peripheral modifiers.

Unambiguous examples of complex event nominals are *ing*-nominalizations.[12] In (81a), the *of*-complement is essential, whilst the possessor is optional. If present, however, the possessor can only denote the Agent (i.e. external argument).[13] Pluralization is impossible, as is the use of any determiner other than *the* or a possessor phrase.

(81)   *a.*   {The/The doctor's} examining of the patient took a long time.
       b.   *The doctor's examining took a long time.

---

[12] A few *ing*-nominalizations have acquired idiosyncratic status as simple event nominals. Thus, *killing*, besides its more verbal use (*the killing of the hostages*), can denote an act of killing (*There were hundreds of killings*). For more on *ing*-nominalizations, see Ch. 10.

[13] Actually, this is not quite true. *Yesterday's examining of the patient* seems acceptable to me. Grimshaw (1990: 57), on the other hand, asserts that temporal possessors can never be associated with an element in argument structure, and so are disallowed as possessors to complex event nominals. Accordingly, she (p. 84) asterisks what to me sounds a perfectly acceptable expression: **Yesterday's defeat of the Europeans*. Even the insertion of the adjective *constant*—diagnostic, for Grimshaw, of a complex event reading—is, to my ears, perfectly compatible with the temporal possessor: *Yesterday's constant examining of the patient*.

 c. *His examinings of the patient took a long time.

 d. *{An/That} examining of the patient took a long time.

Unambiguous examples of simple event nominals are result nominals. These denote the product of a process, or some entity associated with the process. Often, result nominals have idiosyncratic semantic properties, not fully predictable from the base verb. Thus, in (82), *examination* denotes a written set of tasks involved in the examining process. The relevant grammatical facts are that *examination*, in its result sense, is a count noun, it readily pluralizes, an *of*-phrase tends to be unacceptable, and the noun takes the full range of determiners. In addition, the possessor, if present, is open to a range of semantic interpretations. In (82*a*), for example, John could be the examiner or the examinee (in these cases *John* would count as a complement), or even the invigilator who is handing out the examination papers (in this case it would, presumably, be a modifier).

(82)   *a*. {The/John's} examination is eight pages long.

 b. *John's examination of medieval history is eight pages long.

 c. His examinations are eight pages long.

 d. {an/that/some} examination that is eight pages long.

Grimshaw makes the more controversial claim that, even when a derived nominal like *examination* clearly has a process, rather than a result interpretation, the distinction between complex event and simple event nominal still holds. Even though both sentences in (83) could denote exactly the same state of affairs, Grimshaw contends that the sentences differ fundamentally in this respect.

(83)   *a*. The doctor's examination of the patient took a long time.
        [complex event nominal]

 b. The doctor's examination took a long time.
        [simple event nominal]

Examination in (83*a*) is a complex event nominal, whose internal argument receives obligatory expression in the *of*-phrase, while (83*b*) contains a simple event nominal. Diagnostics of the distinction, in addition to the possibility of pluralizing *examination* in (83*b*), include the use of adjectives like *constant*, *frequent*, and *intentional*. These, she claims, are only appropriate for complex event nominals.

(84)   *a*. The constant examination of the patient took a long time.

 b. *The constant examination took a long time.

More surprisingly, perhaps, Grimshaw claims that 'passive nominals' always have a simple event reading, never a complex event reading. Thus, the expressions in (85), like those in (83), also differ with respect to the complex event vs. simple event reading.

(85)   *a*. The examination of the patient took a long time.
        [complex event nominal]

      b. The patient's examination took a long time.
      [simple event nominal]

Grimshaw's position is thus comparable with that of Safir (1987)—see example (50*b*)—for whom the possessor in (85*b*) would be assigned a free thematic interpretation. For Grimshaw (1990: 86), *Reagan's defeat* is not really a passive nominalization at all, or even a nominalization with a preposed theme, it merely denotes a defeat with which Reagan was associated.

As with Safir's account, we again need to examine the evidence for the distinction which Grimshaw draws between simple and complex event nominals, and for the associated distinction between complements, modifiers, and adjuncts. She observes (p. 83), quite correctly, that unambiguous complex event nominals, viz. *ing*-nominalizations, never have passive readings: **the tree's felling*, **the city's destroying*. (This fact, however, could be due to some special properties of *ing*-nominalizations, not shared with derived nouns.) Otherwise, Grimshaw's arguments, and the data on which they are based, are rather questionable. She claims (p. 82) that *murder*, which readily permits a passive interpretation, is an unambiguous simple event nominal that cannot be used as a complex event nominal. For Grimshaw, therefore, *the murder of Julius Caesar* would be ungrammatical![14] She also maintains that passive nominalizations cannot contain adjectives that are diagnostic of complex event readings, such as *constant* and *frequent*. I do not feel, however, that *his constant nomination to that post* would merit an ungrammaticality asterisk. Likewise, she states that passive nominalizations cannot occur with aspectual modifiers like *in three days*, which are supposed to be consistent only with complex event readings. Again, *the city's destruction in only three days* strikes me as unexceptional. She also claims that passive nominalizations with a *by*-phrase—notwithstanding the frequently cited *the city's destruction by the enemy*—are 'essentially ungrammatical' (p. 87). The reason is that simple event nominals, not having an argument structure, do not contain in their semantic structure the notion of an Agent expressible in a *by*-phrase. She (pp. 87–8) therefore queries the grammaticality of the expressions in (86).

(86)   *a*. America's defeat by the Soviet Union.
      b. it's [*sic*] removal by Mary.
      c. the book's publication by the MIT Press.

For Grimshaw, therefore, so-called 'passive nominalizations', as in (85*b*) and (86), are no such thing. The derived noun denotes a simple event, without an argument structure. The possessor therefore does not denote an argument, it is a modifier or complement 'participating in its usual relationship to the head' (p. 88).

Grimshaw has little to say about the Affectedness Constraint, beyond the

---

[14] Grimshaw's example (1990: 82) is **{The/John's} murder of Jack* (Grimshaw's asterisk).

observation that the constraint is 'mysterious' (p. 93). Given her theoretical assumptions, affectedness cannot have to do with argument structure (passive nominals do not have an argument structure). Neither can affectedness be a property of modifiers, since possessor modifiers (as in *John's dog*) are hardly subject to affectedness. Affectedness therefore can only be a matter of lexical conceptual structure, which must 'distinguish affected participants from unaffected in such a way that unaffected lcs [= lexical conceptual structure: JRT] arguments are not subject to the complement interpretation' (p. 94). On this aspect of lexical conceptual structure, however, she has no proposals to make.

In Chapter 9 I suggest that the distinction that Grimshaw draws between arguments, complements, and modifiers can be given a natural conceptual interpretation, having to do with a gradience of 'intrinsicness' of a participant in the designated state of affairs. The demise of a clear-cut distinction between complement and argument puts into question the basis of Grimshaw's equally clear-cut distinction between simple event nominals and complex event nominals, as well as her distinction between a specifically grammatical level of lexical argument structure, and a semantic level of lexical conceptual structure. This is not to say, of course, that all nominalizations come tarred with the same brush. It will be necessary to make syntactic/semantic distinctions amongst nominalizations. These distinctions, however, will need to be based in a more general theory of nominalization.

I should emphasize that my misgivings about Grimshaw's analysis of (85), with its distinction between a complex event and a simple event nominal, should not be taken to imply that I regard pairs of expressions such as *the examination of the patient* and *the patient's examination* as perfectly synonymous. They are not. I will, however, attempt to derive the difference between the expressions from a more general account of the possessive construction on the one hand, and of *of*-complements on the other.

To get some idea of what an alternative account of the distinction between simple event and complex event nominals might look like, we can turn to Lebeaux (1986).[15] Lebeaux addresses the question of what exactly, in a nominalization, gets nominalized. He identifies two main possibilities: that nominalization may apply to V, i.e. to the verb alone, or to V', i.e. to the verb and its internal argument. In the former case, we get the noun *destruction*, which may be used without mention of Agent or Patient, or indeed of any other participant. Nominalization of V' gives *destruction of the city*, in which the internal argument receives obligatory expression. Subsequently, the Agent (external argument) may be attached in a possessor phrase, to give *the enemy's destruction of the city*.

Crucially, therefore, nominalization of V' requires the satisfaction of the thematic relation (usually that of Theme) that is satisfied at the V' level. V'-nominalizations would seem to correspond to Grimshaw's complex event

---

[15] I abstract away from the morphological issues that Lebeaux deals with in his paper.

nominals. They have a process interpretation, they are more 'verbal' in character than V-nominalizations, and the complement is obligatory. (Lebeaux is not clear on whether an objective possessive, like *the city's destruction*, would also count as a V'-nominalization.) Nominalization of a V, in contrast, takes place without satisfaction of any thematic relation. V-nominalizations would seem to correspond to Grimshaw's simple event nominals. Released from their thematic relations, V-nominalizations frequently undergo 'semantic drift' (p. 233), that is, they may take on a range of more or less unpredictable, idiosyncratic values. Thus, *destruction* can take on a result interpretation.

(87)   The destruction extended over several blocks.

Lebeaux notes that certain kinds of clauses, which typically attach at a certain V level, only attach to the corresponding nominalization. Thus, purpose clauses are claimed to attach at the V'-level, not at the V-level. Purpose clauses are therefore only acceptable with a V'-nominalization.

(88)   *a.* the destruction of the city to ensure its powerlessness.
         b. *the destruction to ensure the city's powerlessness.

Likewise, he points out that *while-* and *although*-clauses presuppose, not only nominalization of V', but also the attachment of the external argument.

(89)   *a.* the doctor's examination of the patient while looking out of the window.
         b. ?*the doctor's examination while looking out of the window.
         c. *the examination while looking out of the window.
(90)   *a.* the doctor's examination of the patient although he was busy.
         b. *the professor's examination although the students were reluctant.

A further issue is the somewhat unexpected behaviour of nouns like *criticism* and *proof*. Whereas *the city's destruction* can only have an objective reading, *John*, in *John's criticism*, can be interpreted either as the criticized or the criticizer. To handle cases like these, Lebeaux suggests that some derived nouns have the idiosyncratic property of always being V-nominalizations. These nouns pattern like *picture* and *book*, rather than like *destruction*. Evidence for this analysis comes from that fact that their notional subjects (i.e. possessors) may appear predicatively, as well as in postnominal possessives.

(91)   *a.* The picture of Mary was Bill's.
         b. The proof of the theorem was ours.
         c. ?That criticism of Mary was John's.
         d. *The destruction of the city was the enemy's.
(92)   *a.* that picture of Mary of Bill's.
         b. that proof of the theorem of ours.
         c. ?that criticism of Mary of John's.
         d. *the destruction of the city of John's.

Lebeaux's suggestion that the semantic properties of a derived noun may reflect differences in the scope of the nominalization process is an important insight, broadly consistent with the cognitive grammar account of nominalization that I shall adopt in Chapters 9 and 10. We shall find, however, that a much more differentiated account will be necessary. We shall also need to bring *-ing* nominalizations into the picture, and distinguish these from nominalizations headed by derived nouns.

To conclude this chapter I return, again, to the Affectedness Constraint. We saw that Grimshaw (1990) had little to say about this. Doron and Rappaport Hovav (1991; henceforth D&R), however, develop a theoretical construct employed by Grimshaw, and show how this construct could go some way towards solving the mystery of affectedness. The construct is that of 'event structure' (Grimshaw 1990: 26–7; Pustejovsky 1991*b*). Some verbs, such as *know, pursue*, or *work*, denote an internally homogeneous state, or activity. These we may describe as imperfective verbs. Perfective verbs, on the other hand, typically denote internally complex situations, which may be broken down into two simpler sub-events. Many verbs, for example, denote an activity, which causes, or leads up to, a state. *X constructs Y* involves an activity on the part of X, which results in Y being in existence as a completed whole; *X destroys Y* involves an activity on the part of X, which results in Y ceasing to be an integrated whole. Likewise, *X transfers Y to Z* implies that X performs a certain kind of activity with respect to Y, which results in Y being at Z.

D&R propose to capture the notion of an affected argument as follows: For a verb V with internal argument Y and external argument X, Y is affected if the event structure of V contains a sub-event of which Y is an argument, but of which X is not an argument. By this definition, the internal arguments of *know* and *pursue* are unaffected, since these verbs denote homogeneous situations, which cannot be broken down into sub-events. In contrast, the internal arguments of *construct* and *transfer* are affected, in that these verbs implicate a sub-event involving the internal argument but not the external argument. D&R observe that *transfer* contrasts with the apparently rather similar verb *bring*. *X brings Y to Z* can be broken down into one sub-event in which X performs some activity with respect to Y, and the resultant state, in which X is with Y at Z. The second sub-event involves both Y and X. Consequently, the internal argument of *bring* must be analysed as unaffected.

D&R go on to argue that their characterization of affectedness actually predicts the syntactic consequences of affectedness, with respect to both possessive nominalizations and the middle construction. Both constructions, they claim, involve the same process of 'externalization' of an internal argument, that is to say, the internal argument appears in the syntactic slot normally reserved for the external argument, the grammatical subject in the case of middles, and the prenominal possessor in the case of possessives. Externalization of the internal argument requires that the original external argument be eliminated. The elimination of the original external argument will only be possible in case the event structure of the original predicate contains a sub-event in which the original external argument plays no role. Consequently, it is only affected internal arguments that can appear in passive nominalizations and in middles.[16]

One consequence of this analysis is that externalization results in the creation of lexical polysemy. The event structure of a middle verb is different from the event structure of its transitive counterpart. We would therefore need to say that a verb such as *transfer* is polysemous between its transitive use (*I transferred the money*) and its use in the middle construction (*The money won't transfer easily*). Whatever the merits of the lexicalist analysis of middles, it is far from clear that we should want to recognize two polysemes of the noun *transfer*, the one exemplified in *his transfer of the money to my account*, the other exemplified in *the money's transfer to my account*.

We may also raise, once again, the question of the supposed correlation between objective possessives and middles, more specifically, between affectedness as it applies to possessives, and the role of affectedness in the middle construction. It is, in fact, with respect to middles that D&R's account is particularly open to question. On the one hand, their analysis correctly predicts the possibility of *transfer* appearing as a middle, and the impossibility of *bring* as a middle (*The money won't transfer easily* vs. **The money won't bring easily*). But on their account of affectedness, and its role in the middle construction, *put* ought to form a good middle. The event structure of *X puts Y on Z* contains, as one sub-event, the state *Y is on Z*; this sub-event does not involve X. Yet **These books won't put on the shelf* is very bad. Consider also the verb *interview*. It seems scarcely possible to analyse *X interviews Y* in terms of a sequence of sub-events, one of which involves Y but not X. Yet *interview* forms a perfectly good middle: *Bert doesn't interview very well*.

With respect to possessives, however, D&R's characterization of affectedness does seem to capture some essential properties of the notion. Their definition amounts to this. Given an event of the type denoted by verb V involving entities X and Y, Y is affected if the result of the event can be described solely in terms of Y, without any necessary reference to X. Merely by inspecting Y, we can verify whether an event of the appropriate type has or has not taken place. The result of X constructing Y is that Y is constructed; we can verify whether this sub-event took place merely by inspecting Y. But the result of the hikers avoiding the cliff cannot be stated by reference to the cliff only, nor does inspection of the cliff afford us any opportunity to find out whether it was avoided. Neither

---

[16] There is a certain convergence here with Giorgi and Longobardi's account of the Affectedness Constraint. For Giorgi and Longobardi, too, the possibility of an objective possessor required the 'elimination' of the external argument.

can we verify whether the student studied algebra, or whether Herbie loves Louise, by inspection of algebra, or, respectively, Louise.[17]

These kinds of considerations will be an important ingredient of the cognitive grammar account of possessive nominalizations that I shall develop in Chapter 9.

[17] D&R's approach also offers an insightful account of the different behaviour of *fear* and *fright*. *X fears Y* denotes a state, without structure at the sub-event level, whereas *X frightens Y* presumably involves a sub-event such that Y is frightened. Whence the possibility of the internal argument of *frighten* appearing as a possessor nominal (*Amy's fright*), whereas an objective possessive with *fear* is not possible (**the scarecrow's fear by Amy*).

7 Specificity and Definiteness of Prenominal Possessives

IN this chapter I address one important aspect of the semantics of prenominal possessives, namely their referential properties.

We saw in section 5.1 that in a prenominal possessive expression, the possessor phrase [NP POSS] can be regarded as a kind of determiner to the possessee noun. Determiners comprise such items as the articles (*the, a*), demonstratives (*this, that*), and quantifiers (stressed *some, many, most*). Determiners make a distinctive semantic contribution to the meaning of an NP. Whereas an N or N′ denotes a kind, or category of entity, the determiner establishes reference, that is, it picks out those members or those instances of the category as the entities being spoken about. Three kinds of reference can be distinguished: definite-specific, indefinite-specific, and non-specific. The question here is: If the possessor phrase is a kind of determiner, what kind of reference does it establish?

My purpose in this chapter is, first, to ascertain some of the facts concerning the referential properties of possessives. This is the topic of section 7.2. The evidence supports the view that prenominal possessives generally have specific reference, and are nearly always compatible with definite reference; nevertheless, there are no grounds for excluding in principle the possibility that prenominal possessives may have indefinite, non-specific reference. Definiteness and specificity cannot therefore be regarded as inherent properties of the construction.

Subsequently, in sections 7.3 and 7.4, I look at two attempts to derive the referential properties of possessives from general syntactic principles. Both accounts presuppose a conservative version of X-bar syntax, and both proceed on the assumption that possessives invariably have definite reference. Even leaving aside the factual inaccuracy of this assumption, the accounts turn out to be far from unproblematic. The failure of configurational accounts points to the need for an alternative approach, motivated by semantic and pragmatic considerations. And indeed, we shall find that the referential properties of possessives fall out rather naturally from the reference point account of the construction.

7.1 KINDS OF REFERENCE

Before broaching the main issues, it is necessary to clarify some matters relating to the notion of reference. I shall draw a broad distinction between three kinds of reference. These are differentiated according to whether the speaker has in mind a specific member (or specific members) of a category, and, if so, according to whether the speaker expects the hearer to be able to uniquely identify the specific entity(ies). These distinctions are diagrammed in (1).

(1)

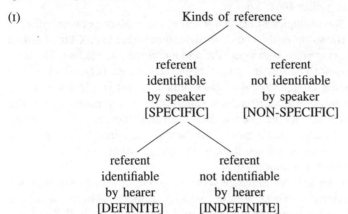

The sentences in (2) (after Dirven and Radden 1977: 218) exemplify NPs with definite, indefinite, and non-specific reference.

(2)   *a.* I bought that house after all. [Definite, Specific]
       b. I bought a nice house. [Specific, Indefinite]
       c. I wish I could find a nice house to buy. [Indefinite, Non-specific]

That house in (2*a*) presupposes that the hearer is able to uniquely identify the house that the speaker is talking about. If this presupposition is not met, the hearer can legitimately enquire after its identity, by asking, for instance, *Which house do you mean?* Observe that it is not strictly necessary that the hearer be able to identify the referent independently of an utterance of a definite NP. Identification may be guaranteed in virtue of information contained in the utterance itself. In the case of (2*a*) it is, namely, the function of the demonstrative *that* to direct the hearer's attention to just that referent that is intended. In (2*b*), on the other hand, there is no expectation that the hearer is able to identify which house was bought; the speaker merely conveys that a specific house was bought. In (2*c*), no specific house is being referred to at all. *A nice house* denotes any arbitrarily selected member of the category 'nice house'. There is no suggestion, even, that a member of this category might actually exist.

Given this last property of non-specifics, one might wonder whether non-specific reference really is a category of reference at all, in that non-specific NPs need not actually 'refer' to entities in the real or discourse world. Givón (1993: 224), for example, speaks of 'non-referring indefinites' for my category of non-specific indefinites. I maintain that non-specifics do have reference, in that they refer to arbitrary instances that may inhabit a 'mental space' distinct from the mental space established by current discourse.[1] In (2c), the 'nice house' exists in the world of the speaker's wishes, but may not correspond to any entity in the 'real world' in which the speaker formulates his wishes. There is therefore no inherent contradiction in speaking of non-specific NPs as instantiating a category of reference (Langacker 1991: 103–7).

We see from the examples in (2) that whereas the contrast between definites and indefinites shows up in the choice of determiner (*that* vs. *a*), the so-called indefinite article is open to both a specific and a non-specific reading. The non-specific reading typically arises in 'opaque' contexts; these are contexts introduced by what Fauconnier (1994: 16) calls 'space-builders', that is, predicates which set up a mental space distinct from, and subordinate to, the parent space. The distinction between specific and non-specific reference does, however, show up in the pronouns. *I want to buy it* means that there is some specific article which I want to buy. In *I want to buy one* there is no specific article that I want to buy, any arbitrarily selected instance will do.

Somewhat problematic for the three-way distinction in (1) are NPs with so-called generic reference. These are NPs which are used, typically in subject position, to make a statement about a category of entities as a whole. Generics, therefore, refer to the type, not to an instance, or instances, of the type. Since they denote entities in 'type space' rather than entities in the 'domain of instantiation',[2] distinctions pertaining to definiteness and specificity fail to apply to generics. Against this, we need to take cognizance of different grammatical strategies for effecting reference to the type.[3] One strategy involves the use of a singular definite: *The cat is a carnivore*. Here, we could say that *the cat* still denotes a definite individual (the expression therefore has definite reference, in the sense introduced), the individual, however, is taken to be representative of the type. Likewise, an indefinite singular (*A cat chases mice*) presents an arbitrarily selected instance as representative of the type. A third strategy is the use of a determiner-less NP—a singular in the case of mass nouns (*Water boils at 100°C*), a plural in the case of count nouns (*Pigs can't fly*). The singular mass noun denotes the mass *per se*, and the plural count noun denotes the total set of possible instantiations. The absence of an overt determiner in these cases again suggests that notions of definiteness and specificity do not strictly apply to generics. Certainly, from a purely formal point of view, the distribution of generics differs significantly from that of canonical definites (*the water, the pigs*). We shall also see that determiner-less generics, when they occur as possessor nominals, have some interesting consequences for the interpretation of possessives.

---

[1] For the concept of mental space, see Fauconnier (1994); also Langacker (1991: 97–8).

[2] The concept 'domain of instantiation' was introduced in section 4.4; see Langacker (1991: 61–4).

[3] For a discussion of some of the problems associated with generic reference and its linguisitic expression, see Lyons (1977: 193–7).

7.2 DEFINITENESS AND SPECIFICITY OF POSSESSIVES

We can introduce the question of the referential properties of possessives by considering some likely paraphrase relations. Intuitively, *the student's dictionary* is roughly equivalent to definite "the dictionary of the student", not to indefinite "a dictionary of the student", even less to "some dictionary (or other) of the student". More problematic are possessives with an indefinite possessor. Does *a student's dictionary* mean "the dictionary of a student", or "a dictionary of a student", and, if the latter, does "a dictionary of a student" imply specific or non-specific reference ("some dictionary or other")? Here, intuitions are far from clear, and for this reason it is useful to be able to turn to various kinds of tests of referential properties.

A test for specificity of reference is the pronoun test. An expression with specific reference may be taken up by the specific pronouns *it/them*, whilst an expression with non-specific reference may be taken up by non-specific *one/ some*. Consider the examples in (3).

(3) *a.* I was looking for a French dictionary, but I couldn't find {it/one}.
     b. I was looking for John's French dictionary, but I couldn't find {it/*one}.

A *French dictionary* could be non-specific (my search would be satisfied the moment I found *any* French dictionary), in which case the expression is taken up by non-specific *one*. Alternatively, *a French dictionary* may denote a specific dictionary (and my search would be satisfied only when I found this one particular dictionary), in which case the expression is taken up by specific *it*. The impossibility of *one* in (3b) shows that *John's French dictionary* can only have the specific reading.

The facts are less clear if the possessor is itself non-specific and/or indefinite.

(4) *a.* I wanted to buy a friend of mine's car, but I couldn't afford {it/*one}.
     b. I was looking for a student's dictionary, but I couldn't find {it/?one}.

The impossibility of *one* in (4a) suggests that *a friend of mine's car* is specific. But in (4b) *one* does seem marginally possible.

One reason for this could be that *a student's dictionary* is actually ambiguous between a prenominal possessive reading, with the structure [[$_{NP}$a student]'s [$_N$dictionary]], and a reading as a possessive compound, with the structure [a [$_N$student's dictionary]]. In the former case, the expression denotes the (a?) dictionary of a student, in the latter case it denotes an instance of a particular kind of dictionary, namely [student's dictionary].

The contrast between 'genuine' prenominal possessives and possessive compounds will be addressed in Chapter 11. One diagnostic test that we shall introduce for distinguishing the two constructions concerns the possibility of adjective insertion. *Second-hand* can modify *dictionary*, but not *student*. Inserting *second-hand* into the prenominal possessive gives us *a student's second-hand dictionary*, insertion into the compound gives us *a second-hand student's dictionary*. Both expressions are fully acceptable, suggesting that *a student's dictionary* is indeed ambiguous between a possessive and a compound reading. Applying now the pronoun test to these expressions, we get the following judgements.

(5)   *a.* I was looking for [a student]'s [second-hand dictionary], but I couldn't find {it/?one}.

     b. I was looking for a second-hand [student's dictionary], but I couldn't find {it/one}.

The compound reading is compatible with both specific and non-specific interpretations (5*b*). However, the prenominal possessive still seems to tolerate, if somewhat marginally, the non-specific reading "some second-hand dictionary (or other) of a student".

Langacker (1991: 168) makes a similar point with respect to the following example.

(6)   I want some teenager's car to enter in a demolition derby.

He comments: 'The speaker need not have any particular car in mind, nor any specific teenager—he may simply want a beat-up old jalopy to enter in the race, and he knows that the car of any teenager is liable to qualify.' The non-specific status of (6) is confirmed by the pronoun test.

(7)   We want some teenager's car to enter in a demolition derby, but up to now we weren't able to find one.

There is still the possibility that (7) has a non-specific reading in virtue of *some teenager's car* being a possessive compound, not a genuine prenominal possessive. However, adjective insertion confirms that the non-specific reading is perfectly compatible with the prenominal possessive. Note the acceptability of (8*a*), in which adjective insertion forces interpretation as a prenominal possessive.

(8)   *a.* We want [some teenager]'s [beat-up car] to enter in a demolition derby, but up to now we weren't able to find one.

     b. We want some beat-up [teenager's car] to enter in a demolition derby, but up to now we weren't able to find one.

This is not to say that *some teenager's beat-up car* is intrinsically non-specific. In a different context, it may refer to a specific car (although *some teenager* need not refer to a specific teenager).

(9)   Some teenager's beat-up car is occupying my parking bay. It was there last week as well.

The question whether possessives may tolerate an indefinite reading has been the subject of some controversy. Jackendoff (1968) had argued that a possessive with an indefinite possessor could itself be indefinite. He suggests, in other

words, that possessives are liable to 'inherit' the indefiniteness of their possessor. Woisetschlaeger (1983) took issue with Jackendoff, arguing that prenominal
possessives invariably have definite reference. Let us consider some of their
arguments.

As evidence for the indefinite reading, Jackendoff (1968) notes that prenominal
possessives may occur in environments which are inconsistent with definiteness.
He cites two such environments: predicative position (10*a*), and existential *there-*
sentences (10*b*).

(10) *a.* She is {a nice girl/*the nice girl/a farmer's daughter}.
      b. Once upon a time there was {a little girl/*the little girl/a farmer's
          daughter}.

In evaluating these examples we should note that Jackendoff uses 'indefinite'
to cover both specific and non-specific indefinites. Indefiniteness, in the sense
introduced earlier, does not entail non-specificity. It may well be the case that
the speaker of (10*b*) does not expect the hearer to be able to uniquely identify
the person denoted by *a farmer's daughter*; the function of an existential *there-*
sentence is, precisely, to introduce new entities into a discourse. These, almost
by definition, will be entities that the hearer is not already able to identify. The
indefiniteness (in this sense) of *a farmer's daughter* does not, however, mean
that the speaker himself may not have in mind a specific member of the appropriate
category.

Jackendoff's examples are problematic for other reasons. I spoke above of *a
farmer's daughter* denoting a 'member' of a 'category'. But which category? Is
a farmer's daughter a member of the category 'daughter', or a member of the
category 'farmer's daughter'? The point is, of course, that *a farmer's daughter*
is structurally (and therefore also semantically) ambiguous between a genuine
prenominal possessive, with the structure [a farmer]'s [daughter] and a compound
reading, a [farmer's daughter]. Again, we can disambiguate the two structures
by insertion of a modifying adjective such as *beautiful*, construed as an attribute
of the daughter, not of the farmer. Adjective insertion gives us the following.

(11) *a.* She is {a beautiful farmer's daughter/*a farmer's beautiful daughter}.
      b. Once upon a time there was {a beautiful farmer's daughter/*a farmer's
          beautiful daughter}.

This rather clear acceptability contrast suggests that in (10) we are dealing with
instances of possessive compounds, not with prenominal possessives; to this
extent, Jackendoff's examples shed no light at all on the issue under discussion.

A further problem with (10) is that it is not the case that the syntactic
environments in these sentences are always inconsistent with definiteness, where
definiteness is diagnosed as the possibility of occurrence of the definite article.
Jackendoff himself (p. 28) notes the acceptability of (12).

(12) She is the daughter of a farmer.

Concerning the possibility of definite NPs in existential *there*-sentences, Woisetschlaeger (1983: 142) cites the following examples.

(13)   *a.* There was the air of the successful businessman about him.
       b. Suddenly, there were the words of a madman tumbling out of his mouth.
       c. There was the strident rhetoric of the far left in all of their campaign literature.

If these contain definite NPs, then so too, according to Woisetschlaeger (pp. 144–5), does (14*a*). Note that the paraphrase in (14*b*) is likewise definite.

(14)   *a.* There was a young man's vigour in his step.
       b. There was the vigour of a young man in his step.

   With respect to the examples in (13), Woisetschlaeger observes that their definiteness

> does not seem to be due to some particular(s) having been previously identified so as to be capable of being existentially presupposed, but rather to some generic concept having narrow enough specifications to qualify for prior identification. (Woisetschlaeger 1983: 142)

Putting this slightly differently, we can say that the sentences in (13) invoke stereotypical situations, whose particulars, although newly introduced in the discourse, are nevertheless fairly predictable to anyone familiar with the stereotype. The particulars are therefore, in a certain sense, already identifiable by the hearer. This approach, I think, is also relevant to Jackendoff's example (10*b*), which raises stereotyped expectations about the characters likely to be introduced into a folk-tale. If these expectations are frustrated, an indefinite is much less acceptable.

(15)   ?Once upon a time there was a farmer's aunt.

   Woisetschlaeger brings further evidence for the obligatory definiteness of possessives. His method is to select environments which, he claims, are inconsistent with indefiniteness, and then to show that possessives are impossible in these environments. Actually, his examples (p. 148) are less than convincing. Amongst the environments which allegedly select for indefiniteness are the prenominal modifiers *unusual* and *different*.

(16)   *a.* {An/*The} unusual news report by a Greek team revealed the full extent to which political reality and political rhetoric had diverged.
       b. *A Greek team's unusual news report revealed the full extent to which political reality and political rhetoric had diverged.
(17)   *a.* {A/*The} different approach by a California commune yielded much better results.
       b. *A California commune's different approach yielded much better results.
       [acceptability judgements Woisetschlaeger's]

The starred sentences seem to me to be only marginally less acceptable than the unstarred versions. And indeed, consultation of the LOB (= Lancaster-Oslo-

Bergen) KWIK corpus of English shows the collocations *the unusual* and *the different* to be, if not especially frequent, then at least possible.[4] The evidence of (16) and (17) is, therefore, inconclusive.

While Woisetschlaeger fails to demonstrate that prenominal possessives must be definite, there could be grounds for claiming that possessives are always compatible with definiteness.

One environment which demands a definite NP is the partitive construction exemplified in (18)–(20).

(18)   three of   ⎰ the men
                    │ those men
                    ⎨ *some men
                    │ *ten men
                    ⎱ *many men

(19)   some of   ⎰ the cake
                  │ this cake
                  ⎨ *a cake
                  ⎱ *some cake (or other)

(20)   some of   ⎰ the money
                  │ this money
                  ⎨ *some money
                  ⎱ *money

The partitive construction may denote a subset of entities selected from a set (18), a portion of an entity selected from a whole (19), or a portion of a substance selected from a mass (20). The larger set of entities, the whole, and the mass, are denoted only by incontrovertibly definite NPs. Significant for our purpose is the fact that prenominal possessives (even those with an indefinite possessor) may also occur in these environments.

(21)   three of   ⎰ John's friends
                    ⎨ a person's friends
                    ⎱ someone's friends

(22)   some of   ⎰ John's cake
                  ⎨ a person's cake
                  ⎱ someone's cake

(23)   some of   ⎰ John's money
                  ⎨ a person's money
                  ⎱ someone's money

The following examples make the same point.

(24)   *a.* A large part of a family's monthly income goes on food and rent.
          (cf. *a large part of a monthly income)

---

[4] The corpus records 6 instances of the collocation *the unusual*, and 26 instances of *the different*.

    b. That's the least important of a person's worries.
       (cf. *the least important of some worries)
    c. Three of a cat's lives.
       (cf. *three of some lives)
    d. Much of an academic's working time is spent on administration.
       (cf. *much of working time)

Consider next certain nominals which demand a definite determiner, proto-typically *the*. Amongst these are expressions headed by a subset of descriptive adjectives: *the rich, the poor, the underprivileged, the Welsh, the Irish.* These are construed as plural, and are understood in a generic sense. The definite article is virtually obligatory; while *these rich, those underprivileged* are perhaps marginally acceptable, **some rich, *three poor, *an underprivileged* are out. Significantly, a possessor phrase (even if indefinite) can replace the definite article.

(25)   Britain's poor, America's Irish, the country's rich, a city's unemployed, a nation's underprivileged

Similar facts hold for NPs headed by certain collective nouns, especially collective nouns which denote a social or professional group: *the aristocracy, the proletariat, the clergy, the press, the police.* These nominals are construed (usually) as plural, they denote the social or professional group as a whole, and determiners other than the definite article are virtually impossible: **some aristocracy* (in the sense "some members of the aristocracy"), **two proletariat* (in the sense "two members of the proletariat"), **two clergy, *this/these press, *a police.* Again, we find that the definite article may be replaced by a possessor phrase, even if indefinite.

(26)   a country's aristocracy, a nation's press, a city's police

It is time to take stock. We have seen that there are good reasons for supposing that prenominal possessives are always compatible with definiteness. However, *pace* Woisetschlaeger, there can be no grounds for asserting that possessives invariably are definite. On the other hand, the possibility of an indefinite or non-specific reading does appear to be dependent on the indefinite or non-specific reading of the possessor nominal.

Let us assume a gradience of definiteness, with indefinite specifics standing between definites on the one hand, and non-specifics on the other. The above discussion suggests the following generalization.

(27)   The possessee may not be lower on the scale of definiteness than the possessor.

The various possibilities are shown in Table 7.1.

The student's dictionary can only have definite reference; *a student's dictionary* (with specific reference of *a student*) can have either definite or indefinite specific reference; while *some teenager's car* (with non-specific *some teenager*) can be definite, specific, or non-specific.

TABLE 7.1. Referential properties of possessors and possessees

possessor	possessee
definite, specific	definite, specific
indefinite, specific	indefinite, specific
non-specific	non-specific

Whilst the generalization in (27) is, I think, consistent with the linguistic data, there is the question of its cognitive motivation. Why *should* possessives have these referential properties? Why, to take our earlier example, does *the student's dictionary* not mean "some dictionary (or other) of the student"?

The reference point analysis provides a plausible answer. On this analysis, a speaker refers to a target entity T by first mentioning a reference point entity R. This summary statement leads one to expect that the intended target will normally be high on the definiteness scale; after all, the very point of the construction is to facilitate identification. But to derive the full details of (27) we need to assume that a speaker, in using the construction, will strive to maximize its efficiency, in accordance with (28).

(28)   Select a reference point which will most effectively guarantee identification of the target.

An effective reference point is one which will delimit the choice of possible targets. In the optimal case, for a given reference point, there will only be one possible target; the reference point is such that there is a *unique relation* between it and the intended target. Take the expression *a man's life*. Since a man has only one life, the expression will uniquely identify the target, given the reference point. *A man's life* is therefore definite. A student, however, is likely to have several books. Still, a speaker might find it useful to characterize 'a book' as one which can be conceptualized from the reference point of 'a student'. Hence, *a student's book* could have indefinite reference. Observe that a further pragmatic principle is involved here.

(29)   Only invoke a reference point if there is good reason to do so.

The 'good reason' is, precisely, the desire to facilitate conceptualization of the intended target. It would go against the very *raison d'être* of the construction if the intended target were lower on the definiteness scale than the invoked reference point.

The notion of mental space is important here, too. A non-specific entity in a subordinate mental space may well facilitate reference to a target entity, also in this subordinate mental space. Such, in fact, seems the most reasonable account of *some teenager's car* in (6). Both the 'teenager' and the 'teenager's car' exist in the subordinate mental space of the speaker's wants, and need not correspond to any specific entities in the world in which the speaker formulates his wants.

It should also be pointed out that the full range of possibilities envisaged by (27) may not always be available for a given expression. *Some teenager's car* can readily be interpreted as non-specific, whereas *a student's dictionary*, and even more, *a friend of mine's car*, resist the non-specific reading. Givón (1993: 227) mentions that encyclopedic knowledge may 'tip the scales' towards a specific or non-specific reading of an indefinite. *A house*, in *She wanted to sell a house*, is likely to be specific, given the presupposition that a person who wants to sell a house probably already owns a house (and, moreover, probably owns just one). But in *She wanted to buy a house*, *a house* is likely to be non-specific, since a potential house-buyer is likely to consider several houses before deciding on a specific house. Pragmatic knowledge, rather than any syntactic facts, also seems to be involved in our earlier examples. Since the number of friends that a person has is likely to be quite small, *a friend of mine* would tend to evoke a specific individual; this, in combination with the knowledge that a person usually has at most one car, favours a specific reading of *a friend of mine's car*. On the other hand, there are countless teenagers in the world, and there is no reason why any one of these should be in the mind of the speaker uttering (6). *Some teenager* is thus likely to have non-specific reference, making possible the non-specific reading of *some teenager's car*.

7.2.1 *Generic possessors*

There is one kind of possessive for which the generalization in (27) does not hold, and which therefore demands some special comments. Consider the expressions in (30).

(30)   students' essays, taxpayers' money, women's rights, men's shoes, people's homes, children's schooling

The possessor is a plural nominal with generic reference, and the expressions inherit the generic reference. If *students*, in (31a), denotes the category of students (within a certain discourse context), so *students' essays* denotes the category of students' essays (again, within a discourse context).

(31)   *a.* [Students] should limit their essays to 10 type-written pages.
       b. [Students' essays] should not exceed 10 type-written pages.

On the reference point analysis, this property should not be too surprising. The generic possessor picks out a type in the domain of type space. Within this domain, the type is invoked in order to facilitate identification of a further type. What makes these expressions unusual, is that they tolerate *only* a generic interpretation.

Thus, expressions with generic possessors may not be used in the partitive construction, suggesting that they are incompatible with definiteness.

(32) *a.* *Some of [taxpayers' money] was used to bribe the contractors.

     b. *I spent the afternoon marking three of [students' essays].

     c. *Many of [men's shoes] are imported.

If we consider how these sentences could be rendered grammatical, we discover that *taxpayers' money*, *students' essays*, and *men's shoes* have much the same distributional possibilities as their head nouns.

(33) *a.* Some (of the) {money/taxpayers' money} was used to bribe the contractors.

     b. I spent the afternoon marking three (of the) {essays/students' essays}.

     c. Many (of the) {shoes/men's shoes} on sale are imported.

In fact, *taxpayers' money*, *students' essays*, *men's shoes* appear to have the status of Ns, rather than NPs. A rough paraphrase of *taxpayers' money* is not the definite NP "the money paid by taxpayers", or even the indefinite "some money paid by taxpayers", but rather the N (or N′) "money paid by taxpayers".

In Chapter 11 I argue that generic possessives as in (30) testify to a blurring of the distinction between the prenominal possessive and the possessive compound constructions, exhibiting some properties of both, but being good examples of neither. To the extent that they can be taken to be genuine prenominal possessives, they are certainly counterexamples to the claim that possessives are *always* compatible with definiteness. On the other hand, we already mentioned the problematic status of generic reference, so it should not be too surprising if possessives with generic possessors should exhibit some unusual properties.

The viability of any account of linguistic data will, to some extent, be contingent upon the availability, and the plausibility, of alternative accounts. I argue here for a cognitive grammar account of the referential properties of possessives. There are, to my knowledge, two proposals which attempt to derive these properties from purely syntactic, configurational aspects. Both proposals assume that possessives invariably have definite reference. Even though this assumption is factually incorrect, we may take it as established that possessives (with the exception of the generics just discussed) are always compatible with definite reference, and generally do in fact have definite reference. If these alternative, syntax-based accounts should turn out to be conceptually flawed, this will indirectly support, if not the account I present here, then at least the need for a non-configurational, semantics-based account.

I discuss these proposals in the next two sections, beginning with the more complex of the two, Woisetschlaeger (1983).

7.3 WOISETSCHLAEGER (1983)

Woisetschlaeger (1983) claims that prenominal possessives, irrespective of the referential properties of the possessor, invariably have definite reference. He explains this property by the following, rather convoluted argument.

In a possessive expression, the possessor phrase [NP POSS] occupies the position otherwise occupied by a determiner. Determiners constitute a closed class. Closed classes frequently permit one of their members to be zero. In such cases, zero receives an unmarked interpretation *vis-à-vis* the other member(s) of the class. The unmarked value within the determiner system is [+Definite]. The absence of a closed-class determiner in a possessive thus causes the expression to be interpreted in accordance with the unmarked value, that is, as [+Definite].

Woisetschlaeger's major premiss concerns the value assigned to the unmarked member of a class. He envisages a situation in which the various members of a closed paradigmatic class fail to 'exhaust' the semantic domain in question (p. 150). This situation is then 'resolved by a zero element', such that '[t]he meaning contributed by the zero element . . . will be that set of semantic values that lie within the domain but which are not the translation of any overt formative'. He (p. 151) illustrates the validity of this principle on the examples of tense and epistemic modality. Expressions with an overt epistemic modal fail to be marked for tense. *There must have been a conspiracy behind that coup* is interpreted with respect to the unmarked value of the tense system, namely 'present'; the sentence conveys an inference valid at the moment of speaking. Conversely, an expression that is marked for tense fails to be marked for epistemic modality. *Bill was tall* is interpreted with respect to the unmarked value of the modality system, that is, as 'factual'.

Even granting all this, Woisetschlaeger's account of possessives fails to convince. Consider, first, his claim that the unmarked term in the determiner system, the one associated with the absence of an overt determiner, is [+Definite]. There are, in English, two kinds of NPs which lack a determiner. First, there are proper names. *John* is obviously definite, as required. The second category comprises NPs with generic reference: *Water boils at 100°C*; *Pigs can't fly*. In defending the thesis that generics have definite reference, Woisetschlaeger (p. 153) refers to Milsark (1974), who draws a broad, two-way distinction between quantifying determiners and cardinality determiners. Quantifying determiners (*the, all, most*, stressed *some*, etc.) presuppose the existence of a class of entities, and designate a subset of the existentially presupposed class. Cardinality determiners (unstressed *some, one* and *a, several*, the numerals, etc.) merely indicate the size of a set, with no existential presuppositions. Since generics are not interpreted in terms of cardinality, and assuming the validity of Milsark's binary contrast, generics 'must somehow fit in with . . . quantification' (p. 153), presumably on the grounds that the set of entities designated by a generic NP is equal to the set of presupposed entities. Woisetschlaeger also brings in the universal quantifier $\forall$. He claims that $\forall$ is 'the only semantic category with which [the zero determiner] is unambiguously associated' (p. 152); conversely, while '$\forall$ is not in all cases realized by the overt determiner *the*, $\forall$ is nonetheless the only semantic category that is unequivocally realized by *the*' (p. 153). The conclusion is that 'if $\forall$ symbolizes a coherent category in terms of definiteness at all, it must be the category [+Definite]' (p. 153). This, then, is the semantic category 'unambiguously' (!) associated with the absence of a determiner.

A first observation on this account is that Woisetschlaeger himself seems not to be too convinced of it! Note the various hedges ('somehow', 'if . . . at all'). He also states, in his footnote 8, that his 'provisional' (p. 152) answer to the question whether the determiner system is associated with an unmarked value, is based on an account of the semantics of determiners which 'seem[s] to me to be ultimately not quite on the right track'. Be that as it may, Woisetschlaeger is proposing, essentially, that definites with *the*, generics, and prenominal possessives form a coherent semantic category, unified by, variously, [+Definite], true quantification (as opposed to cardinality), and the universal quantifier ∀. Whatever the (tenuous) semantic commonality between the categories of *the*-definites, generics, and prenominal possessives, there can be little doubt about their very different syntactic distributions. As we have seen, *the*-definites and generics are distributed very differently, and whilst most possessives pattern like definites, some (those with generic possessors) pattern like generics.

There is another crucial issue. Woisetschlaeger presents his conclusion as a matter of necessity, not as a description of contingent facts, facts 'which could, in principle, have been otherwise' (p. 150). He claims that the association of [+Definite] with the absence of a determiner follows from 'the general theory of grammatical categories'. Could the facts have been otherwise? Woisetschlaeger's argument is intended to show 'that they could not' (p. 150). Yet a cursory glance at some other languages shows that the absence of a determiner need not be associated with definiteness. In Hungarian, determiner-less nominals are indefinite: *ház* "a house"; while definiteness must be phonologically marked: *az ház* "the house". (In Turkish, though, it is the other way round: *ev* "the house", *bir ev* "a/ one house".)

A second stage in Woisetschlaeger's argument rests on the view that [NP POSS] is not a proper determiner. This is why possessives get interpreted as if they lacked an overt determiner, namely as [+Definite]. To the extent that we regard determiners as a closed class, comprising a small, finite number of lexical items (*the*, *a*, *some*, etc.), this claim might go through. *John's* is not a member of a closed class.

Woisetschlaeger's position has, however, been overtaken by subsequent developments within X-bar theory. The theory requires that specifier position be filled by a phrasal category, not by items selected from a lexical category. If the specifier position is occupied by a phrasal constituent, no special significance attaches to whether the position is occupied by an [NP POSS] constituent, or by a phrase headed by one of the lexical determiners. And in more recent elaborations of the theory, the possessive morpheme itself is accepted as a fully paid-up member of the determiner category. There is therefore no basis for claiming that the presence of an [NP POSS] constituent signals the absence of an overt determiner.

We conclude that Woisetschlaeger conspicuously failed in his attempt to derive the definiteness of prenominal possessives from general principles of syntactic organization.

7.4 LYONS (1985, 1986A)

Christopher Lyons (1985, 1986a) makes a more radical proposal for deriving the definiteness of prenominal possessives. He claims that an NP with a filled specifier always has definite reference. That some items traditionally regarded as determiners (such as the indefinite article, as well as unstressed *some* and the numerals) do not impose definite reference is due to the fact that these items do not appear in specifier position, but in modifier position. Consequently, a definite NP like *the mad dog* has the structure in (34), with the definite determiner in specifier position, whereas an indefinite NP like *a mad dog* has the structure in (35), where the indefinite article is sister to N'.

(34)

(35)

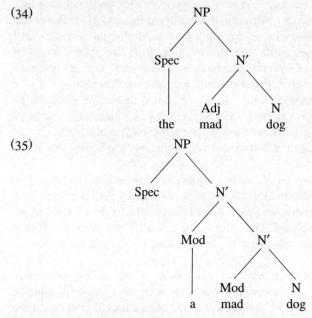

Given these assumptions, the definiteness of a possessive follows from the fact that possessors occur in specifier position.

Some support for this analysis comes from facts of word order. Observe, first of all, that the class of 'true' determiners—those that occupy specifier position and which therefore confer definiteness—corresponds by and large with Milsark's class of quantifying determiners, whereas the class of indefinite determiners—those that occupy modifier position and which do not confer definiteness—

corresponds to Milsark's cardinality determiners. In English, quantifying determiners precede cardinality determiners: *the three boys*, not **three the boys*. On Lyons's assumptions, this is just what one should expect in a specifier-first language like English. We also have an explanation at hand for some co-occurrence restrictions with possessor nominals. As we saw in section 5.1, possessors may be followed by a restricted range of cardinality determiners, as in *my one (and only) friend*, and *his (each and) every move*, but not by definite determiners: **my this friend*. It needs to be noted, however, that a considerable degree of idiomaticity appears to be involved here, also. We have *my every wish* but not **my each wish*, *my three friends* but not **my several friends*. And while *my one friend* is perfectly acceptable, **my a friend* and **my some friends* are completely out.

Lyons (1985) musters considerable cross-linguistic evidence for his hypothesis. In some languages, he claims, the 'parameter' assigning a possessor nominal to the specifier vs. modifier position is set differently than in English. Consider, first, the case of Italian (Lyons 1985: 100). A prenominal possessive adjective in Italian needs to be preceded by an article or demonstrative,[5] whereby it is the article or demonstrative that confers (in)definiteness on the containing NP: *il mio amico* "my friend" (definite), *questo mio amico* "this friend of mine" (definite), *un mio amico* "a friend of mine" (indefinite). There could be good reasons, therefore, for supposing that possessive adjectives in Italian are in modifier position, and so, by Lyons's hypothesis, do not confer definiteness.[6] (Still, the question arises, if *il mio amico* is definite by virtue of the article in specifier position, why should the indefinite article be necessary at all for the indefinite reading? Lyons's thesis would seem to entail that **mio amico* ought to be acceptable on an indefinite reading.)

Special problems arise in connection with Italian kinship terms. We have *mio padre* "my father", *mia sorella* "my sister", *sua cugina* "his/her cousin", not **il mio padre*, **la mia sorella*, **la sua cugina*. These are definite, and so, by Lyons's hypothesis, we must assume that kinship terms idiosyncratically require the possessive adjective to be in specifier position, as in English, not modifier position, as otherwise in Italian.[7] With third person plural *loro*, however, the definite article is obligatory: *il loro padre* "their father", *la loro sorella*, *la loro cugina*. Presumably, then, *loro* is a well-behaved possessive adjective, and always

---

[5] Non-referential uses of possessives do not, however, require the determiner: *Li consideriamo nostri amici* "We consider them our friends", *L'hai accettata come tua collega?* "Have you accepted her as your colleague?" (Lepschy and Lepschy 1977: 116). Being non-referential, these examples presumably do not upset Lyons's hypothesis.

[6] The modifier status of the possessive adjective is also confirmed by the possibility of adverbial modification: *una cosa molto sua* "a very his thing", i.e. "something typical of him" (Maiden 1995: 113).

[7] Giorgi and Longobardi (1991: 241) point out that in very literary registers it is possible for a third-person possessor to occur in a prenominal *di*-phrase: *?Il di lei fratello* "the of her brother", i.e. "her brother"; *La di lui madre* "the of him mother", i.e. "his mother". Here, definiteness has to be assigned by the definite article.

occupies modifier position. But also in the indefinite *una mia sorella* "a sister of mine", the possessive must be assumed to be back in its 'normal' position for Italian, i.e. in modifier position. And when kinship terms are modified by an adjective, or even by a suffix, the definite article again becomes obligatory: *la sua cugina preferita* "his/her favourite cousin", *la mia sorellina* "my little sister". Here, we would have to say that the modifier forces the possessive out of specifier position and back into its modifier position.

Also complicating the picture somewhat are expressions like *casa mia*, in which the possessive adjective is in postnominal position. In *Fuori da casa mia!* "(Get) out of my house!", *casa mia* is definite. By Lyons's thesis, *mia* must be in specifier position. We have to assume that, occasionally, Italian permits the specifier to NP to occur in NP-final position.

Another language discussed by Lyons (1985: 100–2; 1986a: 6) is Spanish. Spanish, in contrast to Italian, has two series of possessive adjectives. One series appears prenominally: *mi libro* "my book". Here, it is claimed, the possessive adjective occupies specifier position, and, as in English, confers definiteness. The other series appears postnominally, in modifier position: *un/el libro mio*. Here, the possessive adjective does not confer definiteness; definiteness can only be induced by the preceding definite article. Of interest, also, is the evidence from languages which do not have articles at all, such as Latin and Russian (Lyons 1986a: 27–9). *Meus liber* (as well as *liber meus*) and *moja kniga* "my book" are definite; the possessive adjective therefore occupies specifier position.[8] (For Latin, we must allow for the specifier to occur both phrase-initially and phrase-finally; for Italian, too, phrase-final specifiers must be allowed, albeit very marginally.) If, however, *moja kniga* is preceded by a cardinality determiner (which occupies modifier position), such as *odna* "one", then the possessive adjective gets demoted to modifier position. *Odna moja kniga* can only be modifier-modifier-noun, not modifier-specifier-noun, and so has the sense "one book of mine", or "one of my books", not "my one book". Likewise, in Latin, *tres tui libri* "three books of yours", *multi sui libri* "many books of his", have only an indefinite reading.

Lyons has proposed a coherent account of the referential properties of possessives, which is supported by evidence from a range of languages. With respect to English, it is based on the assumption that possessives invariably have definite reference. Problematic, therefore, are those possessives (*some teenager's car*) which do seem able to have indefinite, even non-specific reference. For these expressions, on their indefinite reading, it would be necessary to make the *ad hoc* assumption that the possessor phrase appears in modifier position. (On the other hand, for possessives with a generic reading, of the kind *taxpayers' money*, such an analysis could be defended, especially if these expressions are

---

[8] A reader points out to me that Russian *moja kniga* is not invariably definite; it could also be indefinite.

analysed as possessive compounds.) Then there are all those complications introduced by the Italian kinship terms, requiring possessives now to occupy modifier position, now to occupy specifier position. Plank (1992) maintains that these complications do not perforce undermine Lyons's thesis. Possibly, any generalization of the scope that Lyons envisages has to tolerate some idiosyncratic exceptions, especially those associated with specific lexical items. Lyons's account does, however, raise some more fundamental issues, which I want to address. Foremost amongst these is the status and function of specifiers. It is a topic that we already raised in section 5.6.

A main force in the development of X-bar theory has been the desire to draw generalizations across categories. Notions such as head, complement, and specifier are supposed to have cross-categorial validity. It is therefore not just NPs that have specifiers, there are specifiers to VP, specifiers to AP, even specifiers to DP (determiner phrase).

For the category of NP, Lyons proposes that the specifier has a very precise semantic function. It is, namely, the specifier which imposes definite reference. Given the desire to make cross-categorial generalizations, it is legitimate to ask whether a filled vs. an unfilled specifier in noun phrases has analogous semantic effects for other phrasal categories. Only in the case of the so-called inflectional phrase (IP) might there be a case for drawing such analogies. IP (equivalent to S = Sentence in earlier versions of the theory) is headed by an inflectional element, whose complement is a VP and whose specifier is the subject. But while the subject (i.e. specifier to IP) certainly elaborates the semantic content of an inflected VP, it does not establish reference. Reference is established by the inflectional element itself. It is, namely, the inflectional element that grounds the VP, by anchoring it in relation to the here and now, comparable to how a determiner grounds an NP (section 4.4). With respect to other phrasal categories, the analogies with NP are even more tenuous. The semantic role of specifier to a prepositional phrase: [*right*] *into the water*, an adjectival phrase: [*rather*] *fond of cheese*, an adverbial phrase: [*quite*] *independently of me* would seem to have nothing whatsoever in common with the alleged function of the specifier in a noun phrase.

One conclusion could be that the syntactic position of specifier is peculiar to the category of NP—a position entertained by Bierwisch (1988: 3–4). This conclusion, however, goes counter to one of the main motivations of X-bar syntax, viz. the desire to draw cross-category generalizations. By the same token, it will not be possible to derive the special properties of specifier to NP from more general principles of X-bar syntax. If there are no independent grounds for characterizing the properties of a specifier, Lyons's distinction between specifiers, which confer definiteness on an NP, and modifiers, which do not, turns out to be essentially *ad hoc*.

In fact, the proposed distinction between specifiers and modifiers within an NP may not always be clear-cut, anyway. Plank (1992) addresses this issue on the example of the possessive adjectives in German. He points out some subtle facts concerning the declension of possessive adjectives when they occur together with demonstratives.

(36) *a.* in diesem Land   "in this country"
        b. in unserem Land   "in our country"
(37) *a.* in diesem schönen Land   "in this beautiful country"
        b. in unserem schönen Land   "in our beautiful country"
(38) *a.* in diesem unserem Land   "in this our country"
        b. in diesem unseren Land
(39) *a.* in diesem unserem schönen Land "in this our beautiful country"
        b. in diesem unseren schönen Land

(36) and (37) illustrate the standard pattern in the language. Note in particular that the demonstrative and the possessive—both of which confer definiteness—share the *-em* inflection, while the interposed adjective has the *-en* inflection. In (38), we see that the possessive following the demonstrative can take either the *-em* or the *-en* inflection (although the former, according to Plank, is preferred.) In other words, in (38*a*), the possessive inflects just as it would in the absence of the demonstrative, that is, on Lyons's thesis, like a definite specifier. (We could say, therefore, that *diesem* and *unserem* are specifiers in an appositional relation.) In (38*b*), however, the possessive inflects like a modifying adjective (which does not confer definiteness). These same possibilities exist in (39). Again there is a choice between inflecting the interposed possessive as a definite specifier or as a modifying adjective; according to Plank (p. 460), the two options are not associated with any semantic contrast. Contrary to Lyons's thesis, therefore, the choice between specifier and modifier construal of the possessive, in this case at least, has no semantic significance.

There is another, and actually rather puzzling aspect of German possessives that is worth mentioning. This is that the series of possessive adjectives *mein* "my", *dein* "your", etc. (which confer definiteness) inflect like the indefinite article *ein*, and not like the definite determiners *der* "the" and *dieser* "this". (This aspect is obscured in (36), since in the dative singular there is syncretism of the two inflectional series.) Thus, the definite determiners distinguish between masculine nominative *der Mann* "the man" and neuter nominative *das Kind* "the child", whereas the indefinite article (and the possessives) do not: *ein Mann/ mein Mann*, *ein Kind/mein Kind*. Not only this, but the possessives and the indefinite article require that a following adjective takes the so-called strong inflection, whereas the definites require the weak inflection. The contrast shows up in (40) and (41).

(40) *a.* ein schönes Land   "a beautiful country"
        b. unser schönes Land "our beautiful country"
        c. das schöne Land   "the beautiful country"
        d. dieses schöne Land   "this beautiful country"

(41)   *a.* ein schöner Garten   "a beautiful garden"
       b. unser schöner Garten
       c. der schöne Garten
       d. dieser schöne Garten

Even in the case of a full NP possessor, a following adjective still takes the strong inflection.

(42)   *a.* Goethes versammelte Werke.
            "Goethe's collected works"
       b. die versammelten Werke.
            "the collected works"

With a preceding definite determiner, the adjective has the weak inflection (42*b*). Even though prenominal *Goethes* may confer definiteness, and seems to occupy the place reserved for an overt definite determiner, the definite article and the prenominal possessor have different inflectional consequences for a modifier.

Lyons had claimed that the definite and indefinite articles are assigned to different positions within the NP—the definite article going into the specifier position, the indefinite article into the modifier position. To the extent that a prenominal possessor confers definiteness (as it usually does in English, and also in German), it too, according to Lyons, goes into the specifier position. The inflectional evidence of German, however, shows that prenominal possessors, whether full NPs or pronominal forms, tend to pattern like indefinites. The different slots reserved for definiteness-conferring elements and elements which do not confer definiteness might therefore not be so clearly distinguishable after all. Even assuming that the distinction between specifier and modifier is well-founded, the distinction may not always correlate with the ability to confer definiteness.

For various reasons, therefore, Lyons's attempt to derive the definiteness of possessives from their syntactic configuration turns out to be flawed. In conclusion, it is worth considering why such an undertaking was felt to be necessary in the first place. Lyons is quite explicit on this issue. He notes (Lyons 1985: 99) that the notion of possession (understood, presumably, in a rather broad sense, to encompass the various kinds of semantic relation that may exist between possessee and possessor) is neutral with respect to the (in)definiteness of the possessee. There is therefore no reason why, given the identity of the possessor, the possessee should be uniquely identifiable. *Some books belonging to John* and *some books of John's* are indefinite, and in no way semantically anomalous. The definiteness of *John's books*, Lyons claims, cannot therefore be derived from the semantics of possession; it must have a syntactic cause.

This argument, I think, is fallacious. It is true that *John's books*, *some books of John's*, and *some books belonging to John* all invoke a 'possession' relation between the books and John (not necessarily the same relation in the three cases, of course). But this relation is only one aspect of the semantics of the three expressions. *Some books belonging to John* and *some books of John's* both refer to some arbitrarily selected instances of a type specification, which are characterized with respect to John. But in speaking of *John's books* I intend to refer to some specific books, and invoke the relation of the books to John as a means for identifying, amongst the numerous possible referents of *book*, just those that I have in mind. The definiteness/specificity of these expressions is an aspect of their semantics that is in principle independent of the semantics of the possession relation *per se*.

8 Possessors as Topics

IN this and the following chapter, I develop some aspects of the reference point analysis of the possessive construction that was outlined in Chapter 1. Here, I focus mainly on properties of the possessor, or reference point nominal, whilst the main concern of Chapter 9 is the semantic relation between possessor and possessee.[1]

On the reference point analysis, the possessor nominal names a reference point entity, which the speaker introduces as an aid for the subsequent identification of the target entity, denoted by the possessee. A reasonable assumption could be that not every nominal is in equal need of support by a reference point. Conversely, we may expect that not every nominal is equally suited to serve as a reference point. By considering the expected properties of reference point and target, we will be able to formulate a number of predictions concerning the possessor and the possessee, which may then be checked out against the empirical data. Confirmation of the predictions will tend to confirm the correctness of the reference point analysis.

We can, though, imagine a more ambitious aim. This is that the entailments of the reference point analysis could go a long way towards explaining the grammaticality restrictions on possessives that have been reported in the literature, and which we discussed especially in Chapter 6. In fact, my aim, in this and the following chapter, will be to show that the reference point analysis alone is sufficient to explain these restrictions.

8.1 REFERENCE POINTS, TOPICS, AND POSSESSORS

The reference point phenomenon is not restricted to the prenominal possessive construction. It is, as Langacker affirms, a fundamental cognitive ability, 'ubiquitous in our moment-to-moment experience' (Langacker 1993: 5). We have already mentioned some non-linguistic manifestations. Consider again Langacker's own example of the night-time sky (see above, section 1.2). The sky is populated by a multitude of stars. Yet the focus of a person's visual attention is limited to just one small portion of the overhead expanse. How to single out for focal attention one specific star from the vast number of potential candidates? More to the point: How to get a partner to focus *his* attention on just

---

[1] This chapter develops a number of ideas first presented is Taylor (1994*a*, *b*).

this entity? One strategy could be to direct our partner's attention to a salient constellation, such as the Southern Cross, so that he can take his bearings from there. Many other manifestations of the same procedure come to mind. I find a side street on a map by first locating a major thoroughfare; I locate a paragraph in a book by first finding the page, or section, in which the paragraph occurs; in order to strike the 'A' key on my computer keyboard, I must first locate the keyboard, and position myself in front of it.

The use of reference points is not restricted to locating entities in the material world. We also use cognitive reference points to locate concepts in our conceptual world. Just as the material world is populated by countless physical entities, so our mental world is populated by countless mental entities, i.e. concepts. And just as our visual attention can be focused only on a tiny portion of the visible scene in front of us, so mental attention can be focused only on a tiny number of concepts. In order to focus mental attention on just one concept (or, in Langacker's apt metaphor, to 'establish mental contact' with it), it is often necessary to first invoke another concept as reference point. To conceptualize the 'A' key on a keyboard, I must first conceptualize a keyboard. And in order to conceptualize a particular person (or, more pertinently, to enable a partner to conceptualize just this individual), it may be necessary to first invoke, as reference point, a more salient entity, or more immediately identifiable individual.

Given its fundamental role in cognition, it is not surprising that the linguistic manifestations of the reference point phenomenon should be 'numerous and varied' (Langacker 1993: 18). Perhaps its most transparent manifestation is in fragments like the following (Langacker 1993: 5).

(1)   You know that hunk who works in the bank? Well, the woman he's living with just got an abortion.

The point of this utterance is to convey information about a specific woman. The speaker realizes that she cannot simply make a statement about this individual, and expect to be understood. She cannot simply say, out of the blue, *She just had an abortion*, or even, *That woman just had an abortion*. She must first guarantee that the hearer is able to conceptually locate this person. Perhaps, even for the speaker, the woman can only be identified *as* the woman that the hunk is living with, and the hunk can only be identified *as* the one who works in the bank. In other words, 'the bank' (which presumably both speaker and hearer *can* uniquely identify, without further assistance) functions as the reference point for identification of the hunk who works there; the hunk is then the reference point for identification of the woman he lives with.

In this example, the semantic relations between reference points and targets are spelled out explicitly, and at leisure. Furthermore, the reference point function is not associated with any specific grammatical construction.[2] Many languages,

---

[2] We can observe, though, that in (1) the reference points are both named in a relative clause. Cf. Fox and Thompson (1990).

however, do have special constructions which have grammaticalized the reference point function. Such is the 'topic construction' in Chinese and Japanese, exemplified in (2) and (3).

(2) nèi-xie   shùmu   shù-shēn   dà. (Mandarin)
    those   tree   tree-trunk   big
    "Those trees, the trunks are big", i.e., roughly, "Those trees have big trunks"
    [Li and Thompson 1976: 462]

(3) sakana wa   tai   ga   oisii. (Japanese)
    fish   TOP red-snapper SUBJ delicious
    "As for fish, red snapper is delicious", i.e., roughly, "Red snapper is a delicious kind of fish"
    [Li and Thompson 1976: 468]

Chafe (1976: 50) characterizes the 'Chinese-style topic' as an item—usually nominal—in initial position which 'limit[s] the applicability of the main predication to a certain restricted domain'; it 'sets a spatial, temporal, or individual framework within which the main predication holds'. In (2), the predication 'the tree trunks are big' applies only to the set of entities established by 'those trees'. Likewise, in (3), the initial nominal evokes a conceptual domain, i.e. 'fish', against which the following predication is to be interpreted (Langacker 1993: 25).

The English possessive construction also grammaticalizes the reference point function. The possessor nominal, therefore, can be regarded as a kind of 'local topic', which, like the Chinese-style topic, delimits the referential possibility of the possessee nominal—prototypically, down to a single, uniquely identifiable entity (whence the preponderance of prenominal possessives with definite reference). Of relevance here could be the fact that the possessor nominal, like the Chinese and Japanese topics, occupies initial position within the construction.[3]

There are, to be sure, some important differences between the English possessive construction and the topic constructions of Chinese and Japanese. One difference concerns the nature of the target entity. In the possessive, the target is a nominal entity, generally a uniquely identifiable instance. In the topic constructions, the target is a grounded clause, i.e. a process. Furthermore, in the topic constructions, there is no overt morphological marking of the semantic relation between the topic and the predication that follows it. There is nothing in (2) which tells us that *shùmu shù-shēn* "tree-trunk" bears a semantic relation

---

[3] The conceptual affinity between topics and possessors is shown by the fact that sentences like *Elephants' noses are long, Taro's decision is quick* can be rendered in Japanese equally well by the Topic–Subject construction exemplified in (3)—*Zoo wa hana ga nagai* "elephant TOP nose SUBJ long", *Taro wa ketsudan ga hayai* "Taro TOP decision SUBJ quick"—and by a Possessor–Topic construction—*Zoo no hana wa nagai* "elephant POSS nose TOP long", *Taro no ketsudan wa hayai* "Taro POSS decision TOP quick". The two constructions are not exactly coextensive in range, however. The class-inclusion relation in (3) cannot be rendered by a possessive: *Sakana no tai ga oisii* "fish POSS red-snapper SUBJ delicious". (I thank Ken-ichi Seto for these observations.)

to *nèi-xie* "those trees", nor, in (3), is there any encoding of the fact that *tai* "red snapper" is a kind, or hyponym, of *sakana* "fish".[4] In the possessive construction, in contrast, there *is* overt morphological marking of the relation between possessor and possessee, in the shape of the possessive morpheme. Even so, the possessive morpheme does not of itself encode any specific semantic relation. Whether the relation is one of ownership, kinship, whole–part, or whatever, emerges largely in virtue of the semantic content of the participating nominals, it is not inherent in the construction *per se*.

Before proceeding, and in order to pre-empt possible misunderstandings, I should note that in this chapter I am using the term 'topic' to refer to a particular manifestation of the reference point function. A topic, in this sense, crucially has to do with the accessing of mental entities. Other uses of the term are current. While these do share a family resemblance, it may nevertheless be useful to point out some differences of nuance and emphasis.

For example, 'topic' is often used in the sense 'the thing or person about which something is said', in contrast to 'comment', which denotes that which is said about the topic. In this sense, topic and comment have to do with the packaging of information within the clause. Typically—at least in a subject-first language like English—the topic coincides with the grammatical subject of a clause, and the comment with the predicate. In the second sentence in (1), *the woman he's living with* would count as topic, with *just had an abortion* as comment. In this usage, topic and comment coincide with Halliday's 'theme' and 'rheme' (see e.g. Halliday 1970). Observe that a topic, in this sense, need not function as a reference point, neither can the comment, in many instances, be properly considered a target, in that the clausal subject does not have to name an entity which facilitates establishment of mental contact with the remainder of the clause.

Especially in the generative literature, 'topicalization' denotes the phenomenon whereby some element, other than the grammatical subject, appears in initial position in a sentence. (A topicalized element corresponds to Halliday's 'marked theme'.) This element functions as a 'psychological subject' (Halliday 1970: 159), concerning which some statement is made: *John, I can't stand the bastard.* Even an initial clausal subject may be topicalized: *Me, I can't stand him.* Here, the marked topic does seem to take on a reference point function, in that it

---

[4] In this respect, the Chinese-style topic construction differs from some putative English translations, of the kind {*Speaking of these trees/As for these trees*}, *their trunks are big*. Here, the initially named entity *is* grammatically integrated with the main predication, namely, by means of the preposition-like element *speaking of/as for*.

Chinese-style topics do, however, sometimes occur in English, especially in unscripted speech. The following example was heard in the course of a radio interview. Note that *your proposals* is not integrated syntactically into the main predication: *But surely, your proposals, you'll be bound to come in for a lot of criticism.*

In section 5.1 I suggested that topicalized elements bear a relation of complement to the main predication. This account also applies to the example, in that *proposals* elaborates a schematic entity in the semantic structure of *come in for criticism*.

explicitly draws attention to an entity (*John*, *me*) which provides the context for the proper understanding, or proper evaluation, of the main predication. The same goes for the fronting of an adverbial phrase. *On Mondays, lectures begin at 8.30* is a statement about what happens on Mondays, in contrast to the unmarked *Lectures begin at 8.30 on Mondays*, which is a statement about lectures. Likewise, various 'topicalizing' locutions, such as *as for*, *concerning*, *speaking of*, arguably introduce a reference point entity, which specifies the setting for the proper interpretation of a subsequent predication: *As for eating out, I prefer Chinese*.

Other uses focus on the role of the topic in discourse organization. (Givón, in particular, uses 'topic' in this sense.) This use of 'topic' can perhaps be regarded as a specialization of the everyday sense of the word, exemplified in expressions such as *the topic of the conversation*, *the topic of her dissertation*. Here, the topic, or overarching theme of a text (often stated, in written texts, in the form of a title, or heading) provides the general context for the interpretation and integration of the component sections of a text, and to this extent clearly has something of a reference point function. (It is well known that a text can sometimes be rendered virtually incomprehensible if its title is withheld; this is due to the fact that the concepts named in the text cannot be properly accessed if the reference point is withdrawn.[5]) Now, 'topic', in this everyday sense, can be applied, not only to a complete text, but also to segments of a text, to chapters, sections, subsections, and even to paragraphs. A text topic can therefore dominate a hierarchy of more local topics. It is also evident that the local topic will shift as a discourse progresses. On a more fine-grained level still, we might even want to speak of the topic of a sentence, or sentence fragment. Here, the distinction between 'discourse topic', 'sentence topic', and 'reference-point topic' is likely to become blurred. It seems quite consistent with the everyday sense of the term to say that *the woman he's living with* is the 'topic' of the second sentence in (1), and that *nèi-xie shùmu* "those trees" is the 'topic' of sentence (2).

As already remarked, these different uses of topic are best regarded as related by a family resemblance, rather than as discrete and mutually exclusive categories. Often, the discourse-organizing topic will function as a cognitively accessible reference point, while the sentence topic will often coincide with the discourse topic. It is to be expected, therefore, that 'topics', on whatever characterization, will tend to share a cluster of properties which differentiate them from non-topics. Such properties include definiteness, givenness, and animacy (more specifically, reference to human beings). Together, these properties constitute the 'topicality' (or, perhaps more appropriately, 'topicworthiness'[6]) of a nominal, and determine its suitability to function as topic.

I address the question of topicworthiness in the following section, where I

---

[5] For exemplification, see Brown and Yule (1983: 139–40).
[6] For discussions of topicworthiness, see especially Givón (1979, 1984, 1989) and Fox and Thompson (1990).

focus on those aspects of a nominal which render it especially suited to functioning as a reference point in the possessive construction.

8.2 THE TOPICWORTHINESS OF POSSESSOR NOMINALS

Given the reference point analysis, what kinds of properties is a possessor nominal likely to exhibit? What makes a 'good' possessor? An ancillary question concerns the kinds of properties likely to be associated with nouns functioning as possessees.

On the reference point analysis, the possessor is invoked to facilitate identification of the possessee. It is evident that the reference point, by definition almost, needs to be more easily accessible than the target. Were the target as easily accessible as the reference point, there would be no point in using the reference point for its identification. And if the reference point were less accessible than the target, it would be perverse indeed to invoke a less accessible entity to aid the identification of a more accessible entity.

The question of concept accessibility has been addressed in some detail by Wallace Chafe. Drawing on the analogy between the focus of visual attention and the focus of cognitive attention, Chafe distinguishes three possible 'activation states' of a concept: active (i.e. maximally accessible), semi-active, and inactive (i.e. minimally accessible).[7]

> An active concept is one that is currently lit up, a concept in a person's focus of consciousness. A semi-active concept is one that is in a person's peripheral consciousness, a concept of which a person has a background awareness, but which is not being directly focused on. An inactive concept is one that is currently in a person's long-term memory, neither focally nor peripherally active. (Chafe 1987: 25)

These activation states are relevant both to the organization of discourse and to the presentation of information within the clause. For, as Chafe puts it, a speaker 'does not simply thrust concepts forward out of nowhere' (p. 36). As a speaker proceeds to construct a discourse, various configurations of concepts move in and out of the focus of consciousness.

> The usual technique for presenting information is to choose some concept, typically some referent, as a starting point and then to add information about it. As a speaker proceeds to verbalize one focus of consciousness after another, each added piece of information is attached to some other piece that is in some sense already present. (Chafe 1987: 36)

The normal procedure, therefore, is to attach each new concept, i.e. a concept that was previously inactive in the consciousness of the speaker (and which is presumably unavailable to the hearer), to a 'starting point', i.e. a concept that is

---

[7] A more fine-grained taxonomy of activation states is proposed in Gundel *et al.* (1993). For our purposes, the three states discussed by Chafe are sufficient.

already active, or at least semi-active, in the speaker's consciousness (and which the speaker presumes is equally active in the consciousness of the hearer). For Chafe, this 'formatting strategy' underlies the subject–predicate organization of the clause, and, more generally, the manner in which a speaker regulates the flow of information in a discourse.

A similar point has been made by both Prince and Givón. Givón (1990: 897–8) points out that any utterance, if it is to be communicatively successful, needs to appeal to information already known to the hearer, in addition to conveying information not already known. An utterance which conveyed only known information would be redundant, one which conveyed only new information would be incoherent. A speaker therefore presents new information in the context of what he presumes is already known to the hearer, so as to make the new information maximally relevant to the hearer.[8] Prince (1981) notes that when 'brand-new' concepts (that is, concepts that have not been previously mentioned, and which are presumably inaccessible to the hearer) are introduced into a discourse, they typically need to be 'anchored', that is, attached to some other discourse entity, which is accessible to the hearer (p. 236). Thus, in (4), *a rich guy* is anchored by means of the defining relative clause to the discourse referent *I*.

(4)   A rich guy I know bought a Cadillac.

On the assumption that the possessive construction grammaticalizes a special strategy for 'anchoring' the possessee, we may presume that the possessor nominal needs to name an entity that is cognitively accessible, or, in Chafe's words, is 'in some sense already present'. We need to address, therefore, the factors that are likely to render a concept cognitively accessible. There are, I suggest, two aspects that need to be considered. In the first place, a concept may be rendered accessible by the discourse context in which it occurs. This I will refer to as *discourse-conditioned topicality*. We must also consider the possibility that certain concepts, by their very nature, are inherently more accessible than other concepts, irrespective, almost, of discourse context. I refer to this aspect as *inherent topicality*.

8.2.1 *Discourse-conditioned topicality*

A concept may be rendered mentally accessible by the fact that it has already been introduced into the discourse. The concept, therefore, has 'given', rather than 'new' status. Halliday (1970: 163) characterizes given information as information that the speaker assumes the hearer could 'recover', or 'derive' from preceding text or from the situation. Chafe explicitly links givenness with mental accessibility. Given information he defines as information 'which the speaker

---

[8] Givón (1987) uses the term 'grounding' for this function. Grounding, in Givón's sense, corresponds to Prince's anchoring; it should not be confused with the Langackerian notion of grounding, which I adopt in this book.

assumes to be in the consciousness of the addressee at the time of the utterance' (Chafe 1976: 30).

An obvious test of givenness is the recent mention of the concept in preceding discourse. Especially good candidates, we may suppose, will be concepts which, in the everyday sense of the term, constitute the 'topic', or the main theme, of a text. It is not, however, strictly necessary that a concept has been explicitly named for it to have given status. Given status may also attach to concepts that enter a person's focus of consciousness through activation by a 'frame', that is, by a body of knowledge conventionally associated with an already named concept, or with some feature of the situational context (Chafe 1987). Some further expectations are warranted. For example, we may expect givenness to be associated with definiteness. Certainly, with regard to possessives, it will make more sense to select as reference point a uniquely identified entity, than to invoke a non-specific entity, or a class of entities. We can also expect that the given status of a concept will tend to favour the use of pronominal forms. If a concept is presumed to be already in the hearer's focus of consciousness, the speaker may refer to this concept by means of a minimal linguistic expression, that is, by a pronoun.[9]

Specifically, therefore, we can make the following predictions concerning possessor nominals.

(a) Possessor nominals will refer to entities mentioned in recently preceding text.

(b) Discourse, or text topics, will tend to be amongst the preferred referents of possessor nominals.

(c) Possessor nominals will be overwhelmingly definite.

(d) Pronominal forms will be frequent.

A number of empirical studies confirm these predictions.

Let us turn, first, to Cheryl Brown (1983). Brown studied various properties of the nominals which occurred in a continuous written narrative (fifty pages from an Ian Fleming novel). One property that she considered was the 'continuity' of the nominals (or, more precisely, the continuity of their referents) in the discourse. Two assessments of continuity were made, lookback and persistence.

- *Lookback* has to do with the distance, in number of clauses, between the present mention of the referent and the nearest previous mention. In measuring lookback, Brown took a maximum cut-off value of 20. A low lookback value thus indicates that the referent has been recently mentioned in preceding discourse. A value of 20 indicates that the nominal is introducing an entity which, to all intents and purposes, has not been previously mentioned.

- *Persistence* is a measure of the number of consecutive clauses immediately following the present clause in which the referent of the nominal is

[9] In the limiting case, highly topical concepts need not even be explicitly named at all. See the discussion of (30) below.

TABLE 8.1. Discourse continuity of nominals in Subject, Direct Object, Indirect Object, Possessor, and other syntactic positions, in 50 pages of written narrative

	Sub	Dir Obj	Ind Obj	Poss	Other
Average Lookback	6.36	15.97	8.25	3.51	17.09
Average Persistence	1.42	0.23	1.00	1.47	0.22

Source: Brown 1983: 326.

mentioned.[10] A persistence value of 0 indicates that the referent, after its introduction, is immediately dropped from the discourse. Higher values indicate that the referent has an uninterrupted presence in the following clause(s). No maximum cut-off value for persistence was set.

Average lookback and persistence for nominals occurring in various syntactic environments are given in Table 8.1. We see that subject referents not only tend to be given, in that they have been recently mentioned in the discourse, they also persist for between one and two clauses in following discourse. Subjects, in other words, constitute particularly good examples of discourse topics. Subjects are highly differentiated from direct objects. Direct objects introduce entities that tend to be new to the discourse, furthermore, direct object entities tend to be dropped fairly quickly in immediately following discourse. The category 'Other' in Table 8.1 (comprising objects of prepositions, locatives, objects of infinitives, and 'any other use of a nominal which could not be classified in the other four categories'—Brown 1983: 326) also turns out to be highly non-topical. Of special interest to us, of course, are the possessor nominals. These are remarkable in that they exhibit even stronger topicality properties than subjects. On average, possessor nominals have the lowest lookback of any syntactic position, and the highest persistence.

The role of discourse topic was also highlighted by Osselton (1988). Osselton collected examples of prenominal possessives in which the possessor deviated markedly from what he saw as the prototype (a human being who possesses, or owns, the possessee entity), and examined the circumstances which might have motivated the writer to use the prenominal construction. He surmises that the determining factor was 'the general topic upon which the writer of the piece is engaged' (p. 139). Consider one of Osselton's examples.

(5)   More than 15,000 Ford workers were laid off last night ... duty free perks, although the incentive, were not *the dispute's critical issue*.

---

[10] Brown's (1983: 319) definition of persistence is open to misunderstanding. For clarification, I have drawn on the characterization given by Givón (1983*a*: 15), in his essay introducing the volume in which Brown's paper appears.

It is the topicality of *the dispute*—the fact that this is what the text is 'about'—that justifies the possessive *the dispute's critical issue*. Without this supporting context, an alternative wording—*the critical issue of the dispute*—would almost certainly have been preferred.

The givenness of possessor nominals was further confirmed in a quantitative study reported in Taylor (1991*a*). Data for the study were the 240 prenominal possessives that occurred in a corpus of some 13,000 words, compiled from various sources: a biographical narrative, a popular scientific text, an extract from a novel, newspaper articles, and transcripts of spontaneous speech.[11]

The overwhelming majority of possessor nominals in the corpus referred to entities that had already been explicitly introduced into the respective texts. As many as 182 (= 76 per cent) denoted entities that had been mentioned either in the same clause or in the immediately preceding clause. A further 44 (= 18 per cent) denoted entities that had been mentioned further back in a text. Only 14 (= 6 per cent) introduced entities 'out of the blue', without previous mention. But even the referents of many of the out-of-the-blue nominals could be said to have semi-active status (in Chafe's terminology) in the hearer/reader's consciousness in virtue of the context in which the nominals occurred. For example, the first sentence of a newspaper article on Salman Rushdie contained the expression *Britain's younger novelists*. This was the first mention of *Britain* in the text. But given that Rushdie had been named in the title of the text, together with the fact that Rushdie is a British novelist, and the not unreasonable assumption that the text writer could presume that the reader might know this fact, *Britain* acquires semi-active status through the activation of frame-based knowledge. Or consider the title of one of the texts: *Bush's bid to weld US foreign policy*. Standing as it does as the first word of the title, *Bush* is clearly introducing an entity without previous mention. Yet the very context of the title—the top of the foreign news page of a daily newspaper—could serve to render the name of the US President at least peripherally active. A further significant fact is that the headline appeared adjacent to a small head-and-shoulders photograph of the President. The photograph itself therefore served to activate the concept of the President.

Of special interest, too, is the fact that in a number of texts it was possible to identify 'possessor chains', that is, sequences of possessives whose possessor nominals all referred to one and the same entity. Furthermore, this entity could

---

[11] The sources for the corpus were as follows: (*a*) D. Mack Smith, *Mussolini* (London: Granada, 1983): 2,000 words beginning at p. 197; (*b*) C. Blakemore, *Mechanisms of Mind* (Cambridge: Cambridge University Press, 1977): 2,000 words beginning at p. 93; (*c*) I. Murdoch, *The Unicorn* (London: Chatto & Windus, 1963): first 2,000 words of ch. 2; (*d*) Three articles from p. 11 of the Johannesburg daily newspaper the *Star* (16 Feb. 1989), entitled 'Bush's bid to weld US foreign policy' (1,100 words), 'Rushdie, man without a home' (400 words), and 'Islamic revival likened to medieval era' (600 words); (*e*) A 1,400-word article on travel in Portugal, from the *Sunday Star* of 26 Feb. 1989; (*f*) Transcripts 2, 3, 5, 8, and 10 from Crystal and Davy (1975), totalling ±3,500 words.

often be construed as the topic, or main theme of the text. Consider the text about Rushdie. Of the 26 possessives in this text, as many as 21 had as their possessor either the name of the novelist, or the pronominal form *his*. In other cases it was possible to identify more limited topics. Two paragraphs of a text dealing with American foreign policy focused on the man likely to be appointed as Bush's chief adviser on African affairs. The paragraphs in question contained only two possessives, and both had the prospective appointee as the referent of their possessor nominals. A more complex example is provided by the extract from a biography of Mussolini. The main theme of this text was, of course, the dictator himself. But two sub-themes could be discerned. One was the destiny of Italy, the country which Mussolini ruled. The second was Hitler, by whom Mussolini was becoming increasingly influenced. The relative incidence of possessor nominals referring to Mussolini (24), Italy (10), and Hitler (5)—a further 9 possessors referred to other miscellaneous entities—exactly reflects the relative salience of the three concepts in the text.

The corpus also confirmed the prediction of pronominality. As many as 180 (= 75 per cent) of the possessor nominals were pronouns. Furthermore, of the full NP possessors (60 in number), at least 12 were clearly functioning as pro-forms to a previously mentioned nominal. The following example is typical. Here *the country* refers back anaphorically to the previously mentioned *Pakistan*.

(6) After Cambridge, he went to Pakistan, whither his parents had removed. He got a job in *the country*'s new television service . . .

The predicted definiteness of possessors received almost total confirmation, in that all but a tiny handful of possessors had definite reference. Moreover, of the 60 non-pronominal possessors, more than half (37) were proper names, mostly the names of persons (22) and geographical locations (11). Proper names, of course, are prime examples of definite, uniquely referring nominals.

As mentioned, a few possessives did have non-definite possessors. (7) contains one of the very few expressions with indefinite reference; here, the vitality of *any* nation is at issue.

(7) He began to refer . . . to imperialism as the supreme test of a nation's vitality.

In (8), on the other hand, *the* implies generic reference; both *the rat* and *the rat's brain* denote types, not instances.

(8) L . . . described a similar kind of resistance to local injury in the store of information in the rat's brain.

There were, in addition, a couple of expressions that were arguably ambiguous between a prenominal possessive and a possessive compound reading. *A day's ploughing* in (9) could equally well be assigned the structure [a day]'s [ploughing]—in which *a day* would have indefinite reference—or [a [day's ploughing]].

(9) Oxen are led home from a day's ploughing by a woman on foot.

In (10), on the other hand, adjective placement suggests that *publisher's editor* is a genuine compound, not a possessive.

(10) [He] made friends with L.C., a rising young publisher's editor.

The corpus data revealed a further unexpected property of possessor nominals. The overwhelming majority (203, or 84 per cent) were singular rather than plural. In retrospect, this property is not too surprising. In terms of the reference point analysis, it makes good sense to suppose that a single definite entity can better fulfil the reference point function than a plurality of entities.

Some other aspects are worth mentioning for their indirect relevance to the reference point analysis. Consider, for example, the incidence of possessive expressions in the different kinds of texts. The 13,000-word corpus contained 240 possessives, equivalent to one possessive to every 54 words of running text. This overall figure conceals the fact that the spoken text samples differed significantly from the written samples. In the written texts, the incidence of possessives ranged from one every 36 words for the journalistic texts, to one every 49 words for the literary text. In the spoken texts, possessives were between three and four times less frequent. On average, the five samples of spontaneous speech contained one possessive to every 170 words.

The text samples also differed with respect to the complexity of the possessive expressions. The excerpt from the Mussolini biography was a closely knit, informationally dense piece of prose. Many possessives in this text were both semantically and structurally complex, in that the occurrence of derived nouns as possessee was frequent, as was pre- and post-modification of the possessee. Typical examples were *his glib talk about colonial expansion* and *his pride at being advised by such a great man*. These possessives express, in condensed form, a constellation of semantic relations that in more discursive prose might have been expressed by a sequence of finite clauses. The conversational extracts were just the opposite. Possessives typical of these texts were *my pupils*, *their hand*, *my mother*. A well-known feature of conversational English is the low incidence of syntactically complex noun phrases (Crystal and Davy 1969: 112–13). In accordance with this tendency, few of the possessives in the conversational extracts encoded 'sentential' relations. The occurrence, as possessees, of deverbal nouns was rare, as was pre- and post-modification of the possessees.

The reference point analysis suggests a simple explanation of these trends. On the assumption that a possessor nominal serves to facilitate identification of the possessee referent, the low incidence of possessives in conversational English could imply that speakers in face-to-face interaction rarely need to have recourse to the facilitating function of possessor nominals. The reason plausibly has to do with the fact that in live conversation a speaker can monitor her interlocutor's current state of knowledge, from both linguistic and non-linguistic feedback, and so has greater confidence in the hearer's ability to identify the referents of noun phrases without the aid of a reference point. Thus, in one of the conversational

TABLE 8.2. Discourse continuity of possessee nominals

Average lookback (human: N = 7)	20.00
Average lookback (non-human: N = 222)	18.28
Average total lookback (N = 229)	18.34
Average persistence (human)	0.00
Average persistence (non-human)	0.09
Average total persistence	0.08

Source: Brown 1983: 328.

extracts, the speaker could talk of *the children* and *the mother*. In a written text, which lacks the contextual props of live conversation, these nominals would typically need to be further specified, one means for doing so being, of course, the possessive construction.

I have said little so far about the properties of possessees. But if possessors, as local topics, are likely to have given status, we could expect possessees to be exactly the opposite, that is, to be new, and non-topical. A first expectation, therefore, is that possessives will occur predominantly in those sentence positions that are associated with non-topicality, that is, direct object, and the miscellaneous positions grouped under 'Other' in Table 8.1. This is exactly what emerges from Brown's data (Brown 1983: 338). Only 13 per cent of possessives occurred in the topical position of Subject, none occurred in the highly topical position of Possessor, whilst 27 per cent occurred in the non-topical position of Direct Object and 60 per cent occurred in the non-topical positions classified as 'Other'. Further information pertaining to the topicality properties of possessees can be gleaned from Brown's study. This information is summarized in Table 8.2.

We see that possessees overwhelmingly introduce new, previously unnamed entities into the discourse. Their average lookback, in fact, is greater than that of any of the categories in Table 8.1. Furthermore, possessee entities are nearly always immediately dropped from the discourse. In other words, possessee entities are not only non-topical at the time of their mention, they also fail to achieve topicality in following discourse.[12] The crucial point, with respect to

---

[12] The text analysed in Chafe (1987) independently confirms these trends. I reproduce part of it here, omitting pauses, interruptions, and intonation marks, and with normalized punctuation.

I can recall a big undergraduate class that I had, where everybody loved the instructor, and he was a real old world Swiss guy. This was a biology course, and he left all of the sort of real contact with students up to *his assistants*. And he would come into class at, you know, three or f, precisely one minute after the hour, or something like that, and he would immediately open *his notes* up, in front of the room, and he st, and every lecture after the first, started the same way. This was at Wesleyan, when Wesleyan was still a men's school. So every lecture after the first would begin, 'Gentlemen, ze last time ve vere talking about', and then he would, but then you know he would just give a lecture, and there was no real interaction with the students, and then at the end he would close *his notes*, and walk out of the room. And he was the I guess, that is the old world

TABLE 8.3. Properties of possessee nominals in a written narrative (Brown 1983) and an oral autobiographical narrative (Givón 1983c)

	Brown (1983)	Givón (1983c)
Average lookback	18.34	10.29
Average persistence	0.08	2.09

referent continuity, is that *possessee nominals are maximally differentiated from possessors*. The possessor is a *maximally topical* nominal, which functions as reference point for a *maximally non-topical* possessee.

It should, however, be mentioned that some aspects of Brown's data may have been skewed by the nature of the narrative she investigated. We see from Table 8.2 that nearly all (97 per cent) of her possessee nouns denoted non-human entities, and that these had a very low persistence. Givón (1983c) applied the same quantitative measures as Brown to a spoken autobiographical narrative. The main protagonists in this narrative were the narrator himself and his blood relatives. These latter were typically named by means of possessives (*my dad, my great grandfather*). Human possessees thus figure quite prominently in Givón's data. (Unfortunately, no figures are given.) Furthermore, in contrast to Brown's findings, possessees did show a high degree of persistence, 2.09, one of the highest values for any of Givón's categories. Their lookback was also considerably shorter (Table 8.3). In brief, Givón's possessees were very much more topical than Brown's. This difference suggests that possessives invoking kinship relations may have rather different discourse properties than other kinds of possessive, in that they are typically used to introduce, and to keep track of, potentially topical individuals who are identified by their kinship relation to a narrator, or to another discourse participant. I shall mention a possible grammatical reflex of this property later in this chapter.

> style of lecturing,. But he was the the most extreme example I had, I ever had as a student. And he was very good. (After Chafe 1987: 23–4)

Disregarding the compound *men's school*, this text contains just three possessives: *his assistants,* and *his notes* (two tokens). The possessor is in each case the main protagonist in the narrative, that is, the biology instructor. The instructor is introduced towards the beginning of the text, and, according to Chafe, 'this concept came to be treated as given for the remainder of the narrative' (p. 26).

If the possessor is the main protagonist, the possessee entities—the 'assistants' and the 'notes'— are incidental to the main narrative. Neither entity, for example, is mentioned outside the possessive expressions. Nevertheless, according to Chafe, the concepts do have 'semi-active' status in 'peripheral consciousness', in virtue of their role in the 'instructor schema' (p. 30). Although the possessees are non-topical—with respect to both lookback and persistence—they are peripherally associated with the text topic. The possessives serve to identify these somewhat incidental entities by linking them to the main protagonist.

8.2.2 *Inherent topicality*

There is a further property of the data in Taylor (1991*a*) that must be mentioned. This is the preponderance, as possessors, of nominals denoting animate, and more especially human entities. Of the 240 expressions in the corpus, as many as 183 (= 77 per cent) had possessors which denoted human beings.[13] In this respect, also, possessors are maximally distinct from possessees. In Brown's (1983) corpus, possessees were overwhelmingly inanimate (97 per cent). The general pattern, it would seem, is for a human possessor to serve as a reference point for an inanimate target.

Many commentators have noted that the possessive construction 'works best' if the possessor is human (Huddleston 1984: 269–70; Thomson and Martinet 1960: 12). Quirk *et al.* (1985), Hawkins (1981), and Deane (1987) go further, and set up hierarchies of nouns according to their suitability to occur as possessors, with human nouns invariably in first place. These hierarchies appeal to inherent properties of the nouns concerned, not to any properties that the nouns might acquire in virtue of discourse context.

The high incidence of human possessors may simply reflect the fact that human discourse is predominantly 'about' humans. Consequently, in any random sample of texts, we can expect that topicality will attach predominantly to nominals which designate human beings. A second possibility is that preference for human possessors reflects the inherent topicworthiness of human nominals. These nominals function so frequently as topics, not only because human discourse is predominantly about humans, but that, even after specific discourse effects have been factored out, a human noun is going to be more topical than a non-human noun.

Inherent topicality entails that some concepts are automatically more easily accessed than others, regardless of discourse context. The matter receives extensive discussion in Deane (1992: 194–205) in terms of a concept's 'automatic salience'. An automatically salient concept constitutes a 'natural topic' that is always available to anchor the new information content of a phrase, clause, or sentence.

Deane (pp. 194–5) argues that inherent topicworthiness is a function of entrenchment, or frequency of successful use. He discusses several, interrelated factors that are likely to contribute to automatic salience. Amongst these are egocentricity, position in a taxonomic hierarchy, and earliness of acquisition.

- Egocentric concepts are those that are learned, and understood, with reference to the speaker himself, his immediate environment, and his interaction with, and manipulation of, the environment.
- Basic level concepts (Rosch *et al.* 1976, Lakoff 1987, Taylor 1995*b*) are

---

[13] The figure of 183 human possessors excludes place-names that were being used metonymically for persons acting in those places (such as *Italy's technical achievements* in the sense "the technical achievements of the Italian people"). The percentage of possessors with human reference could thus be somewhat higher than the cited 77 per cent.

more entrenched, and therefore more easily accessed, than superordinate and subordinate concepts. They are associated with a rich network of perceptual and sensorimotor information, and can be accessed by many different routes, thereby increasing the opportunities for their successful use.

• Concepts acquired in early childhood are more entrenched than late acquired concepts. Early acquired concepts will be, in the main, egocentric and basic level, comprising notions of the self and of other humans, things associated with the here and now, material objects that are clearly individuated, and objects that can be handled and manipulated.

These various factors conspire to render certain concepts more inherently topical than others. Highest in topicality are human beings. Within this category, the highest position goes to the speaker, other participants in a discourse situation, and named individuals. A speaker's ability to empathize with other humans, to view situations from their perspective, and to attribute to them such subjective notions as intentions, emotions, and viewpoints, will further increase the inherent topicality of human nominals. Intermediate in value are names of higher animals, as well as entities which are characterized primarily in terms of human interaction, such as social institutions, places, and basic level objects. The lowest degree of inherent topicality attaches to abstract concepts, that is, concepts that are non-human, non-animate, non-concrete, non-manipulated, non-individuated, and not tied to the speaker's here and now.

Precisely this kind of topicality hierarchy is reflected in the statistical properties of the possessor nominals in Taylor (1991*a*). As already mentioned, the majority (77 per cent) denote human beings, with a further 5 (= 2 per cent) denoting higher animals. Of the remaining 52 non-animate possessors, the majority denote entities of obvious relevance to human activities and interests, such as geographical or geopolitical entities, i.e. countries (19), continents (2), towns and cities (8), rivers (2), and valleys (5). The remainder denote expressions of time (3), names of cultural institutions (2), and names of human activities (3). Only six denote inanimate objects.

The notion of intrinsic topicality can be read onto some other accounts of possessives. Hawkins (1981) proposes the following hierarchy, claiming that a prenominal possessor must be higher on the hierarchy than the possessee.

(11)   [HUMAN < [HUMAN ATTRIBUTE]] < [NON-HUMAN ANIMATE]
        < [NON-HUMAN INANIMATE]

(11) is clearly a hierarchy of inherent topicality (although Hawkins does not mention this fact), and amounts to the requirement that a possessor must be inherently more topical than the possessee.

A more elaborate 'gender hierarchy' is proposed in Quirk *et al.* (1985: 314). They claim (pp. 322–3) that the higher a noun on the hierarchy, the more it is able to function as a possessor. The gender hierarchy is established on the basis of pronoun substitution, that is, by choice of *she/he* and *who* over *it* and *which*.

Highest on the hierarchy are nouns denoting human males and females (*brother, sister*), which are always substituted by gender-marked pronouns. Next are human common nouns (*baby*) and human collectives (*crowd*), which sometimes take *it* and *which*. Lower still are gender-specific terms for higher animals (*bull, cow*), and names of certain artefacts (*ship*). Least marked for gender are names of lower animates (*ant*), the remaining inanimates (*box*), and presumably the abstracts. By and large, then, the gender hierarchy turns out to be a hierarchy of inherent topicality. Inherent topicality also seems to be involved in departures from the proposed correlation between the gender scale and occurrence as a possessor, as in *Europe's future*, *this year's sales*, *the body's needs*, *my life's aim*. At least some of these departures, Quirk *et al.* (p. 324) suggest, reflect the possessor's 'special relevance to human activity' (in our terms, the concept's egocentricity).

Deane (1987; 1992: 202–4) has invoked inherent topicality as a major parameter in the grammaticality of a possessive. He claims, moreover, that a basic difference between the prenominal possessive and the postnominal *of*-construction has to do with topicality distribution. With declining topicality of the possessor, the prenominal construction becomes gradually less acceptable, while the postnominal construction increases in acceptability.

(12)

decreasing acceptability		decreasing acceptability	
	my foot	↑	the foot of me
	his foot		the foot of him
	its foot		the foot of it
	Bill's foot		the foot of Bill
	my uncle's foot		the foot of my uncle
	the man's foot		the foot of the man
	the dog's foot		the foot of the dog
	the bicycle's handle		the handle of the bicycle
	the house's roof		the roof of the house
↓	his honour's nature		the nature of his honour

8.3 SOME CONSEQUENCES

Having established the relevance of topicality to the semantics of the possessive construction, it is legitimate to enquire whether topicality might not be a factor contributing to the grammaticality judgements on possessives that have been discussed so extensively in the literature. In the remaining part of this chapter I turn to a number of phenomena which plausibly can be attributed to the requirement that the possessor nominal be high in topicality. I begin by considering some of the more central issues addressed in the literature, followed by some more minor restrictions. I should mention at the outset that I am not claiming that the topicality requirement is the only parameter influencing the acceptability of possessives. Some further factors will need to be considered, and will be addressed in the next chapter.

8.3.1 *The Affectedness and Experiencer Constraints*

Experiencer constraint According to the Experiencer Constraint (section 6.2), the possessor to a psychological noun like *love*, *fear*, *fright* may denote the Experiencer of the psychological state, never the Stimulus that causes the state. Whence the grammaticality judgements in (13).

(13)   *a.* Amy's fear of the scarecrow.   *inanimate*   Baby's fear of my ugly face
human   *the scarecrow's fear by Amy.   the screaming police siren
       b. Amy's fright at the scarecrow.
            *the scarecrow's fright of Amy.

The import of the Experiencer Constraint is fully consistent with the topicality requirement on possessors, in that an animate, and prototypically human Experiencer is going to be more inherently topical than the often inanimate, or even abstract Stimulus. Furthermore, if it is correct that empathy contributes to inherent topicality, the Experiencer will always be more inherently topical than a Stimulus, even if the Stimulus should happen to be human. Topicality therefore offers itself as a viable alternative to configurational and argument-structure accounts of the constraint, as proposed by Giorgi and Longobardi (1991), Grimshaw (1990), and others. In fact, an explanation in terms of topicality will be more highly valued than purely syntactic accounts, to the extent that it appeals to very general cognitive processes of concept accessing and discourse organization; the learnability issue that besets syntactic accounts (section 2.10) is thereby circumvented.

Affectedness constraint The situation with respect to the Affectedness Constraint is less transparent. We should need to claim that an affected entity is inherently more topical than a non-affected entity. Such a claim is not, perhaps, indefensible, given the earlier suggestion that manipulable entities, i.e. entities that a person can manually 'affect', are inherently more topical than non-manipulable entities. It is also worth recalling Rozwadowska's Neutral Constraint. According to this constraint, neutral nominals, defined in (14), are banned from possessor position.

(14)   An entity X holds a thematic relation NEUTRAL (N-role) with respect to a predicate Y if
       (i) X is in no way affected by the action, process, or state described by Y,
       (ii) X does not have any control over the action, process, or state described by Y.

Rozwadowska's definition of 'neutral', it seems to me, could serve as a pretty good characterization of inherent non-topicality. The Neutral Constraint amounts to a ban on non-topical possessors.

The topicality hypothesis may be put to the test in a simple way. While inherent topicality is a fixed property of a nominal, discourse-conditioned topicality is a function of context, and therefore variable. We may expect, therefore, that the acceptability of at least some possessives will vary according to context. Cited out of context, the expressions are judged ungrammatical, due to the low inherent topicality of the possessor. When inserted into a context which enhances the possessor's topicality, the expressions may achieve a quite high degree of acceptability.

Consider the following expressions.

(15)   *a.* *the event's recollection.   *my recollection of the event*
      b. *the problem's perception.
      c. *the picture's observation.
      d. *the novel's understanding.
      e. *the film's enjoyment.

These violate both the Affectedness and the Experiencer Constraints. I have taken them, along with their asterisks, from Giorgi and Longobardi (1991: 141), who took them from Rozwadowska (1988), who in turn credits them to Rappaport (1983).

In the course of their discussion of the Affectedness Constraint (which, it will be recalled, is claimed not to hold in Romance—section 6.6), Giorgi and Longobardi want to show that the Italian equivalents of (15) are fully grammatical. In Italian, of course, possessors occur prenominally only if they are pronominalized and incorporated into possessive adjectives. In order to test their predictions concerning Italian, Giorgi and Longobardi thus need to replace the possessor phrases in (15) by possessive adjectives. Then, to establish the intended reference of the pronominalized possessors, they need to contextualize the expressions. To this end, they select a classical topicalizing context. It is ironic that Giorgi and Longobardi fail to notice that topicalizing the possessors of the Italian sentences contemporaneously increases the acceptability of the English glosses. Here are Giorgi and Longobardi's Italian sentences, along with their English glosses.

(16)   *a.* A proposito di quegli avvenimenti, il loro ricordo ancora mi spaventa.
      "Concerning those events, their recollection still frightens me"
      b. A proposito di quel problema, la sua percezione varia da individuo a individuo.
      "Concerning that problem, its perception varies from person to person"
      c. A proposito di quella fotografia, una sua attenta osservazione rivelerà molti particolari interessanti.
      "Concerning that picture, its careful observation will reveal many interesting details"
      d. A proposito di quel romanzo, la sua comprensione richiede notevoli capacità ermeneutiche.

"Concerning that novel, its understanding requires remarkable hermeneutic skills"

e. A proposito di quel film, il suo pieno godimento è certo riservato a pochi amatori.

"Concerning that film, its full enjoyment is certainly restricted to a few amateurs [*sic*]"

[Giorgi and Longobardi 1991: 141–2][14]

Similarly with *the problem's understanding*, which, again, both the Affectedness and Experiencer Constraints predict to be ungrammatical. The English translation of the French and Spanish sentences in (17), it seems to me, shares with the English glosses in (16) a quite high degree of acceptability. Appropriate context-ualization can render (reasonably) acceptable even *Latin's knowledge*, an expression which, judged in isolation, might seem irredeemably ungrammatical. The same goes for the alleged impossibility (see example (66) of Chapter 6) of an objective reading of *its discussion*.

(17) a. Ce problème est très difficile. Sa compréhension exige beaucoup de travail.

b. Este problema es muy difícil. Su comprensión exige mucho trabajo.

c. This problem is very difficult. Its understanding needs a lot of work.

[Giorgi and Longobardi 1991: 142]

(18) Concerning Latin, I believe its knowledge should be a requirement for all students of Romance languages.

(19) I suggest that the Dean's proposal, and its further discussion, be post-poned for the next meeting of the Faculty Board.

Some readers may have misgivings with some of these English examples. To counter any suggestion that my grammaticality judgements have been coloured by my enthusiasm for the topicality hypothesis, I will cite some attested contra-ventions of the Affectedness Constraint. Standard accounts of English possessives would no doubt asterisk *music's pursuit*,[15] *the conviction's expression*, *the sac-rament's reception*, on the grounds that the possessor entity is unaffected. Here are some examples from the LOB KWIK Concordance. Note that in each case

---

[14] Giorgi and Longobardi (1991: 141) also cite the following example, where there does seem to be a real difference between the acceptability of the Italian sentence and the unacceptability of its English gloss: *A proposito di Gianni, la sua vista mi ha spaventato* *"Concerning Gianni, his sight frightened me" (acceptability judgement mine). The unacceptability of the English gloss is possibly due to the fact that English *sight* does not reify the process or activity of seeing, it is not, therefore, a process nominalization (see below, section 9.3). On my judgement, *my sight of John* does not fare much better than *John's sight by me*. Rather, *sight* may designate the ability to see, as in *John's sight is poor*, or (aspects of) what is seen, as in *It was a pitiable sight*. Neither of these senses is compatible with the context in the English gloss.

[15] Cinque (1980: 96) explicitly contrasts English *pursuit* and Italian *inseguimento*, claiming that the former, but not the latter, is subject to the Affectedness Constraint (*il suo inseguimento* vs. **the fox's pursuit*). It is worth mentioning, however, that at the time of the United Nations' involvement in Somalia, I heard the following on the BBC World Service: [Speaking of Aidid] *The UN, which authorized his pursuit . . .*

the possessor nominal has been pronominalized, and that its intended referent is mentioned in the immediately preceding context.

(20)   Men with the greatest insight into music use one life in *its pursuit* and lack another in which to command words in a way that effectively communicates their musical judgement.

(21)   This conviction of the superhuman ... found *its visible expression* in offerings, sacrifices to the spirits or deities.

(22)   Sometimes criticism is in the form of protest; at others, it simply experiments with emotions and *their expression* in unusual forms.

(23)   the great sacrament, without *whose reception* no man could call himself a Christian

(24)   slogans, *whose repetition* pleases those who use them

(25)   the new large generators, *whose safe operation* at the extreme limit of stability would be beyond the capacity of the human operator

(26)   sexual perversion, *whose naming* fifty years ago would have made a book suspect

(27) is a striking counterexample to the Experiencer Constraint, in that the possessor ('statue') constitutes the Stimulus.

(27)   His statue of a man with a child on his shoulders, *whose first impression of brute strength* yields to a sense of uncertain architecture and even pretentiousness.

Several objections may be raised in regard to the above data:

(*a*) Granted that the English examples are indeed acceptable, the examples merely document the acceptability of *its pursuit, their expression*; they say nothing of the acceptability of *music's pursuit, the emotions' expression*. The objection is invalid. It is certainly true that acceptability is enhanced if the possessor is pronominalized.[16] Pronominalization is simply a reflex of the discourse-conditioned topicality of the respective concept. But pronominalization does not of itself change the semantic relation between possessor and possessee. The import of the Affectedness and Experiencer Constraints is to ban from prenominal position all nominals bearing certain semantic relations to the possessee. Whether the possessor happens to be a full NP or a pronoun has no bearing on the nature of the semantic relation.[17]

---

[16] Browsing in the LOB Concordance, I found only one (admittedly, rather odd-sounding!) counterexample to the Affectedness Constraint with a full NP possessor: 'From that time forth, she lived in the past and *three years' recollection* offers a sort of companionship although it has no future.' This is a counterexample only on the assumption that *three years* designates what was recollected, rather than the time span of the recollecting activity. The latter interpretation is unlikely, given that *recollection* is singular (cf. *three years' recollections*).

[17] Grimshaw (1990: 179, n. 14), noting that pronominalizing the possessor can sometimes improve acceptability, and observing that the phenomenon has 'never been explained', speculates that pronominal possessors may constitute 'some kind of second-order system' in English. The topicality hypothesis both explains the effect, and undercuts the need for a 'second-order system'.

(*b*) Even though the English glosses in (16) are not as bad as the decontextualized expressions in (15), they still remain somewhat marginal, perhaps, compared with the easy acceptability of *my recollection (of those events), John's perception (of the problem)*. Again, the objection is invalid. The asymmetry in acceptability is an expected consequence of the asymmetry in inherent topicality of Experiencer and Stimulus. Given the inherent topicality of Experiencer, we may expect the one reading to be readily available, regardless, almost, of discourse context, while the other reading is sanctioned only if supported by a specially favourable discourse context.

(*c*) Violations of the constraints require special contextual conditions, and are in any case rather rare compared to the easy acceptability of the Romance examples. The typological difference between English and Italian thus remains, even though it is not perhaps as clear-cut as Giorgi and Longobardi want to maintain. Again, this need occasion no surprise. Possessive adjectives in Romance are not strictly comparable to English possessors, even when the latter are pronominalized. There is no reason to suppose, for example, that adjectives in general, or possessive adjectives in particular, are subject to a topicality requirement.

(*d*) A more serious objection is that some readings remain obdurately unavailable, regardless of discourse context. No amount of contextual manipulation is able to sanction an objective reading of *Louise's love*, and this despite the fact that *Louise*, being a human nominal, is already high in inherent topicality. Nor does a topicalizing context facilitate an objective reading of *John's recollection*. Here, English does seem to differ significantly from Italian. (28*b*) is much worse than (28*a*), although the Italian equivalent of (28*b*) is unproblematic.[18]

(28)   *a*. Concerning those events, their recollection still frightens me.
       b. *Concerning John, his recollection still frightens me.
       c. A proposito di Gianni, il suo ricordo ancora mi spaventa.

These examples suggest that while the topicality of the possessor may be an important condition on the acceptability of a possessive expression, topicality may not be the whole story. In the next chapter, I propose a further requirement on possessor nominals, which is largely independent of the topicality requirement.

In the meantime, though, it might still be worthwhile to pursue the possible role of topicality in the unacceptability of (28*b*). In an act of recollection, *those events* can only be construed as Stimulus, not as Experiencer. On the other hand, it is equally feasible for a person to be either Experiencer or Stimulus. Given two possible semantic roles of the possessor, it could be that in (28*b*) the more

---

[18] On the other hand, *memory* does tolerate an objective reading. Note how, in the following example from Oscar Wilde's *The Picture of Dorian Gray*, context serves to topicalize 'the picture'. 'There was only one bit of evidence left against him. The picture itself—that was the evidence. He would destroy it. Why had he kept it so long? Once it had given him pleasure to watch it changing and growing old. Of late he had felt no such pleasure. It had kept him awake at night. When he had been away, he had been filled with terror lest other eyes should look upon it. It had brought melancholy across his passions. *Its mere memory* had marred many moments of joy.'

highly topical role of Experiencer wins out over the less topical role of Stimulus; the possessor nominal, that is, automatically (and obligatorily) receives that *'experiencer'?* semantic interpretation that is consistent with its status as topic.

Hawkinson and Hyman (1975) document a comparable phenomenon in Shona. In double object constructions in Shona, the first object—the one which immediately follows the verb—is reserved for the more topical entity. Hence, in causatives, the secondary Agent is normally placed before the Patient.

(29) *a.* Murame a-ka-rov-es-a   mwana muti.
     man   he-PAST-hit-CAUSE-IND child   tree
     "the man made the child hit the tree"

     b. Murame a-ka-rov-es-a   mukadzi mwana.
     man   he-PAST-hit-CAUSE-IND woman   child
     "The man made the woman hit the child"

In special discourse contexts (discussed by Hawkinson and Hyman in terms of 'marked topic'), postverbal position may be occupied by the Patient. However, this possibility exists only if secondary Agent and Patient differ sufficiently in animacy for it to be obvious who is affecting what.

(30) Murame a-ka-rov-es-a   muti mwana.
     man   he-PAST-hit-CAUSE-IND tree child
     "The man made the child hit the tree"

If secondary Agent and Patient do not differ in animacy—if both, say, are human—then the alternative word order is not possible. (29*b*) can under no circumstances mean "The man made the child hit the woman". Here, the postverbal nominal is automatically (and obligatorily) interpreted as secondary Agent, consistent with the hypothesized topicality of the postverbal position.

8.3.2 *Control phenomena*

I turn next to a phenomenon that has been extensively discussed in the government and binding literature under the rubric 'obligatory control of PRO' (Jaeggli 1986: 618–19; Roeper 1987: 279–80; Giorgi and Longobardi 1991: 134–7). Giorgi and Longobardi go so far as to claim that the grammaticality judgements in question are of such subtlety that the principles underlying them 'would . . . be completely unlearnable under normal conditions' (p. 135). The data therefore 'confirm in one of the strongest possible ways' (p. 137) the reality of the formal principles of Universal Grammar.

At issue are contrasts like the following, and the manner in which the unexpressed subject, *alias* PRO, of the non-finite adjunct clause gets interpreted.

(31) *a.* their destruction of the ship [PRO to collect the insurance].
     b. the destruction of the ship [PRO to collect the insurance].
     c. *the ship's destruction [PRO to collect the insurance].

The claim is that the PRO subject of the *to*-clause must be 'controlled', that is, must be construed as coreferential with an NP which c-commands it. In (31*a*), the 'controller' is the Agent of the action nominal *destruction*, expressed by the possessor, *their*. In (31*b*) the Agent is unexpressed; its argument-role, however, is claimed to be present in the semantic structure of *destruction*, such that the unexpressed Agent, itself possibly PRO, can act as controller. The (31*b*) sentence is therefore understood to mean that whoever destroyed the ship, did so to collect the insurance. In (31*c*), the internal argument of *destruction*, i.e. *the ship*, has moved into Spec position, where the Agent argument is presumed to originate. By Giorgi and Longobardi's 'Argument Uniqueness in Spec' principle, the Agent argument is thereby obliterated, and so is not available for the control of PRO. Whence the ungrammaticality of (31*c*). Precisely the same contrasts hold with respect to the interpretation of participial clauses. The following are based on Giorgi and Longobardi (1991: 135).

(32)   *a.* their detention of the prisoner after promising him impunity.
       b. the detention of the prisoner after promising him impunity.
       c. *the prisoner's detention after promising him impunity.

Here, I want to argue that the grammaticality judgements in question could well be reflexes of topicality. Such a possibility would make it necessary to relativize Giorgi and Longobardi's claims about the 'complete unlearnability' of the principles underlying their judgements of (31) and (32)—and might even cause one to query the need for the underlying principles in the first place!

Givón (1983*a*: 23–4) has drawn attention to the role of topicality in the interpretation of non-finite subjectless clauses. The fact that in the following examples the subject of the non-finite clauses is unexpressed, reflects the status of the unexpressed subject (construed to be identical with the overt subject of the main predication) as a highly topical element; it is, namely, its high topicality that renders it fully predictable, and therefore omissible.

(33)   *a.* I did it *to attract attention.*
       b. *Having finished,* he left.
       c. *Working hard and fast,* he managed to plug the hole.

Such an account coincides exactly with the prescriptive requirement that the understood subject of a non-finite clause be coreferential with the subject of a main clause. Yet 'dangling participles' and 'dangling infinitives' may occasionally be tolerated.

(34)   *a.* Crossing the road, I was knocked down by a car.
       b. (?)Crossing the road, a car knocked me down.
       c. *Crossing the road, the lights turned red.
(35)   *a.* While acknowledging the ingenuity of her argument, it is still legiti-
             mate to raise the following questions.

   b. Without going into details, there is little chance of the proposal being accepted.

   c. Taking all these facts into consideration, it is unfortunately not possible to recommend acceptance of the proposal.

(34*b*) is allowable to the extent that the first person narrator is an inherently topical participant in the discourse (and is, moreover, mentioned, albeit as direct object, in the main predication), and is thus available as the understood subject of *crossing the road*. And while careful speakers and writers would probably try to avoid dangling adjuncts like those in (35), the expressions are readily interpretable, in virtue of the fact that the understood subject of the participles and the infinitives is again the inherently topical 'I', or 'we', of the discourse situation. (34*c*), however, is completely out, since the main clause sets up its own topic ('the lights'), thus deflecting attention away from the understood subject of the participle.

   Returning now to (31) and (32). The (*a*) examples are unproblematic, in that the understood subject of the non-finite clause is readily interpreted as the highly topical possessor. The (*b*) examples are acceptable to the extent that the understood subject is identified with some topical entity that is implied by the discourse context, and is therefore 'in the air', so to speak. This option is not available in the (*c*) examples, for the reason that the prenominal possessor has already presented a topical entity, one, moreover, that is semantically incompatible with the understood subject of the non-finite clause. In one respect, therefore, Giorgi and Longobardi are correct to claim that in the (*c*) examples the semantic role of Agent has been 'obliterated' by the prenominal possessor. I submit, however, that obliteration is not a syntactic process, but reflects the outcome of competing claims on cognitive attention. A person's powers of cognitive attention are limited. Although the Agent is implicit in the semantic structure of *destruction* and *detention*, its status as an accessible, topical entity is defeated by the necessarily highly topical possessor.

   As Giorgi and Longobardi (p. 135) note, intuitions on examples like those in (31) and (32) are somewhat variable. This fact alone should alert us to the possibility that other than purely configurational considerations might be playing a role. For example, to my ears, (*b*)–(*e*) below are not nearly as bad as (*a*).

(36)   *a*. *the city's destruction to prove a point.
          [Roeper 1987: 280]
       b. the paragraph's erasure to appease the censor.
       c. [concerning those art treasures] their sale in order to pay off the family's debts.
       d. [concerning that scandal] its exposure in the press in the hope of embarrassing the government.
       e. [concerning your colleague] his transfer to another department without even first consulting him.

The reason, I suggest, has to do with the coherence of the scenes described in the examples. 'Scandal', 'exposure', 'press', 'embarrass', 'government'—these words alone are sufficient to evoke a familiar, and stereotypical scenario. Familiarity with the scenario is sufficient to activate, in the hearer's focus of consciousness, the one participant in the situation that is not explicitly mentioned, that is, the Agent responsible for the exposure, and who acts with the intention of embarrassing the government. To this extent, the very content of (36*d*) conspires to render the notion of Agent accessible. This topical entity is then available to function as the unexpressed subject of the adjunct phrase. Nothing of this sort applies to (36*a*). Here we have a truly bizarre concatenation of event and purpose, which fails to activate any stereotypical scenario in the mind of the hearer, or any notion of an Agent which might be responsible for instigating it.

8.3.3 *Embedded possessives*

A possessor nominal may itself have the internal structure of a possessive. Even multiple embedding of possessives is possible.

(37)   *a.* [John]'s wife.
      b. [John's wife]'s mother.
      c. [John's wife's mother]'s friend.
      d. [John's wife's mother's friend]'s baby.

Langacker (1993: 27–8) discusses such examples in terms of a chaining of reference point–target relations. The initial reference point serves to identity a target, which then becomes a reference point for the identification of a further target, and on so. Embedded possessives are thus analogous to chained locatives, in which each location becomes the point of departure for identifying the next location.

(38)   The Lexicostatics Museum is across the Plaza, through that alley, and over the bridge.

The possibility of possessive embedding, however, is largely restricted to possessives headed by human relational nouns, especially kinship terms. Other possessives tend to be precluded from functioning as possessors. Halitsky (1975: 291) cites the following examples, which he marks as ungrammatical.

(39)   *a.* *[the peasants' rebellion]'s outcome.
      b. *[Kennedy's assassination]'s effect on the country.
      c. *[America's invasion of Cambodia]'s failure.

Halitsky proposes to derive the ungrammaticality of (39) from a general structural constraint, his 'Specifier Recursion Hypothesis', which bans recursion of possessives in specifier position of an NP. The constraint was motivated by certain parallels between sentences and noun phrases. On Halitsky's assumption that a

Subject is a Specifier to VP, the constraint forbids recursion in subject position also: *That that John smokes bothers Bill is obvious.*

Of course, the Specifier Recursion Hypothesis incorrectly predicts the ungrammaticality of (37). Halitsky is thus led to propose an entirely *ad hoc* modification to his constraint, namely, that recursion in Specifier position is disallowed just in case a 'grammatical relation' holds between the constituents of the embedded possessive (1975: 292, n. 11), whereby 'grammatical relation' will need to be defined 'in some principled way so as to exclude relations of kinship, class-membership, etc.'. By 'grammatical relation' is meant, presumably, an argument relation, of the kind holding within a possessive nominalization. But counterexamples, even to this modification of the Specifier Recursion Hypothesis, are not difficult to find. Consider the following, in which the relation expressed in *his readers, his supporters,* and *your critics* is presumably a 'grammatical' relation.

(40)   *a.* The author maintains [his reader's interest] right to the very end.
       b. The politician tried to satisfy [his supporters' aspirations].
       c. Don't be too discouraged by [your critics' remarks].

Note that in these examples, the embedded possessor is denoted by a pronoun (also that the embedded possessee is animate). Even the expressions in (39) become significantly better, it seems to me, simply through pronominalization of the embedded possessor.

(41)   *a.* ?their rebellion's outcome.
       b. ?his assassination's effect on the country.
       c. ?our invasion's failure.

Whether a possessor appears as a full NP or as a pronoun ought to have no bearing of the validity of Halitsky's constraint, whether modified or not. For whatever the nature of the relation obtaining between *the peasants* and *rebellion* in (39*a*)—whether the relation be a 'grammatical' relation or a 'non-grammatical' relation—precisely the same relation obtains within *their rebellion* in (41*a*).

The possibility of using a pronoun is a symptom of topicality. That mere pronominalization of the possessor can increase acceptability suggests that the source of the grammaticality judgements in (37) and (39) might well lie in topicality. In fact, the joint studies of Brown (1983) and Givón (1983*c*) that were reviewed in section 8.2.1 suggest the obvious explanation of the contrast. Consider, first, the starred examples in (39). Brown's (1983) study showed that possessor and possessee are maximally differentiated by topicality: the possessor names a maximally topical entity, whilst the possessee is not only non-topical at the time of its mention, possessees typically fail to achieve topicality in following discourse. In virtue of this last property, possessives are likely to be especially infelicitous in the highly topical position of possessor. We can approach this in another way. On the topicality thesis, *the peasants' rebellion's outcome* presupposes the topicality of *the peasants' rebellion*, which in turn presupposes the topicality of *the peasants*. But if the discourse context has rendered both *the peasants* and *the peasants' rebellion* topical, a speaker would have no reason at all to refer to the outcome of the rebellion by means of the expression *the peasants' rebellion's outcome*! It would be sufficient for her to say, quite simply, *the rebellion's outcome*, *its outcome*, or even *the outcome*. It is difficult, therefore, to imagine any discourse context in which *the peasants' rebellion's outcome* would be an appropriate thing for a speaker to say.

What, then, of the acceptability contrast between (39) and (37)? A glance at Table 8.3 gives the answer. We already noted in connection with Givón's (1983c) study that possessives denoting kinship relations may have different discourse properties than possessives denoting inanimates, in that kinship possessives are used to introduce, and to keep track of, individuals who are accessed in terms of their relation to a central participant (the narrator, in Givón's text). It is just these kinds of possessives—possessives which identify a potentially topical individual by invoking a kinship or other kind of interpersonal relation—that lend themselves to possessive embedding.

It seems reasonable to conclude, therefore, that the possibility of possessive embedding reflects aspects of topicality distribution, it has nothing at all to do with configurational constraints, of the kind proposed by Halitsky. In fact, I would go further, and cite Halitsky's 'Specifier Recursion Hypothesis', and its modification, as a textbook example of the futility of attempts to devise formalistic, configurational accounts of linguistic phenomena which are clearly grounded in general cognitive processes of referent identification and referent tracking.

8.3.4 *Plural possessors*

The text-based study reported in Taylor (1991a) revealed that the majority of possessives had, as their possessor, a singular definite NP. I suggested earlier that this preference for singular number falls out quite naturally from the reference point analysis of the construction, in that a single identifiable entity is likely to be better suited to a reference point function than a plurality of entities.

It is in fact the case that plural nominals do tend to be less felicitous as possessors than singulars. Huddleston (1984: 270) notes, without discussion or explanation, that *the errors' removal from the manuscript* is 'significantly worse' than *the error's removal from the manuscript*. Acceptability gets even worse if the possessor contains a definite plural numeral (42c), an indefinite plural numeral (42d), or a generic plural (42e).

(42)   *a.* the error's removal from the manuscript.
       b. (?)the errors' removal from the manuscript.
       c. ?the ten errors' removal from the manuscript.
       d. ??ten errors' removal from the manuscript.
       e. *errors' removal from the manuscript.

Similarly graded judgements attach to the following examples.

(43) *a.* the city's destruction.
      b. (?)the cities' destruction.
      c. ?the two cities' destruction.
      d. ??both cities' destruction.
      e. *cities' destruction.

(44) *a.* the girl's mother.
      b. (?)the girls' mother.
      c. ?the three girls' mother.
      d. *three girls' mother.
      e. **girls' mother. (in the sense "a/the mother of girls")

We already noted (section 6.7) that Fellbaum (1987: 82) had cited the ungrammaticality of *cities' destruction* (43e) as evidence that possessives headed by deverbal nouns (like *destruction*) can only have an accomplishment reading, not an activity reading. Her account is immediately rendered suspect by the fact that the graded grammaticality judgements in (43) exactly parallel those in (44), where the question of an activity vs. accomplishment reading obviously cannot arise. Furthermore, as already pointed out in Chapter 6, her claim that possessive nominalizations may not have an activity reading could be descriptively incorrect, anyway.

The most economical explanation of the ungrammaticality of *cities' destruction* is therefore in terms of the general unsuitability of a plural, and especially a generic plural, to function as the reference point for the identification of the possessee, in this case, a specific instance of the process of destruction.

8.3.5 *Possessives and relative clauses*

It is well known that a possessor NP may be internally quite complex, as in the following examples.

(45) *a.* [the Queen of England]'s son.
      b. [John's wife]'s mother.
      c. [the people who live across the road]'s new car.
      d. [the house of a friend of mine]'s roof blew off.

Yet it would be an error to assume that *any* NP, irrespective of its internal structure, can function as a possessor. (45c) shows that a possessor NP may contain a restrictive relative clause. Non-restrictive relatives, however, are not permitted.

(46) *our neighbours, who moved in last week's new car.

Topicality offers itself as a plausible explanation of the contrast. Restrictive relative clauses contain information that the speaker supposes is accessible to the hearer (Givón 1990: 645–50); a restrictive relative clause is necessarily topical, and therefore fully compatible with the reference point function of a possessor NP. Non-restrictive relatives are parenthetical assertions, introducing information assumed by the speaker not to be accessible to the hearer. This is not to say that a non-restrictive relative is *per se* incompatible with a topical NP. But the use of a non-restrictive relative with a possessor nominal does conflict with the required topicality of the possessor position, determining the ungrammaticality of (46).

While restrictive relatives, in virtue of their topicality, may readily occur with the possessor nominal, restrictive relatives are not, in general, tolerated with the possessee nominal. The restriction has been noted by Lyons (1986*b*: 124), from whom the following example (along with its asterisk) is taken.

(47)   *John's book that you borrowed.

For myself, I would hesitate to claim that (47) is fully ungrammatical, though it is, certainly, slightly odd.[19] Lyons offers no explanation for this. Again, topicality is likely to be involved. On the one hand, the possessive construction serves to introduce a specific entity into the discourse, namely (*John's*) *book*. This is an entity which the speaker presumes the hearer would not have been able to identify without prior mention of the reference point. (Otherwise, the speaker would not have used the possessive construction in the first place.) At the same time, in using a restrictive relative, (*book*) *that you borrowed*, the speaker presupposes the hearer's familiarity with the fact that the book was borrowed. There is therefore a conflict between the topicality of the relative clause, and the non-topicality of the possessee entity. This conflict explains the (slight) oddity of (47).

We saw in the preceding section that kinship possessives may differ in their topicality properties from inanimate possessives, in that kinship possessives may be used to name potentially topical participants in a discourse. Kinship possessives, therefore, ought to be fully compatible with a restrictive relative. This prediction does seem to be borne out. Other kinds of human relational nouns also tolerate restrictive relative.

(48)   *a.* his sister who works in the bank.
      b. Bill's cousin who lives in Australia.
      c. her students who flunked phonology.
      d. my friends who accepted the invitation.

Not only restrictive relatives, but restrictive prepositional phrases also tend to be infelicitous as modifiers of a possessee nominal. On this issue, intuitions are perhaps even more shaky, and fluctuate according to the identity of the nominals involved (again, suggestive of a semantic-cognitive, rather than a purely configurational explanation). The following contrast is due to Chomsky (1970: 197).

---

[19] Pullum (1991: 769) also notes that prenominal possessors 'slightly lower the acceptability of restrictive relatives', stating that *my book that I told you about* is 'slightly unacceptable'.

(49)   *a.* *John's book on the table.
     b. John's house in the woods.

In his commentary on these examples, Chomsky points to the status of *on the table* as a 'true reduced relative' (p. 197). The example is therefore comparable to the restrictive relative clause in (47). (Chomsky, though, does not enlighten us as to why relatives, whether reduced or not, should be infelicitous in possessives.) Concerning (49*b*), Chomsky merely states that *house in the woods* constitutes 'some kind of nominal constituent'. Presumably, what is meant is that *house in the woods* denotes a kind, or stable subcategory of house—a weekend-house, perhaps. A specific instance of this subcategory may then be legitimately identified by means of the possessive construction. It would be odd, however, to think of 'book on the table'—or, returning to (47), 'book that you borrowed' —as a kind, or subcategory of book. Where a book happens to be, at any moment, is a contingent property of the book, it is not a criterion for the subcategorization of books.

Again, we find that 'true reduced relatives' on kinship and other human relational nouns are perfectly acceptable in possessives.

(50)   *a.* his sister at the University.
     b. Bill's cousin in Australia.
     c. her students with an 'A'.
     d. my friends with invitations to the party.

8.3.6 *Reversability of possessor and possessee*

A final observation: Topicality offers itself as one factor behind the general impossibility of reversing the nominals in a possessive relation (*the girl's hat* vs. **the hat's girl, the car's headlights* vs. **the headlights' car*). This property is fully consistent with the asymmetry between the topical possessor and the non-topical possessee.

9 The Cue Validity of the Possessor

IN this chapter I consider some further entailments of the reference point analysis, especially as these pertain to the semantic relation between possessor and possessee.[1]

We have remarked on several occasions that the possessive construction does not of itself encode any specific semantic relation. Even so, it is not the case that *any* semantic relation is compatible with the construction. Restrictions on the semantic relation of possessor to possessee were in fact a major topic of the literature reviewed in Chapter 6.

We saw in the preceding chapter how some of these restrictions fall out from the requirement that the possessor nominal be topical; this requirement, in turn, is a natural consequence of the reference point analysis. Continuing this approach, I argue here that the restrictions reflect a further requirement on the possessor nominal, one which, again, falls out from the reference point analysis. This requirement concerns the *cue validity* of the reference point *vis-à-vis* the intended target.

possessor   *possessed*

9.1 CUE VALIDITY

It is not at all surprising that a reference point construction should impose restrictions on both reference point and target. We should certainly not expect that any two randomly selected entities can be placed in a reference point relation just in case there exists *some* semantic relation between them. On the contrary, it seems reasonable to suppose that a given entity will be better able to serve as a reference point for the identification of some potential targets than others; ra conversely, that a given target can be more efficiently identified from some reference points than from others. *rather*

Langacker approaches this matter in terms of the reference point's 'dominion'. A *dominion* is characterized as 'the conceptual domain (or the set of entities) to which a particular reference point affords direct access'; the dominion, in other words, comprises 'the class of potential targets' (Langacker 1993: 6). Langacker explicates the notion on a spatial analogy. In a locative expression, such as *the*

[1] Some of the arguments of this chapter were first presented in Taylor (1994*b*).

book on the table, the prepositional phrase *on the table* defines a *search do-main*.[2] This is a region in space to which the locative expression confines the trajector; it is the region to which one must look in order to find the trajector. The dominion of the possessor nominal, Langacker suggests, can be thought of as a 'possessive search domain' (p. 12). The possessive confines the possessee to the dominion of the possessor, and it is to the dominion that one must look in order to conceptually 'locate' the possessee.

While the spatial analogy is instructive, there is a crucial difference between a locative and a possessive search domain. This is that a possessor nominal's dominion, unlike a locative search domain, cannot be exhaustively delimited. It is possible, in principle, to circumscribe, and to visually scan, the spatial region defined by *on the table*, in search of the trajector entity. An analogous operation is not possible with a possessor nominal. What, for example, might be the contents of the possessive search domain established by *John*? There is no coherent answer. The number of semantic relations that may be invoked by a possessive expression is in principle indeterminate, hence the possessor nominal's dominion is also indeterminate. One needs, at very least, to know the semantic category of the target entity. If the target is a 'possessible' entity, such as a watch or car, the search domain is constituted by John's possessions; if the target entity is a kinship term, the search domain is John's family members; if the target entity is a body-part term, the search domain is John's body; if the possessee is an action noun, or a noun denoting a psychological state, the search domain comprises those actions in which John is a participant, or those psychological states in which John is involved.

A possessive search domain is therefore not something that can be established in advance, for any and every possessor nominal. Consider the fact that a speaker, in producing a possessive, manifestly does not start out from reference point R, only then to select a target from the set of entities that might be identified from R. Rather obviously, the speaker starts with the intention of referring to a target entity T, and then selects the reference point most appropriate to this purpose. Likewise the hearer, on encountering a possessive, does not first try to conceptualize the possessor's dominion, only then to select from its contents just that entity that the speaker intends. The hearer takes note of the semantic character of the target, and then, given the identity of the reference point, attempts to identify the target in terms of a semantic relation that can hold between reference point and target.

The question to be addressed in this chapter can therefore be phrased as follows: Given the speaker's desire to uniquely identify the target, what determines the choice of reference point? In addressing this question, I shall pay special attention to the restrictions on possessor nominals that were reviewed in Chapter 6, and that are encapsulated in the Experiencer and Affectedness

---

[2] Langacker attributes the term 'search domain' to Bruce Hawkins (1984).

John's destruction of his back shed took all afternoon

p 709
p 29

Constraints. In this connection, we shall need to ask: Given the speaker's intention to identify target T, why is it that certain entities—entities which, moreover, bear a rather transparent semantic relation to T—are excluded from functioning as reference points?

We already gave a partial answer to this question in the preceding chapter. There, we documented the requirement that the reference point be topical, i.e. that it name a cognitively accessible entity. We also observed that topicality is probably not the only constraint on possessives. No amount of topicalizing context seems able to sanction objective readings of (1).   *ie Louise is the one you /o*

But OK
My love of Louise
My recollection of John

(1) a. *Louise's love. [unacceptable with Louise = Stimulus]
     b. *John's recollection. [unacceptable with John = Stimulus]

(2) a. *the cliff's avoidance. [objective reading of *the cliff*]
     b. the city's destruction. [objective reading of *the city*]—*oK*

Avoidance of the cliff
was crucial to survival

Nor is it likely that the topicality of the possessor determines the acceptability contrast in (2), or the fact that (2b) does not permit a subjective reading of *the city*.

In this chapter I shall pursue the thesis that, in addition to the requirement that it be topical, the possessor nominal needs to be such that it can provide reliable cues for the identification of the target. I refer to this aspect of the possessor as its *cue validity vis-à-vis* the possessee. Coming back to the examples in (1), we shall want to say the Experiencer has high cue validity for the identification of an emotional or cognitive state, whilst the Stimulus that gives rise to the state has virtually zero cue validity. With respect to (2), we shall want to say that an event can be more reliably cued by an entity affected by the event, than by an entity that is unaffected by it, or by the entity that instigates the event.

9.2 RELATIONAL NOUNS IN POSSESSIVES

In order to get a handle on some of the issues involved, I want to take a close look at possessives whose target entity is denoted by a relational noun, such as a kinship term. A remarkable fact about kinship possessives, such as *John's wife*, is that their interpretation is quite determinate. Although *John's car* would normally be taken to refer to the car that John owns, many other interpretations are easily imaginable, especially if certain kinds of background knowledge are available. If it is known that John is a car designer, *John's car* could readily refer to the car that John has designed, not to the one that he owns.

Such shifting interpretations are not available for *John's wife*. The expression can only designate the woman related to John by marriage, it could not refer to a married woman who bears some other relation of association to John. The expression could not, for example, designate the married woman employed as John's secretary, or the married woman with whom John is currently having an extramarital affair. No amount of background knowledge that one might bring to bear on the situation is able to interfere with the rigid interpretation of *John's wife*.

The reason plausibly has to do with the fact that *wife* is an inherently *relational noun*, and with the manner in which a valence relation is established between inherently relational *wife* and the possessor phrase *John's*. Like all nouns, inherently relational nouns profile a thing (in the technical sense of section 4.1). In addition, they construe the designated thing in terms of a relation to another entity. The relation, and the relatum, are not designated by the relational nouns, nevertheless these aspects are salient elements in the unprofiled base of predication of a relational noun. Now, a grammatical relation can be established between two expressions just in case some component of the semantic structure of the one can be construed as identical to some component of the semantic structure of the other (section 4.3). Let us consider, then, the integration of the constituent morphemes *John*, POSS, and *wife* in the possessive *John's wife*.

ie the kinship diagram

In Figure 9.1 I assume the analysis of the possessive morpheme proposed in section 5.6. The possessive morpheme is a kind of determiner, which profiles the grounded entity (the possessee), but which also, in its unprofiled scope of predication, invokes the mental path that a conceptualizer follows in order to identify the grounded instance. The trajector of the possessive morpheme is therefore a schematically characterized instance, while its landmark is a schematically characterized reference point. The lower part of Figure 9.1 shows the integration of *John* and POSS; here, *John* is identified with the landmark of POSS, and is put into correspondence with it. The upper part of Figure 9.1 shows the integration of *John's* and *wife*. Here we see, first of all, that the profile of *wife* is placed in correspondence with the schematic profile of *John's*. More than this, we observe a *maximization of overlap* between the semantic structures of the participating expressions. The unprofiled relation in the semantic structure of *wife* is construed as identical with the unprofiled relation in the semantic structure of POSS, whilst the unprofiled landmark in the semantic structure of *wife* is construed as identical to the unprofiled landmark in the semantic structure of POSS.

Maximization of overlap in the establishment of valence relations was noted in Taylor (1992). In the case in point, maximization of overlap is not only preferred; to the extent that *John's wife* can only invoke a kinship relation, *John* has to be construed as the husband of the designated person. The overlap is therefore *obligatory*.

It is easy to see why this should be so. *Wife*, as an intrinsically relational noun, designates an adult human female, but construes this individual as a participant in an unprofiled relation. Moreover, it is the speaker who *has chosen* to designate this individual by means of the word *wife*; he could easily have chosen another word: *friend*, *mother*, *colleague*, *neighbour*, or, quite simply,

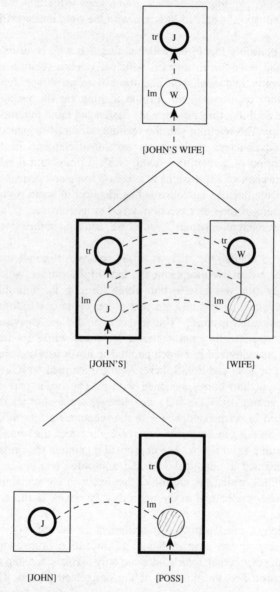

FIG. 9.1. Integration of *John's wife*

woman. The very fact that the speaker has chosen this relational term (*wife*) entails the existence of a relatum (i.e. the husband), to whom the designated person bears the relation. It is this that gives the relatum a high measure of cue validity for the identification of the target. In contrast, all other entities with which the designated person may have some or other relation of association (as friend, daughter, colleague, neighbour, or what not) have minimal, or insignificant cue validity.

Similar arguments can be brought to bear on the interpretation of *the dog's tail, the girl's hat*, in contrast to the general impossibility of **the tail's dog* and **the hat's girl*. The notion of a part, especially a part which typically has no independent existence except as a constituent of a whole, entails the notion of the whole. The notion of the whole is intrinsic to the conceptualization of the part, with the consequence that the whole has high cue validity for the identification of the part. On the other hand, the part has minimal cue validity for the whole. A whole typically consists of many, perhaps even an indefinite number of parts, and (generally) no one part has privileged status in the conceptualization of the whole. Consequently, a part will be highly unsuited to functioning as a reference point for the identification of the whole. Likewise with names of clothing items. The very notion of an article of clothing entails a wearer. The notion of a wearer is therefore intrinsic to the semantic structure of *hat*; the very fact of calling something a 'hat' entails that the entity is wearable. Whence the high cue validity of the wearer with respect to the item of clothing. The notion of a person, on the other hand, does not entail any specific article of clothing; the notion of 'hat' does not figure at all in the semantic characterization of 'girl'. Whence the zero cue validity of *the hat* with respect to *girl*, and the impossibility of **the hat's girl*.[3]

A preliminary conclusion, therefore, is that the possessor nominal is obligatorily identified with some schematically characterized entity in the semantic structure of the possessee nominal. Two problems, however, arise.

(*a*) Many nouns, such as *book, dog, car*, and the like, are not inherently relational. Conceptualization of the entity need not invoke any specific relation to another entity. There is therefore no relatum inherent in the semantic structure of the noun which could function as an optimal reference point. What we find, generally, is that expressions with non-relational possessees are typically interpreted in terms of a relation of possession.

(*b*) Some inherently relational nouns contain, in their scope of predication, more than one unprofiled relatum. Foremost amongst these are nouns derived from transitive verbs, of the kind *destruction, avoidance, recollection*. These

[3] An analysis in terms of cue validity leads to exactly the same conclusion as an analysis in terms of topicality (see section 8.3.6). This does not mean that appeal to cue validity is redundant. On the contrary, the acceptability of *the girl's hat*, in contrast to the impossibility of **the hat's girl*, is multiply motivated. A possessive expression, to be fully acceptable, will need to simultaneously satisfy different kinds of constraints inherent to the possessive construction.

nouns make reference, in their semantic structure, to both the trajector and the landmark of the nominalized process. With these nouns, there are therefore *two* potential candidates for elaboration by a possessor nominal. The import of the Affectedness and Experiencer Constraints is to state the conditions under which these potential candidates may be selected for the possessor role.

I address the second of these issues first. As a preliminary to the discussion, I first say a few words on the nature of deverbal nouns.

9.3 SEMANTIC STRUCTURE OF DEVERBAL NOUNS

Deverbal nouns are characterized by *profile shift vis-à-vis* the base form. A verb, by definition, profiles a relation, more precisely, a process, that is, a relation scanned through time. In a deverbal noun, some facet of the process is reified (that is, is construed as a thing), and put in profile, whilst the relational profile of the verb gets demoted to the unprofiled base of predication.

There are several kinds of deverbal noun. These may be distinguished, in the first instance, according to which facet of the verbal predication is singled out for profiling (Langacker 1991: 23–35). Here, I list some of the major categories.

(*a*) Agent nouns (*invader, narrator, singer*) profile the trajector of the process, the process itself, as well as the schematic landmark, being demoted to the base of predication. Agent nouns are typically marked by the suffix *-er*. We might say, therefore, that *-er* has a schematic nominal profile, which is inherited by the agent noun. The account would be essentially compatible with the analysis of derivational processes that is pursued by Lieber (1983), amongst others. On Lieber's approach, the derivational suffix heads the derived form, and so determines its semantic and syntactic category.

(*b*) Patient nouns (*draftee, appointee*) are analogous to agent nouns, except that they profile the landmark entity. Patient nouns are typically marked by the suffix *-ee*. As with agent nouns, therefore, one could say that the *-ee* profiles a schematic landmark, and confers this profile to the deverbal noun.[4]

(*c*) Result nouns profile an entity that comes into existence as a consequence of the process (*bruise, dent, photograph*). These, and the categories listed below, are not associated with any distinctive morphology.

(*d*) Manner nouns profile the manner in which a process is carried out by the trajector (*walk*, as in *His walk is peculiar, He had a peculiar walk*).

---

[4] The semantics of *-ee*, however, are rather more complex. First, nouns in *-ee* seem able only to denote humans. Furthermore, the suffix not only attaches to transitive verb stems, to denote the person affected by the process, it can also attach to some of the so-called unaccusative intransitives, to denote the person who performs the relevant activity (*returnee, escapee, retiree*), and even to transitives to denote the human trajector (*the convention attendees*). The relevant point seems to be that *-ee* is non-agentive, and may thus profile either the Patient or the Theme, the latter roughly equivalent to Langacker's (1991: 285) 'mover'.

(*e*) Ability nouns profile the ability of the trajector to perform the relevant activity (*speech*, in *His speech returned, He lost his speech*). *his walk, hearing, sight*

In each of the above cases, there is in the semantic structure of the noun *just one* salient candidate for elaboration by a possessor nominal. Consequently, in *the country's invader, the country* is straightforwardly identified as the unprofiled landmark in the semantic structure of *invader*. *The country* thus comes to be interpreted as the the entity that was invaded. Likewise, in *the minister's appointee, the minister* is interpreted as the trajector, that is, as the one who did the appointing. Similarly with *his walk, his speech*, in the examples cited above.

Our special concern here is with another type of deverbal noun. This is the type referred to by Langacker (1991: 24) as an *episodic nominalization*.[5]   *— a jump*

(*f*) An episodic noun reifies a single instance, or episode, of the process. Concurrently, both trajector and landmark are demoted to unprofiled elements in the noun's base of predication. The unprofiled participants—the trajector and the landmark—may then be specified *periphrastically*, by means of a possessor phrase or an *of*-phrase. Our concern here is to identify the conditions under which the first of these possibilities (elaboration by a possessor phrase) is exploited.

The above categories are by no means always clear-cut. In the case of situations having to do with the bringing into existence, or, alternatively, the destruction of an entity, the distinction between a patient and a result noun becomes essentially vacuous. It may also be difficult, in some cases, to draw a clear conceptual distinction between an episodic noun and a result or patient noun. The matter is also complicated by the fact that deverbal nouns are typically polysemous with respect to at least some of the different categories.

Consider, for example, nouns derived from accomplishment verbs. An accomplishment, in Vendler's (1967) sense, consists of an internally homogeneous activity which culminates in a change in state. The verb *destroy* is plausibly regarded as polysemous between a purely activity sense (*They were destroying the city for three days*) and an accomplishment sense, where the activity and the resulting change of state are profiled (*They destroyed the city in three days*). The episodic noun *destruction* can likewise have both an activity and an accomplishment reading. But in addition, *destruction* can have a third reading, which profiles only the result of the activity.

(3)   *a.*   {the destruction of the city/the city's destruction} continued for three days. [Activity]

---

[5] Some further, minor types of deverbal noun can be identified, such as locatives (which denote the place at which a process occurs) and instrumentals (which denote the instrument used in a process). These can perhaps be regarded as idiosyncratic extensions of more basic senses. *Smoker*, in its locative sense "a train compartment for smokers", is plausibly a metonymic extension of the agent sense. Earliest uses of *typewriter* denoted the typist; the instrument reading is plausibly regarded as a metonymic extension.

  b. {the destruction of the city/the city's destruction} took place in three
     days. [Accomplishment]
  c. The destruction that the enemy caused was considerable. [Result]

On the activity and accomplishment readings, *the city's destruction* can have
only an objective interpretation. On the result reading of *destruction*, however,
a subjective interpretation is available (4). This should not be too surprising,
since on its result reading, *destruction* denotes the landmark entity which results
from the process, it does not denote an episode of the process itself. Like patient
nouns, it naturally takes the trajector as possessor.

(4) a. The bomb's destruction extended over several blocks.
     b. The enemy's destruction took many months to repair.

  Some departures from the paradigm illustrated in section 6.2, especially the
possibility of subjective readings of expressions like *John's criticism, the company's donation*, may be plausibly attributed to the fact that the deverbal nouns
in question have result readings alongside the episodic reading. In (5), *took
place* forces an episodic reading; it requires, as its subject, an expression denoting an event, that is, an episodic noun, not a participant in the event or an entity
resulting from an event. We see that the episodic reading of *donation* is consistent only with an objective reading of the possessor. The subjective reading is,
however, possible in (5c), where *donation* has a patient interpretation, denoting
the entity that was donated.

subject of donate

(5) a. *The company's donation took place at a ceremony yesterday. [episodic
        reading; *the company* = Agent] *is the only possible reading*
     b. The money's donation took place at a ceremony yesterday. *(episodic*
     c. The company's donation was valued at $1,000. [result reading]

object of donate

(subject of donate)

The following are similar. Acceptability judgements pertain to a subjective reading of the possessor. We see that the possibility of a subjective reading in each
case correlates with the availability of a result reading of the possessee.

(6) a. John's examination is three pages long. *(result— John*
     b. *John's examination took place yesterday.
(7) a. God surveyed His creation.
     b. *God's creation took place in six days.
(8) a. John's criticism will be published shortly. *(result possible —John did the critic*
     b. *John's criticism took place during the meeting yesterday.

  It is also worth observing that many deverbal nouns, on some of their readings
at least, have semantic values that are not fully predictable from the meanings
of the source verbs. Consider *speech* and *sight*.

  As a mass noun, *speech* may denote the faculty, or ability to speak (9a), or
the manner in which a person speaks (9b).

(9) a. the onset of speech; he lost his speech; after his stroke his speech began
        to return. — *ability*

assessment
evaluation .
John's investigation was careful & meticulous / rapid & superficial) John is subject— process
was published in IJAL /was carefully checked by his supervisor —var

    b. speech training; her speech has improved; her speech is slurred. — *manner*
    c. I'm busy transcribing a passage of aphasic speech.
    d. I'm busy transcribing a speech.— *product of an activity*

Speech may also denote the product of the speaking activity. As a mass noun, *speech* (predictably) denotes the product of the activity construed as an imperfective (that is, as an internally unstructured and unbounded) process (9*c*). As a count noun, however, *speech* does not simply denote the product of a bounded instance (*any* bounded instance) of speaking activity, it idiosyncratically denotes a formal monologue addressed by a person of some importance to an assembled audience (9*d*).

A similar state of affairs holds for *sight*, in that as a mass noun the word may denote the faculty (10*a*), or the ability (10*b*) to see, while as a count noun *sight* denotes (some aspects of) what is seen. As a plural, it idiosyncratically denotes "things worth seeing".

(10)   *a.* He lost his sight as a result of the accident. *(ability to see)*
      b. These spectacles improve my sight. *(ability to see)*
      c. It was an impressive sight.
      d. Have you seen the sights? *(something worth seeing)*

Curiously, neither *speech* nor *sight* have episodic readings. Corresponding to *John spoke those words* we have neither **John's speech of those words*, nor **those words' speech* (*by John*). *John's speech*, it seems, may only have an ability reading (the general faculty of speech is attributed to John), a style reading, or a result reading. Likewise, corresponding to *John saw the film*, we have neither **John's sight of the film* nor **the film's sight* (*by John*).

We have discussed the differentiation of derived nouns according to which facet of the base process the noun profiles. There is a further dimension to nominalization, which we shall explore in greater detail in the next chapter. A brief mention may be appropriate here, however. This concerns what we might refer to as 'degree of reification'. The idea is that derived nouns are fully nominal in character, whilst other nominalizations preserve some of the verbal, or 'processual' character of the nominalized process. The notion of degree of reification will be especially relevant to *-ing* nominalizations in English, to the extent that these may incorporate such typically clausal elements as markers of aspect and voice, and even negation, elements which are, of course, absent from the deverbal nouns discussed above.

9.4 INFORMATIVITY

Episodic nouns make reference, within their scope of predication, to two schematically characterized entities, viz. the trajector and the landmark of the unprofiled process. In principle, therefore, there are two 'elaboration sites' in the *relational* noun's semantic structure, each of which is a candidate for elaboration by a possessor nominal. Yet, it generally happens that one of these unprofiled entities is a stronger candidate for elaboration than the other.

Langacker (1993: 10) has suggested that it is the subject of the nominalized verb that preferentially serves as possessor, by virtue of its 'greater prominence (as primary figure within the profiled relationship)'. The situation, however, is clearly more complex and differentiated. With psychological predicates, it is the Experiencer (irrespective of its syntactic role in the clausal predication) that obligatorily functions as possessor, whence the impossibility of an objective reading of *Louise's love*. With action predicates, it is preferentially the landmark, but only on condition that the landmark is affected by the action: *the city's destruction, *the cliff's avoidance*. The trajector is normally permitted as possessor only if the landmark is already specified in an *of*-phrase: *the enemy's destruction *(of the city)*.

the enemy destroyed the city

In accordance with the thesis being pursued in this chapter, we shall need to say that of the two candidates for elaboration by the possessor, one has higher cue validity for the identification of the possessee than the other. In the case of Herbie loving Louise, Herbie is a more effective cue for the identification of the relational predicate than is Louise; in the case of the enemy destroying the city, the city is the more effective cue; whilst in the case of the hikers avoiding the cliff, the cliff is quite ineffective. — *hikers are the effect means*

Let us consider in more detail what is involved here. Suppose we learn from some source that Herbie loves Louise. Suppose, also, that we want to check on the truth of this information. How would we go about it? Where, in other words, would we look to find out whether the stated relation between Herbie and Louise does, in fact, hold? Rather obviously, we would look to Herbie and enquire about his emotional state. There would be little point in looking to Louise, to see whether she is loved. Louise might not know that she is the object of Herbie's love; possibly, the Louise that Herbie loves exists only in Herbie's imagination![6] Herbie, clearly, provides a much more effective cue to the verification of the relation than does Louise. Or consider, next, a statement that *The enemy destroyed the city*. In order to check out the truth of this statement, our first step would surely be to inspect the referent of *the city*, for visible signs that it had been destroyed; only then might we turn to the referent of *the enemy*, to find out whether they had engaged in a destroying activity. Again, the city (or what was left of it) is a more effective cue for the verification of the information than the enemy. Thirdly, consider *The hikers avoided the cliff*. Here, there would be no point in examining the cliff, to see whether it had been avoided: a cliff that has been avoided looks no different from a cliff that has not been avoided. We would surely turn to the hikers, and attempt to reconstruct their actions with respect to the cliff, and their motives for their actions.

---

[6] *Love*, like many of the psychological verbs (*admire, fear, want, believe*, and so on) is a 'space-builder' (Fauconnier 1994: 16); it sets up a mental space whose inhabitants might not correspond to anything in the parent space. See also Fodor (1979) and Zubizarreta (1987: 30–2).

The cue validity of the respective entities turns on differences in the *inform-ativity* of the relatum with respect to the relation that is to be identified. We may characterize informativity as follows.

(11)   An entity E is informative with respect to a relation R in proportion to the number, and specificity, of inferences that may be drawn with respect to E, given a characterizaton of R.[7]

To the extent that a participant is informative with respect to the relation, that participant will be an effective cue for the identification of the relation.

If we go through each of the three cases discussed above, we shall see that the entity that is the preferred reference point in a possessive turns out to be the more informative participant in the relation, in the sense of (11). Consider the skeletal sentence *X loves* (*hates/fears/admires/knows*, etc.) *Y*. It is evident that we can draw more specific inferences with respect to X than with respect to Y. We infer that X is an animate, sentient creature, prototypically a human being, also that X is in a certain emotional or cognitive state. Concerning Y we can infer practically nothing. Y may be human or non-human, animate or non-animate, concrete or abstract; we can say nothing about the present state of Y; we are not even able to infer the real-world existence of Y, for the object of X's love (hate, fear, etc.) might exist only in X's imagination. Consider, next, a statement to the effect that *X destroyed Y*. Here, it is possible to draw more substantive inferences with respect to Y than with respect to X.[8] Y has undergone a drastic change of state, such that subsequent to the event Y may no longer even be categorized as a 'Y', or at least, not as a good example of a 'Y'. Of X we can infer little, other than that X is an entity that can exert a force, and that force was in fact exerted. We may not infer that X acted intentionally (*X unintentionally destroyed Y* is perfectly coherent), or even that X is animate, let alone human (cf. *The hurricane destroyed the city*). For verbs with non-affected objects, such as *avoid*, the facts are rather different. From *X avoided Y* we infer that X is a rational creature that acted intentionally, that X regarded Y as an obstacle or hindrance of some kind, and that X behaved in a certain manner with respect to Y. Of Y we can say little, other than that Y was an obstacle to X, or, more precisely, that X regarded Y as such. What little we can infer about Y has to be expressed in terms of the intentions and behaviour of X. Y thus turns out to be particularly low in informativity with respect to the avoidance-relation.

Informativity, and its contribution to cue validity, thus exactly predicts the properties of possessives headed by *love*, *destruction*, and *avoidance*. *Love* can only have the Experiencer as possessor, never Stimulus. *The city's destruction*

---

[7] Note that the informativity of E does *not* mean that, given a characterization of E, we may draw reliable inferences about the identity of R.

[8] The argument, of course, only applies to realis sentences, not irrealis sentences of the kind *X will/should/might destroy Y*.

can only have an objective reading (except, of course, when *destruction* functions as a result/patient nominal), whilst **the cliff's avoidance* is simply incoherent.

(The fact that, with *destruction* and *avoidance*, the possessor can have a subjective reading just in case the object is expressed in an *of*-phrase, follows from the present account. In *destruction of the city* and *avoidance of the cliff*, one of the participants in the relation has already been elaborated. There is therefore only one candidate for elaboration by the possessor, namely, the trajector of the process.)

With other action predicates, however, informativity is more evenly distributed between trajector and landmark; we predict, in such cases, that a possessor can have either a subjective or objective reading. This seems to be correct. Consider *invade* and *burgle*. From *X invaded Y* we can infer quite a lot about both X and Y. Y is a country, or territory, whose integrity has been violated; whilst X is an aggressor, with expansionist ambitions. Probably, an objective reading of *the country's invasion* would be preferred. Yet a subjective reading is not difficult to obtain, especially when the possessor is an individual or country whose aggressiveness is well known. We can easily get a subjective reading of *Hitler's invasion*, or, with reference to events of August 1990, *Iraq's invasion*. Likewise with *burgle*. From *X burgled Y* we infer that Y is an entity (a person or property) that has suffered damage of a certain kind, whilst X is a person who has intentionally performed a certain kind of criminal act. Predictably, *John's burglary* can have either a subjective or objective reading.

Note, by the way, that one could not account for the subjective readings of *Iraq's invasion* and *John's burglary* by claiming that *invasion* and *burglary* here have result, rather than episodic readings. (As we saw in (4), even *destruction* easily tolerates a subjective possessor on its result reading.) It is, namely, doubtful whether *invasion* and *burglary* can have result readings at all. *A film of the invasion*, *a photograph of the burglary* will depict some aspect of the invasion or burglary in progress, not the state resulting from the event.

There is some commonality between informativity, as here defined, and the specificity of a predicate's selection restrictions. Keenen (1984: 203) notes that action verbs typically impose much more specific restrictions on the semantic category of their direct objects than on their subjects. This, he suggests, is a consequence of the tighter 'bondedness' of an action and the Patient, than of an action and the Agent. *Break* requires that its direct object be fragile (i.e. 'breakable'), *spill* requires that its direct object be liquid (i.e. 'spillable'), *destroy* that its direct object be destructable. Restrictions on the subjects of these verbs are much less specific. In the case of *break* and *destroy*, the subjects do not even have to be animate, let alone human. On the other hand, *invade* and *burgle* do impose quite specific restrictions on both their subjects and objects.

Psychological verbs impose more specific selection restrictions on the Experiencer than on the Stimulus. The verbs *love, fear, know, bore*, etc. all require that the Experiencer (whether expressed as subject or direct object) be a cognizing entity, prototypically a human being, while there are practically no restrictions at all on the semantic category of the Stimulus. Of interest, also, is the manner in which Stimulus is encoded, especially in association with a derived noun. In the first place, the expression of Stimulus is generally optional. Whereas *the hikers' avoidance*, *the enemy's destruction*, with no mention of what was avoided or destroyed, are conceptually incomplete, *the hikers' fear, the students' bore-dom* are perfectly coherent, even though the reason for the fear or the boredom is not stated. Secondly, if the Stimulus is expressed, as in a prepositional phrase, the deverbal noun often selects a semantically more contentful preposition than the highly schematic *of*.

(12) *a.* desire {*of/for} chocolate.
  b. need {?of/for} chocolate.
  c. boredom {of/at/with} the lecture.
  d. admiration {?of/at/for} the performance.
  e. love {of/for/towards} the children.
  f. fear of the enemy/fear at the prospect.

The phenomenon is attested in other languages, too. In Italian, psychological nouns may take the preposition *per* "for" rather than the *di* "of": *l'amore per i bambini* "love of/for children", *l'odio per Maria* "hatred of/for Mary". We have already seen (section 6.6) that Giorgi and Longobardi (1991: 145), following Anderson (1978), take this as evidence for a distinction between arguments and complements, with 'true' arguments of a derived noun being introduced by the 'dummy' preposition *of* (or *di*), whilst complements are introduced in 'genuine' prepositional phrases, whose head is selected by the predicate. On their thesis, only arguments are available for preposing into possessor position. Whence the general impossibility, in both English and Italian, of Stimulus appearing prenominally as a possessor.[9]

I would interpret the alleged distinction between arguments and complements rather differently, namely in terms of the more peripheral, or *extrinsic* status of the Stimulus in the semantic structure of a psychological noun, as compared, say, to the highly *intrinsic* status of the affected entity in the semantic structure of *destruction*. One symptom of the extrinsic status of Stimulus is the fact that, if the Stimulus is expressed at all, the nature of the relation between the psychological state and the Stimulus may need to be encoded with a fair degree of specificity, i.e. by prepositions other than the highly schematic *of*. Furthermore, as some of the examples in (12) show, the choice between different prepositions can convey subtle semantic contrasts in this respect.

9.5 INTRINSICNESS

The last paragraph has introduced the notion of the intrinsicness/extrinsicness of a participant in a relation. The terms are used in the sense of Langacker (1987a: 160–1). Informativity is related to, but is not always identical with intrinsicness.

---

[9] See example (67) of Ch. 6.

Intrinsicness is a function of *conceptual autonomy* (see section 4.1; also Langacker 1991: 286–91). An entity is conceptually autonomous to the extent that it is possible to conceptualize that entity without making necessary reference to anything outside of the entity itself. An entity is conceptually dependent if conceptualization of the entity needs to make reference (if only schematically) to some other entity, or entities. Relational predicates (such as verbs and prepositions) are conceptually dependent, in that the very notion of a relation necessarily makes reference to the entities that are related. The same, of course, goes for episodic nouns, which reify the temporal relation designated by a verb.

Conceptual dependence and conceptual autonomy are matters of degree. (Probably, there is no such thing as an entity which is *fully* autonomous, in Langacker's sense.) A crucial insight of Langacker's is that, in the case of relational predicates, the elaboration of just one of the entities involved in the relation can often result in a conceptualization with a greater degree of autonomy than would result though the elaboration of the other entity. The entity involved in the more autonomous conceptualization is more intrinsic to the relation.

Langacker (1991: 295–8) illustrates on the example of the sentence *Floyd broke the glass*. He observes that the event may be conceptualized from two complementary perspectives. On the one hand, we construe the event in terms of an independently acting entity (Floyd), whose action directly affects another entity (the glass). Floyd is the energy source, energy flows from Floyd to the glass, resulting in a substantial change in state of the glass (the energy sink). This construal (the 'energetic' construal) underlies the agent–patient/subject–direct object/nominative–accusative pattern of a canonical transitive clause in English (and other 'accusative languages').

On the energetic construal, both participants in the relation (energy source and energy sink) are arguably equally intrinsic to the conceptualization; whence the fact that *break*, as a transitive verb, requires a specification both of Agent and Patient.[10] There is, however, an alternative conceptualization, which rests on the possibility of isolating a conceptually autonomous (or relatively autonomous) component of the event. The 'autonomous core' may be progressively expanded by the incorporation of further elements, whereby each expansion is itself (relatively) conceptually autonomous. In the case of Floyd breaking the glass, the notion of the glass breaking is clearly more autonomous than the notion of Floyd performing an act of breaking. We can conceptualize a glass breaking without invoking any specific cause, as when we say that 'the glass just broke', or 'it broke by itself'. On the other hand, we can only conceptualize Floyd's act of breaking if we make reference to some entity or entities that got broken; we cannot, for example, say **Floyd broke* (with Floyd as Agent). This sentence is grammatically (and conceptually) incomplete, we need, at the very least, to say

---

[10] Even in a passive clause (*The glass got broken*) the Agent is schematically represented in the semantic structure of the past participle, and may be explicitly elaborated in a *by*-phrase.

Floyd broke something, schematically specifying the landmark entity. The autonomous core of the event—the glass breaking—may then be expanded by reference to its cause (some action by Floyd), which in turn may be expanded by a statement of *its* cause . . . and so on. On the autonomous core construal, therefore, the Patient, or landmark entity turns out to be more intrinsic to the relational predicate *break* than the Agent, or trajector, that performs the action.

It must be emphasized that the notion of autonomous core has to do with a person's conceptualization of a situation, not with its objective properties. Objectively speaking, it could be argued that, if an act of breaking on the part of Floyd entails an entity that got broken, then the breaking of a glass equally —*not necessarily* entails some event which caused the glass to break. The glass breaking, and Floyd performing an act of breaking, would both be conceptually dependent, to the same degree, and in comparable ways. We 'know' that a glass does not just break; the event has to have some cause, whether a person's destructive act, or whatever. But by the same token, Floyd's destructive act must also have a cause, which itself has a cause . . . and so on, back to some hypothetical first cause. Likewise, if Floyd's act of swinging a hammer such that the hammer comes into contact with the glass, has an effect, namely the glass's breaking, so also this event (the glass breaking) has an effect (say, injury to the spectators), a state of affairs which has a further effect . . . on so on, to the end of time. The point, of course, is that in their everyday conceptualization of the world, people are not usually concerned with such metaphysical issues. People can, and do, talk about events as self-contained, conceptually autonomous segments of a vast chain of events, with little consideration of their ultimate, or even their immediate cause, nor of their immediate or ultimate effect. It is from this perspective that we can say that a glass breaking is conceptually autonomous.

The autonomous core construal has various linguistic repercussions. In the first place, it underlies ergative case systems. In an ergative system, the affected entity in a transitive clause receives the same case (absolutive, typically marked by zero) as the single participant in an intransitive clause, whereas the Agent in a transitive clause is specially marked for ergative case. In other words, absolutive case is reserved for the autonomous core of an event, whereas ergative case attaches to the element that expands the autonomous core. In a nominative/accusative system, on the other hand, both transitive and intransitive subjects are marked for nominative case, whilst the transitive object is specially marked for accusative case. Thus, in an accusative system, *the glass* receives different case marking in *The glass broke* and in *Floyd broke the glass*.

Although English, at least in its clausal structure, is typically an accusative language, encoding an energetic construal of events, both Williams (1987) and Langacker (1992) have commented on the ergative character of English nominalizations.[11] This aspect is seen in the following examples.

---

[11] For a cross-linguistic survey of ergative-style nominalization, see Koptjevskaja-Tamm (1993: ch. 7).

(13)   *a.* the arrival of the guests/the guests' arrival.
       b. the destruction of the city/the city's destruction.
       c. the destruction of the city by the enemy/the city's destruction by the
          enemy.

An intransitive subject (*the guests*) and a transitive object (*the city*) are encoded
in exactly the same way, either in an *of*-phrase or in a prenominal possessor
phrase, whilst the transitive subject (*the enemy*) needs to be specially encoded
in a *by*-phrase. That, even in a predominantly accusative language like English,
nominalizations should exhibit an ergative construal, should not be too surprising.
In a finite clause, an event is construed dynamically, through time. Furthermore,
in a canonical transitive clause, there is a coincidence of several layers of temporal
organization. The initiator of the event is encoded by the first mentioned nominal,
which in turn is the subject (the trajector) of the clause. Several aspects therefore
conspire to reinforce the energetic construal, from energy source to energy sink,
underlying the nominative/accusative encoding. Nominalization, however, causes
an event to be reified as a static, atemporal 'thing'; almost by definition, we might
say, nominalization removes sequential scanning. Under these circumstances,
an energetic construal becomes far less compelling, thereby making way for
the possibility of ergative marking, based in an autonomous core construal of an
event.

   As these remarks indicate, autonomous core construal has significant repercussions for English nominalizations. Langacker, as we have seen, presents the
notion of autonomous core construal on the example of the verb *break*. Unfortunately, there is no episodic noun derived from *break*, on which we might test
the consequences of autonomous core construal for English nominalizations.[12]
What has been said of *break*, however, readily applies to other action verbs,
such as *destroy, dismiss, assassinate*. These verbs designate events whose
landmark is relatively more intrinsic to a conceptualization of the event than the
trajector, to the extent that the change in state of the landmark entity can be
conceptualized relatively independently of its cause. The derived episodic nouns
pattern in essentially the same way, in that a possessor is preferentially interpreted as the landmark entity, not as the trajector. *The city's destruction, the
ambassador's dismissal, the president's assassination* (on their objective readings)
designate autonomous conceptualizations, in which the possessor elaborates a
highly intrinsic participant in the process. Subjective readings of the possessor
tend to be rejected, because of the conceptual incompleteness of the situations
they denote.

   I spoke earlier of the typically accusative character of English clause structure, which reflects an energetic construal of a situation. There is one type of
clause, however, which does display features of autonomous core construal. In

---

[12] *Breaking*, as in *the breaking of the glass* and *Floyd's breaking of the glass*, is a process, not
an episodic nominalization. Process nominalizations are discussed in Ch. 10.

middles (*The glass breaks easily*), the subject nominal names the highly instrinsic participant in the relation. The role of intrinsicness, both in middles and posses-sives, plausibly lies behind the frequently observed correlation between argu-ment affectedness (as manifested in the possibility of an objective reading of a possessive) and the possibility of a middle. Both phenomena could reflect the fact that a change in state of an affected entity can be conceptualized without intrinsic reference to the cause of the change. Even so, as noted in section 6.6, the correlation between middles and objective possessives is far from perfect. This fact need not be problematic for the account proposed here. The middle is an independent construction, with its own semantics, which may impose special constraints on the kinds of items that may occur in it. As already observed, one requirement on the middle construction could be that the subject must be in some way 'responsible' for the successful outcome of the process (*Bert doesn't interview very well*); the subject, in other words, needs to take on certain agent-like properties.

In the cases so far discussed, the notion of intrinsicness coincides exactly with the notion of informativity. The point is important, in that Langacker (1992) has argued that the schematic meaning of *of* is, precisely, to profile an intrinsic relation. In line with the argument being developed here, he has also stated (Langacker 1993: 13) that 'the more intrinsically one entity figures in the char-acterization of another, the more likely it is to be used as a reference point for it'. To the extent that intrinsicness and informativity are two sides of the same coin, the distribution of *of*-phrases will exactly match the distribution of posses-sor phrases. And in many cases, this is in fact the case. The two expressions in (14) are alike in that each very strongly prefers an objective interpretation.

(14) *a.* the destruction of Rome.
      b. Rome's destruction.

Other action predicates are exactly analogous (*the president's assassination* vs. *the assassination of the president*, *the ambassador's dismissal* vs. *the dismissal of the ambassador*). This is not to say that the two expressions in each case are perfectly synonymous. The *of*-phrase fleshes out the meaning of the head noun, by elaborating an entity that is highly intrinsic to its semantic structure. The function of the possessor phrase is to facilitate identification of the head noun's referent, by naming an entity that not only has to be topical, and therefore inde-pendently accessible to the conceptualizer, but which is also highly informative with respect to the head noun.

The situation with respect to psychological predicates is more complex, in that intrinsicness may not always coincide with informativity. Psychological predicates denote a relation between an Experiencer and a Stimulus. On the one hand, given the greater informativity of the Experiencer, we may suppose that the Experiencer will be more intrinsic to a conceptualization of a psychological state than the Stimulus. The evidence from preposition selection in the (optional) expression of the Stimulus—see the examples in (12)—could support this claim. On the other hand, the evidence from the middle construction is less clear. *Louise bores/frightens/pleases easily* are acceptable, whereas **Louise fears/ admires/loves/knows/amazes easily*, on either a subjective or objective reading of *Louise*, are not. This said, it does seem possible to conceptualize a psychological state both from the point of view of the person who experiences it, and from the perspective of the entity that is apt to engender it. *The lecture was boring, The storm was frightening, Louise is very lovable*—with focus on the characteristics of the Stimulus—display a degree of conceptual autonomy comparable to that of *Herbie was bored, Herbie is frightened, Herbie is very loving*—which focus on the state of the Experiencer. Psychological states, like action events, may be conceptualized from alternative perspectives. Unlike with action predicates, both perspectives may be consistent with an autonomous core construal.

Under appropriate circumstances, therefore, either Experiencer or Stimulus may be construed as intrinsic to a psychological state. Accordingly, with psychological nouns, an *of*-phrase may often introduce either the Experiencer or the Stimulus. One consequence is that with psychological nouns, the distribution of *of*-phrases may not match that of possessor phrases.

(15)   *a.* the fear of the enemy.
       b. the enemy's fear.
(16)   *a.* the knowledge of the students.
       b. the student's knowledge.
(17)   *a.* the love of God.
       b. God's love.

The (*a*) expressions can have both subjective and objective readings, consistent with the possibility that both Experiencer and Stimulus may have intrinsic status. In contrast, the (*b*) expressions can only have subjective interpretations, with possessor as Experiencer, consistent with the greater informativity of Experiencer.

Consider, now, the following, rather more complex paradigm.

(18)   *a.* the boredom of the lecture.   (stimulus)
       b. the boredom of the students.   (experiencer)
       c. *the lecture's boredom.
       d. the students' boredom.
       e. *the students' boredom of the lecture.
       f. the students' boredom {at/with} the lecture.

The (*a*) and (*b*) expressions show that the complement in the *of*-phrase can be construed equally felicitously as Experiencer or Stimulus, whilst the (*c*) and (*d*) expressions show that the possessor can only denote the Experiencer. Of special interest is the contrast between (*e*) and (*f*). In (*e*), the lecture is construed as intrinsic to the psychological state (cf. *The lecture was boring*). On this construal, the Experiencer comes to have the status of a peripheral, and non-informative participant; if expressed at all, the Experiencer would have to appear in a prepositional phrase, headed by a more contentful preposition than schematic *of* (as in *the boredom of the lecture for the students*). On the other hand, with the Experiencer as possessor, the Stimulus takes on a peripheral, extrinsic status. If expressed at all, the Stimulus must appear with a more contentful preposition.

This approach, I suggest, offers a plausible account of the contrast noted by Giorgi and Longobardi (1991: 132).

John's recordings of my favourite pianist

(19) *a.* John's books by my favourite writer.   John's recordings *by my favourite pianist

   b. *John's books of my favourite writer.

These expressions differ from the ones so far discussed to the extent that *books* would not normally be considered an intrinsically relational noun. Nevertheless, given encyclopedic knowledge of what books are, various relations can be imagined, such as between books and their owner, and between books and their author. Both owner and author may serve as reference point (hence the ambiguity of *John's books*). We see, also, that if the author is construed as intrinsic, as in (19*b*), the owner becomes a peripheral and non-informative entity, which cannot serve as reference point.

In spite, then, of the non-relational character of *book*, the ungrammaticality of (19*b*) seems to exactly parallel the ungrammaticality of (18*e*). Observe that this parallelism, if valid, puts into question Giorgi and Longobardi's explanation of (19). For if Giorgi and Longobardi's account of (19*b*) is correct, we should expect the very same account to be applicable to (18*e*). But their explanation of (19) does not carry over to (18*e*).

Giorgi and Longobardi take the ungrammaticality of (19*b*) to follow from their 'Argument Uniqueness in Spec' condition (see section 6.6). Their claim is that *writer*, in its status as Agent, originates in Spec of *books*, and that, on moving into postnominal position, it leaves a trace in Spec. The presence of the trace forbids Spec to be occupied by the possessor *John*. Apart from the fact that this account is problematic even in GB terms (*book* would not normally be considered an argument-taking predicate), argument uniqueness in Spec cannot be the reason for the ungrammaticality of (18*e*). For this to be the case, we would have to say that *lecture* in (18*e*) originates in Spec position of *boredom*, and that its trace in Spec precludes another argument, i.e. *students*, from appearing in Spec. But *lecture* is forbidden in Spec, even in the absence of a postnominal *of*-phrase (cf. **the lecture's boredom*). In terms of Giorgi and Longobardi's own theory (pp. 144–5), the Stimulus *lecture* originates postnominally, as a prepositional complement.

9.6 COMPARISON WITH ALTERNATIVE ACCOUNTS

The notion of informativity (and its contribution to cue validity) has enabled us to arrive at essentially the same results as those predicted by the Affectedness and Experiencer Constraints. More than this, the informativity hypothesis offers a natural explanation for the constraints. Like the topicality requirement presented in Chapter 8, the informativity requirement falls out from the very semantics of the possessive construction, entailing the cue validity of the possessor nominal. In brief, the Affectedess and Experiencer Constraints turn out to be reflexes of more general semantic principles.

Here, I want to suggest that some of the accounts proposed in the formalist, and especially GB literature, might be open to reinterpretation within the present framework.

Consider Giorgi and Longobardi's (1991: 143) explanation of the Affectedness Constraint, discussed in section 6.6. They claim that, if the internal argument of a predicate is unaffected, the external θ-role of the predicate may not be 'erased'. As a consequence, the internal argument may not move into prenominal position (whence the impossibility of *the cliff's avoidance*). The attribute of 'non-erasability' could plausibly be taken as a symptom of the relative intrinsicness of the external argument, as compared to the relative non-intrinsicness of the internal argument. On the present account, this fact alone suffices to explain the non-occurrence of the unaffected, i.e. less intrinsic, and less informative argument in possessor position.

Consider, next, a central topic of Grimshaw (1990), viz. the 'structure of argument structure'. Grimshaw orders the arguments of a predicate with respect to their thematic and syntactic 'prominence'. For the verb *announce*, she (p. 4) suggests the following structure.

(20)   *announce* (Agent (Goal (Theme)))

Agent is the most prominent, and Theme the least prominent argument. Grimshaw contends that thematic hierarchy has many ramifications in the grammar; specifically, argument positions have to be discharged sequentially, starting from the most deeply embedded, or least prominent, and concluding with the outermost, or most prominent. Noteworthy is that Grimshaw, in her monograph, nowhere offers a conceptual clarification of thematic prominence. We can only infer what prominence actually is from the role it is claimed to play. Considering its properties, prominence would appear to be exactly the converse of intrinsicness. That the 'least prominent' (i.e. 'most intrinsic') argument is discharged first, is, of course, fully concordant with the autonomous core construal of a situation, and, to the extent that intrinsicness may be identified with informativity, with the present account of possessives.[13]

---

[13] With action verbs, intrinsicness and informativity do tend to correlate. Psychological verbs, however, are more complex, as already explained. With respect to psychological predicates, such as *fear*, Grimshaw (1990: 8) claims that Experiencer is 'more prominent' than Stimulus, whereas on the present account, Experiencer may be more intrinsic (= less prominent?) than Stimulus. As noted, Grimshaw gives no conceptual characterization of prominence, so it is unclear how one might set about querying her assignment of prominence relations.

Finally, let us turn to Doron and Rappaport Hovav's (1991) proposal to explain the Affectedness Constraint in terms of event structure, which we discussed in section 6.7. On their definition, for a verb V with internal argument Y and external argument X, Y is affected if the event structure of V contains a sub-event of which Y is an argument, but of which X is not an argument. By this definition, the internal argument of *break* and *destroy* is affected, since these verbs will each contain two sub-events, one involving action on Y by X, the other denoting the final state of Y. The internal argument of *avoid*, on the other hand, will be unaffected, since the verb (presumably) contains only a single sub-event, involving only X's behaviour with respect to Y.

In view of what has been presented so far in this chapter, it will be appreciated that the 'sub-event' that legitimizes the notion of affectedness would appear to correspond to the 'autonomous core' construal, and that the affected argument is the highly intrinsic participant in the autonomous core. Given that V designates a relation that involves two participants, X and Y, it is possible, then, to conceptualize V, or at least a sub-event covered by V, solely in terms of Y, without any reference to X. We also have a natural explanation of the little scenarios sketched earlier in this chapter, in which a person attempts to verify the truth of a statement by examination of the participants. We can verify whether X has destroyed Y by examination of Y, thereby appealing to the final sub-event of *destroy*, but we can only verify whether X has avoided Y by examination of X's behaviour with respect to Y.

Doron and Rappaport Hovav's account, then, appeals essentially to the notion of the relative intrinsicness of the arguments in a relation, as manifested in the possibility of an autonomous core construal involving only one of these arguments. I have argued, however, that the crucial property of possessor nominals is not so much intrinsicness, as informativity. And there are certainly cases in which the notion of a sub-event involving only the internal argument fails to account for the objective readings of a possessive. Consider the possibility of objective readings of *Kuwait's invasion* and *John's burglary*. I do not think that one could plausibly maintain that X *invades* Y, or X *burgles* Y, comprises a sub-event involving only Y but not X.

Although some of the formal devices proposed in the literature may be amenable to a cognitive/semantic interpretation, there remains a fundamental difference between the two approaches. Formal constraints, like those proposed by Giorgi and Longobardi and by Doron and Rappaport Hovav, make categorial predictions of grammaticality. Cognitive/semantic constraints, in contrast, are inherently variable, and context-dependent. We saw in Chapter 8 how the Affectedness Constraint may be overridden by discourse-conditioned topicality. Likewise, the informativity of a reference point with respect to the target is not a fixed, invariant property, but may be modified by various contextual circumstances.

Compare the following expressions.

(21)   *a.* John's burglary.
   b. John's attempted burglary; John's daring burglary; John's well-planned burglary.
   c. John's burglaries; John's daring burglaries; John's well-planned burglaries.

John's burglary can have both a subjective and an objective reading. A subjective reading becomes more likely if *burglary* is modified by certain kinds of adjective, or if *burglary* is pluralized. The salience of the subjective reading seems to be due to a switch of focus away from the victim and towards the criminal. A *daring burglary* is such in virtue of the daring of the criminal; the expression tells us little else about the victim, other than that he was burgled. The victim is therefore decidedly less informative with respect to a 'daring burglary', or a 'well-planned burglary', than is the criminal. Likewise with the plural noun. In speaking of 'burglaries', focus again tends to shift to a characterization of the criminal as a habitual practitioner of the activity, and away from the victim. The burglar is therefore a more efficient cue for the identification of multiple acts of burglary than is a multiple victim.

The pattern illustrated in (22) occurs with quite a number of deverbal nouns. In the following, a subjective reading seems much more likely for the (*b*) expressions than for the (*a*) expressions.

(22)   *a.* the ambassador's dismissal.
   b. the ambassador's dismissals.
(23)   *a.* John's murder.
   b. John's attempted murder.
(24)   *a.* the policeman's arrest.
   b. the policeman's many arrests.

John's attempted murder can hardly be interpreted in the sense that someone attempted to murder John. The reason, clearly, is that the notion of 'attempted murder' tells us about the would-be murderer, not about the intended victim. Hence, the would-be murderer is a more effective cue for an identification of an attempted murder than the would-be victim. Likewise with (24*b*). There is certainly nothing conceptually incoherent in the idea of a person (even a policeman) being arrested many times. But given a series of arrests, we are more likely to draw inferences about the efficiency, or eagerness, of the policeman, than about the misfortunes of a suspect.

9.7 REPRESENTATIONAL NOUNS

The preceding sections have focused mainly on episodic nouns. Here, I want to mention some further consequences of the intrinsicness/informativity thesis, namely with respect to representational nouns.

A representational noun designates an artefact which represents, in some medium, another entity. Some representational nouns, such as *photograph*, can be regarded as result nominals, which designate the artefact which comes into existence as a result of some activity denoted by a base verb (in this case, the verb (*to*) *photograph*). Many representational nouns, however, are not derived. There is, for example, no verb to which *statue* can be related. Some examples of representational nouns are given in (25) and (26).

(25) portrait, photograph, statue, biography, history
(26) sketch, painting, sculpture, story, tale

The semantic structure of a representational noun makes reference, in its unprofiled base, to the creator of the artefact, and to the entity that the artefact represents. As with episodic nouns, there are two potential candidates for elaboration by a possessor nominal. We note, however, a significant difference between the nouns in (25) and those in (26). Compare, for example, *portrait* and *sketch*.

(27) *a.* John's portrait. [*John* = creator or represented object]
    b. a portrait of John. [*John* = represented object]
(28) *a.* John's sketch. [*John* = creator]
    b. a sketch of John. [*John* = represented object]

The *of*-expressions confirm that in both cases the represented object may be construed as intrinsic to a conceptualization of the representational artefact. Likewise, we see that in both cases the creator can function as a reference point entity. But when it comes to the represented object serving as reference point, we note a curious asymmetry. In the case of *portrait*, the possessor can readily [*John's portrait*] designate the thing that is represented, an interpretation that is less easy to obtain with *sketch*.

The difference is plausibly attributable to the greater informativity of the represented object to the nouns in (25) compared to the nouns in (26). Consider the case of *portrait*. What, after all, motivates a person to characterize an artefact as a 'portrait' in the first place, rather than as a 'sketch', 'painting', 'picture', or whatever? Obviously, it is the fact that a portrait, by virtue of the very meaning of the word, is meant to be a visual representation of some specific person. Given that something is a 'portrait', a 'statue', a 'history', we may draw quite reliable inferences as to the nature of the represented object. Consequently, the represented object may readily function as a possessor reference point. On the other hand, a sketch, painting, story, etc. could be a representation of just about anything.[14] The thing represented, although intrinsic to the noun in question (a

as in John's sketch,

[14] In the case of a sketch, painting, story, etc. the represented object may exist only in the imagination of the creator, in the mental space of the representation. *Sketch*, and the other nouns in (27), are therefore akin to the space-building predicates mentioned in n. 6. On the other hand, a portrait, photograph, history, etc. is supposed to depict some real-world entity(ies).

sketch *has* to be a sketch *of* something), has lower cue validity for the identification of the artefact.[15]

Significantly, when the nouns in (25) focus on the style, medium, or aesthetic value of the representation, that is, on qualities of the artefact that reflect on the creator rather than on the represented object, the depiction reading tends to become inaccessible. In each of the following, John is <u>preferentially</u> the creator (or owner), not the person represented.

(29)   *a.* John's black-and-white photograph.
      b. John's award-winning photograph.
      c. John's true-to-life portrait.
      d. John's two-volume biography.
      e. John's recently published biography.
      f. John's marble statue.

Pluralizing the representational noun further enhances the creator reading. *John's black-and-white photographs* can scarcely mean "the black and white photographs depicting John".

As with psychological nouns discussed earlier, representational nouns testify to the need to distinguish intrinsicness and informativity. (One consequence is that the reading of a <u>prenominal possessor</u> need not coincide with the reading of an *of*-complement.) A similar conclusion emerges from a glance at *information nouns*. These may be regarded as a subcategory of representational nouns, in that they denote linguistically encoded information about things, events, states of affairs, etc. *Story* and *tale*, listed in (26), are information nouns in this sense. Some further examples are given in (30).

(30)   news, review, report, précis, survey, draft, account, version, statement, declaration

Intrinsic to these nouns is the notion of the content of the <u>represented information</u>. Predictably, the content may be stated in <u>a prepositional phrase</u>, introduced by *of*: *news of the war*, *an account of the accident*, *a version of the events*, *a précis of the main points*, *a draft of the proposal*.

Depending on the semantics of the noun in question, various entities are potentially informative reference points. Take the case of *news*. News is not only information about events; what turns information into 'news' is the fact that the information is 'new', that is, previously unknown, as well as important. Given that some information has been categorized as news, we may infer that it became known at a certain time, probably also that it emanated from a certain source. Consequently, the source and the time of its release can have high cue validity.

---

[15] I do not claim that the represented object can *never* feature as a possessor to the nouns in (26). A reader offers the following fictitous newspaper headline, pointing out that its acceptability (if it *is* acceptable) depends upon specific encyclopedic knowledge pertaining to possessor and possessee: GIOCONDA'S PAINTING STOLEN FROM LOUVRE! Still, I think one's first inclination, on encountering this, would be to assume that Gioconda is the artist!

Whence the fact—noted in section 1.1.2—that *yesterday's news* need not be *news of yesterday*. The *of*-phrase states the content of the news, the prenominal possessor may denote either the content, or the time at which the news became known. Likewise, *John's news* need not be *news of John*. The possessor can name either the content of the news, or its source. However, as with *photograph*, *statue*, and so on in (29), if *news* is modified such that the focus shifts to properties of the news *as* news (concerning, for example, its newness or its potential interest), a content reading of the possessor becomes less likely. *John's old news* is preferentially old news that John brought, not old news about John. Likewise *yesterday's alarming news* is alarming news that became known yesterday, rather than alarming news about yesterday.

9.8 POSSESSION AND UNIQUENESS

We have looked at several examples in which a non-intrinsic entity can function as a reference point. In each case, an encyclopedic conception of the target comprises some reference to the role of the possessor entity, such that the possessor can function as a valid cue for the identification of the possessee, in accordance with the informativity thesis in (11).

But now, a special problem arises. This concerns the relation of *possession* that may hold between reference point and target, as, for example, in *John's car*. We could, of course, claim that a full semantic characterization of *car* will incorporate, alongside much else, the notion of a car as a possessible entity. Given the predominance of the possession relation in the intepretation of *John's car*, we would have to go further, and claim that the notion of an owner is highly salient, even that it is intrinsic to a conceptualization of *car*. But this, surely, is incorrect. A car is not *primarily*, or *intrinsically*, a possessible entity. It is significant that *of*, a preposition which profiles an inherent relation, is generally awkward with a relation of possession. *This photograph of John* (where John is the person represented) is fine, whereas *this car of John* sounds very bad. And the expression is only slightly improved if the complement of *of* is made heavier: *this car of the people who live next door*. Much better would be to explicitly spell out the possession relation: *this car which belongs to the people next door*.

In line with the thesis being pursued in this chapter, I shall nevertheless argue that, in the case of non-relational entities like a car, the legal owner is a natural reference point, with high cue validity for the identification of the referent.

The basic function of the possessive construction is to facilitate the identification of the target, given the identification of the possessor. A speaker, therefore, will tend to choose a reference point such that, given the reference point, and the semantic type of the target, there will typically be only one potential referent of the possessee nominal.

Inability to uniquely identify the intended target, given the reference point, can sometimes cause a possessive to be rejected as ill-formed. The following examples are due to Hayase (1993).

(31)   *a.* *the city's road.
       b. the city's roads.
       c. the city's best-paved road.

The city's road instantiates the whole–part relation that is attested in so many possessive expressions (*the car's headlights, the man's hand, the cat's tail*). What renders it unacceptable is the fact that a city is likely to have very many roads, such that (31*a*) is virtually useless as a means of uniquely identifying a specific road. (*A city's road* is just as bad.) On the other hand (31*b*) is perfectly acceptable, since the target is now the totality of the roads in the city. Observe that (31*a*) may be rendered acceptable by modification of *road*, such that the potential target is restricted, ideally down to a single instance. This is achieved, in (31*c*), by means of the superlative *best-paved. Best-paved* states a criterion for singling out just one of the many potential referents of *road*, identifiable from the reference point. Hayase cites several examples in which modification of the possessee serves precisely this function. Note that the following tend to become unacceptable if the material in parentheses is omitted.

(32)   America's *(most exciting) city, the world's *(most popular) singer, the town's *(first) telegrapher, the world's *(seventh ranked) lightweight

The city's road may also become acceptable if contextual information can narrow down the referential possibilities of *road*. If only two roads are under discussion, one in the city, one in the country, the possessive may fulfil its uniquely identifying function.

(33)   Since the two roads run through the same type of marshy terrain, maintenance on *the city's road* must be just as difficult and expensive as that on *the country's*. [Hayase 1993: 156]

   Also instructive are the following examples, again from Hayase.

(34)   *a.* the circle's diameter.
       b. the circle's radius.
       c. *the circle's arc.

Diameter and *radius* denote unique properties of a circle. On the other hand, a circle has indefinitely many arcs, of indefinitely many lengths. In the absence of contextual information which could restrict the referential potential of *arc*, (34*c*) will be judged ill-formed.

   It should be borne in mind that the criterion of unique identifiability may sometimes be relaxed. Certainly, in a monogamous society, *John's wife* is uniquely identifying. But in stating that *My sister is getting married next week*, I do not necessarily imply that I have only one sister, or even only one marriageable sister. Likewise, in speaking of *the policeman's arrest*, I do not commit myself to the proposition that the policeman was arrested only once, nor (on the subjective construal) that the policeman carried out, in the course of his career, no more than one arrest. And *my grandfather* is perfectly acceptable, even though each person, perforce, has two grandfathers.

Still, in such cases, the number of potential referents is typically quite small; if a person talks of *my sister*, the potential referents—given encyclopedic knowledge about the typical size of families—will number two or three, perhaps, at the very most. It would be quite normal for a university lecturer to say that she is having problems with *her Ph.D. student*, but odd for her to say that there are problems with *her undergraduate student*. The number of Ph.D. students of any single lecturer rarely exceeds half a dozen, whilst the number of undergraduate students could run into hundreds.

The issue is not peculiar to possessives. Use of the definite determiner *the* also presupposes unique identification. Nevertheless, I can perfectly well say that *the people next door* are making a lot of noise, even though there are two sets of 'people next door'—those to the left, and those to the right. Strictly speaking, *the people next door* is not uniquely identifying. Similarly with possessives. If I say that *our neighbours* are moving out tomorrow, I probably mean that only one set of neighbours, to one side of us, are moving out. For many practical purposes, therefore, failure to uniquely identify is not considered unduly problematic. It is sufficient merely to characterize the intended referent in terms of its role in a relation to the reference point entity.

In other cases, there may in fact be quite a large number of potential referents. If the conversation turns on a certain person, I could volunteer the information that she was *my student* in 1980. Very likely, there exist several hundred people who might qualify for the designation *my student in 1980*. Or consider (35).

(35)   The suspect's photograph appeared in all the newspapers.

This sentence could be consistent with the existence of a large number of photographs of the suspect. In fact, if we were to attempt a paraphrase of *the suspect's photograph*, the indefinite "*a* photograph of the suspect" might well be considered more appropriate than the definite "*the* photograph of the suspect". (To this extent, the sentence might be construed as a counterexample to generalization (27) of Chapter 7). The point in (35), of course, is that it is actually immaterial *which* of the photographs was published, provided only that it was a good likeness. The crucial aspect is that the intended referent is characterized in terms of its role in a relation to the reference point.

We can now return to the question raised at the beginning of this section, namely, the status of the possession relation as the predominant, or default, interpretation of many possessives. A relationship of possession is an option only in the case of non-relational nouns. These are nouns which display a quite high degree of conceptual autonomy, and which do not of themselves invoke an inherent relation to another entity. For a possession relation to be entertained, the target entity also needs to be of the kind that people normally own and use, that is, in the main, physical objects and consumer goods. Even so, as remarked at the beginning of this section, it would be wrong to claim that these entities are primarily conceptualized in terms of their possessability.

The privileged status of the possession relation, I suggest, follows from a rather special property of the relation itself. This is that a possession relation is typically an *exclusive* relation between a thing and a person. While a person may have a large number of possessions, each item is typically possessed by only one individual. The owner, moreover, has exclusive rights of access to the thing owned. There are, it is true, exceptions to this prototypical situation. Certain items may be subject to joint ownership (a house can be jointly owned by husband and wife), whilst other entities may be subject to communal ownership. In general, though, if something is *mine*, it cannot at the same time also be somebody else's.

For each item, then, there will usually be one, and only one 'possessor'. The possessor has optimal cue validity for the identification of the 'possessed'. It is the exclusiveness of the possession relation that renders it highly compatible with the identifying function of the possessive construction.

10 *Ing*-nominalizations

In this chapter I address the use of the possessive morpheme in association with deverbal *V-ing* forms, as exemplified in (1).

(1) *a.* the enemy's destroying of the city.
     b. the enemy('s) destroying the city.

These expressions differ significantly from the possessive nominalizations that have been addressed so far. They also differ markedly from each other. Most obviously, in (1*a*), the landmark entity, corresponding to the direct object of the base verb, is introduced by the preposition *of*, whilst the possessive morpheme on the trajector nominal (corresponding to the verb's subject) is obligatory. In (1*b*) the notional direct object occurs without *of*, and the possessive morpheme on the notional subject appears to be optional. Given that cognitive grammar rejects the notion of optional morphemes—phonological material whose presence has no import on the semantic value of a complex expression—we shall need to recognize two distinct constructions in (1*b*), one with the possessive morpheme, one without. The constructions with which we shall be concerned, then, are as follows.

(2) *Type A*: the enemy's destroying of the city
     Type B: the enemy's destroying the city
     Type C: the enemy destroying the city

(Later in this chapter, we shall see that there are good reasons for regarding Type C expressions, of the form [NP V-ing . . .], as ambiguous between two distinct constructions. I reserve discussion of this issue for section 10.4.)

    First, a few words on terminology and on the incidence of the constructions. Two (homophonous) *ing*-forms are traditionally recognized in English—the gerunds and the present participles (Sweet 1898: 120–5). The distinction appears to be based largely on the nominal vs. relational profile of the *V-ing* form. 'Gerund' is the traditional designation of the nominal forms that occur in subject and object position of a verb, or after a preposition (*Running is healthy, I dislike running, without running*), whilst 'participle' is reserved for the relational forms that occur in progressive aspect (*He is running*), after conjunctions (*while running*), and in various kinds of subordinate phrases (*Running in the park, he got mugged.*) To insist on the distinction could, on the one hand, obscure the essential unity, at a more schematic level, of the two categories (Pullum and Zwicky 1991). On the other hand, at a more delicate level of analysis, the recognition of only two categories turns out to be grossly inadequate. Whilst the term gerund, in its traditional sense, may be appropriately used to designate the *V-ing* forms in a Type A nominalization, the *V-ing* forms in Types B and C have a rather different status, for which no traditional labels exist.

This being the case, naming the three constructions in (2) becomes something of a problem. 'Accusative *ing*-construction' could be an appropriate label for Type C. ('Accusative', because the notional subject, if a pronoun, is obligatorily in accusative form: {*they/them} *destroying the city*. In addition, the label conveniently leaves open the categorial status of the *ing*-form.) Analogously, 'possessive *ing*-construction' appropriately labels both Types A and B. Finding appropriate names to distinguish Type A and Type B is more troublesome. One nomenclature (Lees 1960) distinguishes 'action nominalizations' (Type A) and 'factive nominalizations' (Type B). Langacker (1991: 32) has queried the suitability of these terms, pointing out that the factivity of an expression (that is, whether its content is presupposed to be true, or 'a fact') cross-cuts the distinction. Pullum (1991) uses the term 'nominal gerund phrase' to designate Type B. 'Gerund', however, is best reserved for the *V-ing* form that occurs in Type A. Langacker (1991: 31), for reasons that will be mentioned later, distinguishes 'type nominalizations' (Type A) and 'instance nominalizations' (Type B). Type C, however, could also be called an 'instance nominalization'. Rather than resorting to ever more cumbersome descriptive labels, I shall, as occasion requires, simply refer to the three *ing*-constructions as Types A, B, and C.

Although *V-ing* forms are very frequent in English, possessive *ing*-expressions are not. The 13,000-word corpus of Taylor (1991a) contained only one example.

(3)   the . . . prints upon the wall, which she hoped that no one would object to her removing.

Even here, however, the syncretism of objective *her* and possessive *her* renders (3) ambiguous between a possessive Type B and an accusative Type C expression.

Type A expressions appear to be especially infrequent. In the 340 pages of David Lodge's novel *Small World* (henceforth *SW*), I encountered only two unambiguous examples.

(4)   *a.* the slender gold pencil continues its steady traversing of the page. [*SW* 89]
       b. his persuading of the old woman, Angela, to hide him in Madeline's bed-room. [*SW* 46]

Examples of Types B and C were more numerous.

(5)   *a.* What is the point of our discussing your paper? [*SW* 28]
       b. it might look bad if something happened to him without my lifting a finger. [*SW* 282]
       c. if you will excuse my mentioning it. [*SW* 287]
(6)   *a.* she has no objection to Ronald seeking carnal satisfaction elsewhere. [*SW* 239]

b. All I can think about is him getting the UNESCO chair. [*SW* 309]

c. a far cry from the violet blending its odour with the rose. [*SW* 49]

The distinction between the construction types can sometimes be opaque. For obvious reasons, with *ing*-forms derived from intransitive verbs, the distinction between Types A and B cannot be diagnosed by the presence of *of* before the notional direct object.

(7) *a.* I'd be grateful if you would not mention our meeting here to any mutual acquaintance in England. [*SW* 245]

     b. The odds against its happening like that by chance must be billions to one. [*SW* 39]

On the basis of criteria to be introduced below, (7*b*) turns out to be Type B, whereas (7*a*) could be consistent with both Type A and Type B. (In addition, *meeting*, in (7*a*), could also constitute a non-gerundive result noun.) Also in the case of *V-ing* forms derived from copula verbs, as in (8), we shall need to appeal to further criteria in order to allocate the expressions to Type B rather than to Type A.

(8) *a.* the idea of his being a serious candidate. [*SW* 247]

     b. scarcely a blade of grass to be seen, in spite of its being spring. [*SW* 211]

Ing-forms may, of course, lack an explicit notional subject, whether possessive or accusative; in fact, this possibility probably represents the more usual situation.

(9) there is talk of dragging the lake. [*SW* 273]

Here, the contrast between Types B and C obviously falls away. In point of fact, (9) could be equally compatible with a Type B (*there is talk of their dragging the lake*) and a Type C construction (*there is talk of them dragging the lake*).

10.1 *V-ING* AND NOMINALIZATION

Ing-suffixation to a verb stem is a fully productive, and completely regular process. Apart from the defective modals (*must, ought, shall,* etc.), any verb stem can undergo *ing*-suffixation, with predictable consequences for the properties of the resulting *V-ing* form. There is a striking contrast here with the derived nouns discussed in section 9.3, in that these latter display a high degree of idiosyncrasy, in several respects. Derived nouns are formed by a variety of morphological means, with each verb stem making its own selection. From (*to*) *construct* we have *construction,* from (*to*) *refuse* we get *refusal,* from *establish, establishment,* from *bequeath, bequest,* and so on. Secondly, derived nouns are of different semantic kinds (episodic, result, style, etc.), with each noun typically being polysemous between two or more semantic kinds. Especially striking is the fact that derived nouns frequently take on semantic nuances which are not fully predictable from the meaning of the source verb. *Sight* does not denote an episode of seeing, but the faculty of seeing, or, alternatively, aspects of what is seen (*It was a dreadful sight*); if plural, it has the sense "things worth seeing" (*Have you seen the sights?*). Finally, not every verb has derived nouns, of the various semantic types, associated with it. From *sell* we get the episodic noun *sale*, but there is no episodic noun derived from *buy*. We can talk about *the sale of the house*, but not **the buy of the house*. Conversely, we can say *That house was a good buy*, but not **That house was a good sale*.

All these various aspects point to the high degree of entrenchment of derived nouns of the kind *invasion, destruction*, and so on. Derived nouns constitute established lexical items, each with its own idiosyncratic morphology and semantics. *V-ing* forms, on the other hand, may be freely created; these forms have something of an *ad hoc* status, and, perhaps for this very reason, their semantic properties are fully predictable.

Perhaps the most crucial semantic property of *V-ing* forms is that they impose an *imperfective* construal on the underlying process. This aspect is most evident in their use in the progressive construction. *The volcano erupted* designates a completed event, comprising its various temporal stages, i.e. its beginning, middle, and end. *The volcano was erupting* designates the on-going activity, without reference to the beginning or end. The eruption is construed as an internally homogeneous process, any segment of which is qualitatively identical to any other segment. From this property follow a number of well-known restrictions on the incidence of the progressive in English. For example, predications which are inconsistent with an imperfective construal cannot combine with the progressive. **The volcano was erupting twice last week* is conceptually incoherent, since a succession of two discrete events cannot be construed as internally homogeneous. A further, and actually rather more puzzling restriction, is that predications which are inherently imperfective are also incompatible with the progressive. *John is tall* designates an imperfective situation; **John is being tall* is ungrammatical.[1]

The *ing*-forms that occur in progressives are clearly relational, not nominal in character; they could plausibly be analysed as a kind of predicative adjective, many of which, not unsurprisingly, may also be used attributively. Hence *the erupting volcano, the leaning tower, a screaming child*. The term 'present

---

[1] The standard explanation of this restriction is that a predication which is already inherently imperfective cannot be marked a second time for imperfectivity, as it would be if it combined with the progressive. Yet languages, generally, are not averse to the redundant marking of semantic categories. Saying the same thing twice may be open to censure on stylistic grounds, but it does not normally result in ungrammaticality. A more plausible explanation is that while the progressive *profiles* an imperfective state, it subsumes, in its unprofiled base of predication, some notion of change prior to and/or subsequent to the profiled segment. Consider the contrast between *Where do you live?* and *Where are you living?* Both questions enquire about a person's residence (an imperfective situation). But *Where are you living?*, unlike *Where do you live?*, presupposes that the person has recently changed address.

participle' may be appropriately reserved for this relational variant of *V-ing* forms. The term 'gerund', on the other hand, is appropriate for the nominalization of the relational variant. The relation between gerunds and participles thus turns out to be a case of profile shift.

Nominalized *V-ing* forms, or gerunds, preserve the imperfective character of their relational counterparts. What is nominalized, i.e. construed as a thing, is an internally homogeneous process, rather than a completed event with its successive temporal stages. We might therefore refer to nominal *V-ing* forms as *process nouns*, in contrast to the episodic nouns discussed in section 9.3, which reify the conception of a bounded episode of the process.

Many syntactic aspects of gerunds fall out from this characterization. Since they reify an internally homogeneous process, they function, grammatically, like mass nouns, prototypical examples of which, such as *oil, water, meat*, likewise designate an internally homogeneous 'mass'. On the other hand, episodic nouns, which reify a discrete episode, tend to function like regular count nouns, proto-typical examples of which likewise designate discrete, individuated, countable 'things'.

Thus, an episodic noun like *invasion* displays all the typical properties of a count noun. It may be pluralized, the plural may be construed with partitive phrases such as *a large number of*, the singular may take an indefinite determiner, and so forth.

(10)   *a.* Caesar's two invasions of Britain.
       b. a large number of the invasions.
       c. An invasion was planned.

A gerund may not be pluralized, it is construed with partitive phrases of the kind *a large amount of*, and, like other mass nouns, it may be used without any overt determiner at all.[2]

(11)   *a.* *Caesar's two invadings of Britain.
       b. there was a fair amount of wailing and gnashing of teeth. [*SW* 69]
       c. there is talk of dragging the lake. [*SW* 273]

We should expect gerunds, like other mass nouns, to be incompatible with the indefinite article, and this does, in general, turn out to be the case: **An invading was planned*. The indefinite article is sometimes found, however, especially if a particularized instance of the process is meant; in such cases, the gerund will typically need to occur with some kind of restrictive modifier.

(12)   *a.* It struck them as an arrogant flaunting of American cultural imperialism. [*SW* 276]
       b. it is not a to-and-fro process, but an endless tantalising leading on, a flirtation without consummation. [*SW* 26]

---

[2] Some *V-ing* forms do have the status of episodic nominalizations (*yesterday's killings* vs. **yesterday's murderings*) and result nominalizations (*the city's buildings* vs. **the city's constructings*). These items and their properties obviously have no bearing on the characterization of gerunds proper.

Again, though, there are parallels with some other mass nouns. *Education* is a mass noun. It fails to pluralize (**They received good educations*), it takes the determiners and quantifiers appropriate for a mass noun (*not much education*), but can, exceptionally for a mass noun, occur with the indefinite article, especially if there is modification (*They received a good education*).

10.1.1 *The 'verbal' vs. 'nominal' character of* ing-*nominalizations*

In the presentation of cognitive grammar in Chapter 3, we noted that Langacker postulates a clean distinction between nominal and relational predicates, between expressions which designate things and those which designate relations.

   With respect to their external syntax (that is, the kinds of syntactic environments in which they occur), nominalizations, of whatever kind, are obviously and unambiguously nominal in character. A remarkable fact about *ing*-nominalizations, however, is that with respect to their internal syntax they tend to be rather more verbal (or relational) in character than the possessive nominalizations that were discussed in earlier chapters. Especially Types B and C preserve, in their internal make-up, a number of characteristics of the verbal expressions from which they derive. Semantically, also, forms such as *invading* and *destroying* seem to focus more on the processual character of the nominalized situation, whereas derived nouns, of the kind *invasion* and *destruction*, have taken the process of conceptual reification further. Derived nouns constitute fully independent lexical items, which have to varying degrees drifted loose, so to speak, from the processual construal profiled by the base verb. Possibly, we can see in the more verbal character of *V-ing* forms an iconic relationship with their morphological make-up, in that morphologically, too, *V-ing* forms are 'closer' to the base verb than most derived nouns.

   The 'more verbal' vs. 'more nominal' character of nominalizations was highlighted by Comrie (1976), in his cross-linguistic survey of the syntax of nominalization patterns. He noted, for example, that Czech nominalizations tend to be even more nominal in character than their English equivalents, in that what in English would be a possessor phrase may turn up in Czech as an attributive adjective. In (13), *Husovo* is an adjective, which agrees in case with the head noun, it is not a genitive-inflected nominal; the expression, therefore, has the syntax of a regular [ADJ N] expression.

(13) Husovo upálení.
      "the burning of Huss"

In Classical Arabic, on the other hand, nominalizations are distinctly verbal in character, in that they preserve some of the syntactic aspects of their clausal source. In (14*a*), the Agent appears in nominative case, while in (14*b*), the Patient appears in accusative case. In the English version, of course, both Agent and Patient appear in guises which are peculiar to noun phrases, not to clauses, namely in association with the possessive morpheme, or in an *of*-complement.

(14) *a.* qatlu   muḥammadin   zaydun.
        kill-NMLZ Muhammad-GEN Zayd-NOM
     b. qatlu   zaydin   muḥammadan.
        kill-NMLZ Zayd-GEN   Muhammad-ACC
        "Zaid's killing of Muhammad"

With respect to English, syntactic considerations (to be discussed more fully below) suggest a gradation of nominalizations from most nominal (15*a*) to most verbal (15*e*).

(15) *a.* the enemy's destruction of the city.
     b. the enemy's destroying of the city.
     c. the enemy's destroying the city.
     d. the enemy destroying the city.
     e. (the fact) that the enemy destroyed the city.

I propose to handle the differences between these various nominalization patterns in terms of the 'domain of nominalization', that is, in terms of what, precisely, gets nominalized. The idea was already introduced in section 6.7, in connection with Lebeaux's (1986) distinction between V-nominalizations and V'-nominalizations. (See also Langacker 1991: 31–2.) We can distinguish, in the first place, between the reification of a discrete episode (*destruction*), as in (15*a*), and the reification of an imperfective process (*destroying*), as in (15*b*). In both cases, unprofiled participants in the process (the notional subject and the notional direct object) are available for optional periphrastic specification, either in a possessor phrase, or in a postnominal prepositional phrase. In the case of a Type B nominalization, of the kind *the enemy's destroying the city* (15*c*), what is nominalized is a more fully specified process, viz. *destroy the city*, where the landmark is a specific individual that undergoes destruction—whence Langacker's (1991: 31) term 'instance nominalization'. Here, periphrastic specification is limited to the naming of the trajector entity in an optional possessor phrase, specification of the notional direct object being obligatory. Significantly, type B nominalizations may incorporate some further elements of the verb phrase, such as markers of polarity, aspect, and voice: *the city's not having been destroyed by the enemy*. With respect to Type C, *the enemy destroying the city* (15*d*), nominalization reifies a conception of a fully specified, yet ungrounded, process; again, markers of polarity, voice, and so on, may be incorporated into the nominalization: *the city not having been destroyed by the enemy*. Finally, if nominalization applies to a fully grounded clausal predication, we get, of course, a tensed *that*-clause: (*the fact*) *that the enemy destroyed the city* (15*e*).

Before looking in more detail at the three *ing*-constructions, it is worth pointing out that degree of conceptual reification appears to underlie Grimshaw's distinction between 'complex event nominals' and 'simple event nominals', discussed at length in section 6.7 (see Grimshaw 1990: ch. 3). Grimshaw, it will be recalled, claimed that complex event nominals preserve, in their semantic structure, the aspectual properties of the reified process. We might take this to mean that the nominalization retains some of the processual character of the nominalized pre-dication, that is, the event is construed with respect to its successive temporal stages. Complex event nominals are therefore distinctly verbal in character. This property could account for the characteristics of complex event nominals that Grimshaw highlights, especially the fact that complex event nominals, like verbs, have an argument structure, entailing the obligatory expression of the internal argument in an *of*-phrase, and the optional expression of the external argument in a possessor phrase. She also points out (pp. 54–6) that complex event nominals do not pluralize, and tolerate, as determiners, only *the* or a possessor phrase (or, more marginally, zero). In this respect, therefore, complex event nominals are more restricted in their distribution than regular mass nouns. To the extent that *ing*-nominalizations, for Grimshaw (pp. 49–50), are invariably complex event nominals, the examples in (12), where a gerund takes the indefinite article, show that this last claim could be factually incorrect. (I return to this topic below, arguing that with respect to the determiners that they take, gerundial *ing*-forms do in fact function like full-fledged mass nouns.)

If *ing*-nominalizations, for Grimshaw, are invariably complex event nominals, she claims (p. 47) that derived nouns like *destruction* and *invasion* are typically polysemous between a complex event and a simple event reading. Simple event nominals (of which result nouns are unambiguous examples) do not have an argument structure; possessors and prepositional phrases do not satisfy argument positions, but have the status of optional complements or modifiers. Simple event nominals are therefore fully noun-like in character. Depending on their semantics, they may have mass or count status (and, if count, may pluralize), and they take the full range of determiners appropriate to their mass/count status.

Although the notion of the more verbal character—both syntactically and semantically—of complex event nominals seems basically correct, Grimshaw's account has some rather strange consequences. According to the distinctions which she draws, the (*a*) expressions below (which, in virtue of the presence of the internal argument in an *of*-phrase, together with their status as singulars, have to exemplify complex event nominals) differ fundamentally from the (*b*) and (*c*) expressions, which have to exemplify simple event nominals.

(16)   *a.* the destruction of the city.
       b. the city's destruction.
(17)   *a.* Caesar's invasion of Britain.
       b. Caesar's two invasions of Britain.
       c. Britain's invasion(s) (by Caesar).

Destruction and *invasion*, in (16) and (17), are therefore polysemous, in a quite fundamental way. On the other hand, the two expressions in (18) and in (19) would turn out to be essentially identical, in that in both *destruction* and *destroying*, *invasion* and *invading*, would count as complex event nominals. (At any rate, whatever differences there might be between these two nominalization patterns, Grimshaw does not address them.)

(18) *a*. the enemy's destruction of the city.
      b. the enemy's destroying of the city.
(19) *a*. Caesar's invasion of Britain.
      b. Caesar's invading of Britain.

But this has to be wrong. The two expressions in (18), surely, differ in a more fundamental way than those in (16)! The main difference concerns the aspectual character of the nominalization. (18*a*) reifies an event, construed through its temporal stages, whereas (18*b*) focuses only on the medial stage, construing it as an imperfective process, without invoking its beginning or end. Whilst Grimshaw makes what is a basically correct distinction, she draws it in the wrong place; she also fails to make some other, equally necessary distinctions.

10.2 TYPE A: *THE ENEMY'S DESTROYING OF THE CITY*

In terms of its internal syntax, this is the most nominal of the *ing*-constructions under discussion. As examples (18) and (19) show, the *V-ing* forms *destroying* and *invading*, like the derived nouns *destruction* and *invasion*, behave like full-fledged nouns. Both take a prepositional complement, and both may be preceded by a possessive determiner. Furthermore, both kinds of items may be modified by an attributive adjective (20). In contrast, Type B nominalizations require modification by an adverb (21). It is, in fact, on this basis that the expressions in (7*b*) and (8) would be assigned to the Type B pattern (22).

(20) *a*. the enemy's sudden destruction of the city.
      b. the enemy's sudden destroying of the city.
(21) the enemy's {*sudden/suddenly} destroying the city.
(22) *a*. the odds against its {*sudden/suddenly} happening like that by chance.
         [cf. (7*b*)]
      b. the idea of his {*sudden/suddenly} being a serious candidate. [cf. (8*a*)]
      c. in spite of its {*sudden/suddenly} being spring. [cf. (8*b*)]

One difference between the *V-ing* forms and the deverbal nouns is the fact, already mentioned, that the *V-ing* forms are invariably mass nouns, whereas derived nouns may be either mass and count. *Pace* Grimshaw, I see no reason to regard the *V-ing* forms in a Type A nominalization as anything other than full-fledged mass nouns. Grimshaw's (1990: 56) claim that they are incompatible with determiners, other than *the* or a possessor, is without basis. In addition to the examples already cited in (12), note the following example with *that*.

(23) the gratuitousness of that giving of herself. [*SW* 76]

Grimshaw (p. 54) does, however, allow that complex event nominals may occur without any determiner at all, citing (24) as an instance. Observe that gerunds, in analogous environments, are also acceptable without a determiner (25). This possibility further strengthens the claim the gerunds (and other complex event nominals) are regular mass nouns.

(24) Assignment of difficult problems always causes problems.
(25) *a.* Assigning of difficult problems always causes problems.
     b. Shooting of rabbits is illegal.
     c. Constant singing of loud songs is something I don't like.

In spite of their uncontroversial nominal character, the *V-ing* forms in Type A nominalizations nevertheless do preserve various traces of their verbal origin. Consider, for example, the name sometimes given to the Type A construction, viz. 'action nominalization'. The term reflects the fact that the construction is compatible only with inherently perfective situations. Inherently imperfective situations, such as those designated by the verbs *know, remember, resemble*, do not permit action nominalizations. This restriction is, of course, identical to that associated with the progressive.

(26) *a.* their destroying of the city.
       They are destroying the city.
     b. the pencil's steady traversing of the page.
       The pencil is steadily traversing the page.
     c. Porphyro's persuading of the old woman.
       Porphyro is persuading the old woman.
(27) *a.* *their knowing of the answer.
       *They are knowing the answer.
     b. *my remembering of the incident.
       *I am remembering the incident.
     c. *John's resembling of his brother.
       *John is resembling his brother.

Other kinds of nominalization are not subject to this restriction. Type B nominalizations (*their knowing the answer*), as well as derived nouns (*their knowledge of the answer*), are fully compatible with imperfectivity. This special restriction on Type A expressions points to the close affinity between the relational present participle and the nominal gerund, and confirms the idea that the gerund reifies an internally homogeneous activity. To this extent, also, the term 'action nominalization' is misleading. The semantic import of the construction is not to designate an action, but to construe a normally perfective situation as an imperfect activity.

A further significant property of Type A expressions is that, unlike many derived nouns, the gerund can only have an active reading. There are no Type

A nominalizations corresponding to the objective readings of (28*a*) and (29*a*).

(28)   *a*. the city's destruction (by the enemy).
       b. *the city's destroying (by the enemy).
(29)   *a*. the students' boredom (with the lecture).
       b. *the students' boring (with the lecture).

In other words, in a Type A nominalization, the possessor obligatorily designates the notional subject of the nominalized process. The idea of the transitive process is therefore still very salient in the semantic structure of the gerund.

Just as the possessor phrase, if there is one, must obligatorily designate the notional subject of the gerund, so, with gerunds derived from transitive verbs, the expression of the notional direct object is usually obligatory. *The enemy's destroying*, or even, simply, *the destroying*, must be judged as conceptually (and syntactically) incomplete. Compare in this respect the full acceptability of *the sudden destruction* (*came as a surprise*) with the incompleteness of *the sudden destroying* (*came as a surprise*). Again, this property seems to reflect the salience of the underlying transitive process (in which the expression of the landmark entity is also obligatory) in the gerund's semantic structure.

This said, it must be recognized that some established *V-ing* forms—such as occur, for example, in idioms and fixed expressions—may sometimes be used without explicit elaboration of the notional object, and do sometimes tolerate, if rather marginally, a passive reading.

(30)   *a*. The proof of the pudding is in {the/?its} eating.
       b. The events lost none of their excitement in {the/?their} telling.

It could be that these *ing*-forms, in virtue of their role in established locutions, have begun to partake of the properties of standard deverbal nouns. Note also the following example, in which the temporal possessor could belie the claim that the possessor to a gerund obligatorily elaborates the notional subject.[3]

(31)   A few days' living in this place would see off the remainder of his bank balance. [*SW* 274]

Again, a plausible explanation is that *living* (cf. its use in the standard locutions *cost of living*, *standard of living*) has begun to take on the properties of an independent derived noun.

We have seen that with respect to the semantic role of the possessor, gerunds differ significantly from a good many episodic nouns. With respect to the semantic roles elaborated by an *of*-complement, there is, though, a remarkable similarity. This concerns the ergative patterning of the *of*-complements (see above, section 9.5). That is to say, the role of the *of*-complement may correspond to the direct object of a transitive verb (32), or to the subject of an intransitive verb (33).

---

[3] Adjective insertion confirms that (31) is a Type A nominalization: *a few days' {extravagant/ *extravagantly} living in this place.*

(32)   *a.* the kidnapping of a well-connected resident. [*SW* 276]
     b. owing to the grounding of the DC-10. [*SW* 272)
     c. *a* learned conversation about the brewing of stout ale. [*SW* 170]
(33)   *a.* Persse heard . . . the banging of the door as the two men left. [*SW* 16]
     b. Morris Zapp is woken by the bleeping of his digital wristwatch. [*SW* 83]
     c. the only sounds are the tapping of Robin Dempsey's fingers on the keyboard of his computer terminal, and the crunching of Josh Collins's potato chips. [*SW* 309]

Should the notional subject of a transitive process be expressed, it would have to appear in other than an *of*-phrase—either in a possessor phrase (*their kidnapping of a resident*) or in a *by*-phrase (*the kidnapping of a resident by the socialists*). As with derived nouns, the ergative patterning of the complement phrases is plausibly regarded as a natural consequence of the atemporalizing effect of the nominalization process itself.

I have mentioned the somewhat infrequent incidence of Type A nominalizations. To conclude this section, it may be worth looking at the special stylistic value of the construction, and some possible reasons for it. Consider again the two attested examples that were cited in (4), repeated below.

(34)   *a.* the slender gold pencil continues its steady traversing of the page.
     b. his persuading of the old woman, Angela, to hide him in Madeline's bedroom.

The first example, in which the *ing*-nominalization functions as a complement to *continue*, incidentally confirms the thesis that the construction offers an imperfective construal of a situation. It is, namely, the 'continuous' character of the process that is doubly at issue. However, the special stylistic value of (34*a*) derives from the fact that a more concise, and less marked wording is available: *the pencil continues steadily traversing the page.* The special quality of the more wordy version lies specifically in the conceptual reification of the activity that it encodes. The activity is designated by a noun, *traversing*, whereby the trajector and landmark entities (the thing that traverses, and the thing traversed) are specified only periphrastically. In fact, the wider context of the example is characterized by a delinking of entities from their natural conceptual partners. A few sentences earlier we read of 'an exquisitely manicured hand', that 'guides a slender gold-plated propelling pencil across lines of print, occasionally pausing to underline a sentence or make a marginal note'. Observe here the use of *hand* without mention of whose hand it is, also the assertion that it is the hand that pauses and underlines, whereas a more normal wording would have the 'possessor' of the hand pausing and underlining. The same artefactuality, I feel, attaches to some of the expressions in (33), in which the notional subject of the gerund appears in a periphrastic *of*-phrase. Consider the narrative context of (33*c*). The Computer Centre of the fictitious Darlington University is the scene of Robin

Dempsey's incipient nervous breakdown. We read again of body parts—'the shoulders', 'the jaw', 'the small eyes'—delinked from their natural possessor. In this 'charged atmosphere', the 'tapping' and the 'crunching' become autonomous entities, whose source is specified only periphrastically.

The stylistic value of (34*b*) is somewhat different. Its wider context is relevant.

He skimmed quickly through the early stanzas about the coldness of the weather, the tradition that maidens who went fasting to bed on St Agnes' Eve would see their future husbands in their sleep, the abstractedness of Madeline, with this intention in mind, amid the feasting and merrymaking in the hall, the secret arrival of Porphyro, risking his life in the hostile castle for a glimpse of his beloved, his persuading of the old woman, Angela, to hide him in Madeline's bedroom, Madeline's arrival and preparations for bed . . . He read on through the description of the delicacies Porphyro laid out for Madeline, his attempts to wake her with lute music, hovering over her sleeping figure; Madeline's eyes opening on the vision of her dream, and her half-conscious address to Porphyro. (*SW* 45–6)

The protagonist mentally reviews the sequence of events narrated in Keats's poem *The Eve of St Agnes*. The events and circumstances are not presented in a series of finite clauses, they are not, in other words, construed dynamically, through conceived time. Rather, they are designated by a string of nominalizations, with little overt linkage between them. The narrative is thereby atemporalized, creating a kind of stream of consciousness presentation. We might even want to see an affinity between the imperfectivizing effect of the nominalizations, and the use of imperfective verbal aspect in free indirect speech, extensively documented and discussed in Banfield (1982).

10.3 TYPE B: *THE ENEMY'S DESTROYING THE CITY*

This construction, often referred to as a factive nominalization, exhibits a curious mixture of both nominal and verbal properties. No doubt for this very reason, it has been the object of considerable interest from syntacticians.[4]

While the external syntax of the construction is very definitely that of a nominal, its internal syntax is predominantly that of a verb phrase. Thus, the notional direct object (if there is one) appears adjacent to the *V-ing* form, without intervening *of*, and modification of the *V-ing* form is achieved by an adverb, not by an adjective.

(35)   the enemy's ruthlessly destroying the city.
       Cf. the enemy's ruthless {destroying/destruction} of the city.

Furthermore, nominalization can apply, not only to the verb stem itself (to give, e.g. *destroying*), but also to a passive verbal group (*being destroyed*), and to a verbal group which incorporates markers of anteriority (*having destroyed*) and

---

[4] See e.g. Horn (1975), Jackendoff (1977: ch. 9), Abney (1987: ch. 3), Pullum (1991), and Blevins (1994).

negation (*not having destroyed*). Even modal elements (provided they are designated by non-defective verbs) may be nominalized (*having to destroy, being able to destroy*). Consequently, Type B nominalizations can in principle achieve a quite high degree of internal complexity.

(36)　*a.* in spite of [my having told you].
　　　b. because of [your application's having been repeatedly turned down].
　　　c. without [my having had to tell you].
　　　d. the reason for [your not having been informed].

These various aspects of the construction suggest that what is being nominalized, in a Type B nominalization, is a full-fledged verb phrase, complete with direct object, adverbial modifier, and markers of anteriority, modality, and polarity. The notional subject, however, need not be expressed at all. In fact, subjectless nominalizations are probably the norm.

(37)　*a.* He was so used to [receiving invitations] that [refusing them] was by now a reflex action. [*SW* 163]
　　　b. his performance is enhanced by [having the original backup tracks as accompaniment]. [*SW* 293]

Note, in these examples, the absence of a determiner to the *ing*-nominalization. Insertion of a determiner would result in ungrammaticality.

(38)　*a.* *A refusing an invitation was a reflex action.
　　　b. *The having the original backup tracks enhanced his performance.

Very marginally, perhaps, a demonstrative is tolerable.

(39)　*a.* ?This refusing the invitation is something you'll regret.
　　　b. ?That having the original backup tracks enhanced his performance.

The only fully acceptable determiner is, in fact, a possessor phrase, which, predictably, serves to elaborate the notional subject of the nominalized process.

The use of the prenominal possessor phrase is the only truly nominal aspect of the construction's internal syntax. But if the internal syntax is predominantly verbal, Type B expressions very definitely have the external syntax of a noun phrase. The construction can figure as the nominal complement of a preposition.

(40)　*a.* instructions about [handing them over]. [*SW* 281]
　　　b. Did you tell any of our political friends about [his being married to Désirée Byrd]? [*SW* 289]

It may function as the subject or direct object of a verb.

(41)　*a.* I hope you didn't mind [my having a go at you just now]. [*SW* 30]
　　　b. [His being married] is of no significance.

And it is involved in subject–auxiliary inversion.

(42)　*a.* Did [my having a go at you just now] upset you?
　　　b. Was [his being married] known to his kidnappers?

A further remarkable fact about Type B nominalizations, in contrast to Type A, is that they do not impose an imperfective construal on the reified situation. In fact, Type B nominalizations appear fully to preserve the aspectual properties of the nominalized verb phrase. Inherently perfective situations (cf. *The volcano erupted twice*) are fully compatible with the construction.

(43)   [Speaking of the volcano] Its suddenly erupting twice within a week was unexpected.

Type B nominalizations are also fully compatible with inherently imperfective situations. In this respect, the construction differs radically from both Type A nominalizations and from progressive verb forms.

(44)   *a.* in spite of [its being spring].
       b. because of [his being too inexperienced for the position].
       c. the possibility of [its happening twice].

The only restriction, it would appear, on the scope of Type B nominalizations concerns progressive *be* and emphatic *do*. From *He is worried about it* we get *his being worried about it*. But there is no **his being worrying about it* corresponding to *He is worrying about it*. *He does worry* does not sanction *his doing worry, neither does *He does not worry* sanction **his doing not worry*.[5]

Let us summarize the differences. In the case of a Type A expression, such as *the enemy's destroying of the city*, what is nominalized is schematic conception of a kind of process—hence Langacker's (1991: 33) term, 'type nominalization'. The reified process is designated by *V-ing*, that is, by a gerund. The gerund, we have seen, has close affinities with the present participle. It reifies an imperfectly construed process, and, as such, has mass noun status. As with any other inherently relational noun, entities that participate in the reified process may be periphrastically specified, either in a prepositional phrase, or, additionally, in the case of the notional subject, in a possessor phrase. The possessor phrase fulfils its usual function of grounding the expression, by anchoring the reified process to an individual construed as a reference point.

Apart from the special semantic properties contributed by the gerundial *V-ing* form (such as the imperfective construal that the gerund imposes), a Type A expression is assembled in much the same way as the possessive nominalizations discussed in earlier chapters. Some aspects of the constituency of a typical example are shown in (45). Here, I diagram the way in which the constituent elements of *the enemy's destroying of the city* are put together. The underlined elements constitute the profile determinant at each level of constituency. Observe that nominalization (by means of *ing*-suffixation) occurs on the innermost element *destroying*. Just as, in the case of agent nouns like *singer*, we can say that the *-er* suffix contributes its nominal profile to the derived noun (and may

---

[5] The impossibility of *his doing worry is plausibly explained by the fact that auxiliary *do* is defective (there is no *to do worry*, either). The restriction on progressive *be* is more puzzling.

thus be said to head the derived noun), so, in the case of a gerund, the -*ing* suffix gives its nominal profile to the *V-ing* form, and can thus be analysed as the head of the gerund.[6]

(45)

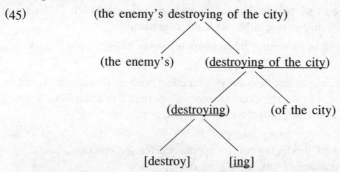

In contrast, Type B nominalizations preserve many of the characteristics of a verb phrase. What is nominalized is a conception of a process which already incorporates the landmark entity, adverbial modifiers, and markers of anteriority, mood, and polarity. Whence Langacker's (1991: 34) term, 'instance nominalization'. Any differences between the finite clause *The enemy destroyed the city* and the nominalization *the enemy's destroying the city*, or *the enemy's having destroyed the city*, follow from more general properties of clausal and nominal predications. The finite clause designates a process, conceived through time. The process is grounded with respect to the speaker's here and now; in the case in point, it is asserted that the process took place, at a time remote from the time of speaking. The nominalization reifies a conception of a fully specified instance of the process, without however carrying any implication that the instance has, or will, take place. The nominalization is (optionally) grounded by the possessor nominal, which anchors the instance to the trajector entity. Even so, the construction carries with it no presupposition of the factuality of the grounded instance. It is easy to imagine a situation in which the grounded instance is not 'a fact', but a possibility.

(46)   The possibility of [the enemy's destroying the city] is remote.

To this extent, the term 'factive nominalization' is an inappropriate level for a Type B nominalization.

In (45) I sketched some aspects of the constituency of a Type A nominalization. Bearing in mind its internal syntax, a Type B expression can be assigned the constituency outlined in (47).

---

[6] In (45), I follow Langacker's (1987a: 313) convention and denote established units by square brackets, and novel units by round brackets.

(47)

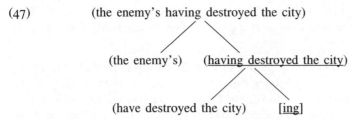

(47) captures the fact that nominalization applies to a fully specified VP. As with Type A expressions, the nominalization gets its nominal character from the *ing*-suffix. The nominalization is therefore headed, once again, by *ing*. The *ing*-suffix, however, does not attach directly to the verb stem, but takes as its complement a full VP. Consequently, *having* does not have the status of a constituent in (47). Whence my reluctance at the beginning of this chapter to apply the terms gerund and participle to the *V-ing* form in a Type B nominalization. Furthermore, not being itself a constituent, the *V-ing* form need not have the distinctive semantic properties of a gerund (nor, of course, of a participle).

It is worth observing that some recent developments in X-bar syntax have come up with a not dissimilar analysis. Thus Abney (1987: 222–5) proposes that in a Type B nominalization, the *ing*-morpheme takes the VP as its complement, the resulting expression being an NP, whereas in a gerund (which is an N), *ing* takes V as its complement. We already noted some similar convergences between the cognitive grammar analysis of functional heads (such as the plural morpheme, as well as the possessive morpheme), and the analyses proposed by linguists who accept the very different theoretical presuppositions of X-bar syntax.

10.4 TYPE C: *THE ENEMY DESTROYING THE CITY*

We have already observed that the possessive morpheme in a Type B nominalization often appears to be optional. Consider the following two examples.

(48) *a.* All I can think about is [him getting the UNESCO chair]. [*SW* 309]
     b. the idea of [his being a serious candidate]. [*SW* 247]

Switching oblique *him* and possessive *his* in these examples has minimal consequences, either for the grammaticality of the expressions, or for their semantics.

(49) *a.* All I can think about is [his getting the UNESCO chair].
     b. the idea of [him being a serious candidate].

The possessive form is most frequent if the notional subject is a pronoun.

(50) *a.* if you will excuse [my mentioning it]. [*SW* 287]
     b. Did you tell any of our political friends about [his being married to Désirée Byrd]? [*SW* 289]
     c. I hope you didn't mind [my having a go at you]. [*SW* 30]

With full NPs, the non-possessive form is strongly preferred. In fact, in *Small World*, I failed to find a single example of a Type B nominalization with a full NP possessor.

(51)   *a.* The Greeks don't approve of [people kissing in public]. [*SW* 244]
    b. He was aware of [the girl pulling a coverlet from the bed]. [*SW* 326]
    c. It makes me mad to hear of [girls getting knocked up]. [*SW* 46]
    d. a far cry from [the violet blending its odour with the rose]. [*SW* 46]
    e. a sense of [things moving to a crisis]. [*SW* 309]

The above examples, it seems to me, would be only marginally acceptable with possessor subjects (?*They don't approve of people's kissing in public*), although pronominal possessors (*They don't approve of our kissing in public*) would be unobjectionable. And while possessive *its* (*in spite of its being spring*) is attested, possessive *there's* is completely out. There can be no question, in the following example, of appending the possessive morpheme to *there*.

(52)   He muttered something about [there being some people whom he wanted to meet]. [*SW* 332]

Let us leave aside for the moment the semantic value of a Type C nominalization. Given the constituency in (47) of a Type B nominalization, the analysis of Type C is quite straightforward. In terms of its internal structure, a Type C nominalization is even more clausal in character than Type B. If a Type B nominalization reifies a fully specified verb phrase (fully specified, that is, in all respects except for grounding by means of tense), a Type C nominalization reifies a fully specified clause, inclusive of its subject nominal (although, again, exclusive of grounding by tense).

(53)   (the enemy destroying the city)

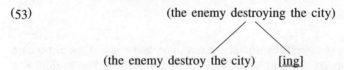

           (the enemy destroy the city)   [ing]

Again, the nominal character of the composite expression is guaranteed by the nominal profile which it inherits from its head, *ing*.

One curious aspect of Type C nominalizations is that the notional subject, if a pronoun, invariably appears in the objective, rather than the subjective form.

(54)   *a.* {*He/Him} getting the UNESCO chair would be unthinkable.
    b. {*She/Her} mentioning that was unpardonable.

This property is plausibly related to the ungrounded status of the nominalized clause. Clausal grounding involves tense marking on the finite verb, as well as number agreement between the tensed verb and the clausal subject. Both aspects are lacking in a Type C nominalization. If we regard the choice of the subjective form also as an intrinsic aspect of subject–verb agreement, the absence of the subjective form in the nominalization is to be expected.[7] An exactly comparable state of affairs is encountered in another construction, exemplified in (55).

(55) *a.* Me write a novel! You must be joking!
       b. Him get the UNESCO chair! Over my dead body!

Here the verb appears in its base form, without grounding and without number agreement with the subject. In addition, the subject is obligatorily in the objective form.[8] The construction differs from a Type C nominalization in that it is verbal (i.e. relational) rather than nominal in character. It resembles the nominalization, however, in that it presents only the conception of a situation, without anchoring it in time or reality.

The semantic difference between a Type B and a Type C nominalization is likely to be very small. Mostly, the choice between elaborating the notional subject subsequent to nominalization (Type B), or nominalizing the clause complete with its subject (Type C), will entail only a negligible semantic contrast. Whence, no doubt, the impression that the presence of the possessive morpheme in a Type B expression is optional. Still, we need to explain why the possessive morpheme is preferred in certain cases (for example, when the notional subject is a pronoun), and disallowed in others. Topicality may be one of the factors involved. We saw in Chapter 8 that the topicality of the possessor is an important requirement on prenominal possessors. It could be that the possessive construal of the notional subject is an option just in case the notional subject is high in topicality. This condition is certainly met whenever the subject is denoted by a pronoun, especially a personal pronoun.

But stylistic considerations, of various kinds, are undoubtedly relevant, also. Type B nominalizations have a 'bookish' feel to them, and the marking, by means of a possessive, of the relation between the nominalized verb phrase and its notional subject smacks of studied correctness. (It is perhaps not by chance that David Lodge puts (50*b*)—*his being married to Désirée Byrd*—in the mouth of a character who is not a native speaker of English.) This aspect could help explain the relatively high incidence of possessor subjects in routine phrases, of the kind *I hope you don't mind my saying so.* Another factor favouring the possessive pronouns—and here I am being *very* speculative!—could be the quite widespread feeling (an unfortunate spin-off of prescriptive disapproval of the objective form in predicative expressions of the kind *It's me*) that the objective forms *me, him,* etc. are somehow lacking in prestige, and are to be avoided whenever possible (cf. Gowers 1954: 147). This kind of sentiment possibly lies behind the curious incidence of subjective *I* in environments in which *me* would be required even by the prescriptive grammarians (a notorious example: *between*

---

[7] In GB theory, this aspect is attributed to the absence of INFL, the element which, it is said, assigns nominative case to the subject.

[8] For an illuminating discussion of this construction, see Fillmore *et al.* (1988).

you and I). This sentiment would certainly favour the studied avoidance of objective *me* in expressions of the kind *If you don't mind my saying so*.

A further factor disfavouring the possessive with full NP subjects could be the homophony, with singular nouns, of the possessive and the plural morphemes. Hence, the use of a Type B construction with a singular subject would be ambiguous for the hearer (*the girl's pulling a coverlet from the bed*). Conversely, with a plural subject, the possessive morpheme would be no more than an orthographic mark, of no phonological significance (*It makes me mad to hear of girls' getting knocked up*).

In spite of what appears, in many cases, to be a purely stylistic contrast between type B and type C expressions, there are circumstances in which the choice of an accusative over a possessive subject is obligatory, and cannot therefore be put down to stylistic preference. Consider, for example, the bracketed expressions in (56). These function as subordinate clauses, which stand in a temporal or even causal relation to the main clause.

(56)   *a*. [The enemy(*'s) having destroyed the city], we had to rethink our strategy.
       b. [There(*'s) being nothing more to discuss], the meeting was closed.
       c. [It (*Its) being spring], the weather ought to be getting warmer.
       d. [The position(*'s) having been advertised], there was much speculation as to who would be applying.

The construction type exemplified in (56) does not require the overt elaboration of the subject of *V-ing*. In (57) the unexpressed subject is construed as identical with the overt trajector of the adjacent clause.[9]

(57)   *a*. Having destroyed the city, the enemy continued their advance.
       b. Having advertised the position, the committee waited for the applications to come in.
       c. Working in the garden, Janet discovered a lizard.

The subordinate expressions in (56) appear to have the form of a Type C nominalization. However, the impossibility of a possessor subject strongly points to the non-nominal character of the expressions; and on other grounds, too, these expressions are not plausibly analysed as nominals. What, then, is their correct analysis?

Discussing example (57c), *Working in the garden, Janet found a lizard*, Langacker (1991: 424–5) attributes to *ing* precisely the same value that it has in the progressive construction (*She was working in the garden*); *ing* merely serves to atemporalize the processual predicate to which it attaches. According to Langacker, therefore, the *ing*-clause does not specifically designate an interclausal relationship; that this sentence is understood to involve a relation of temporal contiguity is due, he says, to properties of the overarching construction, whereby

---

[9] The unelaborated trajector corresponds, of course, to PRO of GB theory.

the time span evoked by *working in the garden* is equated with the scope of predication for the temporal profile of the main clause (*Janet found a lizard*).

I would hesitate to equate all instances of subordinating *ing* in (56) and (57) with progressive *ing*. Observe, for example, the compatibility of subordinating *ing* with an inherently imperfective predication, as in (56c): *it being spring*. This shows that the *V-ing* form should not be identified with the one that occurs in the progressive (**It is being spring*). Rather, we need to attribute to the *ing*-clauses a structure comparable to that sketched in (53), whereby *ing* attaches to a fully specified, yet ungrounded clause, which it takes as its complement. *Ing*, however, does not have a nominal profile; rather than nominalize the clause to which it attaches, *ing* merely imposes an atemporal construal. (Just as, in section 10.1, we recognized the gerund as a nominal variant of the participle, the two variants being related by profile shift, so now we recognize a subordinate *ing*-clause as a relational variant of a Type C nominalization.) Following Langacker, we may say that the subordinate and main clauses may enter a valence relation, to the extent that the first specifies the scope of predication for the temporal profile of the latter.

There are some further contexts in which the presence vs. absence of the possessive morpheme with a *V-ing* form is by no means optional. Compare the (*a*) and (*b*) sentences below.

(58)   *a.* I appreciate {him/his} repairing my TV set.
       b. I watched {him/*his} repairing my TV set.
(59)   *a.* I remember {them/their} breaking into my car.
       b. I caught {them/*their} breaking into my car.

The impossibility of the possessive in the (*b*) sentences suggests that the landmark of *watch* and *catch* is of a different kind from the landmark of *appreciate* and *remember*. What is appreciated, or remembered, could be a kind of situation, described in a nominalized clause. Significantly, both verbs may be followed also by a *that*-clause, which reifies a fully grounded process, as well as by *it*, which is schematic for the clausal landmark.[10] (In the (*a*) sentences, therefore, *it* and the following *that*-clauses are in apposition.) These possibilities are not available with *watch* and *catch*.

(60)   *a.* I appreciate (it) that he repaired my TV set.
       b. *I watched (it) that he repaired my TV set.
(61)   *a.* I remember (?it) that they broke into my car.
       b. *I caught (it) that they broke into my car.

---

[10] This is not to say that a *that*-clause is synonymous with a *V-ing* complement. The *that*-clause designates a fact, which may be apprehended by the intellect, whilst the *ing*-complement focuses more on the process as experienced. *I remember them/their breaking in* is appropriate only if the speaker personally witnessed the event, and recalls the experience at the time of speaking. *I remember that they broke in* would be appropriate even if the speaker had not personally witnessed the break-in, but had learned of it through a third party.

Furthermore, the situation that is appreciated or remembered may be topicalized, to appear as a clausal subject. This possibility is not available with *watch* and *catch*.

(62) *a.* {Him/His} repairing my TV set is something I much appreciate.
      b. *{Him/His} repairing my TV set is something I attentively watched.
(63) *a.* {Them/Their} breaking into my car is something I vividly remember.
      b. *{Them/their} breaking into my car is something I fortunately caught.

What is watched, or caught, is not a situation *per se*, but an individual, more specifically, an individual engaged in a process. In the (*b*) sentences of (58) and (59), *repairing my TV set* and *breaking into my car* are plausibly analysed as participial, i.e. relational constituents, which modify the head nouns *him* and *them*. These considerations suggest the following structure.

(64) *a.* I watched [him] [repairing my TV set].
      b. I caught [them] [breaking into my car].

But the analysis suggested for *watch* and *catch* could also be indicated for *appreciate* and *remember*. What is appreciated or remembered could also be, not so much a situation, but an individual that participates in the situation. Whereas the possessive nominalizations in (58*a*) and (59*a*) have only the constituency in (65), the expressions with objective pronouns could be structurally ambiguous, as shown in (66) and (67).

(65) *a.* I appreciate [his repairing my TV set].
      b. I remember [their breaking into my car].
(66) *a.* I appreciate [him repairing my TV].
      b. I appreciate [him] [repairing my TV].
(67) *a.* I remember [them breaking into my car].
      b. I remember [them] [breaking into my car].

The plausibility of a participial analysis, in any given case, could well be a factor favouring the use of a non-possessive subject in a nominalized clause. Consider one of our earlier examples.

(68) It makes me mad to hear of girls getting knocked up. [= (51*c*)]

What is it that makes the speaker of (68) so mad? It could be hearing of a certain kind of situation, designated by a nominalized clause, *girls getting knocked up*. Equally, what makes him mad could be hearing of 'girls', characterized in terms of their involvement in a certain kind of activity, namely 'getting knocked up'. In this case, *getting knocked up* would count as a participial modifier of *girls*. The same goes for the following example.

(69) There was always a chance of some writer taking a poke at a critic. [*SW* 175]

11 Possessive Compounds

THERE are good reasons why we should want to regard the expressions in (1) as ambiguous, both structurally and semantically.

(1) *a.* the woman's magazine.
     b. the girls' school.
     c. the man's shirt.
     d. the driver's licence.

On one reading, these expressions instantiate the prenominal possessive construction that has been our main focus of attention so far. On this reading, *the woman's magazine* denotes a specific magazine, identified from the reference point of 'the woman'.[1]

On an alternative reading, *woman's magazine, girls' school, man's shirt, driver's licence* have a status akin to that of nominal compounds. A 'woman's magazine' is a kind of magazine, a 'girls' school' is a kind of school. The two structural possibilities can be represented as follows.

(2) *a.* prenominal possessive: [the woman]'s [magazine]
     b. possessive compound: the [woman's magazine]

Our first concern in this chapter will be to characterize possessive compounds, in contradistinction to prenominal possessives.[2] Having done this, we shall see that for quite a number of expressions the distinction is far from clear-cut. Not only this, the distinctiveness of possessive compounds *vis-à-vis* non-possessive compounds will also turn out, in many cases, to be somewhat blurred. The evidence of prenominal possessives, possessive compounds, and non-possessive compounds suggests that these constructions have a prototype structure, with some expressions being 'good examples' of a construction, others being more 'marginal' examples. Indirectly, therefore, the evidence from these three constructions validates the notion of syntactic construction itself.

---

[1] This chapter develops ideas first presented in Taylor (1995*a*),

[2] My category of possessive compounds corresponds to Quirk *et al.*'s (1985: 322) 'descriptive genitives' and to Poutsma's (1914–16: 40) 'classifying genitives' (the latter in contrast to 'identifying genitives'—my prenominal possessives). I use the term possessive compound in order to emphasize the dual affinity of the construction, to prenominal possessives on the one hand, and to regular nominal compounds on the other.

II.I POSSESSIVE COMPOUNDS: A CHARACTERIZATION

First, let us briefly review the main characteristics of the prenominal possessive. On the possessive reading of *the woman's magazine, the woman* constitutes an NP, which, in association with the possessive morpheme, functions as a kind of definite determiner to *magazine*. The possessor nominal can be internally quite complex; the possessee, also, may readily be pre-modified (although post-modification may be subject to various restrictions).

(3) a. [the woman sitting opposite]'s [magazine].
     b. [the young girl]'s school.
     c. [the man]'s [dark blue shirt].
     d. [the drunken driver]'s [recently issued licence].

On the basis of these considerations, we proposed, in Chapter 5, the following schematic structure for prenominal possessives.

(4) [$_{NP}$[$_{DET}$NP POSS] [N']]

With regard to the semantics of the construction, we argued that the import of the possessor nominal is to facilitate identification of the possessee, by mention of a reference point entity that is cognitively accessible (and which is therefore high in topicworthiness), and from whose perspective the referent of the possessee nominal may be identified. On its possessive reading, therefore, [*the woman*]'s *magazine* denotes a specific magazine, identifiable from the perspective of the first mentioned nominal. We emphasized that the nature of the semantic relation between possessor and possessee is not inherent to the possessive construction, but is, rather, determined by various considerations of a semantic-pragmatic nature. Nevertheless, the relation of possession, in the everyday sense of the term, does emerge as the default interpretation, in many cases. But even though "the magazine that the woman has in her possession" may be the dominant, or default interpretation of [*the woman*]'s *magazine*, many others are equally plausible, such as "the magazine that the woman is reading", "the magazine that she edits", "the magazine that she writes for", and so on.

On the alternative reading of *the woman's magazine*, [woman's magazine] constitutes a kind of compound noun, which is headed by *magazine*, and in which *woman's* serves as a kind of restrictive modifier. The modifier nominal would appear to be an N, or possibly an N', in that some limited pre-modification is permitted (5), although post-modification is not (6).

(5) a. a [gifted children]'s school.
     b. an [old people]'s home.
(6) a. *a [children who are gifted]'s school.
     b. *a [people who are old]'s home.

More extensive pre-modification is not possible (7), nor may the modifier contain a determiner (8).

(7) *a.* *an [exceptionally gifted children]'s school.

    b. *a [very old people]'s home.

(8) *a.* *a [the gifted children]'s school.

    b. *a [the old people]'s home.

However, the modifier may itself be a possessive compound.

(9) *a.* a young [driver's licence] holder.

    b. the [spider's web] layout of the streets.

    c. a recipe for [bird's nest] soup.

The head of a possessive compound would appear to be an N. Whilst a possessive compound may itself be headed by a nominal compound (10), adjectival modification of the head noun is not possible; compare in this respect (11) and (12). In (11), *famous* and *expensive* modify the compound expressions *deaf children's school* and *boys' school*, respectively. In (12), *famous* and *expensive* modify only the head of the possessive compound.

(10) *a.* an [old people]'s [retirement home].

    b. a men's [shoe shop].

    c. a boys' [grammar school].

(11) *a.* a famous [deaf children]'s school.

    b. an expensive [boys' school].

(12) *a.* *a [deaf children]'s [famous school].

    b. *a [boys]' [expensive school].

Lieber (1992: 84) proposes, as a test of compoundhood, the criterion of inseparability: 'the elements of a compound in English may not be separated by an intervening modifier of any sort, at least not without eliminating the compound's meaning'. The impossibility of (12) is therefore crucial evidence for the compound status of *deaf children's school* and *boys' school*.[3]

These considerations suggest the following schematic structure for possessive compounds.

(13) [$_N$[N'] POSS [N]]

The semantics of a possessive compound follows from its status as a noun, not a noun phrase. A possessive compound denotes a type of entity, not an instance of a type. Generally, the designated type is a subcategory of the type denoted by the head noun, whereby the modifying noun suggests how the referential possibility (or 'intension') of the head noun is to be circumscribed. As with prenominal possessives, the nature of the semantic relation between head noun and modifier is not determined by the construction itself, but is open to pragmatic interpretation.

---

[3] A *boys'* [*private school*] might appear to be a counterexample. On the other hand, the position of primary stress suggests that *private school* is not construed as an adjective–noun expression, but has acquired the status of a conventionalized nominal compound. In this respect, the behaviour of *private school* exactly parallels *grammar school* in (10c).

Unlike with prenominal possessives, however, compound expressions tend to have conventionalized unit status within the lexicon, with fixed, and sometimes quite unpredictable semantic values. Whereas, on its possessive reading, [*the woman*]'*s magazine* could invoke any one of an open-ended set of pragmatically plausible relations between the magazine and the woman, the compound [*woman's magazine*] conventionally denotes a special subcategory of magazine, namely, the category of magazines intended for an adult female readership, rather than, say, magazines that are edited by women, or magazines for which women write. And, as mentioned, the conventionalized senses of some possessive compounds may be quite unpredictable. *Cat's eyes* ("glass reflectors separating traffic lanes") are not a subcategory of eyes.[4]

Following on the above characterizations, we may note some further points of contrast between prenominal possessives and possessive compounds. In the next section we shall appeal to these aspects as diagnostics of the status of an expression as prenominal possessive or possessive compound.

(*a*) In a prenominal possessive, an initial determiner is construed with the possessor nominal. A determiner before a possessive compound must be construed with the maximal nominal constituent. The possibility arises, therefore, that number agreement with an initial determiner can disambiguate the two constructions. A compound reading of *this woman's magazines* is excluded, since singular *this* cannot be construed with plural [*woman's magazines*]; likewise, a possessive reading of *these woman's magazines* is excluded, since plural *these* cannot be construed with singular *woman*. The two expressions, therefore, can only be construed as follows.

(14)   *a.* [this woman]'s magazines.
       b. these [woman's magazines].

(*b*) A comparable state of affairs holds with respect to the construal of an initial adjective. In a possessive, an initial adjective can modify only the possessor, not the possessee. With a compound, an initial adjective may modify either the modifying nominal, as in *a* [*young girls*]' *school*, i.e. "school for young girls", or it may modify the entire compound, as in *an expensive* [*girls' school*], i.e. "a school for girls, which is expensive". Whereas *the young woman's magazine* could have both possessive and compound readings, *the woman's torn magazine*—given the general impossibility of adjectival modification of the head of a compound—can only have a possessive reading. On the other hand—given that *torn* is a semantically inappropriate modifier of *woman*—the *torn woman's magazine* can only have a compound reading.

(15)   *a.* [the woman]'s torn magazine.
       b. the torn [woman's magazine].

---

[4] Note, for example, the rather frequent use of possessive compounds as popular names of plants: *old man's beard, goat's beard, traveller's joy, elephant's ear, daisy* (< *day's eye*), *lamb's lettuce*. Many speakers appear to interpret *cowslip* (< *cū+slyppe*, i.e. "cow slobber") as "cow's lip".

(*c*) An important contrast concerns the referential status of the initial nominal (Kay and Zimmer 1990). In a prenominal possessive, the possessor is a grounded nominal, which denotes an individual, often a uniquely identifiable individual, or individuals. There is therefore the possibility of co-reference with a pronoun (16*a*). In addition, a hearer may legitimately request clarification concerning the identity of the individual denoted by the possessor nominal (16*b*).

(16) *a.* I found [that woman$_i$]'s magazines, but as far as I know, she$_i$ has not read them.

   b. A: I found [that woman$_i$]'s magazines.

   B: Whose$_i$ magazines did you say you had found?

In the compound, the initial nominal names a type of entity, not an individual. The possibility of co-reference is therefore not available (17*a*), nor is it possible to enquire into the identity of the possessor (17*b*).

(17) *a.* *I found those [woman$_i$'s magazines], but as far as I know she$_i$ has not read them.

   b. A: I found those [woman$_i$'s magazines].

   B: *Whose$_i$ magazines did you say you had found?

Symptomatic of its status as a type specification is the fact that the modifier typically lacks the plural marker, even though a phrasal paraphrase might well contain a plural (a *woman's magazine* is a "magazine for women").[5]

(*d*) There is a potential phonological contrast between the two constructions. Possessive compounds, like most nominal compounds, tend to have primary stress on the initial, i.e. modifying element: *a [wóman's magazine]*, *a [dríver's licence]*. Prenominal possessives, like most noun phrases, tend to have primary stress on the final element, i.e. on the possessee: *[the woman]'s magazíne*, *[the truck driver]'s lícence*. The contrast is potential, rather than actual, in that stress levels are influenced by many factors in addition to constituent structure, such as contrast, importance, and newness of information. The evidence from stress location must therefore be evaluated with caution.

Having emphasized the distinctiveness of the two constructions, we also need to enquire into their commonality. Both phonologically and orthographically, the *'s* that occurs in *[the woman]'s magazine* would appear to be exactly the

---

[5] Langacker (1991: 75) discusses the distinction drawn here, pointing out that the singular grounded nominal *the cat* involves 'a type conception construed as being anchored at a particular location in the domain of instantiation and specifically limits the profile to this particular instance'. Singular *cat* in the compound *cat lover*, on the other hand, 'represents the conception of a type per se, and since it lacks the notion of instantiation, the question of quantity does not arise (hence the number of cats subjected to the affection of a *cat lover* is completely indeterminate)'.

In the course of this chapter, we shall see that the distinction is not always as clear-cut as I (and Langacker) have presented it. Anticipating somewhat, we can say that the difference between *an [insider report]* and *an [insider's report]*—the latter construed as a compound—is that while *insider* merely 'represents the conception of a type per se', ungrounded *insider's* does give some salience to the notion of a single individual who made the report, without at the same time 'specifically limiting the profile to this particular instance', i.e. without specifically designating an individual.

same entity as the one which occurs in *the* [*woman's magazine*]. A question of some interest, therefore, is whether the possessive morpheme has the same semantic value in the two constructions—or at least, if not the same value, then semantic values that are in some respect similar, such that both can be regarded as instances of a single, more schematic meaning.

In point of fact, many syntactic theories would be unable to recognize even a formal identity of the possessive morpheme in the two constructions. Consider the following approaches, which we reviewed in Chapter 5.

(*a*) According to Chomsky's 'genitive rule' (section 5.4), the possessive morpheme is a semantically empty element that gets inserted into the following syntactic environment.

(18)   [NP____X']

We have already had reason to criticize this approach. But even assuming its correctness, the genitive rule will apply only to prenominal possessives, not to compounds, since compounds do not instantiate the environment in (18). (Compounds are [N____N], or, arguably, [N____N'], not [NP____N'].) Some quite different rule would be needed to generate possessive compounds. On the classical GB account, therefore, there can be no structural identity (and *ipso facto* no semantic identity) between POSS in prenominal possessives and POSS in possessive compounds. They would, in other words, be chance homonyms.

(*b*) Traditional grammars have regarded the possessive morpheme as a marker of genitive case. This account is problematic for both prenominal possessives and possessive compounds. While case may well be a property of noun phrases, case morphemes themselves normally attach to nominal heads (section 5.2). In the prenominal construction POSS does not attach to the noun head, but to whatever item comes last in the noun phrase. Compounds raise a complementary problem. While POSS, here, does attach to a noun (obligatorily, since the modifying noun may not itself be post-modified), the assumption that POSS is a marker of genitive case would entail that case is a property of nouns, not of noun phrases. Only, then, by relaxing, in different ways, our understanding of case, can POSS be regarded as an exponent of genitive case. With the prenominal construction, we would have to allow that case morphemes can attach to practically any word class; with possessive compounds, we would have to allow that case can be property, not only of noun phrases, but also of nouns.

(*c*) The possessive morpheme has been regarded as an adposition, to be assimilated to the category of prepositions (section 5.5). On this approach, [NP POSS] is a modifying phrase, headed by POSS, and with NP as the complement of POSS. Whatever the merits of this analysis with respect to prenominal possessives (and as we saw, it does capture some properties of the construction), it is inappropriate for possessive compounds. By general principles of X-bar syntax, complements must be maximal projections. But the modifier in a possessive compound is not a maximal projection, and is therefore not eligible to be the complement of POSS. Hence, the possessive morpheme in *the* [*woman's magazine*] cannot be analysed as the same item as the identical sounding morpheme in [*the woman*]'*s magazine*.

(*d*) A similar conclusion falls out even more forcefully from some recent versions of X-bar syntax, which analyse POSS as a determiner, the possessor as its specifier, and the possessee as its NP complement (section 5.6). This analysis is simply not available for possessive compounds. [*Woman's magazine*] is a noun, not a noun phrase. As such, it cannot be analysed as a DP, even less can it be said to be headed by a determiner.

A remarkable conclusion, therefore, is that the possessive morpheme in compounds has to be a completely different kind of entity from the possessive morpheme in prenominal possessives.[6]

This rather bizarre[7] conclusion can, I think, be avoided on the cognitive grammar account, in that the approach makes it possible to capture the essential unity of the two uses of the possessive morpheme, whilst still making explicit the differences between them. Their unity lies in the reference point relation; the difference lies in the instance vs. type status of the reference point and target. In the prenominal construction, the possessor denotes an instance, which serves as a reference point for the identification of a further instance. In the compound, the initial nominal (which it would not be incoherent to call also the 'possessor') designates a type, which serves as a reference point for the identification of a further type, that is, it invokes one kind of entity with respect to which the target type is identified. Langacker (1993: 36–7) draws an analogy with the sentence topics of Chinese and Japanese. Like *sakana* "fish" in *Sakana wa tai ga oisii* "As for fish, red snapper is delicious" (see example (3), Chapter 8), the possessor in a compound 'specifies a domain of knowledge that must be accessed in order to properly interpret the second noun (the target)'.

Some further characteristics of the two constructions fall out. Since, in a compound, both possessor and possessee name a type, not an instance, the possibilities of modifying the two nominals are limited. Especially restrictive modification (which serves to narrow the referential possibilities of a nominal, in the limiting case down to a single instance) will tend to be awkward with a type specification. Secondly, since in the compound we are on the plane of type,

---

[6] Croft (1990: 32) suggests yet another approach to the possessive morpheme. This is to regard it as a 'linker'. Croft characterizes a linker as a normally invariant morpheme, which occurs in a highly restricted syntactic environment, and which contrasts, if at all, only with zero. The linker-analysis would certainly be applicable to both prenominal possessives and possessive compounds. However, it completely begs the question of the semantic value of the morpheme, it fails to explain its occurrence in two distinct syntactic environments, and says nothing about its contribution to the overall meaning of possessives and compounds. This said, the notion of a 'linking' element could be appropriate for some semantically bleached possessives. See below, section 11.3.

[7] It is bizarre not only intuitively, but for good empirical reasons, too. In section 11.2 I present evidence for the fudging of the two constructions. This evidence would be incomprehensible on the assumption that the prenominal possessive and the possessive compound had nothing substantial in common.

not instance specifications, we have a ready explanation for the often conventionalized sense of a possessive compound. In the prenominal possessive, attributes of the instances may be relevant to an interpretation; furthermore, prenominal possessives are assembled in accordance with referential requirements of ongoing discourse. In the compound, only a generic understanding of possessor and possessee is involved, consequently the compound will tend to designate a fairly stable type, unaffected by specific circumstances. A further difference follows. A strong requirement on prenominal possessors is that they be topical, that is, that they designate cognitively accessible entities, typically entities that have already been introduced into the discourse (Chapter 8). We can only make sense of [*the woman*]'*s magazine* if 'the woman' can already be identified. There is no such requirement with compounds, since compounds designate a conventionalized type. [*Woman's magazine*] does not require, for its understanding, identification of the referent of *woman*, since *woman* does not in fact refer to any particular woman. We can therefore talk about the type [*woman's magazine*], without it being the case that 'women' have already been a topic of preceding discourse.[8]

Consider, finally, the profile of the possessive morpheme in the two constructions. I have taken the line (section 5.6) that in the prenominal construction, POSS profiles the schematic possessee. Since the schematic possessee is an instance, a possessor phrase [NP POSS]—subject to constraints that will be discussed in section 12.1—may be used pronominally (19a). On an analogous account of the compound construction, we can say that POSS likewise profiles the schematic possessee. Since, in the compound, the possessor phrase [N POSS] profiles exactly the same entity as the possessee [N], the relation between them is one of apposition. But since [N POSS] designates a type, not an instance, its pronominal use is completely ruled out (19b).

(19)   *a.* This is John's car./This car is John's.
       b. *This is a boys' school./*This school is boys'.

11.2 THE FUDGING OF POSSESSIVES AND COMPOUNDS

Many languages fail to distinguish morphologically between compounds and possessives. (Zulu is such a language, as will be clear from an examination of example (9) of Chapter 1.) In English, however, the distinction between prenominal possessives and possessive compounds seems quite clear. While recognizing the commonality between them, I have cited both syntactic and semantic evidence for this clear-cut distinction.

---

[8] In confirmation, the reader may turn to the text from Chafe (1987), cited in n. 11 of Ch. 8. The text contains the possessive compound *a men's school*. In contrast to the prenominal possessives in the text (*his assistants, his notes*), in which the possessor is the highly topical main protagonist of the story, *men's school* is used without any previous mention of 'men'.

I now discuss several types of expressions which suggest that the distinction between prenominal possessives and possessive compounds may not be so clear-cut, after all. The evidence suggests that the clean distinction that was drawn in the preceding section may be defensible only to the extent that we concern ourselves with 'good examples' of the two constructions.

11.2.1 *Onomastic possessives*

Consider the following expressions.

(20)   Halley's comet, Ockham's razor, Hobson's choice, St Valentine's day, Parkinson's disease, St Vitus' dance, Zeno's paradox

In terms of our earlier characterization of prenominal possessives (4) and possessive compounds (13), these expressions would have to be analysed as prenominal possessives, with the structure [NP[NP POSS] [N]]. The possessor nominals name a specific individual, and are therefore plausibly regarded as definite NPs, while the expressions as a whole may be used without an initial determiner, suggestive of their status as NPs.

(21)   *a.* We watched in vain for [NPHalley's comet].
       b. Some progress has been made in treating [NPParkinson's disease].
       c. We were faced by [NPHobson's choice].

Semantically, however, the expressions in (20) diverge markedly from prenominal possessives, as characterized above. In a prenominal possessive, the possessor nominal names a cognitively accessible entity, which serves as a reference point for the subsequent identification of the possessee referent. To identify the intended referent of *John's aunt*, a person must first be able to identify the referent of *John*; indeed, this referent would normally have given status, in virtue of its already having been introduced into the discourse. And should a person not be able to identify the referent of *John*, he may legitimately ask, 'Whose aunt are you talking about?' Talk of *Halley's comet*, however, does not presuppose prior acquaintance with Edmund Halley, nor is the expression *Halley's comet* restricted to contexts which have rendered the astronomer and mathematician a topical, i.e. cognitively accessible individual. And it would be quite inappropriate for a person who does not know what *Halley's comet* refers to, to come up with the query 'Whose comet is that?' It looks as if *Halley*, in *Halley's comet*, while it undoubtedly names a historical individual, is not fully referential, in the manner of *John*, in *John's aunt*.

In other respects, too, the expressions in (20) resemble compounds, rather than possessives. Observe that the expressions have conventionalized unit status, and are usually listed as such in English dictionaries. If it were a genuine possessive, *Parkinson's disease* would be open to a range of pragmatically plausible interpretations, to be determined according to context. The expression should be able to denote *any* disease that a certain Parkinson happens to be suffering from, just like 'genuine' possessives, of the kind *James Parkinson's disease, Dr Parkinson's debilitating disease*.

Furthermore, in certain contexts, the expressions in (20) clearly do have the status of Ns, not NPs, as shown by the presence of determiners, and by the construal of the adjectives.

(22) *a.* We watched in vain for the much-talked-about [_NHalley's comet].
     b. Some progress has been made in treating the debilitating [_NParkinson's disease].
     c. We were faced by the usual [_NHobson's choice].

Needless to say, this kind of pre-modification is impossible with genuine possessives.

(23) *a.* *the loquacious [John's aunt].
     b. *the debilitating [Dr Parkinson's illness].
     c. *the sprained [Jill's ankle].

One way of dealing with these facts might be to set up a special subcategory of onomastic possessives. Members of this category would have conventionalized unit status, with respect to both form and meaning. They would have the status of definite NPs, and would refer to a unique entity, or unique kind of entity, named after its inventor, discoverer, founder, etc. The expressions in (22) could be derived by the more general principle whereby uniquely-referring article-less NPs can sometimes be used as count nouns (*the much-talked-about John Smith*).

The proposed subcategory would share some characteristics of both prenominal possessives and regular possessive compounds. This fact suggests a more insightful approach. This is to identify prenominal possessives and possessive compounds as ends on a continuum, and to situate the onomastic possessives in (20) at an intermediate point on the continuum. Aspects defining the continuum would include (i) the status of an expression as NP or N; (ii) its referential status; (iii) the referential status of the possessor nominal; (iv) the requirement for the possessor nominal to be topical; and (v) the conventionalized unit status of an expression.

To hypothesize a continuum entails that expressions can be located at slightly different points on the continuum. With respect to onomastic possessives, this prediction seems to be correct. The expressions in (24*a*), in virtue of their status as NPs and the definite reference of the possessor nominal, certainly stand towards the possessive end of the continuum. On the other hand, the superficially parallel expressions in (24*b*) stand towards the compound end of the continuum.

(24) *a.* Beethoven's Ninth, Schubert's Unfinished, Dante's *Inferno*.
     b. Achilles' heel, Adam's apple.

Talk of *Achilles' heel* does not entail the topicality, or require prior mention, or even knowledge, of the individual, Achilles. Furthermore, both expressions in

(24*b*) invariably have the status of Ns, not definite NPs. As such, they must be preceded by a determiner.

(25) *a*. Status is the businessman's Achilles' heel.
      b. *Status is Achilles' heel for the businessman.
(26) *a*. Fred has a protruding Adam's apple.
      b. *Adam's apple is protruding.

If it is correct that onomastic possessives can occupy different regions on the continuum, it ought to be possible for a given expression to move along the continuum, in the process of conventionalization, for example. We can observe this very process in Chomsky's Preface to his *Knowledge of Language* (1986). When Chomsky first introduces the terms *Plato's problem* and *Orwell's problem* as labels for 'two problems concerning human nature' (p. xxv), the expressions have the character of true possessives, in that they denote the problems which the individuals, Plato and Orwell, grappled with. A few pages later, the expressions have begun to take on the character of compounds. Consider the following.

(27) Plato's problem, then, is to explain how we know so much, given that the evidence available to us is so sparse. [Chomsky 1986: p. xxvii]

The present tense, as well as references to *we* and *us*, indicate that it is not Plato who had the problem under discussion (cf. *My problem is to explain* . . .); rather, *Plato's problem* has become the conventionalized name for a kind of problem, which is no longer identified with reference to the individual, Plato. An even clearer example is found a couple of paragraphs later, where Chomsky talks about 'this case of Orwell's problem' (p. xxvii). This construction is not possible with genuine possessives (cf. **this case of my problem*). In fact, Chomsky explicitly states that the 'case of Orwell's problem' that he is discussing goes beyond the specific problem that George Orwell himself addressed.

11.2.2 *Indefinite and generic possessors*

In Chapter 8 I cited a text-based study (Taylor 1991*a*) which showed that the overwhelming majority of possessive expressions have, as their possessor, a nominal with definite reference. Definiteness accords well with the required topic-worthiness of the possessor nominal. This is not to say that possessives with indefinite, or even non-specific possessors are ungrammatical. But since these kinds of nominals are likely to be low in topicality, possessives with indefinite or non-specific possessors will constitute somewhat marginal examples of the construction. It is precisely these marginal examples that, again, point to a fudging of the distinction between possessives and compounds.

Consider the following examples.

(28) *a*. I spent an hour reading a student's essays.
      b. Reading a student's essays is something I hate doing.
      c. Reading students' essays is something I hate doing.

Number agreement of the initial determiner shows that the expressions in (*a*) and (*b*) must be analysed as possessives: [a student]'s essays, *a [student's essays]. But whereas in (*a*) *a student* would probably have specific reference, i.e. the speaker is referring to the essays of a specific individual, in (*b*) *a student* could well have non-specific reference, i.e. the speaker is referring to the essays of *any* student. In (*c*), *students* has generic reference, i.e. the entire category of students (within a situational context) is meant. Now, in virtue of its generic reference, the possessor in (*c*) comes very close, semantically, to the modifying possessor of a compound, in that it denotes a kind of entity, rather than an instance, or instances, of the kind. In fact, it turns out that *students' essays* could be analysed equally well both as a possessive and as a compound. Consider the following possibilities of adjective placement.

(29)   *a.* I hate reading handwritten [students' essays].
       b. I hate reading students' [handwritten essays].

These are equally grammatical. Moreover, the sentences are, to all intents and purposes, semantically equivalent.[9]

Consider another example of the same phenomenon.

(30)   The archaeologists discovered fragments of a man's skull.

A non-specific reading of *a man* would be more plausible here than a specific reading. On the non-specific reading of the possessor, *a man's skull* denotes a skull characterized with respect to its relation to some arbitrary member of the category 'man'. Essentially the same semantic interpretation results if we analyse *man's skull* as a compound. What was discovered were fragments of a specific exemplar of a subcategory of skull, namely, '(male) human skull'. To the extent that 'a [man's skull]' is the same kind of thing as '[a man]'s [skull]', the alternative parsings, once again, fail to correlate with any significant semantic contrast.

Let us pursue, nevertheless, the question whether there might still be grounds for preferring the one structural analysis over the other. Consider, first, the evidence of adjective insertion. Taking *forty-year-old* as a modifier of *man*, both (31*a*) and (31*b*) are possible parsings.

(31)   *a.* [[a forty-year-old man]'s [skull]].
       b. a [[forty-year-old man]'s [skull]].

On the other hand, the strangeness of (32*b*) could suggest that we are dealing with a compound, not a possessive.

(32)   *a.* a forty thousand-year-old [man's skull].
       b. *[a man]'s [forty thousand-year-old skull].

---

[9] Any semantic difference between them reflects what Langacker (1987*a*: 476) calls alternative 'compositional paths'. See also the discussion in section 7.2.1.

And yet the possessor nominal can tolerate a co-referential pronoun—a property, as we saw earlier, of possessives, not of compounds.

(33)   The archaeologists found a forty thousand-year-old man$_i$'s skull. It is not known how old he$_i$ was when he$_i$ died.

Another property of *a man's skull* which would align the expression more with possessives than with compounds, is the fact that if *skull* is pluralized, *man* tends to be pluralized, also. Note the oddity of (34*a*).

(34)   *a.* ?several man's skulls.
       b. several men's skulls.

'Number concord' between between *skull* and *man* does not, of itself, rule out a compound interpretation. Both (35*a*) and (35*b*) are possible parsings.

(35)   *a.* [several men]'s skulls.
       b. several [men's skulls].

Still, the need for a plural modifier does point, once again, to the weak referentiality of the modifying noun. Each man has only one skull (in the inalienable sense of 'have'). If there are several skulls, there were also, perforce, several men. To speak of 'men's skulls' is to evoke the conception of a discrete number of men, corresponding to the number of skulls. The possessive nominal does not therefore merely denote a type specification (cf. the earlier discussion of *woman's magazine*), it evokes the conception of a number of instances of the type.

   If number concord between possessee and possessor suggests a prenominal construal, adjective insertion points in the opposite direction, towards a compound interpretation.

(36)   *a.* several forty thousand-year-old [men's skulls].
       b. *several men's [forty thousand-year-old skulls].

And there is a final twist. The neutral location of primary stress is *a man's skúll*, *several men's skúlls*, that is, on the final nominal, suggesting that we are here dealing with prenominal possessives!

   Where does this leave us? On both semantic and structural grounds, there seem to be no compelling reasons for opting either for a possessive or for a compound analysis of *a man's skull*. It is not that the expression is ambiguous between the two readings. If it were genuinely ambiguous, *a man's skull* ought to behave both like a full-fledged prenominal possessive (on the one reading), and like a full-fledged possessive compound (on the other reading). The important point, rather, is that *a man's skull* is somewhat marginal with respect to both categories. It is marginal *vis-à-vis* the prenominal possessive in that the possessor is indefinite and non-specific, and the possessee may not be freely modified (the expression, therefore, has something of unit status). It is marginal *vis-à-vis* possessive compounds in that the modifying noun preserves traces of referentiality.

As with the expressions discussed in 11.2.1, it again seems reasonable to locate *a man's skull* on a continuum ranging from prototypical possessives to prototypical compounds.

11.2.3 *Status as NP or N*

One diagnostic that we introduced for distinguishing prenominal possessives and possessive compounds concerned the possibility of adjective insertion; in a compound, the possessee may not be pre-modified by an adjective. This restriction was justified on the grounds of the ungrammaticality of (12): **a deaf children's famous school*, **a boys' expensive school*. However, certain kinds of adjective may sometimes be inserted into what look like nominal compounds, especially compounds that are names of articles of clothing. These expressions also put in question the clear-cut distinction, which we also made earlier, between the NP status of prenominal possessives and the N status of compounds.

Consider, first, the structure of *a pair of pants*. Although the syntax resembles that of a partitive construction, the expression cannot be regarded as a genuine partitive. A partitive denotes a smaller number/amount selected from a larger set/amount. *A pair of pants* denotes a single article of clothing, not a set of just two items selected from a larger set.

The *pair*-construction is required because *pants* (along with other nouns like *shorts, jeans, overalls, scissors, binoculars*) is obligatorily plural. *My pants, some jeans* are therefore unspecified with respect to the number of designated items. The *pair*-construction enables us to specify the number of items: *one pair of pants, several pairs of jeans*. Here, *pants* and *jeans* are reasonably regarded as nouns, not noun phrases, to which *a pair of* functions as a kind of determiner.

If it is correct that *a pair of pants* has the approximate structure $[_{DET}$a pair of] $[_{N}$pants],[10] the same, presumably, goes for *a pair of men's pants*. *Men's pants*, being an N, not an NP, must therefore be a compound, not a prenominal possessive. But now consider adjectival insertion.

(37)   *a.* a pair of [dark blue men's pants].
      b. a pair of [men's dark blue pants].

Both are acceptable, and they are to all intents and purposes semantically equivalent. The first is unproblematic, in that the position of adjectival *dark blue* is consistent with a compound construal of *men's pants*. But what about (37*b*)? The bracketed phrase occurs in an environment which requires an N, and yet

---

[10] A comparable analysis is indicated for *a lot of money, a lot of people*. Here again the syntax resembles that of the partitive construction. While *a lot of* can certainly be used in a genuine partitive (*a lot of the money that was stolen, a lot of the people who were invited*), it too has acquired the status of a kind of determiner, i.e. *money* and *people*, in *a lot of money, a lot of people*, are Ns, not NPs. Note, for example, that *a lot of people* is obligatorily construed as plural, as required by the plural status of *people* (*A lot of people have arrived*), not singular, as might be expected if the expression were headed by *a lot*. See also Langacker (1991: 88–9).

adjectival position is consistent only with a possessive (i.e. NP) construal of *men's pants*.[11]

The following examples raise the same kind of problem.

(38) *a*. They stole a pair of [my jeans].

     b. Lily was wearing a pair of [her mother's Italian shoes].

These might appear to contain examples of genuine partitives. *My jeans* and *her mother's Italian shoes* certainly do look like definite plural NPs (prenominal possessives, in fact), which denote a larger set from which the smaller set (*a pair*) is selected. But this, of course, is not what the sentences mean. (38*b*) does not mean that Lily was wearing two shoes selected from the larger set designated by *her mother's Italian shoes*. It means that she was wearing a pair of Italian shoes, selected from the various pairs of shoes (Italian and others) that her mother had. And concerning (38*a*), I do not think that the sentence necessarily entails that I had more than one pair of jeans; the sentence could be consistent with a situation in which they stole my one and only pair of jeans. There could be reason, therefore, to take the bracketed expressions in (38) to be Ns, not NPs. But their status as Ns would conflict with their internal structure as prenominal possessives, i.e. NPs.

In these examples, then, we have what appear to be prenominal possessives (i.e. NPs) being used in a syntactic environment reserved for nouns. Also from the point of view of their external syntax, the distinction between compounds and possessives can blur.

11.3 POSSESSIVE AND NON-POSSESSIVE COMPOUNDS

So far I have considered possessive compounds in contrast to prenominal possessives. I now want to look more closely at possessive compounds in their status as compounds.

It was possible, in section 11.1, to draw a principled distinction, on both structural and semantic grounds, between (examples of) prenominal possessives and (examples of) possessive compounds. Symptomatic of the distinction was the existence of minimal pairs, of the kind [*the woman*]*'s magazine* vs. *the* [*woman's magazine*], [*my driver*]*'s licence* vs. *my* [*driver's licence*]. Continuing the phonological analogy, the relation between possessive and non-possessive

---

[11] A possible explanation of (37*b*) is that *men's* is no longer construed as a possessive at all, but as an attributive adjective. Note the marginal possibility of *men's* being used predicatively: ?*These pants are men's; those others are boys'*. (Having written out this example, I must say that the apostrophes do not look quite right; this is perhaps further confirmation that *men's* is not really a possessive.) Regular possessive compounds do not permit this construction: **This school is boys'*; **This magazine is woman's*. On this account, the possessive morpheme has been bleached of its semantic content. If the account is correct, it testifies to a further fudging of the category of possessor nominals, in this case between possessive modifiers and adjective modifiers.

compounds might be more accurately described, on a first approach, at least, as one of complementary distribution.

The relation between possessive and non-possessive compounds is not one of *strict* complementary distribution. We do get, if rather infrequently, minimal pair contrasts between possessive compounds and non-possessive compounds. The situation, though, is complicated by the fact that the criteria for distinguishing possessive from non-possessive compounds are, in many cases, anything but clear, and often appeal to highly unstable aspects of prescriptive orthographic conventions. Rather than take the line that orthographic instability reflects people's uncertainty as to the content of the prescriptive rules, I shall argue instead that it reflects the inherent fuzziness of the categories to which the prescriptive rules are meant to apply.

We have already observed (section 5.2) that nominal compounding is an extremely productive process in English. Here we are concerned with nominal compounds whose first element is itself nominal. The initial element may be a simple noun, a more complex nominal phrase, and even a possessive compound.

(39) *a.* some [dog] food.
   b. a [cat] lover.
   c. the [Charles and Di] syndrome.
   d. [salad and soup] suppers.
   e. a [model cities] programme.
   f. an [Italian restaurant] chain.
   g. the [informal business] sector.
   h. the [spider's web] layout of the streets.

Lieber (1988), from whom some of these examples are taken, points out (p. 206) that the modifying nominal must receive a generic interpretation. It is for this reason that the modifying nominal lacks a determiner, and usually a marker of plurality as well.

On both structural and semantic grounds, there would seem to be every reason to assimilate possessive compounds to the broader category of nominal compounds, the only difference being, in fact, the presence vs. absence of the possessive morpheme. In nominal compounds, generally, the modifying element serves to limit the referential possibilities of the head noun. *Dog food* denotes a kind of food, namely, food intended for consumption by dogs; *gifted children's school* denotes a kind of school, namely, a school catering for gifted children; *woman's magazine* denotes a subcategory of magazine, comprising those magazines which are intended for an adult female readership.

If it is correct that possessive compounds are a subcategory of noun–noun compounds, the basic question must be: What motivates the presence of the possessive morpheme in just some noun–noun compounds, but not in others?

As suggested at the beginning of this section, possessive compounds are in rough complementary distribution to non-possessive compounds. Note, first, that there are some classes of noun–noun compound in which the possessive marker is prohibited. One such class comprises so-called 'synthetic' compounds, in which the modifier stands in a thematic relation, usually that of Patient, to the head noun. A person who molests children is a *child molester*, not a **child's molester*, or a **children's molester*. A second class comprises compounds where the two nominal constituents are in apposition. A *woman doctor* is a doctor who is a woman; the expression contrasts with *woman's doctor* (or *women's doctor*), i.e. "doctor for women". Likewise, *student nurse* "nurse who is a student" vs. *student's nurse* (or *students' nurse*) "nurse for students".

Leaving aside these cases, a second observation seems warranted. This is that the occurrence of the possessive morpheme correlates fairly reliably with the animacy of the modifying nominal. With human nouns, the possessive marker is generally obligatory. We have *woman's magazine*, not **woman magazine*, and countless more.

(40) man's shop (*man shop), women's college, child's play, driver's licence, Mother's Day, housemaid's knee, writer's cramp, master's degree, witch's broth, printer's ink, potter's wheel, shepherd's pie, ploughman's lunch

Even so, there are quite a few exceptions to this generalization. Contrasting with *woman's magazine* (where the possessive morpheme is obligatory), we have *girlie magazine* (without the possessive morpheme). We talk of the *driver's seat* of a car, but ask someone to get into the *passenger seat* (**passenger's seat*). Here are some further examples.

(41) guest room (cf. children's room), staff room, granny flat, baby clothes (cf. children's clothes), baby carriage, baby food, child labour, slave trade, adult education, passenger train, mother tongue, mother wit, escort agency, bride price

If the modifier noun is inanimate, or abstract, the possessive is generally impossible. We have *nature reserve, letter box, bicycle wheel, car tyre, aeroplane engine*, not **nature's reserve, *bicycle's wheel*, etc. Again, there are a few exceptions: *ship's engine* rather than *?ship engine*, in contrast to *car engine*, not **car's engine*.

(We might observe in parentheses that the gender hierarchy of Quirk *et al.* (1985: 314), mentioned in section 8.2.2, could be relevant to some of these cases. The gender hierarchy is based on the possibility of replacing a noun by the gender-specific pronouns *he/she*, instead of *it*. According to Quirk *et al.*, the higher an item on the hierarchy, the more likely it is to take the possessive morpheme. Although a human noun, *baby* occupies a relatively low position on the hierarchy, since it is possible to refer to a baby as *it*. Accordingly, we have *baby carriage*, and other compounds with *baby*, which lack the possessive morpheme. On the other hand, although inanimate, a ship is generally referred to as *she*. Whence *ship's engine*, and several more: *ship's papers* (cf. *car papers*), *ship's captain* (cf. *aircraft pilot*), *ship's cook*, *ship's boy*, *ship's chandler*.)

With non-human animates, there is considerable variation. The possessive marker is standardly used in *hen's egg* (**hen egg*) and *bird's egg* (**bird egg*), but not in *ostrich egg* (**ostrich's egg*), *goose egg* (**goose's egg*) and *fish eggs* (**fish's eggs, *fishes' eggs*). Compare also *lamb's wool* (**lamb wool*) with *horse hair* (**horse's hair*); *pig's trotter* (**pig trotter*) with *chicken breast* (**chicken's breast*); and *bird's nest* (**bird nest*[12]), *lion's den* with *dog kennel* (?*dog's kennel*), *ant hill*, and *pig-sty*. Sometimes, both possibilities coexist: *duck egg* alongside *duck's egg*, *dog hairs* alongside *dog's hairs*, *sheep liver* alongside *sheep's liver*.

Thus far, I have tacitly assumed that possessive compounds can be reliably identified as such, and distinguished from non-possessive compounds. Yet the basis for the distinction is actually far from unproblematic. The problem stems from the fact that, when attached to a singular noun, the possessive morpheme is phonologically identical to the regular plural morpheme; and when attached to a regularly formed plural noun, the possessive morpheme has no phonological realization.

These phonological facts would be of no great import, perhaps, were it the case that noun–noun compounds invariably have, as their modifier, a noun which lacks a plural marker. In such a situation, the presence of a medial *s* would unambiguously diagnose a possessive. Now, it is, of course, true that in noun–noun compounds the modifying nominal generally does lack the plural marker, a fact which reflects the type-referential status of the modifying element. A *dog lover* is a person who loves dogs in general, not someone who loves a single dog; *cat food* is food to be given to cats; a *hen house* is a construction for housing hens, and so on. The plural marker may be missing even if the modifier contains a plural numeral: a *twenty kilometre(*s) hike*, a *ten dollar bill*, a *five year plan*. Even *pluralia tantum*, such as *groceries* and *trousers* (which, when used referentially, are obligatorily plural) may occur without the plural marker.

(42)   grocery store, trouser suit, suspender belt, expense account, rate-payer, dish washer,[13] oatmeal, noodle salad, curd cheese, scissor sharpener

Plural modifiers, however, are by no means uncommon. Here are some examples that I have observed.

(43)   sports magazine, sports reporter, greetings card, arms race, goods train, accounts clerk, wages clerk, futures speculation, records office, sales figures (cf. export figures), complaints department, suggestions box (cf. letter box), careers adviser, parks board, the small ads section (of a newspaper), systems analyst, applications programmer, projects manager, communications satellite, telecommunications engineer, admissions office, University Grants Committee, small claims court

---

[12] But note *bird nest soup* alongside *bird's nest soup*.

[13] *Dish*, in *dish-washer*, is not the singular count noun *dish* "shallow plate", but the singular form of the *plurale tantum dishes* "crockery, cooking and eating utensils".

Apart from those compounds whose first noun has an irregular plural not ending in *s* (*child's play*, *children's playground*), a medial *s* cannot therefore be taken as fully reliable evidence for the presence of the possessive morpheme. A compound of the form [N₁—s—N₂] has, namely, three possible analyses. [N₁—s] could represent a singular noun + POSS; a (regular) plural noun; or a (regular) plural noun + POSS. While phonologically indistinguishable, the three possibilities are, of course, disambiguated in the orthography, with respect to the use, and the location, of the apostrophe.

Orthographic practice, however, is by no means consistent. Variations in the use of the apostrophe suggest that one and the same phonological form may be construed, alternately, as a non-possessive compound, a possessive compound with a singular possessor, and as a possessive compound with a plural possessor. The variation is particularly evident in informal written texts (public signs, advertising copy, etc.). Shopping expeditions provide ample opportunities to compare the incidence of *boys shoes* and *boys' shoes* (and even *boy's shoes*!), *girls dresses* and *girls' dresses*, *ladies fashions* and *ladies' fashions*. Even on a university campus we may see *Students Union* next to *Students' Union*. Many more examples of this kind of variation are cited in Sklar (1976) and Barfoot (1991). More authoritative written sources display the same kind of variation. Collins English Dictionary has the entry *magistrates' court*, COBUILD cites *magistrate's court*, while Barfoot (1991: 124) reports having seen *Magistrates Court* 'in Margate and elsewhere'. The *OED* of 1989 has the entry *Jews' harp*, whereas the *New Shorter OED* of 1993 has the entry *Jew's harp*. The *Shorter OED* of 1933 gives *trades-union* (where *trades* is said to be a plural) alongside *trade-union*. However, in the course of the same dictionary's entry for *craft* we have *trade's union*. In the *New Shorter OED*, this has been changed to *trade union*.

Instability in the use of the apostrophe, especially with respect to a presumably plural modifier, probably has several causes. It is worth remembering, first of all, that the use of the apostrophe as a possessive marker on plural nouns is a relatively recent innovation (see Sklar 1976, for documentation). While the possessive apostrophe with singular nouns was frequent in the seventeenth century, and its use was standardized by the mid-eighteenth century, uncertainties with plural possessives persisted until well into the nineteenth century. In fact, the prescriptive rules as we know them today became fully standardized only towards the end of the last century.[14]

As documented by Sklar (1976), the apostrophe has had other functions alongside its use as a possessive marker. Its oldest use has been to mark the elision of a letter or sound, still current today in verbal contractions (*I'm, isn't*). Possibly, the rise of the apostrophe with singular possessors, in the seventeenth century, reflected the perception that *the king's daughter* was an elided form of

---

[14] Arguably, possessive morphology is still not fully standardized, even today, as witnessed by uncertainties about the possessive forms of polysyllabic nouns ending in a sibilant (*Dickens' novels* vs. *Dickens's novels*).

the king his daughter. More interesting, from our perspective, is the use of the apostrophe to mark the morpheme boundary between a noun stem and the plural marker, especially in cases where the simple addition of an *s* might result in unusual-looking orthographies. Thus, in the eighteenth century, the apostrophe was regularly used in plurals of noun stems ending in *s* (*genius's*) or in a vowel (*comma's, idea's, folio's, quarto's*). The practice still survives in the non-standard spellings *potato's* and *tomato's*, so frequently seen in greengrocers' shops as plurals of *potato* and *tomato.* Jespersen (1909–49: vi. 253–4), too, noted the use of the apostrophe to avoid unusual-looking plurals (*the why's and where-fore's, pro's and con's, p's and q's*). Especially frequent, still, is the use of *'s* to form the plurals of numerals and abbreviations: *the 1980's, a man in his 60's*; while linguistics texts abound with *NP's* and *VP's* as the plurals of *NP* and *VP.*

The two different uses of the apostrophe—as a marker of the possessive and of the plural—come into head-on conflict with respect to just those expressions with which we are here concerned, namely, nominal compounds containing a medial *s.* Some English speakers (or, rather, writers) manage the conflict by adopting one of two, very different strategies. One strategy is to generalize the use of the apostrophe as a means of separating a noun stem from an affixal *s*, whether this be a possessive or a plural. Hence, to return to the greengrocer's, we not only have *potato's* and *tomato's*, but also *lettuce's* and *onion's*; or, to cite the subtitle of Barfoot (1991): *You know what hairdresser's are like.* The other has been to avoid the use of the apostrophe altogether, especially with plural nouns. Whence *gents hairdressers, cows milk, Readers Admissions Office*, as well as *menswear* and *childrens playground* (all attested examples, cited in Barfoot 1991). The last two examples are particularly significant, since the apostrophe is missing even after an irregular plural. With some justification, Barfoot (p. 124) speaks of a situation of 'complete flux', reflecting a 'basic instability' in the use of the apostrophe.

Complaints about the use (and misuse) of the possessive apostrophe are frequently heard. Burchfield (1992: 79) cites an American college professor who 'claimed to have inserted at least 50,000 apostrophes in the written work of his students in a single semester, and to have moved or removed a similar number'. And yet, as Barfoot (1991: 124) points out, the rules for the use of the possessive apostrophe are 'clear enough', and should be familiar to anyone with even a modest education. Why, then, the instability? After all, anyone who can tell a singular from a plural noun ought to be able to use the possessive apostrophe correctly!

But this, of course, is precisely the point. With respect to nominal compounds, it is often by no means obvious whether the initial nominal is singular or plural, or, in the latter case, whether it is possessive or not. In other words, a major cause of the orthographic instability, at least with compounds, could be genuine uncertainty as to the proper construal of a compound containing a medial *s.* The orthographic variability exhibited by *magistrate's court, magistrates' court*, and *magistrates court* is not simply a consequence of people's ignorance of the prescriptive rules, or their failure to abide by them, it also reflects the absence of clear-cut criteria for distinguishing a possessive from a non-possessive compound, and, in the case of a possessive compound, one with a singular possessor from one with a plural possessor.

The example *menswear*, recognized by the *OED* (second edition) of 1989, raises a further issue. This is that possessive compounds may undergo a process of lexicalization, resulting, not only in the omission of the possessive apostrophe, but also of the word space. Other compounds have travelled the same path. According to the *OED*, *craftsman* was once written as two separate words: *craftes man*, and replaced the now obsolete *craftman*. Also according to the *OED*, the medial *s* in *seedsman*, *salesman*, *townsman*, *tradesman*, *yachtsman*, *landsman*, and *swordsman* (which replaced the now obsolete *swordman*), was once a 'genitive' appended to a singular noun. Presumably, the *s* in *ratsbane* had a similar origin (the *OED* merely states that *ratsbane* derives from *rat + bane*). It is doubtful whether a modern speaker would want to construe any of these words as possessive compounds. The spelling *menswear* could suggest that not even this word is perceived to contain a possessive. The medial *s*—clearly not a marker of the plural—has more the status of a linking element, similar, in fact, to the 'Fugen-*s*' that links the components of many compound nouns in German, and related languages.[15] Support for the 'linking-*s*' analysis could come from examples where a medial *s* has been inserted in comparatively recent times. One example is *bridesmaid* (a nineteenth-century innovation), which contrasts strikingly with *bridegroom*.

The distribution of the possessive morpheme in nominal compounds is essentially a question of how speakers (or, more accurately, writers) interpret a compound. In spite of considerable variation, reflecting, partly, on the multifunctionality of the apostrophe itself, but also on the inherent fuzziness of the linguistic categories involved, the situation with the use of the apostrophe is not one of total chaos. Patterns in the construal of compounds are certainly discernible. Compare the expressions in (44). The expressions are meant to have a compound interpretation, i.e. "man responsible for sales", "box in which suggestions may be placed", "shoes designed for girls", and "college for accommodating women". The orthographies, I suggest, are the 'standard' ones, acceptable to literate, educated speakers who are fully conversant with orthographic prescription.

(44) *a.* salesman/*sales man/*sales' man/*sale's man.

  b. suggestions box/*suggestions' box/*suggestion's box.

---

[15] German has compounds like *Bundespräsident* "Federal President", *Staatstheater* "state theatre", where the linking *s* looks like the remnant of a genitive inflection. However, the linking *s* occurs not only after singular nouns of masculine and neuter gender (which take a suffixed *s* in genitive case), but also after singular nouns of feminine gender (which do not): *Arbeitsgesetz* "labour law", *Arbeitsgericht* "labour court". In Afrikaans (where nouns do not bear a genitive suffix), a linking *s* is also frequent: *arbeidswetgewing* "labour legislation", *gesinsmotor* "family car".

    c. girls' shoes/(?)girls shoes/*girl's shoes.
    d. women's college, *womens college.

Phonologically, the expressions are exactly parallel, in that in each case there is a medial *s* before the modified noun. Semantically, the modifier in each case serves to delimit the referential possibilities of the modified. In each case, too, the modifier can, and in the case of (44*d*), must, be construed as plural. But only in (*c*) and (*d*)—optionally, perhaps, in (*c*), obligatorily in (*d*)—is the apostrophe used.

We can now return to the question posed at the beginning of this section: What motivates the presence of the possessive morpheme in just some noun–noun compounds, but not in others? My suggestion is that a possessive construal is favoured just in case the compound exhibits features which are characteristic of prenominal possessives. Various aspects are involved.

(*a*) As we have seen, one factor favouring possessive construal is the animacy, more specifically, the humanness of the modifier noun. There is an obvious parallel here with prenominal possessives. We saw in Chapter 8 that in prenominal possessives the overwhelming majority of possessor nominals are in fact human. This accords with the reference point function of the possessor, and with the ensuing requirement that possessor nominals be highly topical.

(*b*) A possessive construal is favoured to the extent that the semantic relation between modifier and modified is one which, *mutatis mutandis*, could be expressed in a prenominal possessive. (Barfoot 1991: 128 speaks, in this connection, of the degree of 'possessiveness' of the relation between modifier and modified.) Various factors determine the appropriateness of a prenominal possessive, not only the topicality of the possessor, but also its informativity, that is, its cue validity with respect to the possessee. It would be odd to identify a box from the perspective of a slip of paper that gets inserted into it; a 'suggestion' has minimal cue validity for the identification of a 'box'. The impossibility of the prenominal possessive *[*the suggestion*]'s box* matches the inappropriateness of a possessive construal in *a [*suggestion's box*], or *a [*suggestions' box*]. On the other hand, it would be perfectly normal to identify a college from the perspective of people who study there. That people study there is, after all, part of the encyclopedic characterization of *college*. The appropriateness of the prenominal possessive *her college* thus matches the possessive construal of *a [*women's college*]*.

Exceptions to the animacy hierarchy are especially instructive. Compare *woman's magazine* with *girlie magazine*. It is natural to identify a specific magazine from the perspective of a person who is likely to read it (and to buy it); part of the encyclopedic characterization of 'magazine' is that magazines are things that people read. It would be odd, though, to identify a magazine by reference to a person whose photograph appears in it; *magazine* is not a representational noun, inherently characterized as a medium for the photographic representation of people without their clothes!

(c) A crucial aspect is the degree of referentiality of the modifier noun, i.e. the extent to which the modifier noun invokes the conception of an instance (or instances), rather than a type. Again, exceptions to the animacy hierarchy are particularly revealing. Compare *driver's seat* and *passenger seat*. The 'driver's seat' of a car is meant for a unique individual, in the sense that for each car, there is only one person who takes on the role of 'driver'. 'Passenger', however, is a role that can be filled by practically anybody. Likewise with *children's room* vs. *guest room*. A house or apartment may be occupied by a family, which in turn may comprise children. The 'children's room' of a house is meant for those specific individuals who are 'the children' (of the family living there). On the other hand, the 'guest room' is meant for anybody who happens to be staying in the role of 'guest'. Note also that you could refer to a room as a 'guest room' even though no guest had ever stayed there. Your house could also have a 'granny flat'—that is, a separate apartment suitable for an aged parent—even though 'granny' has never actually lived there. But it would be odd to say that your house has a 'children's room' if you have no children. Likewise, a 'passenger seat' of a car is so named, not because any specific 'passenger' or 'passengers' have sat there, but because it is meant for anyone who should happen to be a passenger.

Lack of referentiality also seems to motivate the absence of possessive morphology in synthetic compounds. To say that a person is a 'child molester' is to characterize them as a certain kind of person, it is not to invoke the notion of any particular child, or children, who have been molested. Having already molested *some* child (or children), a child molester is likely to molest *any* child. And a 'potential child molester' has not actually molested anybody. Likewise with *woman doctor* and *student nurse*. Here the modifier has purely a descriptive function, *woman*, in *woman doctor*, being roughly equivalent to 'female'.

The importance of referentiality can be demonstrated on a minimal pair contrast. In the following, both a possessive and a non-possessive compound are acceptable.

(45) We now bring you a disturbing {insider report/insider's report} on what is happening in the country.

Adjective construal in *a disturbing [insider's report]* confirms the compound status of *insider's report*. Arguably, however, *insider* exhibits some degree of referentiality, in that the report is one which has come from a single person, the 'insider'. The non-possessive compound *insider report* lacks this element of referentiality. An *insider report* is merely a report, of the kind that only insiders can come up with. Compare the (perhaps marginal) acceptability of co-referential *he* in (46*a*) with the impossibility of co-reference in (46*b*).

(46)   *a.* (?) We now bring you a disturbing insider$_i$'s report, in which he$_i$ describes the latest happenings in the country.

   b. *We now bring you a disturbing insider$_i$ report, in which he$_i$ describes the latest happenings in the country.

There is a similar contrast in (47).

(47)   Valuable {collector items/collector's items} have been stolen.

Collector's items invokes the conception of an individual collector, who might be interested in collecting the kind of items in question. *Collector items* merely categorizes the items in terms of their collectablity.[16]

   This last example raises again the question of the proper construal of medial *s*. COBUILD dictionary cites *collector's items*, although *collectors' items*, and even *collectors items*, might be equally feasible. The referentiality of the modifying noun may possibly lie behind the choice between these alternatives. That is to say, singular construal in *collector's items* could be motivated by the fact that collecting is typically a solitary, rather than a group activity; the notion of 'collecting' thus invokes the conception of an individual engaging in his hobby, alone. On the other hand, *collectors' items* could be justified on the grounds that different kinds of items are likely to appeal to different collectors. The contrast is especially clear in *child's play* and *children's room*. Something that is *child's play* is so easy that even a child (any child) could do it. The expression clearly invokes the notion of a single child, whereas *children's room, children's playground* invoke a plurality of children. Likewise, *women's college, women's studies* invoke the notion of a plurality of women. On the other hand, our earlier example of *woman's magazine* (which, of course, coexists with *women's magazine*) might be motivated by the fact that magazines are typically bought, and read, by single individuals, not by groups. It is along these lines also, I suspect, that the choice of singular vs. plural modifier in non-possessive compounds might be motivated. A *grocery store* sells items of a certain kind, collectively characterized as 'groceries'. An *accounts clerk* has the job of keeping 'the accounts', that is, the accounts of the company he works for.[17]

   The examples *insider('s) report* and *collector('s) item* prompt a further observation. This is that *collector item* and *insider report* have the flavour of innovations

---

[16] Compare also *townsman* and *countryman*. Although *townsman* has been lexicalized, and is probably no longer perceived as a possessive, we can perhaps trace the medial *s* to the idea that a 'townsman' is an inhabitant of *a* town (one town out of indefinitely many), whereas a 'countryman' inhabits 'the country', construed as an unbounded region. Even so, a considerable degree of idiosyncrasy surrounds the issue. For example, medial *s* is missing in *town hall, town crier, town council*.

[17] These last remarks are very speculative. As observed in n. 16, there is no denying that the conventionalized shape of a nominal compound is subject to a good deal of idiosyncrasy, which may not be fully susceptible to semantic explanation. Other incidental aspects may be involved. For example, plural construal in *goods train, means test, futures speculation*, may be due to the desire to avoid the ambiguity of *good train, mean test, future speculation*.

vis-à-vis collector's item and *insider's report*.[18] Other examples of the same trend can be cited. *Doll's house* (the form recorded in *OED* and COBUILD) appears to be giving way to *doll house*. The *OED* cites *dog's ear* "turned down corner of a page" (and even the verb, *to dog's ear*) as the principal form, while a more modern dictionary (Collins) gives *dog-ear* as the main form. One even hears *driver licence*, in place of the more normal *driver's licence*.[19]

It is plausible, therefore, that the move to a non-referential modifying noun, and the associated loss of the possessive marker, reflects increasing conventionalization of an expression. One might, in fact, propose a continuum of conventionalization, from a true prenominal possessive with a definite possessor, through a prenominal possessive with an indefinite possessor, to a possessive compound, and finally to a non-possessive compound.

(48)   *a.* [the driver]'s licence → [a driver]'s licence → a [driver's licence] → a [driver licence]

   b. [the student]'s essays → [a student]'s essays → [students' essays] → [student essays]

Alternatively, the final stage of conventionalization could consist in the omission of the word space, with retention of the medial *s*, which, however, is no longer construed as a possessive marker: *trade's man* → *tradesman*, *men's wear* → *menswear*.

Our earlier discussion of *Plato's problem* illustrated the beginning of this very process. From a genuine prenominal possessive, *Plato's problem* came to designate a kind of problem. (Further conventionalization would give us non-possessive *the Plato problem*). The following example is also instructive. It is taken from an eye-witness account of the Soviet invasion of Finland. The passage dates from 1940, at which time Molotov, the Soviet foreign minister, was no doubt a well-known, and therefore potentially topical individual, such that the 'cocktails' that were thrown at the Soviet tanks could be named after him.

(49)   ... we were regaled with stories about the damage which had been done by 'Molotov's bombs'. Everyone apparently speaks of them in this fashion, and when the aeroplanes are heard to be dropping their deadly cargoes, the people say 'Molotov is barking again.' Similarly, when the soldiers attack the Russian tanks, they call their rudely-made hand grenades 'Molotov's cocktails.' (Citrine 1940: 41)

In this passage, *Molotov's cocktails* stands close to the possessive end of the continuum. But now, more than half a century later, as memories of the historical individual, Molotov, have faded, the possessive construal has fallen away.

---

[18] Example (47) was heard in a television news broadcast. At the beginning of the broadcast, reference was to the theft of *valuable collector's items* (*collectors' items*?). Later in the same broadcast, reference was to the theft of *collector items*.

[19] Also *worker grievances, employer abuses, worker protests* (examples from *Time*, 27 June 1994, p. 30).

Home-made petrol bombs are now universally referred to by the conventional-ized, non-possessive compound, *Molotov cocktails.*

11.4 SYNTACTIC CONSTRUCTIONS AS PROTOTYPE CATEGORIES

I began this chapter by showing the need to distinguish, on both semantic and structural grounds, between prenominal possessives and possessive compounds. As the discussion proceeded, the distinction turned out to be anything but clear-cut, with various kinds of expression having an uncertain status between the two categories. Then, focusing on nominal compounds, we found that the possessive marker is licensed just in case the nominal compound exhibits some of the properties of a prototypical prenominal possessive.

The facts suggest a continuum from prenominal possessives, through posses-sive compounds, to non-possessive compounds. Such a state of affairs creates serious problems for many theories of syntax. 'Classical' theories of syntax presuppose clear-cut categories, with membership in these categories being a simple matter of either/or. Whilst it is allowed that an expression may have two different readings, as determined by two alternative parsings [X Y] [Z] and [X] [Y Z], it is not possible, within classical theories of syntax, to claim that an expression simultaneously exhibits some properties of the structure [X Y] [Z] *and* some properties of the structure [X] [Y Z]. Yet some of the examples we have discussed point to the need for precisely this kind of approach. An alter-native is to regard syntactic constructions as prototype categories, with central members, and more marginal members.

Research on prototype categorization (Rosch 1978; Geeraerts 1989; Taylor 1995*b*) has been concerned, first and foremost, with the referential possibilities of selected, and usually nominal, lexical units. A consistent finding has been that the extensions of many words, such as *red* (Heider 1971), *bird* (Rosch 1975), *cup* (Labov 1973), comprise items of different degrees of representativity in the respective categories. Some colours are judged better examples of 'red' than others, some birds (e.g. robins) are 'birdier' than other birds (e.g. penguins), some cups come closer to our notion of a 'typical cup' than others. Secondly, for many of the words that have been studied (though not for all: a penguin, after all, is still a bird, even if not a very representative one), the boundaries of their extensions turn out to be fuzzy. Whereas a 'good red' is unequivocally distin-guishable from a 'good orange', and a 'prototypical cup' is a quite different kind of entity from a 'prototypical bowl', the sets of entities that may be designated by *red* and *orange*, *cup* and *bowl*, in fact merge into each other, with entities near to the periphery of the one category having marginal status in the adjacent category.

While the prototype structure of (many) extensional categories is empirically

TABLE 11.1. Some characteristics of prenominal possessives, possessive compounds, and non-possessive compounds

Prenominal possessives	Possessive compounds	Non-possessive compounds
referential (usually definite), i.e. 'instance specification'	non-referential, i.e. 'type specification'	non-referential i.e. 'type specification'
possessor nominal referential (topical, and usually definite)	possessor nominal non-referential, or weakly referential	modifier nominal non-referential
possessor nominal often human or animate	possessor nominal almost always human or animate	modifier nominal typically non-human
possessor and possessee may be pre- and post-modified	little possibility of modification of head noun or modifier	little possibility of modification of head noun or modifier
variable interpretation	conventionalized interpretation	conventionalized interpretation
final stress	initial streess	initial stress
written with word space and apostrophe	written with word space and apostrophe	with lexicalization apostrophe and word space may be omitted

well documented, the significance of prototype categorization for general linguistic theory has been queried. For it is by no means obvious that the fuzzy boundaries and degrees of representativity that characterize word extensions should necessarily have any consequences at all for 'core' areas of linguistic enquiry, such as syntax, morphology, and phonology. These components of the grammar could still conform to 'classical' models of categorization, with categories defined by a conjunction of necessary and sufficient conditions for category membership, where category boundaries are sharp, and all members of a category have equal status within the category. And even with respect to lexical semantics, it has been suggested that fuzzy boundaries and degrees of representativity may simply be reflexes of verification procedures applied to word extensions, whereby intensions (roughly: 'meanings') may continue to be defined in classical terms (Osherson and Smith 1981; Leech 1981: 120; Tsohatzidis 1990a). For the notion of prototype to have any substantial impact on linguistic theory, it would be necessary to establish that the very categories of linguistic description, such as lexical and syntactic categories, themselves exhibit prototype structure.

This chapter has provided just this evidence with respect to syntactic categories.

On the one hand, prototypical examples of prenominal possessives, possessive compounds, and non-possessive compounds may be readily identified and distinguished. Yet many expressions have a somewhat marginal status with respect to these categories, and may even testify to a blurring, or an overlapping, of the constructions, in a manner reminiscent of Labov's cups and bowls.

The evidence of possessives therefore validates the notion of syntactic construction itself, whose prototype is characterized in terms of a cluster of properties, pertaining to syntactic, semantic, and phonological (as well as pragmatic, and perhaps even orthographic) aspects (Table 11.1). Just as cups may diverge, in different ways, and to differing degrees, from the 'cup prototype', so a complex syntactic expression may diverge from a construction prototype. And just as a particular vessel may be hard to categorize unambiguously as either a cup or a bowl, so an expression may have an unclear status between two contrasting constructions, having some characteristics of both, but being a good example of neither.

12 Other Possessive Constructions

IN this chapter I deal with three further possessive constructions, each involving the use of a possessor phrase [NP POSS]. In each case, the possessor phrase is used independently of a postposed possessee noun.

(a) The possessor phrase is used pronominally: *My car is old but [John's] is new*; *[Theirs] is that big house up there on the hill.*

(b) The possessor phrase is used predicatively: *This car is [John's]*; *Is this coat [yours] or is it [somebody else's]?*

(c) The possessor phrase is used in a postnominal *of*-phrase: *a friend of [John's]*, *a student of [Chomsky's]*, *that perpetual grumbling of [his].*

I refer to these constructions as the pronominal possessive, the predicative possessive, and the postnominal possessive, respectively.

The constructions have several things in common. One is the use of the special forms *mine*, *yours*, *hers*, *ours*, and *theirs* instead of *my*, *your*, *her*, *our*, and *their*. Another is that the possessive form *its* (i.e. *it* + POSS) tends to be exceedingly rare in all three environments—so rare in fact that one might be inclined to say that the form is prohibited: **Its has arrived*, **This one is its*, **one of its*.[1]

A pivotal issue that we shall need to address is the syntactic category of the [NP POSS] constituent in the three constructions, and the manner in which this constituent enters into valence relations with its neighbours. Essentially, this is a question of whether the possessor phrase has a nominal or a relational profile. I shall, in fact, argue that in all three constructions, [NP POSS] has exactly the same semantic value as it has in prenominal possessives, that is, that it has a nominal profile, which designates a schematic instance of the possessee.

This being the case, a major problem concerns the restrictions on the kinds of semantic relations that are compatible with the three constructions. For it is not the case that to each prenominal possessive there exists a corresponding pronominal, predicative, and postnominal expression. Where the relation is one of possession, understood in a fairly literal sense, all three constructions are acceptable.

---

[1] Quirk *et al.* (1985: 362) do, however, cite a couple of examples, involving contrastive *its* in parallel constructions: *History has its lessons and fiction has its*; *She knew the accident was either her husband's fault or the car's: it turned out to be not his but its.*

(1)   *John's shirt*
    a. John's was more expensive than mine.
    b. This shirt is John's.
    c. a shirt of John's.

With kinship relations, predicative possessives are impossible, though postnominal possessives are fine. Pronominal possessives, though, generally require some special supporting context, as provided, for example, by a conjunct expression.

(2)   *John's sister*
    a. ?My sister is still at University, but John's graduated last year.
    b. *This sister is John's.
    c. a sister of John's.

Nouns which invoke other kinds of interpersonal relations, such as *friend, colleague, neighbour*, pattern in a similar way. Finally, subjective and objective relations, such as occur with episodic nominalizations, are sometimes (marginally) acceptable with the pronominal possessive, but not at all with the predicative construction; subjective relations are (marginally) acceptable, in some cases, in the postnominal construction.

(3)   *John's arrest*
    a. ?John's was unlawful.
    b. *The arrest was John's.
    c. ??an arrest of John's. [unacceptable if John = Patient]

In general, then, it appears that the pronominal possessive has the widest application, although its usage range still falls short of the usage range of the prenominal construction. The predicative possessive is the most restricted, being compatible only with a relation of possession (or something close to it). The postnominal construction is of intermediate applicability. The postnominal construction has a further property, which sets it apart from all the other possessive constructions. This is that some of its uses (such as *that husband of mine*) can acquire affective overtones, usually, but not always, deprecatory. Any fully adequate analysis of the postnominal possessive will have to take account of this special property.

12.1 THE PRONOMINAL POSSESSIVE

I begin with what is perhaps the most straightforward of the three constructions, the pronominal use of [NP POSS]. Here are some examples.

(4)   *a.* Every man has his price. [Mine] is one hundred grand a year and no duties. (*SW* 195)
    b. The little girl put her sticky hand in [Philip's]. (*SW* 223)
    c. So I earn a living from the telly. Adapting my own novels or [other people's]. (*SW* 181)

    d. When we heard that the University was going to give you an honorary
    degree, we decided to make [yours] the first complete corpus on our
    tape archive. (*SW* 183)

    e. Nobody, he assures Thelma, will know what they are doing under the
    blankets. "All I'm going to do under [mine] is sleep," Thelma says. (*SW*
    90)

There can be no doubt about the nominal character of the bracketed expressions in (4). This aspect is fully in accordance with our analysis of [NP POSS] as a determiner, whose nominal profile designates a schematic instance of the possessee (section 5.6). In a standard prenominal possessive, the schematically designated instance acquires conceptual substance through unification with the adjacent possessee nominal. In the absence of an explicit possessee, the schematic instance acquires conceptual substance by being identified with some salient entity in the current discourse.

Observe that in this respect, [NP POSS] behaves distributionally exactly like many other determiners. The demonstratives *this*, *that*, *these*, and *those*, and quantifiers such as *all*, *many*, *some*, and *each*, can also stand alone as nominals, in which case they, too, designate schematically characterized instances, whose conceptual substance has to be supplied from the current discourse situation. In fact, the ability of a determiner to stand alone as a fully grounded nominal is one of the standard arguments in favour of the thesis that determiners are nominal in character, and that, in virtue of their being distributionally equivalent to full noun phrases, they in fact constitute the head of a noun phrase (Hudson 1984: 90–1; Hewson 1991: 322–3).

Problematic for the determiner as head thesis are, of course, the most frequent of the English determiners, *the* and *a(n)*. Whereas in Romance and Germanic,[2] the definite and indefinite articles can be used pronominally, this is not so with *the* and *a(n)*. One explanation for the exceptional status of the articles in English could be that these items are so lacking in conceptual substance (*the* is unspecified even for number) that they absolutely require elaboration by an adjacent nominal. Their conceptual dependence matches their phonological dependence. *The* and *a(n)* are clitic-like elements; they are generally unstressed, and therefore need to attach to an adjacent phonological host. Demonstratives (*this*, *that*, etc.) and the numeral *one* may plausibly be regarded as their phonologically strong counterparts, standing in for the articles when a pronominal element is required. Hudson (1984: 91) even suggests that *the* could be regarded as an allomorph of *it* and *they*, on the grounds that the article and the pronouns are in complementary distribution. The relation is supported by diachronic evidence. As is well known, the definite articles, in Germanic and Romance, evolved, through phonological

---

[2] Thus, German *der*, *die*, *das* (and their case-marked equivalents) double as articles to noun phrases and as pronouns, while in French, the forms *le*, *la*, *les* serve both as articles and as clitic object pronouns.

weakening, from demonstratives, whilst the indefinite article evolved from the cardinal numeral 'one'.

The proposal that some of the English determiners come in pairs of 'strong' and 'weak' forms, with the strong forms obligatory in pronominal contexts, also ties in with some properties of the possessor phrase. As already noted, *my*, *your*, etc. have special forms in the pronominal construction (as well as in the other two constructions studied in this chapter). *My*, *your*, etc. may be plausibly regarded as phonologically dependent, clitic-like elements, which require the phonological support of a following item, whilst *mine*, *yours*, etc. are the phonologically independent forms. Some support for this analysis comes from the fact that even in the pronominal construction the weak form must be used if it is accompanied by a phonological host, such as intensifying *own*.

(5)   I now make my living by adapting other people's novels, as well as {mine/ my own}, for television.

The same goes for the predicative and postnominal constructions.

(6)   This money is {mine/my own}; some money of {mine/my own}

It is not therefore any semantic properties of the pronominal construction *per se* (nor of the other two constructions studied here) that render the strong forms obligatory; the decisive factor, rather, is the phonological environment.[3] There is some diachronic evidence, too, for the correctness of this account. Prenominal *my* and *mine* used to be distributed (in the early Middle English period) rather like modern English *a* and *an*, the former appearing before a consonant, the latter before a vowel: *mī fader* but *mīn arm* (Sweet 1891: 344). The contrast, at this stage in the language's history, was purely phonological.[4]

As documented in the examples in (4), the pronominal possessive is especially felicitous when the 'understood' possessee is an underived noun, and the implied relation between possessor and possessee is one of possession, or something quite close to it. In addition, kinship terms, and other interpersonal nouns (*friend*, *colleague*, etc.) are marginally acceptable in the construction. Derived nouns, however, tend to be rejected as the understood possessee. What could be the reason for these restrictions?

I drew attention in Chapter 9 to the multiple construal relations that (in the

---

[3] An alternative account can be imagined (and which would be consistent with the view—which we have rejected—that [NP POSS] has a relational profile). This is to analyse the additional phonological material in *mine, yours*, etc. as instantiating a nominal element, with the approximate semantic value of "one", "ones". Such an account may well be valid for Afrikaans. The possessive morpheme in Afrikaans is *se* /sə/: *Dit is Jan se Auto* "This is John's car". Pronominal possessives require the additional phonological element /n/, plausibly cognate with the indefinite article *'n*: *Dit is Jan s'n* /sən/ "This is John's"; *Johannesburg se weer en Kapstad s'n* "Johannesburg's weather and Cape Town's". With respect to English, however, the absence of any additional phonological material in possessor phrases with full NP possessors strongly argues against the generality of such an account for English, and for this reason it should be rejected.

[4] On the subsequent competition of the strong and weak forms *mine/my, thine/thy* in Early Modern English, see Schendl (1993).

prenominal construction) exist between a possessor phrase and an inherently relational noun which it grounds. As shown in Figure 9.1, correspondence lines link not only the profiles of the possessor phrase and the possessee, but also various unprofiled elements, both nominal and relational, in the semantic structures of the two constituents. Now, the pronominal use of the possessor phrase profiles only a schematic notion of the possessee. There are obviously no unprofiled elements within the semantic structure of this schematically designated instance. Consequently, there is no possibility of multiple correspondence relations between the possessor phrase and the understood possessee. For this reason, inherently relational nouns will tend to be rejected as the understood possessee. Nevertheless, derived nouns as the understood possessee are not totally ruled out, especially when the understood possessee is contextually salient in virtue of previous mention, as is the case in (7).

(7)   Bill's arrest was unlawful, and so was John's.

The following also seem to me to be marginally acceptable.

(8)   *a.* ?Germany's invasion of Poland and Italy's of Albania.
       b. ?Poland's invasion by Hitler and Albania's by Mussolini.

Consider also cases of conjoined possessor phrases.

(9)   *a.* [John and Bill]'s arrest.
       b. [John's] and [Bill's arrest].
(10) [Poland's] and [Albania's invasion] by, respectively, Germany and Italy.

There is a subtle contrast between (9*a*) and (9*b*). The former denotes the arrest of John and Bill together, whereas (9*b*) suggests two separate arrests, that of John and that of Bill. In the first case, *John and Bill* is a compound constituent, whereas in (9*b*) *John's* can plausibly be taken as a pronominal possessive, whose understood possessee is *arrest*. The constituencies of the two expressions are as indicated. Likewise in (10), two separate invasions are designated—Poland's and Albania's—whereby *Poland's* may also be regarded as a pronominal possessive.

   The examples in (7)–(10) are of interest to the extent that they could suggest an alternative account of the pronominal possessive, one which would make it possible to circumvent, if so desired, the analysis developed here. This is in terms of the 'gapping' of the possessee nominal, as proposed by Jackendoff (1977: 116). Gapping involves the deletion of some portion of one expression when it is phonologically identical to some sequence in a conjoined, and syntactically parallel expression. An explanation in terms of gapping carries with it no entailments as to the syntactic category of the gapped element (in our case, the possessee noun), nor of the status of the elements remaining after gapping has taken place (in our case, the remaining NP POSS string). In fact, one of the more problematic aspects of gapping is that the gapped element, and the elements remaining after gapping, may not actually have the status of syntactic constituents at all.[5]

In support of the gapping analysis, observe that the above examples are acceptable only on condition of strict syntactic (and semantic) parallelism between the conjuncts. The following are scarcely possible.

(11) *a.* *John's was an arrest which was reported in all the newspapers.
      b. *Poland's was the invasion that started World War II.

On the other hand, not all uses of pronominal possessives are compatible with the gapping analysis. In (12), there is no conjunct from which the understood possessee could be supplied. The only requirement on the interpretability of *yours* and *theirs* is that the understood possessee, i.e. 'corpus', or 'house', has to be derivable, somehow, from the discourse context.

(12) *a.* We decided to make [yours] the first complete corpus on our tape archive. [cf. (4*d*)]
      b. [talking of houses] [Theirs] is that big one up there on the hill.

At best, then, gapping is an option only for a limited amount of the data. A more general account, along the lines developed here, is therefore to be preferred. Not only is the account more general in its coverage, it also explains why a special supporting context (as supplied by a conjunct) is necessary when the understood possessee is a derived, and semantically complex noun.

12.2 THE PREDICATIVE POSSESSIVE

The predicative use of the possessor phrase [NP POSS] is subject to heavy semantic restrictions. As examples (7)–(10) have shown, pronominal *John's*, in the intended sense "John's arrest", and even *Albania's*, in the sense "Albania's invasion", may be acceptable with an appropriate supporting context. The corresponding predicative uses of the possessor phrases, as in (13), are totally out.

(13) *a.* *The arrest was John's.
      b. *The invasion was Albania's.

The following also demonstrate the incompatibility of the predicative construction with semantic relations that are perfectly acceptable in prenominal possessives.

---

[5] Thus, in *John invited Mary, and Bill, Sue*, the gapped clause [Bill, Sue] is not a recognizable syntactic constituent. Langacker's (1991: 485–90) account of gapping appeals to the notion of 'phonological coinstantiation', whereby a phonological sequence may simultaneously instantiate components, not necessarily adjacent, of two (or more) structures at a more abstract level. While the notion of phonological co-instantiation can readily account for 'non-constituent coordination', as in the above example, Langacker (1991: 485) points out that some alleged cases of non-constituent coordination may be more apparent than real, especially in view of the 'potentially quite variable' understanding of constituency in cognitive grammar.

(14) *a.* This is my {sister/neighbour/friend}.
      b. *This {sister/neighbour/friend} is mine.
(15) *a.* I repaired the car's {headlights/windscreen/brakes}.
      b. *The {headlights/windscreen/brakes} that I repaired were the car's.
(16) *a.* We learned about Bill's {murder/conviction/release}.
      b. *The {murder/conviction/release} that we learned about was Bill's.

Even in cases where the predicative construction is acceptable, there may still be restrictions on its semantic interpretation.

(17) *a.* This is John's photograph.
      b. This photograph is John's.

John's photograph has at least three salient readings: a photograph belonging to John, a photograph created by John, and a photograph depicting John. The predicative expression (17*b*) very strongly invokes only the first of these relations. Likewise, to say of a car that it 'is John's' strongly suggests that the car is one which John owns, or is entitled to use, rather than, for example, the car that John designed (but does not actually own or use).

The predicative possessive thus appears to be compatible only with a relation of possession, or something very close to it; to say of X that it 'is Y's' is to predicate ownership of X by Y, or, failing ownership in the strict legal sense, to state that Y has privileged rights of access to X. No other semantic relation appears to be available.

Since only animate creatures—prototypically human beings—can own things, the non-occurrence of predicative *its* is to be expected. Nevertheless, it would be wrong to rule out predicative *its* in principle. The following example was heard in the course of an SABC news item, which reported that a stretch of highway—a favourite, it would seem, with Cape Town's traffic police—did not in fact come under the city's administration.

(18) Cape Town's most profitable speed trapping area may not be its to trap in.

Here, the relation between the municipal authority and the territory that it administers is construed as a relation of ownership, thereby sanctioning the predicative possessive *be its*.

In the following, I want to argue that the restriction to a relation of possession falls out from some general properties of predicative constructions, in interaction with the specific semantic properties of the possessor phrase.

Let us make a digression (whose relevance will soon become apparent), and compare the attributive (or prenominal) and predicative (or postnominal) uses of adjectives. Only a subset of adjectives can be used predicatively in a sense corresponding to their attributive use; moreover, for many adjectives, the predicative use is compatible with only one of the readings that may be associated with the attributive use. A *red house* is unproblematically a house that 'is red'.

Red can be used both attributively and predicatively in its basic colour-denoting sense. But only on the reading "agèd colleague" can an *old colleague* be described as colleague who 'is old'. In the sense "former colleague", or "colleague of long standing", the predicative use of *old* is ruled out. And, of course, many adjectives cannot be used predicatively at all. A *former colleague* is not a 'colleague who is former', and a *fake Picasso* can hardly be described as a 'Picasso which is fake'. There is an obvious parallel here with possessives, in that only some semantic relations are compatible with the predicative construction.

It is worth emphasizing that in the case of both adjectives and possessives, the semantic restrictions on predicative uses are not dependent upon the presence of a copula verb. In the predicative constructions in (19), which lack a copula, *old* can only mean "advanced in years", whilst (20) invokes only a relation of ownership.

(19)   *a.* They considered my colleague old.
       b. My colleague old? You must be joking.
(20)   *a.* They thought the photograph John's.
       b. This photograph John's? You must be joking.

Likewise, (21) and (22), which invoke readings incompatible with the predicative constructions, are equally ungrammatical.

(21)   *a.* *They considered my colleague former.
       b. *My colleague former? You must be joking.
(22)   *a.* *They thought {this sister mine/this arrest Bill's}.
       b. *{This sister mine?/This arrest Bill's?} You must be joking.

That we are dealing with essentially the same kind of phenomenon with both possessives and adjectives, is suggested also by the following example, which involves both an adjective and a possessive.

(23)   *a.* That is my old car.
       b. My car is old.
       c. That old car is mine.

(23*a*) has two distinct readings. On the one reading, *my old car* designates a car which is old, and which I currently own. These semantic relations are compatible with a predicative adjective (23*b*) and a predicative possessive (23*c*). *My old car* could also designate a car which I used to own, but which I no longer own. In this case predicative expressions are inappropriate. The car need not 'be old', nor, of course, is the car now mine.

Adjectives, then, raise essentially the same kinds of problems as possessives. If *an old car* is a car which is old, why can we not say that *a former colleague* is a colleague who is former, or that *a fake Picasso* is a Picasso which is fake? Likewise, if *my car* is a car which is mine, why can we not say that *my sister* is a sister who is mine, or that *John's arrest* is an arrest which is John's?

The case of adjectives is discussed in some length in Taylor (1992). There I distinguish between the 'absolute' and 'synthetic' readings of an adjective. An absolute reading is one which is compatible with both attributive and predicative uses, whilst a synthetic reading is incompatible with predicative uses. A fundamental aspect, it is argued, concerns the manner in which an adjective enters a valence relation with the noun it modifies. An adjective profiles a relation between a schematically characterized thing (the adjective's trajector) and a region in some domain (the adjective's landmark) (see section 4.2). In the case of the adjective *red*, the domain is that of colour space, for *old* it is the domain of time, whereby the adjective's trajector is construed as having been in existence for a period of time in excess of some norm (set by reference to the kind of entity in question). On the absolute reading of an attributive adjective, there is a simple correspondence between the profile of the noun and the adjective's trajector. In *red house*, the trajector of *red* is elaborated by the nominal profile of *house*, whilst on the absolute reading of *old colleague*, the person designated by *colleague* is construed as having been alive for a period of time in excess of the norm (for human beings).

On a synthetic reading of an [ADJ N] expression, there is a more complex relationship between noun and adjective, involving multiple correspondence relations between entities in the semantic structure of the noun and in the semantic structure of the adjective. In *old colleague*, on the readings "former colleague", "colleague of long standing", the relational character of *colleague* is crucially involved. With "colleague of long standing", it is not the colleague *qua* person that is old, what is at issue is persistence, up to reference time R, of the relation between the designated person and an unprofiled relatum. On the reading "former colleague", at issue is the existence, at a time previous to reference time R, of the colleague-relation, a relation which now, at R, no longer exists; the person designated by *colleague* has, as it were, outlived his participation in the colleague-relation. Or, to take another example (from Vendler 1967: 176), *beautiful dancer*, on its absolute reading, merely characterizes the designated person as beautiful, without reference to the semantic structure of *dancer*, whilst on its synthetic reading ("one who dances beautifully") there is an intrinsic reference to the unprofiled activity in the semantic structure of *dancer*. In the first case, what is beautiful is the dancer *qua* person, in the second case, it is the dancer *qua* dancer.

In the predicative construction, there is no possibility of multiple correspondences between the noun and the adjective. In fact, in the predicative construction, there is no direct valence relation at all between noun and adjective. In attributive [ADJ N] the adjective's trajector is a noun, that is, a type specification. The attributive adjective combines with the type specification to give a semantically more complex type specification. On the other hand, the trajector of [be ADJ] is an NP, that is, a fully grounded instance. Predicative [be ADJ] ascribes a certain property to this fully grounded instance specification.

The difference between noun and noun phrase, between type and instance specification, is crucial. *Picasso* (in the metonymic sense "painting by Picasso"), and *fake Picasso*, both designate a type of entity, whilst *a Picasso* and *a fake Picasso* designate instances of the types. In speaking of *a Picasso* or *a fake Picasso*, the speaker has categorized the designated entities as, respectively, 'a Picasso' and 'a fake Picasso', and commits himself to their existence (at a certain reference time and in the appropriate mental space[6]). It would therefore be incoherent to say of a painting *This Picasso is fake*. Having categorized a painting as 'a Picasso', a speaker cannot reasonably go on to state that this Picasso is not (really) a Picasso.[7] Similar arguments apply to the impossibility of *My colleague is former* and *My colleague is old* in the sense "the designated person used to be my colleague". Having categorized a person, at reference time R, as 'my colleague', I cannot reasonably say of this person that he/she is no longer my colleague at R.

The above observations suggest the following generalization: *Grounded nominals are semantic islands*. By this I mean that non-profiled entities in the semantic structure of a nominal are insulated from interaction with the semantic structure of expressions with which the nominal combines. When a nominal enters a valence relation, only the profile of the nominal may be put into correspondence with the relevant substructure of a neighbouring constituent. If I say of my colleague that he is old, *is old* is not able to evoke the relational character of *colleague*, by conveying, for example, that the relation between the colleague and myself has endured for a long period of time. In terms of its integration with *is old*, *my colleague* is construed as a non-relational entity. *Is old* can only convey the oldness of my colleague *qua* human being (the profile of *my colleague*), not with respect to the colleague's status as a participant in an unprofiled relation with myself. Likewise, to say *The dancer is beautiful* is to assert only that the dancer *qua* person (the profile of *the dancer*) is beautiful, not that she/he dances beautifully.[8]

---

[6] The notion of mental space was introduction section 7.1. Note that some adjectives specifically invoke mental spaces which are imaginative, fictitious, counterfactual, or in some other way 'unreal': *a would-be actor, an imaginary illness, a fictitious uncle, a possible objection, an alleged incident, a non-existent Frenchman*. If used predicatively, these adjectives give rise to the same kind of anomaly as *This Picasso is fake*.

[7] In contexts which involve a juxtaposition of inconsistent mental spaces, *This Picasso is fake* could have a coherent interpretation, along the lines "This painting, which everyone designates as 'a Picasso', is in reality, as I have myself just ascertained, not a Picasso". For discussion of similar examples, see Fauconnier (1994: 12–5).

[8] The island nature of grounded nominals shows up in the fact that unprofiled entities in the semantic structure of a nominal may not normally serve as antecedents to an anaphoric expression. (But see Deane 1992: 40–1 for a discussion of some counterexamples.) In (1) below, *him* cannot be construed as co-referential with the unprofiled relatum in the semantic structure of *colleague* (although in the expression *his colleague*, such a relation of identity between 'he' and the unprofiled relatum *does* obtain). Sentence (1) cannot mean "The designated person X, who is the colleague of some non-specified person Y, spent many hours working with Y": (1) *A colleague spent many hours working with him*. Likewise with the following example from Postal (1969): (2) *Max is an orphan and he deeply misses them*. Although *orphan* makes reference, in its semantic structure, to the deceased parents of the designated person, *them* cannot refer back to the unprofiled parents.

It is precisely this characteristic of nominals, I suggest, that lies behind restrictions on predicative possessives. Whereas in the prenominal construction, the possessor nominal typically (and in some cases, obligatorily: section 9.2) exploits the relational character of the possessee, this kind of interaction between possessor and possessee is missing from the predicative possessive. *Photograph* is a representational noun (section 9.7) which designates a kind of artefact, but which also makes schematic reference, in its semantic structure, to the creator of the artefact, and to the entity that the artefact represents. These unprofiled elements may be elaborated by a prenominal possessor, as in *John's photograph*, on its various readings. But in *This photograph is John's* there can be no valence relation between unprofiled entities in the semantic structure of the nominal *this photograph*, and elements in the semantic structure of *is John's*. The relational predicate *is John's* takes, as its trajector, only the profile of its nominal subject. Only the photograph, in its status as a physical object, is John's.

Predicative possessives are therefore restricted by and large to non-relational nouns: *This car is mine, This watch is hers, This shirt is his*. In such cases, the only semantic relation that can be established between possessee and possessor is the default relation of possession, or ownership (section 9.8). If the semantic relation of ownership is conceptually incoherent (if, in other words, the possessee is a non-possessible entity), the predicative possessive is judged to be ungrammatical: **This colleague is mine, *The arrest was John's, *The destruction was the city's, *That perpetual grumbling was his*. Not even the whole–part relation is possible: **This tail is the cat's, *These headlights are the car's*.

I stated earlier that the differences between the attributive and predicative constructions do not lie in any properties of the copula *per se*. Neither can the differences be attributed to any substantive difference between the semantic content of [ADJ] vs. [be ADJ], or of [NP POSS] vs. [be NP POSS]. As shown by examples (19)–(22), the special properties of predicative adjectives and predicative possessives are not dependent at all on the presence of the copula verb. What, then, *is* the contribution of the copula verb? Langacker (1991: 65) has argued that *be* merely designates a highly schematic stative relation; 'it profiles the continuation through time of a stable situation characterized only as a stative relation', whereby the nature of the relation is 'maximally unspecific'. When *be* combines with an adjective such as *old*, the adjective gives conceptual substance to the schematic relation profiled by *be*, whilst *be* imposes its profile (that of a temporally extended relation) on the composite structure. In other words, *old* and *be old*—or, more generally, [ADJ] and [be ADJ]—profile *exactly the same relation*, the only difference being that with *be old* the relation is construed as extending through time, whereas with *old* the relation is atemporal.

We would like to be able to offer an exactly analogous account of [NP POSS] and [be NP POSS].

In 5.5 I considered the possibility of attributing a relational profile to [NP POSS]. On this analysis, POSS would be a preposition-like element, which profiles the relation between its trajector (the possessee) and its landmark (the possessor); in other words, [NP POSS] would have a semantic structure comparable to that of a prepositional phrase. A relational analysis of [NP POSS] would have a definite advantage in the context of the present discussion, in that it would neatly account for the extensive parallels between [be ADJ] and [be NP POSS]. Just as, in the case of [be ADJ], the relation profiled by the adjective gives conceptual substance to the highly schematic stative relation profiled by *be*, so, in the case of [be NP POSS], we could say that the relation profiled by the possessor phrase elaborates the schematic relation of the copula. In both cases, integration with the copula imposes a temporal profile on the relation, the relation, in other words, comes to be construed as continuing, unchanged, through time.

In 5.6, however, I argued against this analysis of [NP POSS], and proposed that the possessor phrase be assigned a nominal profile, specifically, that the possessor nominal designates a schematically characterized possessee. Now, the idea that [NP POSS] is nominal rather than relational in character is not in itself problematic for its use in the predicative construction. The predicative construction is compatible not only with predicative adjectives (24*a*)—as well as, of course, with other relational predicates, such as prepositional phrases[9]—but also with predicative nominals (24*b*).

(24)   *a*. This car is old.
       b. This car is a Mazda.

(24*a*) even admits of a nominal paraphrase.

(25)   This car is an old one.

One approach to the contrast in (24) would be to recognize two distinct senses of the verb *be*. In the predicative adjective construction [be ADJ], the verb merely designates a highly schematic stative relation, its semantic structure being otherwise devoid of conceptual content. In the predicative nominal construction [be NP], *be* would be somewhat richer in content, in that it designates a relation of identity between its trajector and landmark.[10] The trouble is, the relation of identity is not dependent upon the presence of the copula.

(26)   This car a Mazda? You must be mistaken.

An alternative account, proposed by Langacker (1991: 64–6), is to claim that in the predicative nominal construction, the predicative nominal itself acquires a relational profile, profiling a relation of identity between a to-be-specified trajector and its landmark. The identity relation is not, of course, a relation between two distinct individuals, but between two conceptions of one and the

---

[9] As in *The car is in the garage*. Prepositional phrases, like adjectives, denote atemporal relations. Their integration with the copula is exactly analogous to the integration of an adjective with the copula.

[10] Cf. the standard logical view that 'the *is* of identity is one thing, the *is* of predication another' (Quine 1990: 36).

same individual. (The relation is therefore one of apposition.) The identity relation consists precisely in the correspondence of the two conceptions. In stating that *This car is a Mazda* one and the same individual is construed in two different ways, first, as a specific car, identifiable to both speaker and hearer, secondly as a random exemplar of the type 'Mazda'. The establishment of an identity relation is tantamount to categorizing the car as a member of the category of Mazdas.

Pursuing this analysis with respect to predicative possessives would compel us to attribute a relational profile to the possessor phrase [NP POSS]. The relational profile, however, is quite different to that entertained in section 5.5. There, the relation profiled by [NP POSS] was the possessive relation between the trajector of POSS (the possessee) and its landmark (the possessor). Assuming the inherently relational character of [NP POSS] as discussed in 5.5, a rough paraphrase of *This car is John's* would be "This car is of John". On the present account, the relation is one of identity between the trajector of [be NP POSS] and the schematic possessee designated by [NP POSS]. *This car is John's* thus establishes an identity relation between the referent of *this car* and a schematically characterized entity designated by *John's*. The overall result is to characterize *this car* as one which belongs to John. A rough paraphrase would be "This car is John's one", or, closer to standard English, "This car is John's car", where the double appearance of 'car' in the paraphrase nicely captures the correspondence relation between the clausal trajector *this car* and the schematic possessee profiled by *John's*.

12.3 THE POSTNOMINAL POSSESSIVE

The postnominal possessive (*a friend of John's*) has long been something of a mystery. One of its more puzzling aspects is the fact that the 'possessive'—or 'genitive'—relation appears to be doubly marked, first by the preposition *of*, second by the possessive morpheme POSS. Older grammarians commonly referred to the construction as the 'double genitive' (Curme 1931: 75–7), whilst Sweet (1898: 54) and Poutsma (1914: 77), evidently seeing little motivation for the double marking, called it the 'pleonastic genitive'. Fowler (1926), that astute commentator on English usage, cited the construction as an example of what he called the 'sturdy indefensibles' (p. 573): he found the construction 'plainly illogical' (p. 399), but nevertheless one that was so well established in the language that he thought it unlikely that it could ever be prescribed out of existence.

And indeed, the construction has been around for quite some time. Shakespeare used it: *a bastard of the king's* (*King John* II. i. 65), *this dotage of our general's* (*Antony and Cleopatra* I. i. 1), as did Chaucer: *an officer | of the prefectes* (*The Second Nun's Tale*, ll. 368–9). I have already cited—Chapter 5, example (42a)—an example from Wyld (1936: 318), dating from 1418: *a man of the Ducs of Orliance*.

The alleged 'pleonastic' character of the construction can be easily disposed of. We need only cite the clear semantic contrast that is associated in the following examples with [of NP] vs. [of NP POSS].

(27) *a.* a portrait of John.
      b. a portrait of John's.
(28) *a.* a student of Kant.
      b. a student of Kant's.

In the (*a*) expressions, the *of*-phrase introduces an entity that is intrinsic to the semantic structure of the head noun; the portrait depicts John, and the student specializes in Kant. Here, *of* has its basic value of profiling an intrinsic relation. The (*b*) expressions are very different. Here, the relational character of the head noun is hardly at issue at all. John could be the owner (or creator) of the portrait, Kant could be the person who taught the student. In other cases, the contrast is more subtle, as in (29). Christopher Lyons (1986*b*: 136) stated that his intuitions 'do not detect any difference of meaning'; the two expressions, for him, 'seem to be completely synonymous' (p. 129).

(29) *a.* This man is a friend of Mary.
      b. This man is a friend of Mary's.

Consider, though, the nature of a friendship relation. Normally, the relation is reciprocal. In such a situation, 'X is a friend of Y' entails 'Y is a friend of X'. Assuming a reciprocal relation of friendship between 'Mary' and 'this man', the sentences in (29) do turn out to be semantically equivalent (which is not to say, *pace* Lyons, that they are exactly synonymous.) But friendship need not be reciprocated. If such is the case, a clear contrast certainly does emerge in (29). If I am 'a friend of Mary', I have extended my friendship to Mary; consistent with the account of (27*a*) and (28*a*), the intrinsic relational sense of *friend* (and of *of*) is here at issue. But if Mary has not extended her friendship to me, I do not count as 'a friend of Mary's'. The contrast is exploited in the following (invented) dialogue, from Erades (1975: 81).

(30) A: Who told you that?
      B: A friend of your father's.
      A: If he says such things, he is not a friend of my father, whoever he may be.

The contrast becomes somewhat more transparent if we slightly change the wording of (29).

(31) *a.* This woman is a friend of the prisoner. That's why she wants to help him.
      b. This woman is a friend of the prisoner's. That's why she is also under suspicion.

And with *enemy* the contrast is even more evident. *An enemy of the Bishop* need not be *an enemy of the Bishop's* (and *vice versa*).

A first conclusion from these examples is that the postnominal possessive has much more in common, semantically, with the prenominal possessive than it has with postnominal [of NP]. Disregarding its grounding properties, *a student of Kant's* is clearly to be aligned, semantically, with *Kant's student*, not with *a student of Kant*.[11] Another conclusion, which I shall follow up later in this section, could be that the very substantial semantic difference between [of NP] and [of NP POSS] not only reflects the special contribution of the possessive morpheme to the latter construction, it also has to do with the fact that *of* has different semantic values in the two constructions.

I mentioned the affinities between prenominal and postnominal [NP POSS]. There is another construction with which the postnominal possessive shows some remarkable affinities. This is the appositive *of*-construction. Compare the following.

(32)   *a*. the City of London.
       b. the city of London.

The first denotes a part–whole relation, *the City* being the name of the financial district of London. In the second example, *the city* and *London* refer to one and the same entity, but characterize it in different ways.[12] For this reason the two nominals can be said to be in apposition.

Now, the appositive *of*-construction can take on some very distinctive affective overtones (usually negative, but not necessarily so), especially if the first noun is an emotionally-charged epithet.

(33)   *a*. that scoundrel of a man.
       b. this bitch of a problem.
       c. an angel of a child.

Precisely the same kinds of affective overtones may attach to the postnominal possessive.

(34)   *a*. that worthless husband of yours.
       b. this boring job of mine.
       c. those beautiful eyes of hers.

Affective overtones are present even if the emotive adjectives in (34) are omitted (although without the adjective, the emotional nuance is left unspecified).

---

[11] Admittedly, the situation with respect to *John's portrait* vs. *a portrait of John's* and *a portrait of John* (and similarly with *Mary's friend, the Bishop's enemy*, etc.) is less clear-cut. This is largely due to the range of different interpretations available for the prenominal construction. *I am the Bishop's enemy* could have both a subjective interpretation (the Bishop has feelings of enmity towards me) or an objective interpretation (I have feelings of enmity towards the Bishop). Only on the first reading do I count as 'an enemy of the Bishop's'.

[12] Cf. the so-called descriptive genitive of Latin: *urbs Romae* "the city of Rome". There is a fossilized prenominal expression in English which is based in the appositive relation: *Dublin's fair city*, i.e. "the fair city of Dublin". Poutsma (1914–16: 41), in fact, had recognized the 'genitive of apposition' as a distinctive subcategory of genitive relation, citing such examples as *Tweed's fair river* and *treason's charge* (see section 1.1.2).

That husband of yours would still (probably) be deprecatory, whilst *those eyes of hers* could be associated with a range of emotions, from infatuation and adoration, to fear, anxiety, or loathing. But whatever the interpretation, the expression is certainly not emotionally neutral. Note also, in this connection, the aggressive connotations standardly associated with the formulaic question in (35).

(35)　What business is it of yours?

A further similarity between the appositive and the postnominal possessive constructions is that both tend to occur with determiners (such as a demonstrative or an indefinite article) other than the definite article *the*. *The scoundrel of a man* and *the husband of hers*—with the definite article *the*—while not impossible, are probably less normal than with a demonstrative.

The affinity between the two constructions is further underlined by the fact that the one can be embedded into the other, whereby each seems to reinforce the affective overtones of the other.

(36)　*a.* that bastard of a husband of mine.
　　　b. this bitch of a life of ours.
　　　c. that angel of a daughter of yours.

These affinities could be a clue to the correct analysis of the postnominal possessive, in its various uses (including its non-emotive uses). I shall, in fact, take the line that the construction instantiates an apposition relation.[13]

I mentioned at the outset the puzzling nature of the construction. Not surprisingly, various (incompatible) syntactic analyses have been offered. Chomsky (1970: 202), it will be recalled (section 6.1), derived *that picture of John's* from *John's picture*, which in turn was derived from *that picture that John has*.[14] The derivation was meant to capture the affinity between the postnominal possessive

---

[13] A similar line is taken by Jespersen and Hudson. Jespersen (1909–49: iii. 19) refers to the postnominal construction as the 'appositional genitive'; he lumps *that long nose of his* together with *the three of us* and *the City of Rome*, stating that the function of *of* in all three is to 'join two words which are notionally parallel'. Hudson (1990: 279–80), too, takes the *of* in the postnominal possessive to be a marker of apposition, arguing that in *a hat of Fred's*, both *a hat* and *Fred's* refer to the same entity (the hat), and adding that *a hat of Fred's* 'has a semantic structure which could also be expressed by *a hat which is Fred's*'. However, I disagree with Hudson when he claims that *Fred's hat* and *the hat of Fred* share 'precisely the same' semantic structure (p. 279). For me, *the hat of Fred* is essentially ungrammatical (section 9.8).

[14] The details of the derivation are quite complex. Chomsky proposes the underlying structure in (1) below, where X and Y represent pre- and post-article elements, such as demonstratives (and presumably, also, indefinites, though how an indefinite could be reconciled with *the* is not clear): (1) *X-the-Y picture that John has*. The prenominal possessive then emerges as: (2) *X-John's-Y picture*. Assuming the presence of a demonstrative in (1), this element cannot receive overt expression in the configuration in (2). We cannot have **that John's picture*, or **John's that picture*. The presence of such an element in the prenominal transform would then trigger NP postposing, to give (3) *X-the-Y picture of John's*. This would then need adjusting to give *that picture of John's*. The point of all this elaborate machinery is that with regard to the grounding of the possessee (i.e. *picture*) the postnominal and prenominal constructions are roughly in complementary distribution.

and the non-intrinsic reading of a prenominal possessive (cf. my earlier remarks on *a student of Kant's* and *Kant's student*). As explained in Chapter 6, transformations of the scope that Chomsky had postulated in his 1970 paper soon went out of favour, and a number of non-transformational analyses were advanced. Anderson's (1984) analysis was mentioned in section 6.3. She construed the possessor phrase, i.e. *Bill's* in *this desk of Bill's*, as the specifier to an empty N'. The possessive morpheme has semantic content, and assigns the thematic role of Possessor to *Bill*. The *of*-phrase she construes as a kind of adnominal modifier, analogous to the *of*-phrases in *a book of fifty pages*, *that house of straw*. In *this desk of Bill's*, the head noun *desk* is thereby characterized in terms of its ownership, whereas in *a book of fifty pages*, *that house of straw*, the head noun is characterized in terms of length, and material substance, respectively.

The notion of a specifier to an empty N' could possibly be translated into cognitive grammar concepts; we could equate, for example, the empty N' as the schematic entity designated by the [NP POSS] determiner, *alias* specifier. To this extent, Anderson's account of [NP POSS] could be compatible with my own. More dubious is Anderson's assimilation of postnominal [of NP POSS] to the more general class of postnominal prepositional adjuncts. One difference is that *of fifty pages*, *of straw* may be used predicatively (*The book is of fifty pages*, *The house is of straw*); this is not possible with the possessive phrase: **The desk is of Bill's*. Anderson, then, fails to make some crucial distinctions between different kinds of postnominal phrases. Possibly, this reflects a reluctance to consider *of* to be a meaningful morpheme, a view which forestalls any investigation of its semantic contribution to different constructions.

If Anderson took [of NP POSS] to be a kind of restrictive modifier, another approach has been to align the postnominal construction with partitive expressions (Jackendoff 1977: 116–19). Again, it is assumed that the [NP POSS] constituent is the specifier to an empty N'. On this analysis, *a friend of John's* has roughly the same syntactic structure (and an analogous semantic interpretation) as *one of John's friends*, that is, the designated friend is selected from the set of John's friends. This analysis has been criticized on various grounds by Christopher Lyons (1986b). Some of Lyons's objections concern the distribution of different kinds of nouns in the two constructions. For example, the partitive construction tends not to permit as its head noun the kinds of nouns that so readily occur in the possessive construction. While we can have *several books of mine*, a partitive headed by *several books* is scarcely possible (**several books of those*). Perhaps the most telling of Lyons's arguments, however, for the distinctness of the two constructions is the fact that the postnominal possessive has a partitive interpretation only circumstantially, not inherently. *A friend of mine* might well suggest that I have more than one friend, the particular friend in question being selected from this larger set. But this interpretation has more to do with encyclopedic knowledge pertaining to the noun *friend*, and to its use

with the indefinite article, than with the semantics of the postnominal possessive.[15] (*I bumped into a friend in the cafeteria* could also be taken to mean that
I have more than one friend.) But, as Lyons (p. 128) points out, *a friend of mine*
would not be inconsistent with my having only one friend. Furthermore, many
examples of the postnominal construction are clearly not partitive at all. *That
husband of Berta's* does not entail that Berta has more than one husband, the
particular husband in question being picked out from the larger set.

One of Lyons's main concerns is the distribution of the postnominal possessive. He observes that, with regard to the grounding (not Lyons's term!) of the
possessee, the postnominal construction is in rough complementary distribution
with the prenominal possessive. Secondly, with regard to the kinds of nominals
that can occur as possessor and possessee, he claims that postnominal [of NP
POSS] is in rough complementary distribution with postnominal [of NP].

The first observation is certainly valid, up to a point. Prenominal possessives
generally (though as we showed in Chapter 7, by no means exclusively) have
definite reference. The grounding properties of prenominal [NP POSS] are thus
roughly comparable to those of the definite determiner *the*. *The*, however, is just
the determiner which tends to be infelicitous with the postnominal construction
(**the book of John's*).[16] Definite expressions of this kind become fully acceptable if there is some restrictive modification of the head noun (*the book of
John's that you borrowed*). Precisely this kind of restrictive modification tends
to be unacceptable with the prenominal construction (?*John's book that you
borrowed*; see section 8.3.5). Likewise, demonstratives and indefinites are permitted in the postnominal construction; these are determiners which cannot be
included into the prenominal construction. As Lyons (1986*b*: 124) succinctly
puts it: 'The preposed construction has the meaning that the postposed construction would have with *the*, if it could occur with *the*.'

It is worth pausing for a moment on Lyons's talk of 'complementary distribution' (p. 124) between pre- and postnominal possessives. The term is taken
from structural phonemics. If two phones are in complementary distribution, we
are entitled to regard them, at a more schematic level of phonological description, as instances of the same entity, that is, in traditional terms, as allophones
of the same phoneme. By analogy, if two syntactic constructions are in complementary distribution, we may be entitled to consider them to be identical, at a
more schematic level of representation. Whilst I would hesitate to draw this conclusion in the form in which I have stated it, there are undoubtedly many affinities,

---

[15] The point was also made by Erades (1975: 78–9), in his comments (first published in 1952)
on what he claimed was 'the view most frequently advanced' concerning the postnominal possessive, i.e. that it 'has a partitive sense'. In confirmation, he notes that the Dutch expressions *een
vriend van me* "a friend of me", *welke zuster van je* "which sister of you", *een huis van m'n vader*
"a house of my father" could 'equally suggest more friends, sisters or houses', in spite of the absence
of possessive markers on the Dutch nouns.

[16] One should not be too dogmatic on this point, however. Note the following authentic example:
The point of Strawson's is an interesting one (Wheatley 1969: 230).

as already pointed out, between pre- and postnominal possessives, certainly more affinities than between postnominal [of NP POSS] and postnominal [of NP].

Lyons, however, also argues for the complementary distribution of [of NP POSS] and [of NP]. This is much more dubious. In the first place, to describe the contrast in purely distributional terms turns out to be rather difficult. Certainly, some generalizations can be made. Postnominal possessors are overwhelmingly human; non-relational head nouns with human possessors overwhelmingly prefer the possessive construction (*that puppy of Anne's*/*that puppy of Anne*); relational head nouns (including part-terms, but excluding kinship and interpersonal terms) take a non-possessive complement (*a funnel of the ship*/*a funnel of the ship's*). There is also a strong tendency for a postnominal pronoun (if human) to appear in the possessive form, whatever the semantic relation (*a brother of his*/?*a brother of him*).[17]

Given his assumption that [of NP POSS] and [of NP] are in complementary distribution, Lyons is able to claim that the two constructions are in fact the very same (p. 137). He takes cases like (29), repeated below as (37), as additional support for the claim.

(37)   *a*. This man is a friend of Mary.
       b. This man is a friend of Mary's.

As we have seen, Lyons denies that there is any semantic contrast here. To continue the phonological analogy, he takes *of Mary* and *of Mary's* to be in free variation. Two phones in free variation in a given environment, with no associated semantic contrast, can be taken as instantiations of the same phoneme. The conclusion, again, is that [of NP] and [of NP POSS] instantiate the very same construction.

Concerning the specific details of Lyons's proposal, he assumes (like Anderson) that the postnominal possessive is 'exactly like any descriptive PP in the compl[ement] of an NP' (1986*b*: 128). But unlike Anderson and Jackendoff, who located the possessor phase in the specifier position to an empty N', Lyons takes [NP POSS] to be a regular nominal (i.e. NP) complement of *of*. The distinguishing feature of the construction, for Lyons, is that the preposition *of* may, in special circumstances, assign genitive case (instead of the more usual objective case) to its NP complement, genitive case being realized by the possessive morpheme. The circumstances which trigger genitive case marking by *of* are 'rather complex', even 'unclear'. This, Lyons tells us, is not too surprising, given the 'highly marked and exceptional' (p. 137) nature of the phenomenon.

Some objections to this analysis have already been mentioned in the course of my presentation. (I need hardly go into the questionable mechanics of genitive

---

[17] Again, one should not be dogmatic on this issue. Note the following examples: 'The *Sunday Times* and the *Observer* have asked for a photograph of you ... All I could find was an old snap of you at the seaside in shorts.' (*SW* 226–7) *A Photograph of yours* and *an old snap of yours* would be quite incongruous here.

vs. objective case assignment, associated, moreover, on Lyons's view, with no semantic contrast.) As noted, the alleged example of free variation (37) turns out to be no such thing. Moreover, there is the much more transparent minimal pair contrast between *a portrait of John* and *a portrait of John's*. Consider also the fact that the two kinds of *of*-phrase can readily co-occur, in either sequence (38).

(38)   *a.* a portrait of John's of Bill.
       b. a portrait of Bill of John's.
          [Lyons 1986*b*: 134]

But neither kind of *of*-phrase can co-occur with itself.

(39)   *a.* *the portrait of John of Bill.
       b. *a portrait of John's of Bill's.

We could hardly ask for more convincing evidence that [of NP] and [of NP POSS] are *not* mere morphological variants of one and the same construction.

Langacker (1991: 176; 1995: 70–2) has also addressed the curious postnominal construction, and it is his analysis that I turn to next. Recall that Langacker's account of prenominal possessives differs somewhat from the one that I have pursued in this book, in that he takes the possessive morpheme, and hence also the possessor phrase [NP POSS], to be basically relational in character. As a relational predicate, [NP POSS] profiles a relation between its trajector (the possessee entity) and the possessor, whereby the possessee is located within the dominion, or search domain, of the possessor.

As the complement of *of*, however, [NP POSS] is clearly nominal, not relational.[18] Langacker therefore postulates a semantic variant of the possessor phrase. Rather than profiling a relation to the possessor, it now profiles the dominion defined with respect to the possessor. Concretely, [NP POSS] now designates the set of potentially 'possessible' entities that can be accessed from the reference point of the possessor.

Langacker points out that analogous reifications of relational notions are frequent throughout the grammar. The very existence of nominalizations, he observes, presupposes the reification process. Whilst nominalization usually involves some special morphological marking, reification is also encountered with prepositional phrases, where it is not associated with any special morphological marking.

(40)   *a.* the dust [under the bed].
       b. [Under the bed] is dusty.
       c. Take the book from [under the bed].

In (*a*), *under the bed* is clearly relational. But in (*b*), the same expression has a nominal character; it functions as the grammatical subject of the sentence, and

---

[18] I am informed that in substandard American English expressions of the kind *a friend of John's's* /dʒɒnzəz/ may occur (although I myself have not encountered such examples). On the assumption that the possessive morpheme attaches exclusively to noun phrases, the double occurrence of the possessive morpheme in such examples indirectly confirms the view that *John's* in *a friend of John's* is nominal, not relational.

now names a region in space, not a relation between some entity and a region. Earlier (section 4.1), I also argued that in examples like (c), in which a preposition takes what looks like a PP complement, the complement (i.e. *under the bed*) likewise designates a region, and that, in this environment, it also functions grammatically (and conceptually) as a nominal.

A crucial aspect of Langacker's account lies in the semantic value attributed to *of*. Langacker (1992) has argued that the schematic meaning of *of* is to profile an inherent relation. This meaning is most clearly displayed in *of*-complements to relational nouns (*destruction of the city, student of Kant, portrait of John*). The preposition has a number of more specific values, each of which can be regarded as an elaboration of this more general value. Its prototypical value is to profile the part–whole relation, as in *the tip of my finger, the bottom of the jar* (the tip is an intrinsic part of the finger, the bottom is an intrinsic part of the jar). Other values include the thing–substance and thing–quality relations, as in *a ring of gold, a man of integrity* (what it is made of is an essential quality of the ring, the attribute of integrity is an essential quality of the man). Another use is to profile an identity relation—this corresponds to what I have called the appositional use of *of*—as in *the state of California, the crime of shoplifting* (the more precise characterization is intrinsic to the more schematic characterization).

The specific value that Langacker (1991: 176; 1995: 70) attributes to *of* in the postnominal possessive is its prototypical value, that is, it profiles the intrinsic relation between a part (the possessee) and a whole (the dominion). In *a friend of Jill's*, the 'friend' bears a part–whole relation to the dominion, or search domain, defined with respect to Jill. In accordance with the reference point function of the possessor, a correspondence is established between the trajector of *of* and a target entity located within the preposition's landmark, that is, the dominion of the possessor. The 'friend' is thereby identified with a target entity within the dominion.

In essence, Langacker appears to be proposing a variant on the partitive account of the postnominal possessive. True, the account does not entail that the designated friend is selected from the larger set of Jill's friends. *A friend of Jill's* therefore does not mean "one of Jill's friends". Rather, the friend is construed as one of an indefinite number of entities that can be accessed from the reference point, Jill. A somewhat closer paraphrase could be "a friend that Jill has". Still, by invoking the part–whole sense of *of*, together with the notion of dominion, which comprises the set of entities that can be accessed from the reference point, the analysis does entail an identity, at a schematic level, between postnominal possessives on the one hand, and other examples of the part–whole relation, such as *one of Jill's friends, some of the peas, the centre of the lawn*, on the other. I have already discussed some reasons for querying this postulated identity.

For my own analysis of the construction, I assume that [NP POSS] in the postnominal construction has *exactly the same value* that it has elsewhere in the grammar, that is to say, it profiles a schematic instance of the possessee, identified from the reference point of the possessor. *Of* is appositional, that is, it profiles an identity relation between its trajector and landmark (characterized with different degrees of specificity). The schematic profile of [NP POSS] is thereby identified with the entity profiled by the trajector of *of*. Observe that in the prenominal construction, there is an analogous identification of the profile of [NP POSS] with the entity profiled by the possessee nominal. Disregarding matters of definiteness, therefore, *a friend of Jill's* turns out to have exactly the same conceptual content as *Jill's friend*.

The affinity between the prenominal and postnominal constructions that we noted at the beginning of this section thus receives a natural explanation. That the two constructions are in rough complementary distribution, as Lyons observes, follows from their grounding properties. The prenominal construction grounds the possessee directly, via the possessor; for reasons explained in Chapter 7, the construction generally has definite reference. In the postnominal construction, in contrast, the possessee is grounded independently of the possessor. The construction is therefore compatible with various referential statuses of the possessee that are either inconsistent with the prenominal construction (such as indefiniteness, in case the possessor is definite[19]), or which cannot be overtly marked in the prenominal construction (such as deictic reference, as expressed by demonstrative determiners).

This analysis has a somewhat unexpected, and possibly unorthodox, consequence. The view that the postnominal possessive instantiates an appositional relation entails that the constituency of *a friend of Jill's* is not (41*a*), but (41*b*). On the other hand, *a friend of Jill* unambiguously has the structure in (42).

(41)   *a.* a [$_N$friend of Jill's]
       b. [$_{NP}$a friend] of [$_{NP}$Jill's]
(42)   a [$_N$friend of Jill]

The apposition relation in *a friend of Jill's* is between two fully grounded nominals, *a friend* and *Jill's*, whereby the appositional relation itself is encoded by the preposition *of*. In other words, *of Jill's* is not a prepositional complement of the noun *friend*. In *a friend of Jill*, on the other hand, *of Jill* is a regular complement of *friend*, elaborating a notion schematically represented in the semantic structure of *friend*.

This account easily explains the heavy restrictions on the kinds of nominals, and the relations which they entail, that are compatible with the postnominal construction. In the prenominal construction, there is a direct valence relation between [NP POSS] and the possessee noun. Consequently, the possibility exists for multiple correspondence relations between various subcomponents of the semantic structures of [NP POSS] and the possessee. These kinds of multiple correspondences characterize expressions whose head is a derived noun, and whose possessor is intrinsic to it (*the city's destruction*). In the postnominal

---

[19] This aspect follows from (27) of Ch. 7.

construction, the correspondence between the possessee and [NP POSS] is mediated by the preposition *of*. The identity relation is between the profiles of fully grounded nominals, the possessee and [NP POSS]. On the assumption that nominals are semantic islands (section 12.2), there can therefore be no correspondences between unprofiled entities in the semantic structures of the two items. Consequently, the postnominal construction cannot tolerate the multiple correspondence relations characteristic of possessive nominalizations. Whence the impossibility of **a destruction of the city's*, **an arrest of Bill's*, **an invasion of Albania's*. In the previous section, an analogous account of the impossibility of *the destruction was the city's*, *the arrest was Bill's*, *the invasion was Albania's* was presented.

Nevertheless, some intrinsically relational nouns, especially kinship and other interpersonal terms (*brother, friend, client, colleague*), do tend to be rather frequent in the postnominal construction. Why should this be? One explanation could be that these nouns potentially have a much greater degree of conceptual autonomy than nominalizations of the kind *destruction*, *arrest*, and *invasion*. Recall our earlier account of *a friend of Mary's* in contrast to *a friend of Mary*. The latter explicitly activates the relational character of *friend*, in that *of Mary* elaborates an intrinsic component of the semantic structure of *friend*. In *a friend of Mary's* it is Mary who considers the designated person to be 'a friend'. Mary is the reference point, and the focus shifts to an entity that can be identified from her perspective. The relational character of *friend* is not at issue, in that *of Mary's* fails to elaborate any unprofiled element in the semantic structure of *friend*.

Pursuing this approach a little further, we might claim that in some cases the relational character of a nominal may actually be suppressed. Consider (43).

(43)   *a*. that husband of mine.
        b. those eyes of hers.

We have already observed that *that husband of mine* is (probably) deprecatory. The negative nuance could be due to the fact that the designated person is being construed as a non-relational entity; the husband becomes simply one of the person's goods and chattels! The effect need not be only deprecatory, of course. *Those eyes of hers* seems to construe the eyes as autonomous objects, to be admired (or feared, or whatever) in their own right, not as an intrinsic part of a larger whole.

These observations bring us to the affinities between the postnominal construction and other instantiations of the appositive *of*-construction. Apposition itself is an important and widespread phenomenon, whose grammatical ramifications are quite extensive. Some of its manifestations are exemplified in (44).

(44)   *a*. [Jack] [the Ripper].
        b. [we] [the people].
        c. a [killer] [dog].
        d. [the fact] [that whales are mammals].

I have bracketed the elements in apposition. In each case we have two nominal expressions, similar with respect to their grounding properties, each of which designates one and the same entity, describing it in different ways. The nominals are in apposition in that they combine to form a higher-order constituent which profiles exactly the same entity as each of its components (Langacker 1991: 432). Langacker (1991: 149) even analyses the quantifying uses of *all* and *both* as instances of apposition.

(45)   *a.* [all] [those kittens].
       b. [both] [the starting defensive tackles].

The quantifying nominal profiles a schematically characterized set of individuals, whilst the second constituent lends conceptual substance to this characterization. We might even say that the prenominal possessive displays elements of apposition, in that, on my analysis, [NP POSS] and [N] each designates the same entity, and combine to form a more complex nominal. The prenominal construction diverges, however, from standard apposition in that the constituents differ in their grounding properties. [NP POSS] is inherently grounded, whilst [N] is, of itself, ungrounded.

   In the appositive *of*-construction, we again have two conceptions of one and the same individual. In one variant of the construction, the second nominal offers a more precise specification of the referent of the first nominal. (Note that in (44) and (45), the second nominal also tends to be richer in conceptual content than the first.)

(46)   *a.* [the state] of [California].
       b. [the crime] of [shoplifting].
       c. [a distance] of [10 miles].
       d. [the idea] of [going there alone].

In another variant, the first nominal is an epithet, which of itself merely expresses an emotional attitude towards a schematically characterized entity. Again, the second nominal adds conceptual substance to this schematic entity. The examples in (47) repeat those in (33).

(47)   *a.* [that scoundrel] of [a man].
       b. [this bitch] of [a problem].
       c. [an angel] of [a child].

The postnominal possessive, in its status as an appositive construction, is unusual only to the extent that the initial nominal is typically richer in conceptual substance than the second. And, of course, there is no reason why apposition should be restricted to only two conceptions of the same entity. [*That bastard*] *of* [*a husband*] *of* [*mine*] integrates three conceptions of one and the same individual.

13 Possession

WE come, finally, to the topic of possession. Traditional grammarians have long given the name 'possessive' to the various constructions that have been our concern in the preceding chapters; it is also the name that I have chosen in this book over its main competitor, 'genitive'. Yet the reader will have noticed that the notion of possession has not played a particularly prominent role in the presentation. On the contrary, I have sought maximally general, schematic characterizations of the possessive constructions; these sanction a wide range of specific relations between possessor and possessee, the availablility of any one of which depends, in large measure, on the semantic content of the constituent nominals. The relation of possession is just one of many kinds of semantic relation that may hold between possessor and possessee, of no special significance, it could appear, in the semantics of the various constructions.

On the other hand, I have spoken, in various places, of possession as the 'default' value that certain expressions, such as *John's car*, receive. Futhermore, in apparent contradiction to the approach I have taken in this book, there are compelling reasons why the notion of possession does have to be accorded a rather prominent status in the semantics of possessive constructions. The aim of this chapter is to resolve the seeming contradiction between, on the one hand, a maximally schematic approach, which accords no special status to the possession relation, and, on the other, the undoubted salience of the possession relation to the semantics of possessive constructions.

13.1 POSSESSION

First, we need to clarify the notion of possession. As a concept of everyday discourse, the notion is complex and multi-faceted, as the extended discussion in Miller and Johnson-Laird (1976: 558–83) shows.

Possession involves a relation between two entities, a possessor and a possessee. Elsewhere (Taylor 1989: 679; 1995b: 202), I have suggested that the relation can be appropriately characterized in terms of a cluster of independent properties, whose frequent or typical co-occurrence constitutes an 'experiential gestalt', in the sense of Lakoff and Johnson (1980: ch. 14). Lakoff and Johnson explicate the notion of experiential gestalt on the example of causation. Contrary to the position of many semanticists, who take 'cause' to be a semantic primitive that enters into the semantic form of a great many lexical items, Lakoff and Johnson analyse cause as a cluster of aspects, grounded in experience, which together define paradigmatic, or prototypical causation. Because the gestalt is complex (in the sense that many different aspects are involved), there arises the possibility of a differentiated understanding of cause; depending on the circumstances of individual cases, some aspects of the gestalt can be foregrounded, others can be backgrounded, or even suppressed. Cause thus turns out to be 'family resemblance' category, unified by a criss-crossing of similarities, rather by a common defining feature, or set of common defining features.

With respect to the possession relation, the following aspects can be identified.

(1) *The possession gestalt*
   a. The possessor is a specific human being.
   b. The possessed is an inanimate entity, usually a concrete physical object.
   c. The relation is exclusive, in the sense that for any possessed entity, there is usually only one possessor. On the other hand, for any possessor, there is typically a large number of entities which may count as his possessions.
   d. The possessor has exclusive rights of access to the possessed. Other persons may have access to the possessed only with the permission of the possessor.
   e. The possessed is typically an object of value, whether commercial or sentimental.
   f. The possessor's rights of access to the possessed are invested in him through a special transaction, such as purchase, inheritance, or gift, and remain with him until the possessor effects their transfer to another person by means of a further transaction, such as sale or donation.
   g. Typically, the possession relation is long term, measured in months and years, not in minutes or seconds.
   h. In order that the possessor can have easy access to the possessed, the possessed is typically located in the proximity of the possessor. In some cases, the possessed may be a permanent, or at least regular accompaniment of the possessor.

We can readily think of countless examples of paradigmatic possession, in which each of the above aspects is present. But because the possession gestalt is complex, the possibility exists that various kinds of relations can be construed as deviations—some slight, some more substantive—from the paradigm case. The linguistic consequences of this state of affairs are of some interest.

In the first place, we can identify various linguistic resources which are available for the designation of a relation of paradigmatic possession. These resources, however, are not completely synomymous. On the contrary, they tend to highlight only some aspects of the paradigmatic relation, at the expense of others. These resources thus become available for encoding relations which deviate, in different ways, and in differing degrees, from the paradigm case.

Consider, first, the paradigmatic relation, and its linguistic expression. As mentioned, there are a variety of linguistic means available to the speaker of English for this purpose. In addition to the possessive constructions that we have been considering (*This is my car*, *This car is mine*), these resources include verbs such as *have*, *own*, and *belong to*. Moreover, many predicates invoke paradigmatic possession as one aspect of a more complex semantic structure. *Give* and *take*, *lend* and *borrow*, *sell* and *buy*, *bequeath* and *inherit*, *lose* and *find* designate some of the different ways in which possession can be transferred; *lack* designates the absence of a possession relation between its trajector and landmark; *need* and *want* can denote the desirability of a possession relation coming about, and so on.

In certain contexts, there might appear to be little to choose between the alternative possession-denoting resources. *This car is mine* entails *This car belongs to me*, and vice versa; in many cases, *I have a car* could be roughly equivalent to *I own a car*. Whilst we can observe here a contrast in trajector–landmark alignment, as well as some differences in definiteness, there is a very real sense in which these expressions all share a common conceptual content, identifiable with the possession gestalt of (1).

Having said this, we must recognize that the different expressions do tend to highlight different facets of the possession gestalt. *Own* focuses on the legality of the possession relationship, as sanctioned by an appropriate transaction, cf. (1*f*). *Have*, on the other hand, highlights the accessibility, or immediate availability of an entity, cf. (1*h*). Often, ownership, encoded by *own*, and accessibility, encoded by *have*, go hand in hand. If I 'own' an umbrella, I can usually be said, also, to 'have' an umbrella, and vice versa. Yet the two aspects are in principle independent of each other. If I lend my umbrella to you, then you 'have' the umbrella, even though I still 'own' it. The separability of the two aspects becomes even more apparent if we contrast *He owns a gun* and *He has a gun*. The former designates the possession relation in its legal aspects, whereas the latter means that the person has easy access to a gun (possibly, he is already holding it, ready to shoot). In certain circumstances, the utterance of *He has a gun* could be taken as a warning ('He is liable to shoot'), the legal ownership of the gun being irrelevant to the force of the utterance.

Whereas (*to*) *own* is very much restricted in its usage range to designating a possession relation in its legal aspects, *have* may be used in a wide range of contexts, some of which bear only a very tenuous relationship with paradigmatic possession. In the first place, *have* is readily used of non-human possessors. A dog 'has' a bone, it does not 'own' it. Secondly, the possessed entity need not be a physical object, nor even an entity of any commercial value. A person (and a dog) 'has' a name. Again, *own* would be quite inappropriate here. The following examples exhibit an increasing distance from paradigmatic possession.

(2)   *a.* Do you have a bank account?
       b. The house has three bedrooms.
       c. You have a lot of patience.
       d. We have a lot of crime in this city.
       e. I have some work to do.
       f. I have to go to town this afternoon.
       g. The guests have arrived.

Accessibility, and exclusive rights of access, as sanctioned by a special kind of transaction, are at issue in (2*a*). The relation deviates from the paradigm, mainly because a bank account is not a physical object, nor is it, of itself, an object of any value, commercial or otherwise. Neither, of course, can 'possession' of a bank account be transferred to someone else; you cannot 'give', 'lend', 'bequeath' it to someone else, neither can someone 'steal' it from you. Sentence (2*b*) invokes a whole–part relation, and while one cannot say of a whole that it 'owns' its parts, there is, nevertheless, some affinity to aspects of paradigmatic possession. A whole–part relation is necessarily a long-term one (1*g*), and subsists for as long as the whole, in its present form, exists. It also involves proximity; a part is necessarily close—maximally close, in fact—to the whole of which it is a part (1*h*). Exclusiveness (1*c*) is also at issue, in that a part is usually associated with only one whole. However, the requirement that the 'possessor' (observe how the term is becoming increasingly anomalous!) be human has been lifted; inanimates also can 'have' parts. In (2*c*), the 'possessed' is no longer a physical object. Nevertheless, a property of an individual is a necessary accompaniment of the individual; the relation is usually also a long-term one, and subsists for as long as the individual (in its present form) exists.

With (2*d*) we are even further away from paradigmatic possession. What is at issue here is merely the pervasive presence of some phenomenon within a certain environment. (Note that *we* in (2*d*) is understood in a generic sense.) In (2*e*) the 'presence' of some task to the subject of *have* implies the obligation of the subject to perform that task. In (2*f*) this nuance has become fully grammaticalized, in that *have* (*to*) conventionally denotes an obligation on the part of the subject of the verb to perform the activity designated by the verb's complement. *Have* as a marker of anteriority, as in (2*g*), exemplifies another grammaticalized use of the verb. Perfective *have* denotes the present relevance of the designated situation; *The guests have arrived*, in contrast to *The guests arrived*, entails that the guests are now here. Present relevance may be plausibly seen as an extension of the notion of accessibility (1*h*); the guests' arrival is currently 'available'. At issue, however, is not the relevance of the situation to the subject of *have*, but its relevance to the participants in the interaction, i.e. the speaker and hearer. (We return to this aspect of (2*g*) later in this chapter.)

The above paragraphs have sketched the outline of a prototype account of the polysemy of *have*. The account presupposes a 'basic' sense of the verb, rooted in some aspects of the possession gestalt, and a chain of 'extended' senses, radiating out from the basic sense. The prototype account captures the relatedness of the different uses, and thus offers an explanation for how it is that a morpheme, one of whose uses is to denote possession, can also, in other contexts, denote whole–part relations, obligation, and anteriority.[1] As pointed out in section 3.4, however, the postulation of a range of specific meanings does not of itself preclude the feasibility of a schematic sense, which covers the range of specific uses. Langacker (1993: 16), in fact, suggests that the schematic sense of *have* can be found in the reference point phenomenon that is so crucial to the semantics of possessive constructions. The trajector of *have* denotes an entity construable as a reference point, whilst the landmark is an element located within its dominion. The differences between *have* and the possessive morpheme follow from other properties of the two predicates. First, there is the question of trajector–landmark alignment. The trajector of *have* corresponds to the possessor, whereas the trajector of POSS is the possessee. Secondly, *have* is a verb, which profiles the continuance through time of the relation between trajector and landmark, whilst the relation invoked by POSS is atemporal. A third, and crucial difference lies in the fact that the possessive morpheme serves to ground the possessee, whereas in *have* expressions the possessee is an independently grounded nominal. Whilst the verb designates the relation between possessor and possessee, the possessive morpheme does not designate the relation at all, it invokes the relation, in its unprofiled semantic structure, as one aspect of its grounding function.

Leaving aside these differences, the commonality between *have* and the possessive morpheme is no doubt a major reason why a good many possessive expressions can be loosely paraphrased by means of *have*. More importantly, however, my above remarks on the semantics of *have* raise the question of whether an analogous, prototype account of the possessive morpheme might not also be both feasible and plausible. Prototype accounts have been undertaken by Taylor (1989), Durieux (1990), and Nikiforidou (1991). In earlier chapters, too, I have spoken of the possession relations 'and relations that are close to it'—a turn of phrase which presupposes a possession prototype, and deviations therefrom.

13.2 PROTOTYPE ACCOUNTS OF POSSESSIVE RELATIONS

Prototype accounts of the possessive construction are motivated by the desire to bring some kind of order to the *ad hoc* taxonomies of traditional grammars. By proposing that the kinds of relations compatible with the possessive morpheme

[1] As a descriptive statement, a prototype account makes no claims concerning diachronic or synchronic processes. Even so, it is worth mentioning that modern English *have* is cognate with English *heave*, German *heben*, and Latin *capire*, suggesting that the diachronically basic sense had to do with 'holding', 'grasping', and 'manipulating'. There could be grounds for supposing that the range of uses of the modern English verb are indeed extensions of a historical sense, which designated one aspect of the possession gestalt.

constitute a case of 'structured polysemy' (Nikiforidou 1991: 149), they attempt to explain why it is that one and the same linguistic form can come to be compatible with so many, and such highly diverse, semantic relations.

Nikiforidou's account was reviewed in section 1.1.2. I must emphasize again that my misgivings about her account do not pertain to the feasibility of the prototype programme *per se*, but to her implementation of it. As noted in the earlier discussion, Nikiforidou postulates a number of metaphorical extensions from the possession prototype, largely on the basis of what she takes to be analogous metaphorical extensions of the basic possessive sense of *have*. The above remarks on *have*, however, indicate that there are no reasons for regarding the extended senses of *have* as in the least metaphorical. The use of *have* to denote a whole–part relation, for example, exploits only some aspects of paradigmatic possession; while these aspects may well be attenuated in the whole–part relation, there are no grounds for supposing that the relation is construed metaphorically in terms of paradigmatic possession. Moreover, it could still be feasible to postulate a highly schematic, general sense of *have*, with which the range of specific senses are compatible.

Taylor (1989) proposes a more modest prototype approach. The semantic relations encoded by *the dog's bone*, *the secretary's office*, *John's train* ("the train John is travelling on"), *John's furniture* ("the furniture John has made"), *the factory's chimney*, and *the car's road-holding ability* are seen as increasingly distant from the possession prototype (pp. 680–1.) *John's train* conforms to the prototype in that John has rights of access to the train he is travelling on, the possessor is human, the possessed is inanimate, and the possessor is in close proximity to the possessed (at least, for the duration of the train journey). The relation diverges from the prototype in that the possessor's rights over the possessed are rigidly circumscribed, the relation is non-exclusive, and it is short-term. On the other hand, other relations that are compatible with the possessive construction, such as kinship, as well as subjective and objective relations, are not so obviously related to the possession gestalt at all. On a prototype approach, these would have to be regarded as *very* marginal examples of the possession prototype, linked to the prototype mainly in virtue of the exclusivity of the possessor–possessee relation (cf. (1c)). As noted in Taylor (1989: 681), such a conclusion is not entirely satisfactory. It not only goes against intuitions, it is also inconsistent with the high productivity of the possessive construction with relational and derived possessees.

Durieux (1990) proposes a more elaborate prototype account. He identifes, not one, but three main gestalts: Possession, Whole–part, and Source (or Origin). (Of these three, however, possession is still regarded as primary.) These gestalts are linked in virtue of such aspects as spatial proximity, rights of access, and conceptual dependence (pp. 65–8). Even so, there remain some possessive relations which cannot reasonably be related to any of the three gestalts. Durieux mentions the case of objective possessives. He observes, *contra* Nikiforidou, that it makes no sense to say that *South Africa's exclusion from the Common-wealth* testifies to a metaphorical construal of possession: 'one cannot have, lose, receive, or gain exclusions' (p. 74); there is 'no conceptual similiarity (not even one based on metaphor)' (p. 75) between such expressions and paradigmatic possession. To account for cases like these, Durieux, following Taylor (1989), appeals to the exclusivity of the possessor–possessee relation. It is this aspect of the possession prototype that carries over into objective possessives, thus enabling the construction to fulfil its referential function of guaranteeing the unique indentification of the target entity.

Prototype accounts presuppose the reliable identification of the prototype. To propose a prototype account of possessive relations requires that one of the many relations invoked by the possessive morpheme is singled out as basic, from which all other senses can be related, in some way or other. The three studies reviewed above independently selected the possession relation as basic. However, other possibilities could certainly be entertained. With this in mind, let us consider Kuryłowicz's account of case categories in Indo-European.

Kuryłowicz (1964) distinguishes between two kinds of case categories: 'grammatical' cases and 'concrete' cases (p. 179). The grammatical cases (nominative and accusative) serve to encode syntactic relations within a transitive clause; these are relations that in a caseless language such as English are encoded largely by means of constituent order within the clause. The concrete cases, such as instrumental, ablative, and locative, encode semantic relations between a nominal and other aspects of a clausal predication; these are relations that in caseless languages are typically encoded by lexical means, by prepositions, for example. Of special interest to us is Kuryłowicz's treatment of genitive. Surprisingly, perhaps, he classifies the genitive as a grammatical, not as a concrete case (p. 183). Just as nominative and accusative encode grammatical relations within the clause, so the genitive encodes grammatical relations within a nominalization. *Occisio hostis* "the killing of the enemy" is ambiguous between a subjective and objective interpretation. Genitive case is here functionally equivalent to nominative and accusative in a transitive clause.

Kuryłowicz (p. 14) further distinguishes between the 'primary' and 'secondary' uses of a linguistic resource. The primary uses are determined by the language system, whereas the secondary uses, although derived from primary uses, are more dependent on a specific context than on the value of the item within the system. The distinction is brought to bear on the genitive. Whereas the primary use of the genitive is grammatical, in the sense explained above, all other uses 'are founded as *secondary* upon its *primary* syntactical function as *genetivus subiectivus (obiectivus)*' (p. 184). Amongst the secondary uses are the obligatory occurrence of genitive case in the NP complements of certain verbs, as well as a range of adnominal uses outside a nominalization; these latter encode a variety of semantic relations, including, of course, the relation of possession. Kuryłowicz explains as follows.

Action and agent nouns govern the *subjective* and *objective* gen[itive] as long as there exists a morphological bond between them and the corresponding personal verb. Once this bond is loosened, the internal relation between the determining and the determined noun is apt to change. The loss of purely *syntactic* motivation entails the increase of the role of the *semantic* context, i.e. of the meaning of the two nouns. Hence the different sub-groups of the adnom[inal] gen[itive], which may be looked upon as semantically conditioned variants of the subjective and objective gen[itive]. (Kuryłowicz 1964: 187; author's emphasis)

As far as I am aware, no latter-day adherent to prototype theory has seriously pursued the possibility that the prototypical sense of genitive case is to denote grammatical relations within a nominalization. Although Kuryłowicz says little about the mechanisms for deriving secondary variants from the primary uses, a prototype account along these lines is by no means unthinkable. Leaving aside the differences, discussed at length in Chapter 5, between the genitive case of Indo-European languages and the possessive morpheme of modern English, such an account could probably be made to work for the possessive morpheme, also. Let us postulate that the basic sense of the possessive is analogous to a 'genetivus subiectivus', i.e. it designates the relation between a notional subject and a nominalized process. In a transitive process the subject typically initiates, and controls the process; it is, on Langacker's account of transitivity, the energy source. The notion of control would then provide the conceptual link between the subjective sense and the possession relation, in that a possessor typically has control over his possessions. Whereas Nikiforidou (1991) analysed the subjective relation as a metaphorical extension of possession, it would be no less plausible to construe possession as an extension of the subjective relation.

Intuitively, however, this account does not feel correct; the subjective relation within a nominalization is not plausibly regarded as the basic sense of the possessive morpheme (nor, perhaps, of genitive case in Indo-European languages). It is important to consider why this should be so. On what basis can we substantiate the centrality of the possession relation, and the corresponding peripherality of the subjective relation?

One procedure might be to appeal to frequency of occurrence. Unfortunately, there is little evidence that the possessive construction is more frequently associated with the possession relation than with other semantic relations. Durieux (1990) analysed a corpus of 500 prenominal possessives. These were selected from the over 5,400 expressions in the LOB corpus, on the basis of their interpretability and their representativity for the various registers of the corpus (p. 33). Whilst the assignment of these expressions to the various taxonomic types is likely to entail a certain margin of error, Durieux's figures are nevertheless suggestive. He reports (p. 59) that only 30 expressions (6 per cent of the corpus) were open to the paraphrase "have in one's possession", while as many as 91 (= 18 per cent) denoted an 'agentive' relation to a 'verbal noun'. A reanalysis of the corpus used in Taylor (1991a) has confirmed the relatively low incidence of paradigmatic possession. Only 7 (= 3 per cent) of the 240 expressions in the corpus denoted a relation of paradigmatic possession; slightly relaxing the conditions of paradigmatic possession, so as to include a person's temporary rights of access to an entity (as in *her chair*, in the sense "the chair in which she is sitting") caused this figure to rise only to 16 (= 7 per cent). On the other hand, subjective relations of a possessor to a deverbal noun comprised 44 expressions (= 18 per cent). These figures are almost identical to Durieux's, and suggest that paradigmatic possession may not be particularly frequent after all.[2] For example, in both Taylor's and Durieux's corpora, expressions denoting a possession relation were outnumbered by expressions denoting kinship and other interpersonal relations; these constituted 8 per cent of Durieux's corpus, and 11 per cent of Taylor's. These data raise, in a particularly acute form, the question of how we can motivate the possession relation as more basic, than, say, the kinship relation, or indeed than the subjective relation.

A more promising approach is to look at order of acquisition. Embryonic possessives appear very early in the acquisition process, and, according to Roger Brown, are used frequently and productively by 20 months. Brown's comments are pertinent.

The high frequency and apparent productivity of the possessive construction in child speech suggests that children are required in their behaviour to distinguish between objects belonging to one person or another and objects belonging to no one in particular. Much detailed interaction in our transcripts suggests that children have primitive local notions of property and territoriality which they express with the possessive. The idea seems to be that the possessor has prior rights of use or access to his possessions, rights that supercede those of any other member of the family. This appeared most dramatically in our materials when Adam warned Ursula Bellugi, who was about to sit in Daddy's chair: *No, no Daddy chair, home soon.* (Brown 1973: 233)

Brown's observations suggest that early child possessives invoke semantic relations which cluster closely around the relation of paradigmatic possession. Brown, in fact, notes that even whole–part relations (*dog tail*, *Mommy nose*) are relatively infrequent in early speech, whilst more abstract, 'thematic' relations, as exemplified by *America's discovery*, or even *the ship's captain*, do not occur at all (p. 233). A glance at the numerous examples from early speech cited in Radford (1990: 88–9) confirms Brown's observations on the kinds of semantic relation that they invoke.

Brown makes a further and for our purposes very significant observation. He suggests that possessives constitute a means for generating unique names for objects, in that the construction makes it possible to distinguish objects of the same kind according to who has rights of access to them. In this respect, early

---

[2] Possibly, the figures for paradigmatic possession are skewed by the fact that both Taylor and Durieux relied heavily on written data. As mentioned in section 8.2.1, the possessives in spontaneous speech tend not to encode clausal relations.

child possessives already document the reference point function of the adult construction.

> It is interesting to think of [possession] in relation to unmarked common nouns and to nouns marked with the definite article. Thus *chair* is the name of any instance of a certain class; *the chair* is a name for a specific instance identified by uniqueness or prior attention or entailment or any of a number of devices ... The definite article serves to create names more specific than the class name but it is what might be called a floating temporary specifier, since any chair whatsoever can become *the chair* for a time, reverting to its non-specific status as *a chair* whenever attention shifts. Possessions like *Mommy chair* or *Daddy chair* are nonfloating, permanent specifiers which name an entity more specifically than its class name can do. (Brown 1973: 232)

The prototype account of possession relations, such as are found in Taylor (1989), Durieux (1990), and Nikiforidou (1991), share with taxonomic accounts a focus on the semantic relations between possessor and possessee, to the neglect of the construction's discourse function. Brown's comments are important in that they not only point to the developmental primacy of the possession relation, they also show that the emergence of the construction is closely tied up with its reference point function.

This aspect of the child language data suggests a more fruitful approach to the centrality of the possession relation, and its status *vis-à-vis* the schematic meaning of the possessive construction.

13.3 THE SUBJECTIFICATION OF POSSESSION

In this final section I want to propose that the reference point function involves a subjectification of some aspects of paradigmatic possession.[3] This account may help us to reconcile the paradoxical aspects of the possessive construction that we highlighted at the beginning of this chapter. On the one hand, the construction is compatible with a range of semantic relations which seem to have little or nothing to do with possession, even on a *very* broad understanding of the concept. At the same time, the relation of paradigmatic possession does appear to be central to the semantics of the construction—even though the reasons for its centrality are anything but obvious.

I use the term subjectification in the technical sense of Langacker (1990b). Langacker distinguishes between an 'objective' and a 'subjective' construal of an entity. An entity is construed objectively if it is the 'object' of conception, while subjective construal obtains when an entity is an inherent (though unprofiled) aspect of the conceptualization process itself. (Langacker draws a useful analogy with the role of a pair of spectacles in vision. If I take off my glasses and hold them in front of me, I view them 'objectively', as the object of perception. But

---

[3] This section develops a suggestion made to me by Dirk Geeraerts.

when my glasses are sitting on my nose, they play a role in the perception process itself; they are construed 'subjectively', and cease to be the object of perception.) Thus, the notion of the 'ground' (i.e. the context of the speech event) is an inherent aspect of any grounded predication. Yet a grounded expression (such as a definite nominal, or a tensed clause) does not explicitly designate the ground; the ground is therefore construed subjectively, in that it is necessarily invoked by the conceptualizer in the process of grounding. On the other hand, the very expression *ground*, as well as expressions which designate aspects of the ground, such as *here, now, me, you*, do designate the ground, and aspects of it, objectively.

A couple of examples will illustrate the linguistic significance of the distinction. Consider the two uses of *over* in (3) (Langacker 1990*b*: 21).

(3)   *a.* They hiked over that hill.
      b. The village is just over that hill.

(3*a*) presents an objective construal of the trajector's motion through time; the trajector (*they*) successively occupies a series of places whose overall configuration is designated by the prepositional phrase *over the hill*. Arguably, *over the hill* in (3*b*) designates exactly the same spatial configuration as it does in (3*a*). There is, however, no actual motion involved in (3*b*). What the sentence means is that an observer can conceptually locate the village by tracing a mental path 'over the hill', starting from some unspecified point of origin; probably, though not necessarily, the origin of the mental path coincides with the place of the speaker and hearer. It is not therefore the trajector (*the village*) which moves 'over the hill'; the motion is an aspect of the conceptualization process itself. The following examples (Langacker 1990*b*: 19) are similar.

(4)   *a.* The balloon ascended rapidly.
      b. Beyond the 2,000-metre level, the trail ascends quite rapidly.

In (4*a*) *ascend* profiles the objective motion of the balloon, through time, whereas the situation described in (4*b*) does not involve objective motion at all; the sentence describes the static, imperfective configuration of the trail. The use of *ascend*, however, does evoke subjective motion on the part of the conceptualizer, who mentally scans the trail upwards from the 2,000-metre level.

Langacker (1990*b*) proposes that grammaticalization—the process whereby a lexical item evolves into a grammatical morpheme—is often accompanied by subjectification, that is to say, a component of an objectively construed scene comes to be identified with some aspect of the conceptualization process itself. At the same time, the meaning of the erstwhile lexical item becomes more schematic, and less intimately connected with the rich conceptual content of its original value.

For an example, we can turn to the sentences in (2), which illustrate the progressive attenuation of the supposed basic sense of the verb *have*. The final sentence in (2)—*The guests have arrived*—represents a qualitative break with the six preceding examples. In (2*a–f*) there is a real sense in which the landmark of *have* is 'present', or 'accessible' to the trajector of the verb. But in *The guests have arrived*, it is not only that the notion of accessibility has become attenuated to yield the notion of 'relevance', the relevance is not the relevance of the arrival to the persons who arrived, but the relevance of the whole predication (the guests' arrival) to the participants in the speech situation, at the time of utterance. The relevance relation does not hold objectively between the designated participants in the situation, it holds subjectively between the situation and the conceptualizer.

(2*g*) exemplifies a grammaticalized sense of *have*; the verb functions as a marker of anteriority, signalling the present relevance of a past situation. A similar phenomenon is attested by (*be*) *going to* as a means of referring to future time. It is a common observation (e.g. Lakoff and Johnson 1980: ch. 9) that the use of motion verbs for the encoding of temporal relations rests on a metaphorical construal of time. One important conceptual metaphor construes time as a static medium, and the passing of time as movement forward through the medium. *We go into the future with confidence* is a fairly stereotypical exploitation of this metaphor.

One conventionalized value of the present progressive (*I'm staying at home this evening, She's flying to Sydney tomorrow*) is to denote a present intention on the part of the trajector to engage in an activity in the near future. This conventionalized value of the present progressive, in association with the spatial construal of time, yields one reading of (5). On this reading, it is the subject of (*be*) *going to*, i.e. Mary, who intends to get pregnant in the near future.

(5)   Mary's going to have another baby.

This reading still evokes an objective construal of motion, even though the motion in question is metaphorical. But there is another reading of (5) which has nothing to do with the present intention of the subject of the verb. On this reading, the sentence encodes a prediction, formulated by the speaker on the basis of his observation of Mary's being visibly pregnant. It is not Mary's present intention which 'goes' into the future, it is the speaker's prediction, which takes *him* into the future. This aspect is even more evident in examples such as *It's going to rain.*. This can only be a prediction based on present evidence. There can obviously be no question of 'it' intending to move metaphorically into the future and rain. Rather, the metaphorical movement is on the part of the conceptualizer. In this sense, again, the idea of movement entailed by (*be*) *going to* has become subjectified.

These examples illustrate a further aspect of grammaticalization. When *have* and (*be*) *going to* designate objectively construed relations, there are quite heavy restrictions on the kinds of items that can function as the verbs' trajectors. When (*be*) *going to* conveys a present intention to perform a future activity, the subject of the verb must obviously designate a conscious entity, prototypically a human being, to which it is possible to attribute present intentions for future actions. But when the motion into the future is on the part of the conceptualizer, such a restriction on permissible subjects no longer applies. In fact, as a means of encoding a speaker's prediction about the near future, (*be*) *going to* can take just about any nominal as its subject. The same, of course, goes for *have*, when it serves to encode the present relevance of a past situation.

Let us now turn to the relation of possession. There are various means available in English to encode an objective construal of a possession relation. These include the verbs *own, have,* and *belong to.* Especially *own* and *belong to* encode relations that are fairly close to paradigmatic possession, as characterized earlier. If something *belongs to* me, or if I *own* it, the item is readily accessible to me; I am entitled to use it, to manipulate it, to dispose of it, as I please. But a prenominal possessive, such as *John's car,* does not actually encode the relation of possession between the car and John. The point of the expression is to convey the *accessibility of the target to the conceptualizer, given the reference point.* The notion of the accessibility of the possessee to the possessor, an important facet of paradigmatic possession, has been subjectified, and has to do with the accessibility of the target entity, *via* the reference point, to the conceptualizer.

It is this aspect, I suggest, which crucially differentiates the prenominal construction from postnominal *of*-expressions, in spite of the rough equivalence, in many cases, between the two wordings (*the company's director* vs. *the director of the company*; section 1.2). It also differentiates the English prenominal construction from its equivalents (involving, for example, genitive case, or a prepositional phrase) in many other languages. In spite of the rough translation equivalence of English *the neighbour's car* and German *das Auto des Nachbarn,* the adnominal genitive *des Nachbarn* objectively construes the relation between the car and the neighbour. Admittedly, the relation is specified only schematically, in that an adnominal genitive in German is consistent with a wide range of specific semantic values (section 1.1.3). Schematicity, however, is independent of the objective–subjective distinction. English *the neighbour's car* introduces a subjective component, in that the expression invokes the accessibility of the car to the conceptualizer, given the reference point.

It is the notion of the accessibility of the target which testifies to the importance of the relation of paradigmatic possession in the semantics of the possessive construction. The grounding function of the possessor nominal involves a subjectification of precisely this facet of paradigmatic possession. But once subjectification has taken place, the prenominal construction becomes compatible with all manner of semantic relations which, on their objective construal, have little, if anything, in common with paradigmatic possession.

References

Abbreviations

BLS *Proceedings of the Annual Meeting of the Berkeley Linguistics Society*
CLS *Papers from the Regional Meeting of the Chicago Linguistic Society*

ABNEY, S. P. (1987), 'The English Noun Phrase in its Sentential Aspects', Ph.D. dissertation, MIT. Distributed by MIT Working Papers in Linguistics.

ALTENBERG, B. (1982), *The Genitive v. the of-Construction: A Study of Syntactic Variation in 17th Century English* (Lund Studies in English 62). Lund: CWK Gleerup.

AMRITAVALLI, R. (1980), 'Expressing cross-categorial selectional correspondences: an alternative to the X-bar syntax approach', *Linguistic Analysis*, 6: 305–43.

ANDERSON, M. (1978), 'NP pre-posing in noun phrases', *Proceedings of the North Eastern Linguistic Society*, 8: 12–21.

—— (1984), 'Prenominal genitive NPs', *Linguistic Review*, 3: 1–24.

ANDERSON, S. R., and KIPARSKY, P. (eds.) (1973), *A Festschrift for Morris Halle*. New York: Holt, Rinehart and Wilson.

AUSTIN, J. L. (1979), *Philosophical Papers*, ed. J. O. Urmson and G. J. Warnock. Oxford: Oxford University Press (1st edn. 1961).

BAKER, G. P., and HACKER, P. M. S. (1980), *Essays on the Philosophical Investigations*, i: *Wittgenstein: Meaning and Understanding*. Chicago: University of Chicago Press.

BANFIELD, A. (1982), *Unspeakable Sentences: Narration and Representation in the Language of Fiction*. Boston: Routledge & Kegan Paul.

BARFOOT, C. C. (1991), 'Trouble with the apostrophe: or, "You know what hairdresser's are like"', in I. Tieken-Boon van Ostade and J. Frankis (eds.), *Language Usage and Description: Studies Presented to N. E. Osselton on the Occasion of his Retirement*. Amsterdam: Rodopi, 121–37.

BAUGH, A. C., and CABLE, T. (1978), *A History of the English Language*. London: Routledge & Kegan Paul (1st edn. 1951).

BIERWISCH, M. (1981), 'Basic issues in the development of word meaning', in W. Deutsch (ed.), *The Child's Construction of Language*. London: Academic Press, 341–87.

—— (1983), 'Semantische und konzeptuelle Repräsentation lexikalischer Einheiten', in R. Růžička and W. Motsch (eds.), *Untersuchungen zur Semantik* (Studia grammatica 22). Berlin: Akademie-Verlag, 61–99.

—— (1988), 'On the grammar of local prepositions', in M. Bierwisch, W. Motsch, and I. Zimmermann (eds.), *Syntax, Semantik und Lexikon* (Studia grammatica 29). Berlin: Akademie-Verlag, 1–65.

—— and SCHREUDER, R. (1992), 'From concepts to lexical items', *Cognition*, 42: 23–60.

BLEVINS, J. (1994), 'A lexicalist analysis of gerundive nominals in English', *Australian Journal of Linguistics*, 14: 1–38.

BLOOMFIELD, L. (1933), *Language*. London: George Allen & Unwin.

BOLINGER, D. (1977), *Meaning and Form*, London: Longman.

—— (1979), 'The jingle theory of double -*ing*', in D. J. Allerton, E. Carney, and D. Holdcroft (eds.), *Function and Context in Lingusitic Analysis: A Festschrift for William Haas*. Cambridge: Cambridge University Press, 41–56.

BRESNAN, J. (1978), 'A realistic transformational grammar', in M. Halle, J. Bresnan, and G. A. Miller (eds.), *Linguistic Theory and Psychological Reality*. Cambridge, Mass.: MIT Press, 1–59.

—— (1994), 'Locative inversion and the architecture of universal grammar', *Language*, 70: 72–131.

BROWN, C. (1983), 'Topic continuity in written English narrative', in Givón 1983*b*: 315–41.

BROWN, G., and YULE, G. (1983), *Discourse Analysis*. Cambridge: Cambridge University Press.

BROWN, R. (1973), *A First Language: The Early Stages*. London: Allen & Unwin.

BURCHFIELD, R. (1992), *Points of View: Aspects of Present-Day English*. Oxford: Oxford University Press.

BURZIO, L. (1986), *Italian Syntax: A Government-Binding Approach*. Dordrecht: Reidel.

CHAFE, W. (1976), 'Givenness, contrastiveness, definiteness, subjects, topics, and point of view', in Li 1976: 25–55.

—— (1987), 'Cognitive constraints on information flow', in Tomlin 1987: 21–51.

CHOMSKY, N. (1957), *Syntactic Structures*. The Hague: Mouton.

—— (1965), *Aspects of the Theory of Syntax*. Cambridge, Mass.: MIT Press.

—— (1970), 'Remarks on nominalization', in R. A. Jacobs and P. S. Rosenbaum (eds.), *Readings in English Transformational Grammar*. Waltham, Mass.: Ginn, 184–221.

—— (1973), 'Conditions on transformations', in Anderson and Kiparsky 1973: 232–86 (repr. in Chomsky 1977).

—— (1977), *Essays on Form and Interpretation*. Amsterdam: North Holland.

—— (1980), *Rules and Representations*. Oxford: Blackwell.

—— (1981), *Lectures on Government and Binding*. Dordrecht: Foris.

—— (1986), *Knowledge of Language: Its Nature, Origin, and Use*. New York: Praeger.

—— (1988), *Language and Problems of Knowledge: The Managua Lectures*. Cambridge, Mass.: MIT Press.

—— (1991), 'Some notes on economy of derivation and representation', in R. Freidin (ed.), *Principles and Parameters in Comparative Grammar*. Cambridge, Mass.: MIT Press, 417–54.

CINQUE, G. (1980), 'On extraction from NP in Italian', *Journal of Italian Linguistics*, 1/2: 47–99.

CITRINE, W. (1940), *My Finnish Diary*. Harmondsworth: Penguin.

COMRIE, B. (1976), 'The syntax of action nominals: a cross-language study', *Lingua*, 40: 177–201.

CROFT, W. (1990), *Typology and Universals*. Cambridge: Cambridge University Press.

CRYSTAL, D., and DAVY, D. (1969), *Investigating English Style*. London: Longman.

—— —— (1975), *Advanced Conversational English*. London: Longman.

CURME, G. E. (1931), *Syntax*. (= *A Grammar of the English Language*, vol. iii) Boston: Heath.

DEANE, P. (1987), 'English possessives, topicality, and the Silverstein hierarchy', *BLS* 13: 65–76.

DEANE, P. (1991), 'Limits to attention: A cognitive theory of island phenomena', *Cognitive Linguistics*, 2: 1–63.

—— (1992), *Grammar in Mind and Brain: Explorations in Cognitive Syntax*. Berlin: Mouton de Gruyter.

DIRVEN, R., and RADDEN, G. (1977), *Semantische Syntax des Englischen*. Wiesbaden: Athenaion.

DIXON, R. M. W. (1991), *A New Approach to English Grammar, on Semantic Principles*. Oxford: Clarendon Press.

DOKE, C. (1930), *Textbook of Zulu Grammar*. Johannesburg: University of the Witwatersrand Press.

DORON, E., and RAPPAPORT HOVAV, M. (1991), 'Affectedness and externalization', *Proceedings of the North Eastern Linguistic Society*, 21: 81–94.

DOWTY, D. (1986), 'Thematic roles and semantics', *BLS* 12: 340–54.

DURIEUX, F. (1990), 'The meanings of the specifying genitive in English: a cognitive analysis', *Antwerp Papers in Linguistics*, 66.

EMONDS, J. E. (1976), *A Transformational Approach to English Syntax: Root, Structure-Preserving, and Local Transformations*. New York: Academic Press.

ERADES, P. A. (1975), *Points of Modern English Syntax: Contributions to English Studies*, ed. N. J. Robat. Amsterdam: Swets & Zeitlinger.

ERNST, T. (1992), 'Phrase structure and directionality in Irish', *Journal of Linguistics*, 28: 415–43.

FAUCONNIER, G. (1994), *Mental Spaces: Aspects of Meaning Construction in Natural Language*. Cambridge, Cambridge University Press. First published 1985, Cambridge, Mass.: MIT Press. Translation of *Espaces mentaux* (1984), Paris: Minuit.

FELLBAUM, C. (1987), 'On nominals with preposed themes', *CLS* 23/1: 79–92.

FIENGO, R. (1977), 'On trace theory', *Linguistic Inquiry*, 8: 35–61.

—— (1980), *Surface Structure: The Interface of Autonomous Components*. Cambridge, Mass.: Harvard University Press.

FILLMORE, C. (1968), 'The case for case', in E. Bach and R. T. Harms (eds.), *Universals in Linguistic Theory*. New York: Holt, Rinehart and Winston, 1–90.

—— (1988), 'The mechanisms of "Construction Grammar"', *BLS* 14: 35–55.

—— KAY, P., and O'CONNOR, M. C. (1988), 'Regularity and idiomaticity in grammatical constructions: the case of *let alone*', *Language*, 64: 501–38.

FODOR, J. A. (1980), 'The present status of the innateness controversy', in *Representations: Philosophical Essays on the Foundations of Cognitive Science*. Cambridge, Mass.: MIT Press, 257–316.

—— (1983), *The Modularity of Mind*. Cambridge, Mass.: MIT Press.

—— and PYLYSHYN, Z. W. (1988), 'Connectionism and cognitive architecture: a critical analysis', *Cognition*, 26: 5–71.

FODOR, J. D. (1979), 'In defence of the truth value gap', in C.-K. Oh and D. Dinneen (eds.), *Syntax and Semantics* 11. London: Academic Press, 199–224.

FOLEY, W. A., and VAN VALIN, R. D. (1984), *Functional Syntax and Universal Grammar*. Cambridge: Cambridge University Press.

FOWLER, H. W. (1926), *A Dictionary of Modern English Usage*, rev. Sir Ernest Gowers. Oxford: Oxford University Press.

FOX, B., and THOMPSON, S. (1990), 'A discourse explanation of the grammar of relative clauses in English conversation', *Language*, 66: 297–316.

GAZDAR, G. (1987), 'Generative grammar', in J. Lyons, R. Coates, M. Deuchar, and G. Gazdar (eds.), *New Horizons in Linguistics*, ii. Harmondsworth: Penguin, 122–51.

—— KLEIN, E. H., PULLUM, G. K., and SAG, I. A. (1985), *Generalized Phrase Structure Grammar*. Oxford: Blackwell.

GEERAERTS, D. (1989), 'Prospects and problems of prototype theory', *Linguistics*, 27: 587–612.

GEIGER, R. A., and RUDZKA-OSTYN, B. (eds.) (1993), *Conceptualizations and Mental Processing in Language*. Berlin: Mouton de Gruyter.

GIORGI, A., and LONGOBARDI, G. (1991), *The Syntax of Noun Phrases: Configuration, Parameters and Empty Categories*. Cambridge: Cambridge University Press.

GIVÓN, T. (1979), *On Understanding Grammar*. New York: Academic Press.

—— (1983a), 'Introduction', in Givón 1983b: 5–41.

—— (ed.) (1983b), *Topic Continuity in Discourse: A Quantitative Cross-Language Study*. Benjamins: Amsterdam.

—— (1983c), 'Topic continuity in spoken English', in Givón 1983b: 345–63.

—— (1984), *Syntax: A Functional-Typological Introduction*, vol. i. Amsterdam: John Benjamins.

—— (1987), 'Beyond foregrounding and backgrounding', in Tomlin 1987: 175–88.

—— (1989), *Mind, Code and Context: Essays in Pragmatics*. Hillsdale: Lawrence Erlbaum.

—— (1990), *Syntax: A Functional-Typological Introduction*, vol. ii. Amsterdam: John Benjamins.

—— (1993), *English Grammar: A Function-Based Introduction*, vol. i. Amsterdam: Benjamins.

GOLDBERG, A. (1992), 'The inherent semantics of argument structure: the case of the English ditransitive construction', *Cognitive Linguistics*, 3: 37–74.

GOWERS, E. (1954), *The Complete Plain Words*. London: Her Majesty's Stationery Office.

GRIMSHAW, J. (1990), *Argument Structure*. Cambridge, Mass.: MIT Press.

GROPEN, J., PINKER, S., HOLLANDER, M., GOLDBERG, R., and WILSON, R. (1989), 'The learnability and acquisition of the dative alternation in English', *Language*, 65: 203–57.

GRUBER, J. S. (1976), *Lexical Structures in Syntax and Semantics*. Amsterdam: North-Holland.

GUERSSEL, M., HALE, K., LAUGHREN, M., LEVIN, B., and EAGLE, J. W. (1985), 'A cross-linguistic study of transitivity alternations', *CLS* 21/2: 48–63.

GUNDEL, J. K., HEDBERG, N., and ZACHARSKI, R. (1993), 'Cognitive status and the form of referring expressions in discourse', *Language*, 69: 274–307.

HAEGEMAN, L. (1991), *Introduction of Government & Binding Theory*. Oxford: Blackwell.

HAIDER, H. (1988), 'Die Struktur der deutschen Nominalphrase', *Zeitschrift für Sprachwissenschaft*, 7: 32–59.

HALITSKY, D. (1975), 'Left-branch S's and NP's in English: a bar notation analysis', *Linguistic Analysis*, 1: 279–96.

HALLIDAY, M. A. K. (1970), 'Language structure and language function', in Lyons 1970: 140–65.

—— (1985a), *An Introduction to Functional Grammar*. London: Edward Arnold.

—— (1985b), 'It's a fixed word order language is English', *ITL Review of Applied Linguistics*, 67–8: 91–116.

HARRIS, R. (1981), *The Language Myth*. London: Duckworth.

HARRIS, R. (1988), *Language, Saussure and Wittgenstein: How to Play Games with Words*. London: Routledge.

HARRIS, R. A. (1993), *The Linguistics Wars*. New York: Oxford University Press.

HAWKINS, B. (1984), 'The Semantics of English Spatial Prepositions', Ph.D. dissertation, San Diego: University of California.

HAWKINS, J. (1990), 'A parsing theory of word order universals', *Linguistic Inquiry*, 21: 223-62.

HAWKINS, R. (1981), 'Towards an account of the possessive constructions: *NP's N* and *the N of NP*', *Journal of Linguistics*, 17: 179-392.

HAWKINSON, A. K., and HYMAN, L. M. (1975), 'Hierarchies of natural topic in Shona', *Studies in African Linguistics*, 5: 147-70.

HAYASE, N. (1993), 'Prototypical meaning vs. semantic constraints in the analysis of English possessive genitives', *English Linguistics*, 10: 133-59.

HEIDER, E. (1971), ' "Focal" color areas and the development of color names', *Developmental Psychology*, 4: 447-55.

HEWSON, J. (1991), 'Determiners as heads', *Cognitive Linguistics*, 2: 317-37.

HORN, G. (1975), 'On the non-sentential nature of the Poss-Ing construction', *Linguistic Analysis*, 1: 333-88.

HORNSTEIN, N., and LIGHTFOOT, D. (1987), 'Predication and PRO', *Language*, 63: 23-52.

HOUSEHOLDER, F. (1988), 'The group genitive and type 24 languages', in Nixon and Honey 1988: 381-8.

HUDDLESTON, R. (1984), *Introduction to the Grammar of English*. Cambridge: Cambridge University Press.

HUDSON, R. (1984), *Word Grammar*. Oxford: Blackwell.

—— (1990a), *English Word Grammar*. Oxford: Blackwell.

—— (1990b), Review of Langacker 1987a, *Lingua*, 81: 272-84.

JACKENDOFF, R. S. (1968), 'Possessives in English', in S. R. Anderson, R. S. Jackendoff, and S. J. Keyser (eds.), *Studies in Transformational Grammar and Related Topics*. Waltham, Mass.: Brandeis University, Department of English, 25-51.

—— (1973), 'The base rules for prepositional phrases', in Anderson and Kiparsky 1973: 345-56.

—— (1977), *X̄ Syntax: A Study of Phrase Structure*. Cambridge, Mass.: MIT Press.

—— (1983), *Semantics and Cognition*. Cambridge, Mass.: MIT Press.

—— (1990), *Semantic Structures*. Cambridge, Mass.: MIT Press.

JACOBS, R. A., and ROSENBAUM, P. S. (1968), *English Transformational Grammar*. Lexington, Mass.: Xerox College.

JAEGGLI, O. (1986), 'Passive', *Linguistic Inquiry*, 17: 587-622.

JAKOBSON, R. (1936), 'Beitrag zur allgemeinen Kasuslehre: Gesamtbedeutungen der russischen Kasus', in *Selected Writings*, vol. ii (1991), The Hague: Mouton.

JESPERSEN, O. (1924), *The Philosophy of Grammar*. London: George Allen & Unwin.

—— (1909-49), *A Modern English Grammar*, 7 vols. Copenhagen: Munksgaard and London: Allen & Unwin.

JOHNSON-LAIRD, P. N. (1970), 'The perception and memory of sentences', in Lyons 1970: 261-70.

KAY, P., and ZIMMER, K. (1990), 'On the semantics of compounds and genitives in English', in Tsohatzidis (1990b), 239-46. (1st pub. in *Proceedings of the Sixth California Linguistics Association Conference* (1976).)

KEENAN, E. L. (1976), 'Towards a universal definition of "subject"', in Li 1976: 303–33 (repr. in Keenan 1987: 89–120).

—— (1984), 'Semantic correlates of the ergative/absolutive distinction', *Linguistics*, 22: 197–223 (repr. in Keenan 1987: 166–94).

—— (1987), *Universal Grammar: 15 Essays*. London: Croom Helm.

KEMPSON, R. (1977), *Semantic Theory*. Cambridge: Cambridge University Press.

KIRSNER, R. S. (1993), 'From meaning to message in two theories: cognitive and Saussurian views of the modern Dutch demonstratives', in Geiger and Rudzka-Ostyn 1993: 81–114.

KLAVENS, J. (1985), 'The independence of syntax and phonology in cliticization', *Language*, 61: 95–120.

KOPTJEVSKAJA-TAMM, M. (1993), *Nominalizations*. London: Routledge.

KURYŁOWICZ, J. (1964), *The Inflectional Categories of Indo-European*. Heidelberg: Carl Winter.

LABOV, W. (1973), 'The boundaries of words and their meanings', in C.-J. N. Bailey and R. W. Shuy (eds.), *New Ways of Analysing Variation in English*. Washington: Georgetown University Press, 340–73.

LADUSAW, W. A., and DOWTY, D. R. (1988), 'Towards a nongrammatical account of thematic roles', in Wilkins 1988: 61–73.

LAKOFF, G. (1987), *Women, Fire and Dangerous Things: What Categories Reveal about the Mind*. Chicago: Chicago University Press.

—— and JOHNSON, M. (1980), *Metaphors We Live by*. Chicago: University of Chicago Press.

LANGACKER, R. W. (1982), 'Space grammar, analysability, and the English passive', *Language*, 58: 22–80 (repr. in Langacker 1990a: 101–47).

—— (1987a), *Foundations of Cognitive Grammar*, vol. i Stanford, Calif.: Stanford University Press.

—— (1987b), 'Nouns and verbs', *Language*, 63: 53–94. Repr. in Langacker 1990a: 59–100.

—— (1988a), 'The nature of grammatical valence', in Rudzka-Ostyn 1988: 91–125. Repr. in Langacker 1990a: 165–88.

—— (1988b), 'An overview of cognitive grammar', in Rudzka-Ostyn 1988: 3–48.

—— (1988c), 'A usage-based model', in Rudzka-Ostyn 1988: 127–61. Repr. in Langacker 1990a: 261–88.

—— (1988d), 'A view of linguistic semantics', in Rudzka-Ostyn 1988: 49–90.

—— (1990a), *Concept, Image, and Symbol: The Cognitive Basis of Grammar*. Berlin: Mouton de Gruyter.

—— (1990b), 'Subjectification', *Cognitive Linguistics*, 1: 5–38. Repr. in Langacker 1990a: 315–42.

—— (1991), *Foundations of Cognitive Grammar*, vol. ii. Stanford, Calif.: Stanford University Press.

—— (1992), 'The symbolic nature of cognitive grammar: the meaning of *of* and of *of*-periphrasis', in M. Pütz (ed.), *Thirty Years of Linguistic Evolution: Studies in Honour of René Dirven on the Occasion of his Sixtieth Birthday*. Amsterdam: Benjamins, 483–502.

—— (1993), 'Reference-point constructions', *Cognitive Linguistics*, 4: 1–38.

—— (1995), 'Possession and possessive constructions', in J. Taylor and R. MacLaury (eds.), *Language and the Cognitive Construal of the World*. Berlin: Mouton de Gruyter, 51–79.

LEBEAUX, D. (1986), 'The interpretation of derived nominals', *CLS* 22/1: 231–47.

LEECH, G. (1981), *Semantics*, 2nd edn. Harmondsworth: Penguin.

LEES, R. B. (1960), *The Grammar of English Nominalizations*. Bloomington: Indiana University Research Centre in Anthropology, Folklore, and Linguistics, Publication 12 (various reprintings).

LEPSCHY, A.-L., and LEPSCHY, G. (1977), *The Italian Language Today*. London: Hutchinson.

LEVIN, B., and RAPPAPORT HOVAV, M. (1991), 'Wiping the slate clean: a lexical semantic exploration', *Cognition*, 41: 123–51.

LI, C. N. (ed.) (1976), *Subject and Topic*. New York: Academic Press.

——— and THOMPSON, S. A. (1976), 'Subject and topic: a new typology of language', in Li 1976: 457–89.

LIEBER, R. (1983), 'Argument linking and compounding in English', *Linguistic Inquiry*, 14: 251–86.

——— (1988), 'Phrasal compounds in English and the morphology-syntax interface', *CLS* 24/2: 202–22.

——— (1992), 'Compounding in English', *Rivista di linguistica*, 4: 79–96.

LODGE, D. (1984), *Small World*. London: Penguin.

LYONS, C. (1985), 'A possessive parameter', *Sheffield Working Papers in Linguistics*, 2: 98–104.

——— (1986a), 'On the origin of the Old French strong–weak possessive distinction', *Transactions of the Philological Society 1986*, 1–41.

——— (1986b), 'The syntax of English genitive constructions', *Journal of Linguistics*, 22: 123–43.

LYONS, J. (ed.) (1970), *New Horizons in Linguistics*. Harmondsworth: Penguin.

——— (1977), *Semantics*, 2 vols. Cambridge: Cambridge University Press.

MAIDEN, M. (1995), *A Linguistic History of Italian*. London: Longman.

MILLER, G., and JOHNSON-LAIRD, P. (1976), *Language and Perception*. Cambridge, Mass.: Harvard University Press.

MILLER, J. (1985), *Semantics and Syntax: Parallels and Connections*. Cambridge: Cambridge University Press.

MILSARK, G. (1974), 'Existential Sentences in English', Ph.D. dissertation, MIT.

NESPOR, M., and VOGEL, I. (1986), *Prosodic Phonology*. Dordrecht: Foris.

NEWMEYER, F. J. (1991), 'Functional explanation in linguistics and the origins of language', *Language & Communication*, 11: 3–28.

NIKIFORIDOU, K. (1991), 'The meanings of the genitive: a case study in semantic structure and semantic change', *Cognitive Linguistics*, 2: 149–205.

 NIXON, G., and HONEY, J. (eds.) (1988), *An Historic Tongue: Studies in English Linguistics in Memory of Barbara Strang*. London: Routledge.

OOSTHUIZEN, J., and WAHER, H. (1994), 'On the syntax of the *se*-construction in Afrikaans', *SPIL (Stellenbosch Papers in Linguistics)* 28: 21–43.

OSHERSON, D. N., and SMITH, E. E. (1981), 'On the adequacy of prototype theory as a theory of concepts', *Cognition*, 9: 35–58.

OSSELTON, N. (1988), 'Thematic genitives', in Nixon and Honey 1988: 138–44.

PAWLEY, A., and SYDER, F. H. (1983), 'Two puzzles for linguistic theory: nativelike selection and nativelike fluency', in J. C. Richards and R. W. Schmidt (eds.), *Language and Communication*. London: Longman, 191–226.

PINKER, S. (1989), *Learnability and Cognition: The Acquisition of Argument Structure*. Cambridge, Mass.: MIT Press.

PLANK, F. (1992), 'Possessives and the distinction between determiners and modifiers (with special reference to German)', *Journal of Linguistics*, 28: 453–68.

POSTAL, P. (1969), 'Anaphoric islands', *CLS* 5: 205–39. Repr. in E. Schiller, B. Need, D. Varley, and W. H. Eilfort (eds.) (1988), *The Best of CLS: A Selection of out-of-print Papers from 1968 to 1975*. Chicago: Chicago Linguistic Society, 67–94.

POTTER, M. C., and FAULCONER, B. A. (1979), 'Understanding noun phrases', *Journal of Verbal Learning and Verbal Behavior*, 18: 509–21.

POUTSMA, H. (1914–16), *A Grammar of Late Modern English, for the use of Continental, especially Dutch, students*. Part II: *The Parts of Speech*. Groningen: Noordhoff.

PRINCE, E. (1981), 'Towards a taxonomy of given-new information', in P. Cole (ed.), *Radical Pragmatics*. New York: Academic Press, 223–55.

PULLUM, G. K. (1991), 'English nominal gerund phrases as noun phrases with verb-phrase heads', *Linguistics*, 29: 763–99.

—— and ZWICKY, A. M. (1991), 'Condition duplication, paradigm homonymy, and trans-constructional constraints', *BLS* 17: 252–66.

PUSTEJOVSKY, J. (1991*a*), 'The generative lexicon', *Computational Linguistics*, 17: 409–41.

—— (1991*b*), 'The syntax of event structure', *Cognition*, 41: 47–81.

QUINE, W. V. (1990), *Quiddities: An Intermittently Philosophical Dictionary*. Harmondsworth: Penguin (1st pub. 1987 by Harvard University Press).

QUIRK, R., GREENBAUM, S., LEECH, G., and SVARTVIK, J. (1972), *A Grammar of Contemporary English*. London: Longman.

—— —— —— —— (1985), *A Comprehensive Grammar of the English Language*. London: Longman.

RADFORD, A. (1988), *Transformational Grammar: A First Course*. Cambridge: Cambridge University Press.

—— (1990), *Syntactic Theory and the Acquisition of Syntax*. Oxford: Blackwell.

RAPPAPORT, M. (1983), 'On the nature of derived nominals', in L. Levin, M. Rappaport, and A. Zaenen (eds.), *Papers in Lexical-Functional Grammar*. Indiana University Linguistics Club, 113–42.

ROEPER, T. (1987), 'Implicit arguments and the head-complement relation', *Linguistic Inquiry*, 18: 267–310.

ROSCH, E. (1975), 'Cognitive representations of semantic categories', *Journal of Experimental Psychology: General*, 104: 192–233.

—— (1978), 'Principles of categorization', in E. Rosch and B. B. Lloyd (eds.), *Cognition and Categorization*. Hillsdale, NJ: Lawrence Erlbaum, 27–48.

—— (1987), 'Wittgenstein and categorization research in cognitive psychology', in M. Chapman and R. A. Dixon (eds.), *Meaning and the Growth of Understanding*. Berlin: Springer, 151–66.

—— MERVIS, C., GRAY, W., JOHNSON, D., and BOYES-BRAEM, P. (1976), 'Basic objects in natural categories', *Cognitive Psychology*, 7: 575–605.

ROSS, J. R. (1967), 'Constraints on variables in syntax', Ph.D. dissertation, MIT.

—— (1972), 'Endstation Hauptwort: the category squish', *CLS* 8: 316–28.

ROZWADOWSKA, B. (1988), 'Thematic restrictions on derived nominals', in Wilkins 1988: 147–65.

RUDZKA-OSTYN, B. (ed.) (1988), *Topics in Cognitive Linguistics*. Amsterdam: Benjamins.

RUHL, C. (1969), *On Monosemy: A Study in Linguistic Semantics*. Stony Brook: State University of New York Press.

SAFIR, K. (1987), 'The syntactic projection of lexical thematic structure', *Natural Language and Linguistic Theory*, 5: 561–601.

SAUSSURE, F. DE (1964), *Cours de linguistique générale*, ed. Charles Bally and Albert Sechehaye. Paris: Payot (1st edn. 1916).

SCHENDL, H. (1993), '*My/mine, thy/thine*: aspects of their distribution in Early Modern English', *Vienna English Working Papers*, 2: 111–20.

SEARLE, J. R. (1979), 'Literal meaning', in *Expression and Meaning*. Cambridge: Cambridge University Press, 117–36.

—— (1980), 'The background of meaning', in J. R. Searle, F. Kiefer, and M. Bierwisch (eds.), *Speech Act Theory and Pragmatics*. Dordrecht: Reidel; 221–32.

—— (1983), *Intentionality: An Essay in the Philosophy of Mind*. Cambridge: Cambridge University Press.

—— (1992), 'Consciousness, intentionality, and the Background', in *The Rediscovery of the Mind*. Cambridge, Mass.: MIT Press, 175–96.

SEILER, H. (1983), *Possession as an Operational Dimension of Language*. Tübingen: Narr.

—— (1993), 'A functional view on prototypes', in Geiger and Rudzka-Ostyn 1993: 115–39.

SEPPÄNEN, A. (1980), 'Possessive pronouns in English?', *Studia Linguistica*, 34: 7–22.

SINCLAIR, M., and WINCKLER, W. K. (1991), 'Relevance Theory: Explaining Verbal Communication', *SPIL (Stellenbosch Papers in Linguistics) PLUS* 18: 1–97.

SKLAR, E. S. (1976), 'The possessive apostrophe: the development and decline of a crooked mark', *College English*, 38: 175–83.

SMITH, N. (1989), *The Twitter Machine: Reflections on Language*. Oxford: Blackwell.

SPENCER, A. (1992), 'Nominal inflection and the nature of functional categories', *Journal of Linguistics*, 28: 313–41.

SPERBER, D., and WILSON, D. (1986), *Relevance: Communication and Cognition*. Oxford: Blackwell.

STAROSTA, S. (1988), *The Case for Lexicase: An Outline of Lexicase Grammatical Theory*. London: Pinter.

STOWELL, T. (1989), 'Subjects, specifiers, and X-bar theory', in M. R. Baltin and A. S. Kroch (eds.), *Alternative Conceptions of Phrase Structure*. Chicago: University of Chicago Press, 232–62.

SWEET, H. (1891), *A New English Grammar: Logical and Historical*, Part I: *Introduction, Phonology, and Accidence*. Oxford: Clarendon Press.

—— (1898), *A New English Grammar: Logical and Historical*, Part II: *Syntax*. Oxford: Clarendon Press.

TAYLOR, J. R. (1989), 'Possessive genitives in English', *Linguistics*, 27: 663–86.

—— (1991a), 'Possessive genitives in English: a discourse perspective', *South African Journal of Linguistics*, 9: 59–63.

—— (1991b), 'Things, places, and directions', *Cognitive Linguistics*, 2: 357–60.

—— (1992), 'Old problems: adjectives in cognitive grammar', *Cognitive Linguistics*, 3: 1–36.

—— (1994*a*), 'Possessives and topicality', *Functions of Language*, 1: 67–94.

—— (1994*b*), ' "Subjective" and "objective" readings of possessor nominals', *Cognitive Linguistics*, 5: 201–42.

—— (1994*c*), 'The two-level approach to meaning', *Linguistische Berichte*, 149: 3–26.

—— (1995*a*), 'Fuzzy categories in syntax: the case of possessives and compounds', *Rivista di linguistica*, 6: 327–45.

—— (1995*b*), *Linguistic Categorization: Prototypes in Linguistic Theory*. Oxford: Clarendon Press (1st edn. 1989).

TESNIÈRE, L. (1959), *Éléments de syntaxe structurale*. Paris: Klincksieck.

THOMSON, A. J., and MARTINET, A. V. (1960), *A Practical English Grammar*. Oxford: Oxford University Press.

TOMLIN, R. (ed.) (1987), *Coherence and Grounding in Discourse*. Amsterdam: Benjamins.

TSOHATZIDIS, S. (1990*a*), 'A few untruths about "lie"', in Tsohatzidis 1990*b*: 438–46.

—— (1990*b*), *Meanings and Prototypes: Studies in Linguistic Categorization*. London: Routledge.

TUGGY, D. (1992), 'The affix-stem distinction: a Cognitive Grammar analysis of data from Orizaba Nahuatl', *Cognitive Linguistics*, 3: 237–300.

VAN LANGENDONCK, W. (1994), 'Determiners as heads?', *Cognitive Linguistics*, 5: 243–59.

VAN OOSTEN, J. (1986), *The Nature of Subjects, Topics and Agents: A Cognitive Explanation*. Bloomington: Indiana University Linguistics Club.

VENDLER, Z. (1967), *Linguistics in Philosophy*. Ithaca, NY: Cornell University Press.

WHEATLEY, J. (1969), 'Austin on Truth', in T. Honderich (ed.), *Symposium on J. L. Austin, 1969*. London: Routledge & Kegan Paul, 226–39.

WIERZBICKA, A. (1972), *Semantic Primitives*. Frankfurt: Athenäum.

—— (1980), *The Case for Surface Case*. Ann Arbor: Karoma.

—— (1985), *Lexicography and Conceptual Analysis*. Ann Arbor: Karoma.

—— (1988), *The Semantics of Grammar*. Amsterdam: Benjamins.

—— (1996), *Semantics*. Oxford: Oxford Univerity Press.

WILLIAMS, E. (1981), 'Argument structure and morphology', *Linguistic Review*, 1: 81–114.

—— (1982), 'The NP cycle', *Linguistic Inquiry*, 13: 277–95.

—— (1985), 'PRO and subject of NP', *Natural Language and Linguistic Theory*, 3: 297–315.

—— (1987), 'English as an ergative language: the theta structure of derived nouns', *CLS* 23: 366–75.

WILKINS, W. (ed.) (1988), *Thematic Relations* (= *Syntax and Semantics* 21), San Diego: Academic Press.

WILSON, D., and SPERBER, D. (1986), 'Pragmatics and modularity', *CLS* 22/2: 67–84.

WITTGENSTEIN, L. (1978), *Philosophical Investigations*, trans. G. E. M. Anscombe. Oxford: Blackwell (1st edn. 1953).

WOISETSCHLAEGER, E. (1983), 'On the question of definiteness in "An Old Man's Book"', *Linguistic Inquiry*, 14: 137–54.

WYLD, H. C. (1936), *A History of Modern Colloquial English*. Oxford: Blackwell.

ZUBIZARRETA, M. L. (1987), *Levels of Representation in the Lexicon and in the Syntax*. Dordrecht: Foris.

ZWICKY, A. (1985), 'Clitics and particles', *Language*, 61: 283–305.

Index of Names

Subject Index